MW01688542

The Black and White of American Popular Music

From Slavery to World War II

The Black and White of American Popular Music

FROM SLAVERY TO WORLD WAR II

Vera G. Lee

Preface by Ellis Marsalis

THE BLACK AND WHITE OF AMERICAN POPULAR MUSIC
From Slavery to World War II

Published by Pitapat Press
Third Edition 2012

First edition: Schenkman Books, 2007
Second edition, revised: Xlibris Corp., 2009

For information contact:
Pitapat Press
New Town, Massachusetts
www.pitapatpress.com

Printed in the United States of America

ISBN: 978-0-9663065-4-5

Contents

To My Wonderful Family

Preface

This book brings us a much needed look at jazz. Just as the television series by Ken Burns hoped to start a dialogue, Vera Lee's book will surely become a significant contribution to the too few works on jazz. It is thought provoking, not just another cursory biography.

New Orleans naturally plays a role in the book, just as it would in any work that touches on the history of jazz. Right now that city—my native city—is trying to recover from the worst catastrophes in its two-hundred-and-two-year history: Hurricanes Katrina and Rita. New Orleans will recover, and in spite of the pain Katrina/Rita thrust upon its citizenry, it will thrive once again. Like its music, the city will evolve and eventually take on a different structure. But it will continue to be relevant to itself and the nation. This study is relevant to the musical world and will help to bring jazz, an esoteric experience at best, into more public attention.

The book analyzes racial patterns in American popular music, beginning in 1800 and ending around 1950. Since then the situation in race relations and music has changed conspicuously. For example, back in the 1950s, when I was just starting out as a professional musician, I could not have appeared on the same bandstand with the white instrumentalists who play with me today. In fact, in the South, we couldn't even sit and have a cup of coffee without running into trouble. Today, wherever I go, I can work with whoever fits the bill musically. As Miles Davis said, his musicians can be black, white or blue. None of that matters if they can play.

Over fifty years ago, certain questions posed in this book were lively subjects for debate among critics: How did the races interact in music? What is the importance of each to the history of jazz? What is a black sound and what is a white one? Now, in the twenty-first century, such questions may appear dated. Those so-called critics who insist, for instance, that jazz is a black or white phenomenon are often writing defensively, almost as an act of desperation, and with a personal bias. Today, objectively, we can no longer think in terms of racial uniqueness and ethnicity in jazz. I cannot think in such terms when playing with a guitarist who comes from Israel, an alto saxophonist from Italy and others from assorted cultures around the world. Everything depends on the experience and talent of the players who have taken the time to learn and assimilate the jazz language.

But jazz and its musicians have come a long way, and this book will help one understand better how that happened. Vera Lee has taken on a vast and vital topic and has done justice to it. You may find it provocative and controversial at times, but it is a thoughtful study, thoroughly researched, well written and an important contribution.

Today we are at the beginning of an introspective period in America. This book is certain to help make jazz a major part of the process.

Ellis Marsalis, Professor Emeritus and
Former Director of Jazz Studies
University of New Orleans

Introduction

Many music historians have discussed the roles of the races in American popular music. That is certainly the case when it comes to jazz—a field in which African-American and white musicians have long shared the stage and one in which the question of race inevitably comes into play.

In this book, however, I have used another approach and viewed the subject through a different lens. Specifically, I have sought to reveal patterns of black and white interrelationships in popular music. And the subject is treated in a comprehensive time frame: the period from the early nineteenth century to World War II. Moreover, instead of restricting the study to one particular area, such as jazz, I thought it more useful to demonstrate how certain patterns recur in a variety of fields, such as show business, blues recording, music composing, publishing and dance.

The subject is, of course, too vast to cover definitively in any one book. In the interest of space much has had to be omitted (for instance, a lengthy section entitled "The Great Spiritual Controversy" in which my musical samples disproved an old theory that the spirituals are essentially white). Nevertheless, in staking out what appears to be a wide expanse of virgin territory, I would hope that at least some ground has been broken here and that other writers may find interesting possibilities in this study for further development. It is my feeling that almost any one of the following chapters could form the basis of an entire book.

In treating racial themes, some incendiary issues have had to be dealt with. I have tried to discuss those issues as objectively as possible (although an objective approach runs the risk of offending militants on either side of a question). If, however, I have appeared to favor one race over another, that is simply because it is very difficult to spend great amounts of time and energy delving into this subject without acquiring a deep admiration and empathy for the African Americans who created so much against such overwhelming odds. And even beyond their talent, it is impossible not to delight in personalities such as Eubie Blake, Louis Armstrong, Pops Foster and so many others who further enriched and enlivened research on a fascinating topic.

Wynton Marsalis, in *Jazz*, Ken Burns' video production of 2000, depicted the black and white connections in music as "this strange dance that we've been doing with each other since, really, the beginning of our relationship in America." My study devotes itself precisely to that dance, to tracing its history, probing its nature and its rhythms, distinguishing what each of the two partners, black and white, contributes to or subtracts from the dance and discovering how each meshes or remains out of step with the music and with each other.

* * *

I should like to express my gratitude to Boston College for awarding me a grant in support of this project.

My heartfelt thanks to vocalist/songwriter Didi Stewart, faculty of Berklee College of Music; Peter Clote, saxophonist and Boston College Professor of Biology and Mathematics; Bill Horan, pianist; my son-in-law, Conrad Gees, of the Wayland School System, and my discerning friends, Charles Eichhorn, Benjamin Rice and Gene Piazza, for taking precious time to read and comment on chapters of this book.

Words cannot convey my sense of indebtedness to the incomparable Ellis Marsalis. Exiled from his native New Orleans in the aftermath of Hurricane Katrina, he took time from rehearsing, performing, coaching—and getting his life together—to read this book and bless it with a preface. I am touched and honored by his generosity and his kind words.

I am deeply grateful to Professor M. J. Connolly of Boston College's Slavic and Eastern Languages Department. As Co-director of the Faculty Micro Resource Center, he provided unfailing and invaluable support at every stage of this project.

And many thanks to the first publisher of this book, Joe Schenkman, and his wife Kathryn, who both helped bring this project to fruition.

Finally, a personal word of gratitude to the extraordinary Jack Neuhauser, former Academic Vice President of Boston College, for his interest in this book and his unremitting graciousness.

1

GENESIS

BLACK MUSIC IN A WHITE WORLD

Introduction: Song and Symbiosis

In 1845, an enlightened admirer of African-American slave songs wrote:

> Who are our true rulers? The negro poets, to be sure! Do they not set the fashion, and give laws to the public taste? [A new song] no sooner reaches the ear of a white *amateur* than it is written down, amended . . .[1]

A half century later, composer Anton Dvorák would declare: "In the Negro melodies of America I discover all that is needed for a great and noble school of music."[2]

Such claims may sound a bit high flown to us now, but where popular music is concerned, they are close to the mark. In that field, American composers, instrumentalists, vocalists and entrepreneurs have, indeed, found much of what they needed in African-American music. In fact, over the course of nearly two centuries—through minstrelsy, ragtime, jazz, rock and roll, hip-hop and rap—the major innovations and fashions adopted by whites in popular music have had their roots in the black legacy.

It is not, however, a case of a one-way street with all arrows pointing from black to white. On the contrary, from the time of slavery to the present, white influences have contributed heavily to African-American musical creativity. The white contribution, a force to be reckoned with, has made itself felt every step of the way. Rather than pursue two separate paths, the black and white musics have circled each other as they progressed, symbiotically feeding on one another through the years, ever enlightening, ever enriching, ever frustrating each other.

The role of the races in American popular music cannot be analyzed with mathematical precision. Instead, the complex interweaving of black and white interactions and musical cross-influences may appear as a tangled web, impossible to sort out and assess. Further complicating the picture are factors outside the realm of music—social, economic and psychological factors—that have come into play at every turn. Yet despite such complexities, it is worth our while to take a close look at the relationships between black and white music, to trace their origins, follow their itinerary and probe their mysteries, in order to shed light on the history and development of popular music in America.

The Music of the Slaves

From the first arrival of captured Africans in 1619[3] until the nineteenth century, little was written concerning the songs sung and played by North American slaves. It would be impossible, therefore, to determine exactly how much of Africa remained in that early music or to what extent it had become Americanized. In the eighteenth century some chroniclers did hear and describe native African singing and dancing in areas of South Carolina, Louisiana, New York, Maryland, Virginia and elsewhere.[4] But reports of African music in the colonies were far less prevalent than on the Caribbean islands. For the Negro slaves in the colonies had much less opportunity to perpetuate their African musical heritage. So they would gradually fill the gap by appropriating and processing the music of their masters.

We can assume then that in North America the balance of musical influence between the races ran initially from white to black. The sort of hybrid music invented by the slaves themselves would not be taken seriously by a white population before the nineteenth century. And would not have a marked impact on white musicians until the early days of minstrelsy in the 1830s and 1840s.

But let us start at the beginning.

* * *

Like a precious amulet smuggled from Africa, the one important possession the slaves carried with them to the New World was the gift of music. Certainly, music had played a major role in the various regions from which they came (primarily West African countries in areas from Sénégal to Central Africa). There—no matter what the locale or tribe—song, dance and instrumental music making were integral parts of their daily life: their work, their education, their recreational activities and the numerous ceremonies held for any and every conceivable event.

In the early 1800s, white observers writing of their visits to southern states perpetually commented on the "natural" musical ability of the Negroes, their adeptness at dance and the beauty of their voices. Was it a survival of a strong patrimony transmitted from generation to generation?[5] An art imbibed at their mother's breast? A skill fostered by their lot in life—or all of the above? Whatever the case, there is no denying the preponderance of musical talent among the slaves.

They composed, played, danced and, above all, they sang. They sang at work because they were commanded to by their white bosses who knew that singing made their charges labor faster, harder, longer. And as long as they continued singing, the "massa," his overseer or the black driver in command knew exactly where they were, could be assured they weren't sitting down on the job or planning subversive activities. At times they sang to communicate with each other in the fields or to transmit messages. Then, at night, when the laboring was over at last, they sang to let off steam, abandoning themselves to a frenzied jubilation. Above all, at any moment of the day or night, they sang to ease their pain, to survive. And because music was rooted in their soul.

Where, exactly, did slave music come from and how did it really develop? Volumes have been written in an attempt to answer these questions, but the answers remain ambiguous. Understandably so, because such studies address an oral tradition, an art that scholars could not chronicle and record with anything approaching precision until slavery in America had all but disappeared. Generally speaking, however, music historians agree that those slave songs heard in nineteenth-century America were the fusion of white Euro-American music and echoes of Africa, as practiced and developed by African Americans in bondage.

From White Hymns to Black Spirituals

The slaves of North American plantations were trapped in a cultural limbo. On the one hand, they were increasingly discouraged from speaking their African languages and from practicing their native customs. Yet on the other, they had little or no access to formal instruction in the culture or language of the white population surrounding them. In the first half of the nineteenth century, for example, many slave owners feared that "book-lernin'" would fill their charges' heads with dangerous notions of freedom.[6] For this and other reasons educational opportunities for the bondsmen were slim or non-existent.

As a result, when it came to composing verses for their songs, the transplanted Africans were obliged to use what little English they could muster. And since they had become familiar with the religious and secular songs of their white masters, those compositions—especially the hymns—would serve as a scaffolding on which to build their own music.

From the beginning of the nineteenth century to the end of the Civil War, African Americans in bondage developed and produced the soulful black spiritual we know today. Those decades were marked by an unusually rigid repression of the slaves. For the American Revolution, with its ideals of freedom and equality, had unleashed a stern backlash in the slaveholding South. State and local authorities (composed, naturally, of slave owners)

lang.

x repression

had become increasingly wary of black aspirations to liberation. They and the white citizenry in general lived in fear of violent slave uprisings and were more than a little anxious about the numerous and ongoing desertions of abused and freedom minded bondsmen.[7] So southern states enacted ever more stringent laws granting all power to white masters and depriving the slaves of what little freedom they had.[8] Moreover, during that same period, plantation economics prompted owners to sell their human chattel from one region of the South to another, causing tragic separations between spouses and between parents and children.

American black music, a child of sorrow, was largely born of such catastrophes.

Religion and religious music provided at least a ray of hope for the slaves, albeit only in the next world. For a long time many southern owners opposed any religious indoctrination of their black charges. A good number of them suspected that religion—and contact with anti-slavery preachers—would make their human chattel "uppity" or insubordinate.[9] However, white church activists, Methodists and Baptists particularly, had been bending their efforts throughout the eighteenth century to converting the slave population. They were well aware that, given the Negroes' love of music, hymns and psalms provided the strongest fuel in sparking religious ardor in the bondsmen. That spark was well ignited by the turn of the nineteenth century. Moreover, some slave owners understood that religious sermons, rather than a conduit to revolt, could well serve as a means of keeping the slaves obedient, if not docile.

Negroes in bondage heard, overheard or were informed about religious services and had some knowledge of psalms and hymns sung by white congregations. They spread the sacred word amongst themselves. And they sang the sacred music of their masters, whether in the gallery of a white church—if allowed there—in their own Baptist or Methodist churches, at camp meetings, working in the fields or on the levees, in their hovels or in secret gatherings.

They had found early inspiration in the hymns of the English minister, Isaac Watts. Watts' hymns helped spur the religious movement of the 1730s and 1740s known as the

"Great Awakening." Although some European psalmists before him had attempted to make church music less dull and dreary, Watts succeeded in injecting more life and melody into his compositions, often imbuing them with the flavor of cheerful, lilting folk songs. They stood in sharp contrast to the old majestic psalms and colorless hymnody of the Church of England. The slaves responded enthusiastically, not only to Watts' livelier music but also, deeply, to his message of salvation and relief from suffering.[10]

But most importantly, they responded to the sermons and hymns of Methodist and Baptist revivalist camp meetings, events popular in the North and South during the first half of the nineteenth century, in the period called the "Great Revival." Despite the continuing reluctance of many owners to allow slaves religious education and practice, a large number of bondsmen, as well as free Negroes, were present at those meetings and heard the exhortations of ministers both black and white, their fiery tirades against evil sinners and their promises of eternal salvation for believers. Black attendees gathered by the hundreds in a roped-off section, often outnumbering the white participants. There, religious songs of both races mingled, filling the air with a joyous fervor.

The slaves did not, however, simply memorize and repeat the white hymns, even the most accessible and popular ones sung in the camp meetings and geared to those with little or no education. A mere parroting of the white religious songs would not have appealed to them. For formed by another culture, they had their own penchants and mindset—and what one writer calls their "healthy disrespect for purism."[11] So, consciously or not, they changed the original models until they became unrecognizable, transforming white hymnody into a markedly different genre: their own slave spirituals.[12]

The transformation came about in a number of ways. To begin with, since almost no African Americans could read or write, even if they had wanted to adopt the sacred songs *verbatim* and transmit them faithfully to others, it would have been well nigh impossible. The hymns had to be greatly simplified in order to be shared with and understood by the majority of slaves.

So repetition became an important feature of the spirituals, repetition of phrases and lines very much akin to the constant reiteration of phrases in African chanting. This was not a conscious technique but evolved mainly from a spontaneous and emotional experience within the slave community. For example, in any sort of gathering of slaves, one person, perhaps functioning as a song leader, might sing out a phrase, inspired by an idea or a feeling. He or she might repeat that phrase or another enthusiast would take it up, perhaps adding to it. And the whole group, catching the words, melody and feeling of the phrase might join in, building a song around it.[13]

A typical example:

> Heaven bell a-ring, I know de road,
> Heaven bell a-ring, I know de road,
> Heaven bell a-ring, I know de road,
> Jesus sittin' on de waterside.[14]

Such repetition would help impress the meaning and feeling of the message on those present and would assist them in remembering the song or song-to-be. It might also give the leader or song inventor time to think of the next phrase, one that would finish off the message.

This model of a thrice-repeated phrase followed by a "resolution" phrase would remain a familiar and unique feature of the slave spirituals. The same pattern would later appear in the blues.

To some extent the Protestant white church had also used a technique of repetition in what they referred to as "lining out." That is, in colonial times, in the absence of psalm books, a preacher or leader would call or sing out each line of a hymn, and the congregation would echo it. But in the black spirituals, repetition was not a practical device but a familiar and natural way of sounding out a message. And it would become an intrinsic, organic part of the songs.

The spirituals differed strikingly from white hymnody in other ways as well. To begin with, the language of the black songs was far more concrete and personal. For to communicate the sacred message in a direct and understandable way, the text of the white hymns had to be brought down from its customarily lofty plane to the familiar here-and-now of the Negro slave. So abstractions such as "a mighty fortress is our Lord" or generalizations in the vein of "Jesus, joy of man's desiring," gave way to images such as "Paul and Silas bound in jail," "Jesus lock' de lion's jaw," "I hold my brudder wid a tremblin' han'" or "I an' Satan had a race, hallelu . . ."

And from the start, the spirituals shunned the generalizations of white hymnody and, instead, spoke to the slaves familiarly about their own selves—their physical struggles, heartaches, hopes and aspirations. Each singer and each listener could personally and immediately identify with the situation described. The repeated use of the first person singular (as later in the blues) served to strengthen that intimacy. Rare is the spiritual that does not either begin with "I" or use that pronoun several times in its text. "Nobody Knows De Trouble I've Had," "I Don't Feel Weary," "I Want to Be My Fader's Chillun" and songs cited above are but a few examples of that personalization.

Although the white camp meeting revival songs also made use of the first person singular, as in "Oh when shall I see Jesus," "I want to go to glory," "I will be in this band," the slave songs, as illustrated by the above examples, associated "I" with a concrete individual experience and a deeply felt personal emotion. Clearly, although the slaves adopted the religious subjects of white hymns, they profoundly altered their very substance.

Add to such differences the fact that, unlike the white hymns, the spirituals were open-ended and improvisational, never restrictive or set in stone. For example, just as religious themes infiltrated into their secular music, some of their sacred songs were little more than favorite popular songs with a few religious phrases added here and there. Moreover, as in the later blues, one spiritual might borrow familiar phases and melodies from another. And the improvisational manner in which the songs were created and sung prefigured the loose and freewheeling collective approach of early New Orleans jazz bands.

But what most differentiated black music from white was rhythm; it is most strikingly in the unusual tempo of their songs that the slaves created something truly unique. To explain:

White American music, largely adopted from English sources, held to a steady tempo which emphasized every other beat in the measure. The first and third were strong trochaic beats throughout, as witness the white minstrel composition "Jingle Bells" by J. Pierpont:

> Dásh-ing thróugh the snów
> in a óne-horse ó-pen sléigh . . .

But in contrast, slave songs stressed the ordinarily weak beats in a 4-4 tempo measure (that is, the second and fourth), as in:

> "Cap-*n* . . ." "heb-*n*" "Some ti-*ímes* I feel . . ."

Moreover, the black singers anticipated or delayed beats, creating a far greater elasticity and irregularity than found in the white hymns.

Further and strongly contributing to the uniqueness of the slave songs, were certain Africanisms[15] in the way they were sung, or "performed." For instance, group participation, or "call-and-response," an important facet of African song, played a great role in spiritual singing. The white church may be said to have had its own call-and-response system, with those aforementioned preachers who "lined out" hymns, singing each line before the congregation joined in. But there the resemblance ended. For spiritual singing by the black slaves incorporated call-and-response in a very characteristic way. The slaves would vary their responses, rarely repeating exactly a specific melody or text twice. And they provided their own brand of ornamentation[16] and improvisation on the basic melody.

Taking the black spirituals even farther away from white hymnody was the use of African style instruments. Although—as in the West Indies—local authorities often banned the large hollowed log drums, "talking drums"[17] that could transmit messages from village to village, the slaves sometimes improvised smaller types of drums straddled or held between the knees.

And they conveniently made do with contrivances such as gourd rattles, metal pans, sticks and ox or horse bones for clacking. Melodies could be carried by the banjo, patterned after an African instrument, or the European fiddle. But, when available, percussive instruments helped provide the rhythm that had been so essential an aspect of African music

Finally and most dramatically, African body movements put the slaves' rendering of spirituals in sharp contrast with the singing of white churchgoers. To the horror of puritanical Protestant ministers and straight-laced congregation members, blacks often accompanied their religious chanting with the foot tapping, hand clapping, hip patting and even the sensual body sways[18] commonly practiced in their native Africa.

Such movements were common in the famous Negro "ring shouts" witnessed in regions of the South and North well into the nineteenth century. The word "shout" referred primarily to the moving or dancing, rather than the singing of religious songs. In a style evocative of African dancing, the shout consisted usually of men and women walking counterclockwise in a circle, shuffling, scarcely taking their feet from the floor, but moving shoulders and torso in convulsive body lunges. In many instances, one foot was placed in front of the other, the ball of the forward foot raised, then tapped smartly and repeatedly on the ground or floor. Over several hours, the rhythm might become faster and faster, building up to a frenzy and leading at times to a state of trance.

In the absence of percussion instruments, foot tapping and hand clapping kept regular time to the basic rhythm of the music. They were most often used by bystanders and singers outside the dance, to support or "base" dancers and song leaders. In the clapping, or "patting," as it was called, a person would clap two hands together to the rhythm and might also hit them on the thighs, hips or shoulders. (In secular songs and dances this clapping came to be known as "patting Juba," for it sometimes accompanied the lively *juba* slave dance.)

As late as 1937, George Gershwin, witnessed a religious shout on a visit to isolated James Island, where it had been perpetuated by South Carolina Gullah Negroes. Struck by the patting and tapping, he was especially impressed by the intricate rhythmic patterns of the natives' spirituals, in which the irregular timing and interweaving of musical themes formed a definite, cohesive pattern. That shout inspired him in writing a prayer scene for *Porgy and Bess.*

The Secular Side

In discussing African-American music, historians usually dwell on the legacy of the spirituals but are apt to give short shrift to the slaves' secular music. That is largely because by the mid-nineteenth century, when researchers began in earnest to collect black songs, the move toward religious indoctrination had gained great ground. As a result, many newly converted slaves refused to discuss or provide examples of songs that lay outside the holy sphere of hymns and spirituals. Consequently, collectors and chroniclers have had a more difficult time trying to resurrect the slaves' non-religious music.[19] Yet that music formed an important part of their daily lives—their work songs, rowing songs, field hollers, the "recreational" songs they sang, played and danced to at night, after twelve or more hours of labor, or on Sundays and their all-too-brief annual holidays.

The secular pieces, whether songs of sorrow, work, satire or merriment, contained all the effects that colored the spirituals: repetition, group participation, call-and-response, improvisation, ornamentation, rhythmic invention, often accompanied by patting and African movements. And at times they even included religious phrases and other textual crossovers from their store of spirituals.

One of the most memorable example of the slaves' secular music—certainly the most cited one—is their Sunday singing and dancing in New Orleans' Congo Square.[20] There, through much of the first half of the nineteenth century, the slaves were permitted to perpetuate a musical ceremony rife with rhythms of Africa. Before describing this phenomenon, it would be well to explain how such ceremonies could have taken place, given the restrictions imposed on slaves throughout the South, restrictions which alienated them from their African cultural legacy.

Until the latter part of the eighteenth century, the majority of slaves did not come to North America directly from Africa. Most were taken from Africa to the Caribbean, either permanently or for a holding period before traveling on to southern plantations. Early on, Spain—and to a lesser extent, France—held much of Caribbean territory, until England moved in to acquire a bulk of the colonies in the region. Those Catholic countries were far less preoccupied than Protestant England with suppressing or eradicating the African cultural heritage of their slaves. So in Haiti and other islands of the West Indies, the slave communities—more heavily populated than in the American colonies—tended to continue developing their native African music, and incorporating ancestral rhythms and techniques into the European melodies they heard.

A goodly number of those slaves wound up in New Orleans, many of them coming from the French province of Saint-Domingue in western Haiti.[21] The main Haitian exodus to New Orleans occurred in the 1790s when a mass of slaves in Saint-Domingue revolted, and Napoleon, for practical reasons, granted Haiti its freedom. Thereupon, many white plantations owners in Haiti fled to Louisiana, taking their slaves with them. New Orleans, with its predominantly Catholic French and Spanish heritage and its West Indian component, proved relatively tolerant vis-à-vis the shouts and secular songs of the bondsmen. Thus the African celebrations in New Orleans, documented and described by visitors up to 1835-36.[22]

The Sunday entertainment in Congo Square provided a festive weekly outlet for the slaves and amusement for many an observer. Even after the United States purchased Louisiana in 1803, the American Protestant authorities—despite some puritanical protests—continued to permit the slaves' takeover of the Square. That way they could attempt to keep black revelry under control, restricting it (in 1817) to a certain locale and specific times. And they could also capitalize on the value of the black "performers" as a tourist attraction.

For Sundays in Congo Square were, indeed, exotic events for visitors. There a horde of slaves surrounded by groups of onlookers would walk slowly in circles, shuffling, patting and singing, as in the religious ring shouts described above. Witnessing this event in 1819 architect Benjamin Latrobe pronounced the shuffling sort of dancing "miserably dull," the African style music "an incredible noise," and the songs "uncouth," as the women "screamed a detestable burthen on one single note."[23] Latrobe was not alone in his assessment of the event. In 1845, Edward H. Durell had almost as negative a reaction.[24] Not until after the Civil War would a writer such as G. W. Cable offer an enthusiastic description (Cable's was reconstructed after the fact) of activities at Congo Square.

After 1820 or so the New Orleans slaves participating in the Sunday events had mainly replaced their African music with narrative or love songs in their Creole language. But although such songs may have been more European than African in origin, they were often performed to the rhythms of Afro-Caribbean music. The music, dance and the beat of the drums undoubtedly contained elements of ancient Dahomean Voodoo (or *vodoun*) chants. When that occurred, as the music became faster and faster, some performers would become swept away—even falling to the ground, unconscious—in dances like the Haitian *bamboula*[25] (once connected with zombiism) or the African *calenda* or *calinda*.[26]

Whether in New Orleans or elsewhere, white melodies combined with the Negro rhythms in much of the slaves' secular music. In the 1830s, actress Fanny Kemble distinguished strains of the French "Ah! Vous dirai-je maman?" and the Scottish "Coming Through the Rye" in slave songs on a Georgia island.[27] Later, writer Dorothy Scarborough would find hints of "Polly-Wolly-Doodle," "O Susannah" and other such folk songs in the Negro "Bile Dem Cabbage Down." The authors of *Slave Songs of the United States* also pointed out echoes of white music in some of their selections of secular songs.

Certainly the slaves could have heard and enjoyed the lively English and Scottish, or Anglo-Celtic, airs that slave accompanists played for white cotillions and reels. Or picked up such tunes from sailors and roustabouts while working on the levee or on riverboats. As for the Caribbean songs of Congo Square, some critics have emphasized the fact that many appear to derive from "civilized" white Creole drawing rooms.[28]

But additionally, they had their own recreational and work songs in which the tunes usually confined themselves to a more restricted melodic range, as in African song: their "fiddle-sings," "devil-songs," "corn-songs" and "jig-tunes"[29] and their rowing songs. They had their "Sold Off to Ol' Georgy," their "Clar de kitchin,"[30] "Ole Jaw Bone" and others. And in line with a most African tradition, they continually improvised verses, at times satirical, describing their familiars, present or absent. We find examples of such in chronicles such as Fanny Kemble's *Journey of a Residence on a Georgian Plantation*[31] and James Hungerford's autobiographical novel, *The Old Plantation.*[32]

Even where strains of European tunes could be discerned, the black songs were found to be totally different in text and style. Fanny Kemble saw the secular slave songs (and dances) as a "veritable Jim Crow," an "ineffable black conception"[33] with "astonishingly primitive" words.[34] And Dorothy Scarborough noted that despite a discernable trace of an American or European melody in a particular slave song, it had "a Negro swing to it."[35] Just as listeners and critics discovered originality in the slaves' religious music[36] despite traces of white songs, the same discovery held true for the secular music of the Negroes.

The Roots of Jazz

Today jazz may seem a far cry to us from the singing of the slaves. Yet all the important elements of modern jazz could be found in the spirituals, shouts, field hollers, work songs and recreational songs of African Americans in bondage.

One of the most obvious pre-jazz qualities of the early black music was its characteristic rhythm, a rhythm which, as seen above, broke entirely with white tradition. White listeners were constantly struck by the black musician's "distortion" of the customary tempos or his "violation of the laws of rhythm."[37] Although a number of historians and critics of music have attributed the black innovations to "syncopation," that word does not describe the difference adequately. Indeed, syncopation had long been an integral part of traditional European and American music; it is commonly found in Bach, Beethoven, Mozart and other classical masters. The black contribution lies, rather, in the radical changes the slaves made in the accepted tempo and the original and unusual brand of syncopation generated in those changes.

The usual tempos of white America, adopted largely from English, French, German, Scottish or Irish sources, were either the three-quarters time of polkas, waltzes, schottishes and mazurkas or an even four beats to a measure (in two-quarters or four-quarters time). The slaves favored the four-beat tempo, but, as mentioned above, in their singing they tended to place the stress on the weak beats, the second and fourth rather than the standard first and third. This off-beat stress, which would become the heartbeat of jazz, can be heard in recordings of religious and work songs preserved for generations by Negroes in isolated villages and islands of the American South.[38]

Additionally, they anticipated, delayed or prolonged beats in a most unorthodox manner. For example, in his introduction to *Slave Songs of the United States,* William Francis Allen notes that the slaves' boat songs tend to be sung "just a trifle behind time."[39] Black jazz of the twentieth century has lovingly retained this quality of starting phrases slightly after the beat. One has only to listen to Louis Armstrong's vocals and those of his white disciple Frank Sinatra to be aware of the phenomenon.

The rhythmic irregularities were, to a great extent, provided by singers who carried the melody. As later in ragtime piano, the slaves' novel syncopation was ever counterbalanced by a steady background beat—some sort of drumming or the participants' foot tapping. The interplay of the irregular tempo in the singing, with the steady, basic tapping and with bystanders' hand clapping on the offbeat, the irregular anticipation or delaying of the singers' parts—all of these elements overlapped and combined to produce the irregular syncopation that would be found in ragtime and jazz.

Improvisation added to the pre-jazz nature of the slaves' music. A singer might vary or embellish a song to such an extent that it was impossible for a collector to reproduce it definitively note for note or word for word. Adding to the musical ornamentation and improvisation was the slurring of notes by singers and musicians. A singer would not necessarily remain fixed on one tone but might glide two or more notes down or up the scale—or hold a note, stretching it into the next beat or measure. At the same time, certain syllables might be prolonged, or "milked," as in "no-bo-ó-dy" or "go-ó-one" (gone). These effects—to be developed even further in the decorative singing style of gospel music—would form an intrinsic part of ragtime, Dixieland, blues, swing and rock.

Concerning such proto-jazz improvisations in black folk music, W. C. Handy stated, "The Negro becomes impatient of silences and fills in the rest-spaces with impromptu embellishments of his own."[40] So, he wrote, singers would fill any breaks or pauses with vocal interjections like "Oh lawdy!" much as jazz instrumentalists would later add their own embellishments or riffs in breaks.

One of the most telling descriptions of this improvisational rendering of slave songs is found in the classic anthology, *Slave Songs of the United States.*

> . . . [The singers] seem to follow their own whims, beginning when they please and leaving off when they please, striking an octave above or below . . . or hitting some other note that chords, so as to produce the effect of a marvellous complication and variety, and yet with the most perfect time, and rarely with any discord. And what makes it all the harder to unravel a thread of melody out of this strange network is that, like birds, they seem not infrequently to strike sounds that cannot be precisely represented by the gamut, and abound in slides from one note to another, and turns and cadences not in articulated notes.[41]

In the late 1830s, Fanny Kemble, who had a fine musical ear, noted the unusual rhythmic and melodic interplay in the singing of slave boatmen:

> The way in which the chorus strikes in with the burden [chorus] between each phrase of the melody chanted by a

> single voice, is very curious and effective, especially with the rhythm of the rowlocks for accompaniment . . . [42]

Beyond all these incipient jazz qualities heard in the slave songs, the words themselves often anticipated ragtime and jazz rhythms. It is impossible not to feel the "swing" of such lyrics as "Hebn', hebn', when you get to hebn' gwine to try on yo' robe, gwine to shout all over God's hebn'" or "Rock o' my soul in de bosom of Abraham . . ." If proof were needed of this inherent rhythm of the lyrics, one has only to see and hear Noble Sissle and Eubie Blake's filmed rendition of "Walk All Over God's Hebn.'"[43] Although Blake was a masterful ragtime pianist, he played the song absolutely straight and Sissle sang it in the traditional way. Yet the number had an unmistakably jazzed beat to it.

The actual metamorphosis of black music into ragtime and jazz would not become apparent until the latter part of the nineteenth century. Obviously, however, the basic elements that identify that modern music could already be discovered in the songs of the black slaves. The rhythmic and melodic irregularities, the improvisations and embellishments, the freedom and variety that miraculously blend into a perfectly timed musical entity are what, precisely, lie at the heart of the jazz we know today.

How, exactly, did these pre-jazz traits take root in the spirituals? And what role did the slaves' African heritage play in that process? Again, such questions have no pat answers. However, some light may be shed by pointing to features of traditional African music found in the songs of the slaves.

The African Connection

By the end of the eighteenth century the majority of slaves came to America directly from the western part of Africa,[44] from trading posts along a stretch of coastline of over 2,000 miles, extending from the northern Senegambian region toward the Congo in Central Africa and as far south as Angola. A large percentage of them had been captured from inland regions[45] and brought to the coastal stations in chains to await the devastating "middle passage"[46] across the ocean. On the voyage they were often given musical instruments, sometimes European ones, sometimes African, and forced to dance and sing lest they languish and die before being sold.

Once in North America, those slaves who had survived the voyage were largely discouraged from perpetuating their "barbaric" native songs and dances, and the memory of them would eventually dim. But since music itself could not be eradicated from their lives, the slaves adopted what was most present and available. That, as we have seen, was the music of their white masters. In a process similar to the voodooist's merging of the goddess Erzulie with the Virgin Mary, the slaves infused the white songs with residual traits of their native African music.

The process itself—that is, how, precisely, African music blended with the spirituals—remains a puzzle, with many pieces missing. To cite one problem: in order to be able to tap their African heritage in creating the spirituals, the slaves had to possess, one would assume, 1) a common language which would open the way to cultural communication between them and 2) common denominators in the musics of their native regions—characteristic features that would contribute to making the spiritual a distinctive Afro-American product. However, although the African slaves arriving in North America issued mainly from West and Central Africa, they spoke different languages and in many cases would not have been familiar with the mother tongues of slaves from other areas, even contiguous ones. And secondly, the musical styles of their various tribes and countries were not absolutely identical.

Further complicating the problem, once in bondage in North America the Africans were dispersed among various locales of the South. The average slave on a Georgia sea island would have had little knowledge of the kind of music sung by blacks on a New Orleans levee or a Virginia tobacco farm. Besides, the majority of plantations were actually small farms, often with only one or a handful of slaves working alongside the owner. In such cases, the slaves were cut off from any African community that might have conserved Africanisms, and they were more likely to lose contact entirely with their musical and cultural heritage.

As for the large plantations, those having two or three hundred slaves or more, one might imagine that some of them imported slaves all from the same point of origin, with the same language and culture. For it made economic sense for South Carolina rice growers to buy slaves from the Windward Coast,[47] where Africans had previous experience in wet rice cultivation. Or for North Carolina cattle ranchers to import their bondsmen from Senegambia, with its industry of livestock raising and superior techniques of open grazing. To some extent that did happen. But, generally, a landholder would choose according to the presumed potential of a slave (strength, health, looks, skills) or according to price and availability, rather than a slave's country of origin.[48] So as a result, very often a good-sized plantation or farm housed a heterogeneous crew of African natives.

All these factors would seem to militate against the creation of a common music, unique to the slave community. Yet such a music was, indeed, created. How was it possible?

In the first place, despite apparent handicaps, the slaves were, indeed, able to communicate with each other. Even at the start, newly arrived Africans speaking different languages could succeed in making themselves understood by one another.[49] And in any case, once in North America, they were obliged to speak English. So they quickly developed a pidgin English similar to the brand of speech used in coastal West Africa, where the British had established slave trading posts. (Slaves imported from the British West Indies would already have had some fluency in the pidgin English spoken there). Such an idiom contained a number of traits common to West Sudanese and *bantu* languages of Africa. Forms of pidgin English became prevalent throughout the slaveholding colonies, survived well into the twentieth century in remote areas of the South and may still be heard in the West Indies and elsewhere.[50, 51]

Negroes were especially able to preserve Africanisms in language and culture on very large plantations with slaves numbering in the hundreds. In such cases, being relatively cut off from contact with the outside world, as on sizeable plantations in the West Indies, they were more likely to maintain their traditional customs. And also more likely to develop their own, characteristic form of music.

That music flourished and endured most strikingly in precisely those areas where the slaves had the greatest access to a common language and culture. The South Carolina and Georgia lowlands and Georgia Sea Islands, for instance, have been a fertile source of slave songs found in many collections of spirituals. In such areas, clustered together on remote plantations, African born slaves had already developed an idiom called *gullah*—a corruption of "Angola," whence many of them came. Their language retained much of African syntax and a preponderance of words from *bantu*[52] tongues used in regions of Central Africa. That is, regions that provided the colonies with a great percentage of their slave field workers. This phenomenon of slaves relatively isolated and having a similar place of origin and a common idiom undoubtedly fostered the development of a shared culture and a communal style of music.[53]

And with the aid of a common language black music flourished elsewhere as well, even in an area where the slaves were often less isolated from the white community than in other southern regions. Notably, in Louisiana and especially in the New Orleans area. Africans, largely from Senegambia, came as slaves to Louisiana in the eighteenth century, sent there by the French government, They were joined later by slaves from Saint-Domingue, who were imported to work the sugar crops. Their common tongue was Creole, derived from a West African pidgin language based on French, Senegalese and Portuguese.

The word "Creole," as applied to the slaves themselves, indicated those who had been born in North America rather than in Africa. It would later mainly come to mean the free mixed-blood population of downtown New Orleans, that is, the light-skinned upper crust *gens de couleur* combining assorted strains of African, French, Spanish or Caribbean heritage.[54] However, forebears of such elitist freedmen had, as slaves, communicated with each other through their Creole language. And undoubtedly that tongue fostered an ethnic cohesiveness which would help pave the way for the blossoming of black jazz in New Orleans.

New Orleans itself was a most likely locus for the development of African-American music. On the one hand, it had its communities of slaves with a common language, preserving a common musical heritage on several large plantations. And on the other hand, importantly, that city had the greatest percentage of free Negroes in all of the South. Musicians among those freemen were not necessarily isolated on plantations and farms but played amidst an urban population. It is true that a good percentage of that group were light-skinned Creoles whose repertoire and musical style could be classified as white or European. But a good number of ordinary free Africans (or "raw country" Negroes), such as those working around the wharves and other areas of town, were more likely to keep to their Afro-Caribbean rhythms in song and dance.

In fact, not only free Negroes but the slaves themselves might be heard sounding out their characteristic music in public places—even outside of Sundays in Congo Square. Frederick Douglass said, "A city slave is almost a freeman compared with a slave on the plantation.[55] That seemed to hold particularly true in permissive New Orleans where the bondsmen enjoyed a surprising amount of freedom and mobility. There, slaves hired out by their masters as stevedores or roustabouts were observed singing and dancing on the docks and banks of the Mississippi. And many who were technically slaves continued their rhythmic music making in the saloons, dives and streets of the city and even held their own dances (some of them also brazenly infiltrated the quadroon balls of middle class Creoles).[56]

The music of the New Orleans slaves, as evidenced in the songs that were transmitted and have come down to us, were most often not soulful religious spirituals but secular songs with a marked French flavor, frequently accompanied by African rhythms. Unlike most songs in collections of antebellum black spirituals, those of New Orleans are generally cheerful sounding and humorous. Given the tenor of such songs and the later influence of stirring marches, small wonder that when New Orleanean blacks began to form bands, their music, blues and all, would tend to be lively and upbeat.

Although slave songs of New Orleans had their own personality, with their French tinge by way of the Caribbean, they did not lose the African elements that helped establish and keep the music a Negro product. And well beyond New Orleans and the *gullah* regions, African retentions served to keep slave songs in general a recognizably black phenomenon.

Slave music resonated in multiple areas of the slave world.[57] The markedly Negro sounds were heard and commented on by writers particularly in the pre-Civil War era. In her chronicles, Fanny Kemble described typical Negro songs of the Altamaha area of the Georgia Sea Islands in the 1830s. Later, the compilers of *Slave Songs* included in their anthology Negro spirituals of Maryland, Virginia, Tennessee and other states. Lydia Parrish, Guy Johnson, Nicolas Ballanta, Alan Lomax and others have focused on a diversity of isolated southern areas in which slave songs, with their familiar features, had been preserved and perpetuated. (A number of researchers, for example, have singled out the black community of South Carolina's St. Helena Island, which at one point in antebellum times, had two thousand slaves to two hundred white people). The same characteristics found in slave songs were discovered again and again throughout these various regions.

Even in the antebellum North, the ubiquitous black music reached white listeners and amazed them with its strange uniqueness. For as in New Orleans, slaves in some northern locales were permitted to perform traditional African songs and dances on certain occasions. In Albany, New York, for example, that occasion was the annual Pinkster festival of the late eighteenth century, described by James Eights in 1867.[58]

As for the spiritual, Eileen Southern believed, in fact, that it was the North that gave birth to it, that the genre originated "in the independent black churches of the North, where black congregations, freed from the supervision of white clergymen, could conduct their services as they wished."[59] But if that were so, it would leave another blank in the puzzle, namely, how did the spiritual migrate from the North to remote and isolated communities of the deep South? Even granting a certain mobility, with slaves being traded from state to state, such a north-to-south musical migration would seem problematical.

Despite all the unanswered questions, certain realities remain. First, be it in the North, South or elsewhere, the slaves' music struck white listeners as "Negro music." And secondly, its uniqueness was at least in part due to the African component. Plantation owners may have tried to "cleanse" the bondsmen of their African background. The native songs themselves, those with African words and melodies, may have been forgotten. But as we have seen, African traits did remain in slave music.[60]

That survival may be due in part, to the "re-africanization" of the slave trade in the early nineteenth century, for North America saw the perpetual arrival of new slaves from Africa after the Revolution. According to Ira Berlin, by1810, native Africans composed over a fifth of South Carolinian slaves.[61] Moreover, after the 1808 ban on slave importation from Africa, slaves smuggled into various southern states came mainly from the same areas, the Congo and Angola, regions where forms of *bantu* were spoken.[62] But more importantly, Africanisms were transmitted from generation to generation. Throughout the years, children of slaves could constantly be observed alongside their elders performing identical ring dances and singing the exact same songs as their parents.[63] Whether the survival of African traits in music was the result of demographic re-africanization or of intergenerational transmission, or both, the distinctive sounds of African-American music continued to be heard throughout much of the country.

Let us consider more precisely here the connections between African music and the songs of African-American slaves.

First of all, although the various tribes of West and Central Africa had their own individual local styles of singing and dancing, those songs and dances shared enough common features to come under the rubric of African music. In fact, nearly all locales south of the Sahara and west of Ethiopia have had styles of singing, playing and dancing similar enough to warrant the label "African." The main features of their music, as applicable to slave songs, are the following:

1) African music, like the slave songs, was traditionally an active community enterprise rather than a performance to be listened to passively. As in Africa, where a whole village would participate in making music, so in slave

singing and dancing, an entire group would take part, even if simply clapping to keep time for the music makers.

2) Like slave music, African music made constant use of call-and-response, with a leader introducing the main substance of a song and a chorus chiming in with a familiar refrain. The call-and-response was not executed in exact unison. Often a lead singer would come in before the chorus had ended its chant and also start before the drum music, so there was a constant overlapping of the parts. African-American music would use variations of such techniques.

3) Traditional African music, like slave music, featured polyrhythms, but of a more advanced type. That is, African music might have drums beating several different tempos at the same time—such as 4/4, 6/8 and 3/4—along with interjected beats of singing, clapping and foot stamping. The various tempos were staggered. For instance, two drums would never start on the exact same beat.

   The staggering and interweaving of multiple tempos inevitably created off-the-beat rhythms, which became simplified and more pronounced in the music of the slaves.

4) As with slave songs, there were no silences or pauses in African music. Something happened musically at every moment.

5) Singers of traditional African music, namely the lead singers, improvised much of their singing, as would the slaves of the New World.

6) As in slave music, drumming, hand clapping and foot stomping played an important role in the performance of African songs.

7) African movements and African dancing included the shuffling and sensuous swaying movements executed by American slaves.

8) Some African musical instruments were of the same types as those used by the slaves.

Other common denominators could be added, for instance repetition, the frequent use of vocal glissandos, slurring or stretching of syllables[64]; trills, falsettos, yodels, the flatting and "bending" of certain notes (to be featured, differently, in the blues); the common use of melodies corresponding to the pentatonic scale, and more. The above list, however, adequately demonstrates that traditional African music, did, indeed contain important features to be found in slave music and, later, in jazz.

With all these common traits, one might expect that slave music actually sounded like traditional African music, with its percussive polyrhythms and vocal call-and-response. Unfortunately for researchers, that is not the case (or the puzzle would have far fewer missing pieces). For if we compare traditional African music with the slave songs, we are apt to find little obvious resemblance—especially on initial listening. And for good reason.

To begin with, the slaves, deprived in North America of their ancestral religion—and, in many localities, of their large drums[65]—could no longer call to their ancient gods by using the various rhythms identified with each deity.[66] Even if it had been permitted, the rhythmic evoking of gods, perpetuated in the Caribbean, would have been unthinkable to Christianized North American slaves creating and singing religious spirituals. As for their secular music, traditional African drumming accompaniment was commonly heard only in certain locales, for example, in Congo Square, St. Louis or the Pinkster celebrations in the North. Furthermore, although the slaves developed their own off-the-beat stress in music, it did not resemble the more subtle off-the-beat accents that occurred within the highly complex polyrhythms of African music.

When it came to melody, the slaves were dealing with the European scale used in America, rather than the more nuanced African scale. For example, when African music appears to flatten a note—the fourth or seventh in our scale—it is not really the "blue note" as some scholars have said, for rather than lowering a note by a half tone, as in the blues, African music might lower a note by something more like a quarter tone, possibly even less.

Further, African songs were more limited in melodic range and variety than the spirituals devised by the slaves. For African melody usually had to conform to the rise and fall, or pitch, of tonal languages and could not go beyond the range of ordinary speech. The slaves, on the other hand, early favored African sounding songs of a narrow melodic range but were later undoubtedly influenced by the less confined and more lyrical European type of melodies heard in America.

Finally, African music is more disciplined than slave music. A leader may improvise, but the accompanying singers and drummers come in with their part with great precision rather than with the freedom, abandon and creativity of the slaves. And in the last analysis, although African music may be hot, it does not swing in the sense that a lilting, off-the-beat spiritual could swing and, later, jazz.

In view of such differences, going back to the sounds of traditional African group music may well disappoint those eager to discover a strong and immediate link between Africa and black music created on American soil. For a closer connection, one might do better to compare individual examples of the slaves' work songs and hollers with their African counterparts. A very striking resemblance between two such songs may be heard in "Jim and John," a selection from Alan Lomax's recording of *Roots of the Blues.* There Lomax juxtaposes an American Negro work song with one recorded in Africa, and they seem almost duplicates. However, we cannot know whether the African holler in question actually descends from one contemporaneous with slavery in North America. For unlike traditional African ensemble music, spontaneous individual African work songs and hollers of yore have not been perpetuated as a genre through the years.

How much more obvious, direct and persuasive are the echoes of Africa in twentieth-century black music of the West Indies and Latin America. There the African beat of Ketu religious songs for Osain transferred directly into the habañera of the Cuban slaves and into the tango of Argentina. There the Ketu rhythms for Omolú [67] ♪ ♪ ♪ 𝄾 ♩ ♩ have clearly contributed to Cuba's rumba, mambo and the more recent cha-cha. The calipso of Trinidad, the samba and bossa nova of Brazil and the Latin American conga, popular in the late 1930s, have their African tempos as well, syncopated patterns heard in the ground beat. Finally, for a more authentically African style of call-and-response than heard in the black spirituals or in jazz we have only to listen to Cuba's Buena Vista Social Club's rendering of songs like "El Cuarto de Tula" or "Candela" in the late 1990s.[68]

It seems some sort of miracle, therefore, that the American slaves, distanced as they were from their African musical legacy, had so internalized that legacy as to fuse it quite naturally and spontaneously with the music of their white masters. While taking a different musical path from the Caribbean and the rest of the slave world, they somehow blended the old with the new, unconsciously creating a genre unique in the annals of music. Over the years that original and ever evolving genre would be laughed at, frowned at and eventually imitated and adopted by populations throughout the world.

Notes

1 James K. Kennard, Jr. Article in *Knickerbocker Magazine*, 1845.

2 Article in the *New York Herald,* May 21, 1893.

3 Taken to Virginia from a Dutch ship. The first captured Africans were probably simply indentured servants, eligible for freedom after a specified number of years. But the system of lifetime slavery became an institution soon afterwards.

4 See Epstein, pp. 38-42 and 67 *ff* for some specific reports of African survivals in the slaves' music.

5 In North America, as in Africa, many a slave child, strapped to a mother's back as she worked the soil, heard her chanting her work songs.

6 See, for example, Kemble, *Journal of a Residence on a Georgia Plantation,* p. 166, or Kemble's *American Journals,* p. 68, where she notes that in 1832 "to teach a slave to read or write is to incur a penalty either of fine or imprisonment." In 1800 a bill arose in North Carolina's General Assembly ". . . to prevent all persons from teaching slaves to read or write" (*Ante-Bellum North Carolina,*

p. 543). Such a law did not come into effect there until 1830. See also Olmstead, p. 568 and *passim.*

7 Justifiably so, for their were many attempts at rebellion. Even before the Revolution, in "Cato's Conspiracy" of 1739, around eighty slaves secured arms, killed a guard and walked to Florida from Stono, South Carolina. Forty-four Negroes and twenty-one whites perished when the militia confronted the slaves. But the 1820s and 1830s saw a particularly large number of slave uprisings, including Nat Turner's revolt.

8 For example the fugitive slave laws, strengthened in 1850. Such laws punished runaway slaves and forced them to return to their masters—even after years (in some cases decades) of hiding or living in freedom. And they rewarded any finders, North or South, who turned the escapees in.

9 One of numerous examples of such opposition to religious instruction is seen in Kemble, p. 207, with its account of a slave flogged for having his wife baptized. Revolts inspired by preachers such as Denmark Vesey and the violent Nat Turner gave slaveholders cause enough to fear the effect of the church on slaves. From the eighteenth century and up to Emancipation, other ministers inspired their flocks to insurrection. Few, if any, escaped death at the hands of their pursuers, but southern whites remained wary.

Many slave owners, however, would come to endorse religion and church attendance for slaves. For a number of preachers, both white and black, began to support the institution of slavery from the pulpit, dwelling on Bible passages which emphasized obedience of servant to master.

10 Mention should be made of two other eighteenth-century hymnists, John Cennick (1718-55) and John Newton (1725-1807, of "Amazing Grace" fame), who also composed hymns of great popular appeal.

11 Viv Broughton, *Black Gospel,* p. 20.

12 In this book the word "spirituals" will apply to the slaves' religious music. The term "slave songs" will apply to slave music in general.

13 Lawrence Levine examines other ways in which spirituals evolved from a spontaneous communal experience. See p. 25 *ff.*

14 On occasion white revivalists used that same pattern in their camp meetings but may well have taken it over from their black

congregations. In any case, the model did not become a feature of white hymnody.

15 Although a diversity of music styles existed among Africa's numerous tribal areas, the traits described here were common to the African regions from which the slaves were imported and to other areas of the continent.

16 For a while, ornamentation was extensively used in white revival and gospel hymns but in an exaggerated, virtuoso style that did not become a conspicuous feature of slave songs.

17 So structured as to imitate the language of an African tribesman and send messages through variations in pitch. For instance, the Yoruba language, like Chinese Mandarin speech, is tonal, with one word having several meanings according to pitch (although Yoruban and other African tongues have a less complex system of pitch than Mandarin Chinese, and some languages, such as Wolof, are not tonal). Just as in Mandarin, "ma" can mean "mother" or "horse" at different tone levels, the Yoruba tongue has "fo" signifying "wash" or "break," depending on the level of pitch. A message could then be understood through the drumming of "syllables" at different levels of pitch.

Large drums of any sort became suspect after Cato's rebellion (see note six, above), since, in that incident, singing, dancing and drum beating were used to call the rebellious slaves together.

18 A shimmy-like hip rotation has often formed part of traditional dancing in many parts of Africa. Scandalized observers rarely went so far as to describe their hip movements. But in his accounts of slave life on Saint-Domingue (whence came many New Orleans slaves), Moreau de St. Méry provides ample details concerning those Afro-Caribbean gyrations. See Vol. I, p. 64.

19 Slaves and ex-slaves did generally deem religious songs worthier than the secular ones. But Gilbert Chase (p. 257) held that researchers from the North, abolitionists, focused on the religious music in order to stress the more dignified features of the black race.

20 Formerly "Circus Square" and, later, "Beauregard Square." See Latrobe's 1819 account of Congo Square festivities in *The Journals of Benjamin Henry Latrobe,* Vol III. The charming and frequently quoted description of Congo Square by George Cable (*Century Magazine,* 1886) was not an eyewitness account but one most likely

based on his readings and/or interviews. For that late in the century, the African style dances and songs Cable claimed to have seen and heard in the Square were not longer being presented there.

21 Formerly called Island of Hispaniola.

22 There is some evidence that the Congo Square slave music resumed a decade later, at least briefly (see Kmen, p. 229).

23 P. 204. "Burthen," an archaic form of "burden," simply signified a musical chorus and was used in that sense by Fanny Kemble as well, in referring to the slaves' music. But Latrobe's negative description reminds us that the word derives from Old French "bourdon," indicating a droning musical sound.

24 In *New Orleans As I Found It.* Published under the pseudonym "H. Didimus."

25 Named for the African 'bamboula" drum, made of bamboo.

26 This author actually witnessed such a *vodun* possession in an elegant Back Bay mansion of Boston in the late 1980s. Then, as director of the French Library and Cultural Center in Boston, she invited a Haitian dance troupe to perform on Marlborough Street as part of a Haitian Culture Month. Part way into the program, however, one of the dancers fell into a trance, literally stopping the show.

27 *Journal of a Residence on a Georgian Plantation.,* p. 163.

28 For example, in "Those Congo Melodies," *New York Sun,* September 9, 1909.

29 Listed in *Slave Songs,* p. x.

30 Reportedly adapted in the 1830s by a white circus entertainer. See Sanjek, Vol. II.

31 Pp. 141-2.

32 P. 196.

33 *Journal of a Residence on a Georgian Plantation,* p. 131.

34 *Ibid,* p. 163.

35 *On the Trail of Negro Folk Songs,* p. 125

36 See previous section on spirituals.

37 George G. Foster, p. 142.

38 One of countless examples may be heard in "Tamping Ties," in the archival CD *Negro Work Songs,* where the hammer resounds repeatedly on the offbeat.

39 P. xvi.

40 "The Heart of the Blues," pp. 152 ff.

41 Pp. v, vi.

42 *Journal of a Residence on a Georgian Plantation,* p. 259.

43 Video: *African-American Cinema* , Vol. II. This contains 1923 footage of Sissle and Blake in performance. Sound and images were synchronized, predating the 1927 "talkies" through the groundbreaking process of "Phonofilm."

44 Some, especially in earlier years, had been forcibly shipped to the coast of Africa from deep in the African interior, although by the nineteenth century a large percentage of natives from the interior had migrated westward and taken up residence on the coast.

Although the trend to import slaves directly from Africa had already begun in the eighteenth century, it increased markedly in the nineteenth. This was partly because the government imposed a higher tax on the purchase of slaves from the Caribbean, so it was economically more feasible to go directly to the source. But in any case a great number of slaves were needed for the plantations to turn a good profit. Between 1803 and 1808 South Carolina imported nearly 90,000 slaves from Africa. Even after the 1808 ban on slave trade with Africa, large shipments of slaves from Africa arrived illegally on United States soil.

45 The coastal tribes themselves were not supposed to enslave their own people, for they considered that immoral (although it did happen). So the Fanti people of the Gold Coast (Ghana) might go north, and buy slaves from the Ashanti or take them as prisoners of war or by kidnapping. Then the Ashanti could obtain slaves by warfare, kidnapping or trade with their neighbors to the east and south. And so on. Slaves were sometimes brought to the coast from as far as 300 to 500 miles inland.

46 This trip to the New World represented one leg of the international slave trading between Europe, Africa, the Caribbean and the colonies.

47 Today's Sierra Leone and Liberia.

48 Dizzy Gillespie, quite knowledgeable about this subject, noted, as have others, that plantation owners preferred *not* to have slaves from the same region and with the same language, in order to prevent conspiracies. See *To Be or Not to . . . Bop,* p. 290.

49 Ouladah Equiano, kidnapped in Africa and brought to the coast, said that the languages of the different nations he traversed "did

not differ" greatly and he could pick them up and communicate with people from a variety of tribes (Schneider, p. 20). And the enslaved Mendian people sailing on the Amistad in 1839 all came from different tribes but could understand each others' dialects. That communication enabled them to plot and execute a dramatic and successful mutiny (*Ibid.*, p. 42).

50 See Turner, *Africanisms in the Gullah Dialect.* See also William D. Piersen's discussion of slave linguistics, in which he identifies the Louisiana slave idiom as "an Afro-French Creole based upon a Portuguese-French-Senegalese pidgin brought from the West Coast of Africa in the early eighteenth century . . ." *From Africa to America,* p. 88.

51 Today, a Nigerian native unable to communicate with a fellow Nigerian speaking a different language, will use pidgin English.

52 See, for example, Holloway and Vass, pp. xxiv *ff.*

53 According to Holloway and Vass (p. xxv), "Their Africanisms, shared and adopted by various African ethnic groups of the field-slave community, gradually developed into African-American cooking (soul food), music (jazz, blues, spirituals, gospels), dance, language . . . and arts."

54 For specific information on the New Orleans Creoles see www.loyno.edu/~tlkinnon/creoles.htm and its "Biracial Hierarchy Chart."

55 *Narrative of the Life of Frederick Douglass,* p. 50.

56 Kmen makes many references, *passim,* to complaints of whites relating to the ever-present music making of the slaves and cites vain attempts of the citizenry to stem such permissiveness. *Note*: The slaves' presence at quadroon balls was facilitated by the frequent use of masks.

57 The same holds true for the slaves' dancing. Their "calinda" or "calenda" was danced throughout the days of slavery in nearly every corner of the slave world. See, for example, Epstein, pp. 30-38.

58 Cited in Southern, *Readings in Black American Music,* pp. 41 *ff.*

59 "An Origin for the Negro Spiritual," *The Theater of Black Americans.* Vol. I, p. 93.

60 That survival should not surprise us if we remember that the Negro dialect—despite migration to the North, schooling, access to the

national media and a certain degree of desegregation—has endured throughout the centuries. As has the white southern accent, which was seen in antebellum times as a contamination of the dialect of African-American slaves.

61 Berlin concludes: "The re-africanization of the Lower South with the arrival of saltwater slaves informed all aspects of black life" (p. 133). It stands to reason that this would necessarily include their all-important musical life.

62 See Holloway and Vass for details, p. xxv.

63 Epstein cites Jean Baptiste Du Tertre's description of slaves' intergenerational ring dancing in the Antilles before 1659 and Frederika Bremer's similar description in 1851. She concludes that such accounts tell "much about how this style of dancing was transmitted from one generation to another." P. 44.

64 One of the closest likenesses to effects in the spirituals may be heard in the slurring, stretching and displacement of stress that occurs in "Agolona" on the Yoruba/Dahomean Collection Library of Congress CD: RCD 10405.

65 Drums did continue to be played by slaves in locales such as Louisiana and the Georgia Sea Islands.

66 Stephen Tracy has correctly noted (*Langston Hughes and the Blues*) that slaves could make use of other percussive instruments. Still, the large drum had served as the prime medium for calling to the gods.

67 These rhythms are heard on the Yoruba/Dahomean CD, *op. cit*

68 Although African lyrics are not usually found in Latin American compositions, the Spanish version of the song "Tabu," interpolated in the 1931 Hollywood film of the same name, included the words "Ifá changó obatalaba ochún y yemayá." The phrase is clearly the invocation of well known African gods—and a way of infusing mystery and exoticism into the song.

2

DISCOVERY

FROM BLACK CULTURE TO WHITE COMMODITY

Minstrelsy and the Coon Song

At the turn of the nineteenth century, most Americans thought of black and white musics as two distinct, disparate products. On the one hand, the Negro slaves had their spirituals, their field hollers, work, recreational songs and their homespun jigs. On the other, whites, little concerned with such humble fare, held conservatively to their sentimental ballads and love songs, their amusing ditties, their traditional French, English, Scotch, German or Irish dances. The slave songs and dances, with their amusingly quaint style, struck white listeners as nothing less than exotic. For them, black music was a separate, if not equal, genre.

However, the musical products of the two races were not to remain forever segregated. The slaves, as we have seen, had already used white hymns for fodder. But by the 1830s and 1840s, white musicians were returning the compliment, adopting and adapting black songs and dances. From that moment on, the two musics began feeding on one another in earnest, borrowing and stealing this or that element from the other's repertory.

Mutual admiration? Partly, but other realities lay behind the increasing interactions of black and white music. Most importantly, white musicians and entrepreneurs came to depend on black composers and performers for their originality and style, while, more and more, black musicians found they needed the sponsorship of whites in order to reach the public. Specifically, the white czars of popular music knew they could make money with an infusion of African-American material. They realized that the native black music had commercial potential, that it could appeal to a large public of white consumers. But without the backing of those white entrepreneurs, musicians of color would find it difficult to succeed, or even survive, in the field.

This musical cross-fertilization took a giant step forward when a significant number of white entertainers and entrepreneurs discovered the cultural goldmine of black music. Promptly availing themselves of their newly found mother lode, they set about adapting slave songs and dances to the musical stage. Thereby creating the highly popular American minstrel show.

Minstrelsy in White and Black

Well before the 1840s and minstrelsy, white musicians, English and American, had tapped the talents of southern black slaves and their folk music. Struck especially by the lively recreational songs and dances of the "darkies," admiration and opportunism spawned imitation. White English actors led the way, impersonating the American Negro on the British stage. But white American entertainers soon followed suit, smearing their faces with burnt cork and imitating the speech and mannerisms of southern blacks. In no time, more and more white actors and musicians were taking to the stage in blackface,[69] performing Negro style songs and dances, at times accompanied by banjo, fiddle or tambourine.

Significantly, a song and dance routine entitled "Jim Crow" was one of the first major successes in America of a white entertainer impersonating an African American. After performing the number in various cities of the east, Thomas Dartmouth ("Daddy") Rice achieved fame with it in 1832, at the Bowery Theater in lower Manhattan. According to Rice, he was aping the singing and dancing of a crippled old black stable worker, Jim ("Uncle Jim") Crow. Prancing on stage, Rice sang Crow's animated ditty:

> Wheel about, turn about, do jes so,
> An' ebery time I wheel about I jump Jim Crow.

Not until over a century later, in the 1940s, would the song's title function as a symbol of racial discrimination. At the time, white audiences found the routine nothing but entertaining, and if any black observers considered it objectionable they were hardly in a position to object.

The vogue of white musical entertainers impersonating Negroes found its most popular expression in the introduction of the minstrel show in 1843. At that time four white men calling themselves the Virginia Minstrels (Dan Emmett, Bill Whitlock, Frank Brower and Dick Pelham) offered a "Negro Concert" at New York's Bowery Theater, accompanying themselves on banjo, violin, tambourine and African style animal bone castanets. As Arnold Shaw put it:

> No one could have anticipated or predicted that . . . the quartet would launch a uniquely American form of entertainment—a form . . . that would dominate the popular theater into the twentieth century, and through which America's first major popular songwriters and performers would emerge.[70]

Three years later the Christy Minstrels would give the minstrel show its most familiar shape: After an opening musical number, a white gloved, often white faced emcee called "Mr. Interlocutor" would say to his "black" cast: "Gentlemen be seated." Then, sitting at the center of a semi-circle of minstrels, he would banter with Mr. Tambo (for tambourine) and Mr. Bones (for bone clappers) ensconced in the end seats. After that, the actors would circle in a "walk-around" finale to the first part. Then came the "olio," a variety of solo acts such as songs and instrumentals, virtuoso tap dances, humorous monologues, stump speeches, operatic burlesques or theatrical parodies, all heavily dosed with black dialect. And finally, a reprise of the "walk-around," in which the whole company usually participated.

Throughout such a show, actors and musicians regaled the public with staged images and stylized echoes of plantation life. Performers versed in Negro dialect offered the public an acceptably superficial view of darkies singing and dancing on the levee, Rastuses courting their Lizas, watermelon eating idlers, shuffling and stomping rhythm makers. Stephen Foster added his own romanticized, nostalgic view of southern blacks[71] to the minstrel show in songs such as "De Camptown Races," "Massa's in De Cold, Cold Ground" and, later, "Old Black Joe."

The two main styles of minstrel music were the lively, usually comic, song-and-dance[72] numbers like "Zip Coon" (which would later become "Turkey in the Straw" of hoe-down fame) and sentimental ballads such as "Old Folks at Home" or "Darling Nelly Gray," an Irish style of song transposed to a southern setting. Where music was concerned, early minstrelsy did strive for some degree of authenticity. In the 1840s, for example, the Bryant minstrels appropriated a number of secular slave songs of the South. In fact, some principals of the shows traveled South to seek out the slaves' characteristic music on steamboats, river docks and elsewhere. On stage, entertainers such as Dan Emmett[73] attempted to reproduce actual songs of the slaves—at least to a degree.

However, the search for authenticity was short lived and became a relative rarity on the minstrel stage. Musically, for instance, except for certain Negro banjo "jigs" and possibly some black-inspired dancing, the characteristic off-beat syncopation of slave songs did not occur in white minstrel music. Instead, songs like Dan Emmett's "Dixie," with its regular march time tempo, or Stephen Foster's standards, melodic but rhythmically conventional, stand as the most recognizable products of white minstrelsy's musical repertory.

For minstrelsy was a commercial venture, not an anthropological demonstration, and its product had to be "whitened" to attract and hold a white audience. So rather than attempt to seek out source material, entertainers would simply take English, Scottish or Irish tunes and make up lyrics for them in black dialect. Or they would use ballads and novelty numbers of professional songwriters. As a result, the songs of the minstrel stage were, naturally, better crafted than the typical, more spontaneous, creations of the slaves. And they had a far wider melodic range than the usual black fare, which ran a relatively narrow musical gamut, closer to African songs.

This trend away from indigenous black material became ever more pronounced in the latter years of the nineteenth century, when minstrelsy incorporated much of music-hall and vaudeville fare, even regaling audiences with attractive dancing girls. (In traditional minstrelsy, men in skirts and wigs interpreted any female roles.)

Although the white minstrel shows generated fine songs that endured as classics through the years, all in all, their black component served mainly as a veneer, much like the burnt cork on Caucasian faces.

Black Minstrelsy

Many African Americans of the time were well aware of white minstrelsy and its amusing, often outlandish, portrayal of Negro music makers. Unsurprisingly, it occurred to some of them that if whites could win success onstage as black singers and dancers, they too could present themselves to the public—as the genuine article. And so, after Emancipation, Negro minstrel companies went into full swing, in the big cities and on tour throughout the country.

The two most successful black minstrel troupes of the 1860s were Lew Johnson's Plantation Minstrels and George Hicks' Georgia Minstrels.[74] They and others boasted of having talented ex-slaves among their performers. A few companies, such as the Primrose and West Minstrels and Lew Dockstader's Minstrels, were composed of both black and white entertainers. But whatever the makeup, whether all black or mixed, it was minstrelsy that provided the greatest outlet for black musical talent.

Negro minstrel shows proved enormously popular with the public of both races but could not survive without white sponsorship. The troupes were hampered and hounded by racial discrimination, and a number of white theater owners refused to do business with black managers, no matter how competent and reliable they were. As a result, by the 1870s, all but the most tenacious blacks minstrels had sold their services to whites, who now managed all the major black companies.

But the white impact on the black troupes ran far deeper than simple administration or management. It lay at the very heart of Negro minstrelsy. For from the start and throughout their history, the black minstrels adopted all aspects of the format that had brought success to white entertainers in blackface. In fact, most of them applied burnt cork to their own faces, presenting a uniform skin color, the better to imitate whites imitating blacks. What is more, the Negro minstrels retained the demeaning "darky" stereotypes of the white companies: the ignorant, shuffling and lazy "Jim Crow" character and the dandified, ridiculously social climbing "Zip Coon." After all, those familiar caricatures made audiences laugh.

On the positive side, Negro dancers infused their shows with their incomparable styling, in jigs, buck and wing steps, stop-time moves and dances that helped point the way to tap and soft shoe dancing of vaudeville and musical comedy of the future (see Chapter 15).

Moreover, some gifted black songwriters got their start in Negro minstrel shows—men such as James Bland, Gussie Davis, Samuel Lucas and, later, W. C. Handy. However, the music and lyrics they furnished for those shows could have been written by white musicians. Handy, for instance, did not begin to compose his typically black blues numbers until the 1910s. Meanwhile, Gussie Davis alternated between "coon" songs lampooning the southern blacks or sentimental songs intended for white publishers. James Bland, composer of "Carry Me Back to Old Virginny" and "Oh, Dem Golden Slippers" wrote such beautiful nostalgic songs about the Old South that he was known as the "black Stephen Foster."

One might have expected a greater authenticity, a closer resemblance to the actual slave milieu, in black minstrel shows as opposed to white ones. But Negro minstrelsy, although deemed more "natural" than the white product, mainly perpetuated the sham. A striking example of that sham may be found in the songs of the talented James Bland, who spent his early years performing in black minstrelsy. Bland's songs, sung by black and white entertainers alike, were clearly patterned after the repertoire of Foster and other writers for white minstrelsy. His "In the Evening By the Moonlight" paints an idyllic picture of happy slaves singing and strumming all night long. In "De Golden Wedding" his darkies dance and feast on ice cream, honey, cake, apple brandy and wine. And nary a word about picking cotton with parched throat and aching back or lashes from the overseer's whip.

Even more unbelievably, Bland promoted white minstrelsy's view of a lovable massa and missis, people to be missed when far away and mourned when dead (as in Foster's "Massa's in the Cold, Cold Ground"). Now, in reality, such a sentiment was not unheard of, and after Emancipation, some former slaves interviewed by chroniclers did think back with affection on the kindnesses of a thoughtful master. And a good many plantation owners saw themselves as decent and considerate slave owners, not always happy about leaving slaves to the mercy of a ruthless overseer. But according the bulk of contemporary accounts, the kindly resident "massa" was an exception in the lives of nineteenth-century southern slaves.

One would never know it, however, from Bland's songs. Here, for example, are lyrics from his "Carry Me Back to Old Virginny," published in 1878.

> Massa and missis have long gone before me,
> Soon we will meet on that bright and golden shore;
> There we'll be happy and free from all sorrow,
> There's where we'll meet and we'll never part no more.

Apparently Bland's nostalgic slave had somehow had the good luck of serving a master who didn't whip him and his family, work him until he dropped, separate him from his wife, rape his daughters or sell him downriver. In any case, for Bland, as for other black songwriters of his time, mention of such cruelty would have been horribly out of place.

In the 1870s—at a safe remove—some black minstrels did decry slavery as an institution. And in that decade, on the heels of the Fisk Jubilee Singers' concerts, they also introduced audiences to the Negro spirituals of yore. But, as with Bland, their songs did not detail or describe the actual sufferings of those in bondage.[75] Customarily, the bitter realities were either ignored or sugar coated à la Foster. Black minstrelsy as a popular amusement remained essentially conservative.

A new, more authentic note might have been expected in the musical style of the Negro minstrels. However, that style remained largely standard, the rhythms non-innovative. For example, like the songs of white minstrelsy, Sam Lucas' "Carve Dat Possum," was sung in regular trochaic meter:

> . . . pós-sum méat am góod to éat,
> cárve him tó de héart . . .

As we shall see more fully in the next chapter, exceptions to this rhythmic conservativism could be found in some "Negro jigs" published in white manuals of banjo instruction. By and large, however, the music of black minstrelsy kept to the traditional rhythms of the white sentimental ballad and the rustic hoe-down or the two-step of late minstrelsy.

And so the customary style held sway, as African-American minstrels imitated the sounds of their white black-faced models. That imitation of white minstrelsy by black entertainers would continue as a general rule until the turn of the century,[76] when, finally, the rise of ragtime would give African-American musicians their own identity.

Shameless Caricatures: Coon Songs of Two Races

Today, at a remove of over a century, most of us naturally balk at the demeaning caricatures of Negroes presented in both white and black minstrel shows. But were that stereotyping not bad enough, a musical by-product of minstrelsy—the "coon song" of the 1890s and early 1900s—may be seen, in retrospect, as nothing less than scandalous.

At the time, however—a time when vaudeville was beginning to replace minstrelsy—America was far from becoming politically sensitized to discrimination against minorities. On the contrary, sheet music buyers and theater audiences were highly entertained by the openly contemptuous image of blacks created in the coon songs. They found nothing shocking, for example, in one such number performed by the black-faced Victor Minstrels in 1902, a song in which a cakewalk dance caller warns members of the "blue-blooded aristocracy of Darktown's 400" not to carry their razors onto the dance floor. Otherwise, he threatens, "I'm a gwina cut you down in the flower of your youth."[77] And they wildly applauded white performer May Irwin's boisterous rendition of the ferociously insulting "Bully Song" (1896). In that piece (perhaps originally heard in Mamma Lou's brothel of light-skinned Negresses), coon shouter Irwin claims, in black dialect, that she will cut a certain watermelon-eating bully down with her trusty razor. The term "nigger" recurs countless times throughout that tasteless number.[78]

Ironically, a black songwriter and entertainer, Ernest Hogan, gave the coon song fad its greatest impetus with his highly popular "All Coons Look Alike to Me (1896)."

His title, a phrase undoubtedly current among intolerants since the post-Civil War reconstruction period, came to haunt the author. Hogan felt guilty the remainder of his life for having used it, though a Negro himself. He did justify his choice by explaining, among other things, that the song's text concerned a black woman leaving her man, telling him she could find other fish in the sea and it made no difference what man, since they were all exactly the same.

Nevertheless, the text of the song is deprecating to blacks. For instance, the singer assures her soon-to-be ex-lover that another prospect will be just as good to her "as you, nig! ever tried to be." Although African Americans since the days of slavery had used the word "nigger" among themselves, Hogan included it in a coon song for public amusement. Clearly, as with black minstrelsy, this was a case of a talented black musician climbing on the white bandwagon in order to achieve success.[79]

Hogan was far from the only Negro musician to adopt the coon formula. In fact, a whole spate of coon songs emanated from other black composers. A few examples from the end of the century are Gussie Davis' "That Strange Coon (1895)," "I'm the Father of a Little Black Coon (1897)" and "Nigger, You Won't Go (1898)." The gifted concert pianist, and composer, Blind Boone, added his own coon songs to the dubious legacy. And even a poet such as Paul Laurence Dunbar followed suit, writing lyrics (very mortal ones) to Will Marion Cook's "The Hottest Coon in Dixie (1898)." In 1897, a musical extravaganza written by Bob Cole and Billy Johnson was produced by Cole against incredible odds after concerted boycotting by white musical entrepreneurs. The show wound up playing to packed houses. It's title: *A Trip to Coontown.*

One might seek a rationale for the popular coon stereotype in the fact that entertainers of the day found great humor in caricatures of other ethnic and racial minorities—and that the caricatured minorities joined in the fun. The recent waves of European immigrants to the United States provided much grist for the mill.

The Irish, for example, became likely targets of humor. Although Irish tenors had a romantic aura, novelty singers and vaudeville acts made great sport of old Patty's brogue and his reputed fondness for hard liquor. In the last two decades of the nineteenth century, Irish comics Harrigan and Hart (who had begun their careers in blackface) regaled audiences with one-act farces imbued with a strong Irish flavor.

Elsewhere, the popular Jewish comics, Weber and Fields, performed their so-called "Dutchmen" acts in heavy Yiddish accents. And later, in the twenties, Fanny Brice, also Jewish, would continue the tradition of ethnic self-mockery by singing "Second Hand Rose" in her carefully learned Jewish dialect or farcically associating that dialect with an Indian maiden or a sexy shimmy dancer.

In spite of—or more likely because of—the fact that America was becoming the famous melting pot of diverse cultures, foreign was funny and would remain funny until after World War II, when America became sensitized to prejudicial ethnic stereotyping. So clearly, lampoons of other cultures and races shared the stage with coon stereotyping.

Yet the caricatures of immigrants and foreign nationals were nowhere as insulting and abasing as the image of blacks created by both whites and blacks in popular music. Whether in minstrelsy, vaudeville, on Tin Pan Alley or elsewhere, no other ethnic or racial group was so demeaned or viewed as generally ridiculous, supremely ignorant and downright immoral.

* * *

It was high time for African-American musicians, free at last of their enforced servitude, to rid themselves as well of the mask of minstrelsy and of the debasing caricatures rampant in America's popular music. Although both minstrelsy and the coon song managed to survive well into the 1900s, a new and refreshing black sound had already reached the public ear by the turn of the century. That is when a good number of black musicians came into their own. For that is when the American public discovered the miracle of ragtime.

Notes

69 George Washington Dixon is an example of an American white performing in blackface before the time of minstrelsy. He appeared onstage in Albany in 1827 and was known especially for his renditions of the song "Coal Black Rose."

70 *Black Popular Music in America,* p. 18.

71 As a boy Foster had attended a Negro church with his black female servant. He said that he had used snatches of black songs heard in her company. (See Chase, pp. 287-288.)

72 Since dancing in minstrelsy will be discussed in Chapter 15, these paragraphs on music will be confined to song.

73 See Nathan's informative *Dan Emmett and Negro Minstrelsy.*

74 One of the largest, if not the largest black minstrel company was Callender's Consolidated Spectacular Colored Minstrels.

75 White minstrelsy—although not usually anti-slavery—did offer some exceptions to the rule of silence. For example, J. P. Carter's "Lucy Neal" (1844), from Dan Emmett's repertoire—despite its upbeat tempo—contained a sad message about an enforced parting of black lovers. And a few songs from the Civil War period in Hooley's Opera House, also a white company, similarly addressed the subject of cruelty to slaves.

76 White minstrelsy itself would continue throughout the 1920s, even through the rise of vaudeville. See, for example, the numerous notices and ads in the pages of *Variety Magazine* in that decade.

77 CD, *I'll Dance Till De Sun Breaks Through.*

78 CD, *Music From the New York Stage,* Vol. I.

79 As we shall see in later chapters, the phenomenon would recur throughout the twentieth century.

3

ARRIVAL

THE COLOR OF RAGTIME

Introduction

A radical change took place at the turn of the twentieth century when white Americans discovered black ragtime. By all accounts they had their first big brush with the musical phenomenon in 1893, at the time of the Chicago Exposition. Visitors may well have heard the raggy "jig" playing of black musicians competing in cutting[80] contests not far from the fair's amusement area and in the nearby red light district.

It was a major breakthrough. For rather than perpetuating the hackneyed rhythms of earlier white minstrelsy, ragtime music stood on its own. Its sound, new and exotic to white listeners, contrasted sharply with the familiar patterns of America's mainstream popular music. In little time, that innovative sound would transform popular music and set the general public on its heels. Black ragtime, a sensation at home and abroad, was destined to smooth out over time and become packaged and promoted as "jazz."

Interestingly, white musicians entered the ragtime scene from the earliest days of its exposure. They played and composed ragtime pieces, sometimes in contact with black musicians and in time, in their own white milieu. The white involvement in ragtime, however, bore little resemblance to the previous activity of whites in minstrelsy. For this was no longer an artificial attempt at caricature but an enthusiastic adoption of a new and exciting musical trend. Although early on Tin Pan Alley ragtime songs continued to exploit coon images in their lyrics, songwriters eventually tired of the old stereotypes of minstrelsy and vaudeville. Ragtime did not need them for success.

White composers provided the first flurry of published rags in the 1890s. But they were clearly not the originators of the genre. Even without Max Hoffmann's rag accompaniment, black composer Ernest Hogan's "All Coons Look Alike to Me" (written in 1896, before Hoffmann's music was added) had more off-the-beat ragtime syncopation than many of the so-called "rags" appearing in 1897. For black ragtime, as we shall see, evolved out of a much earlier African-American experience.

White musicians who discovered ragtime at the turn of the twentieth century understood that this was, indeed, black music. In an autobiographical sketch, white pianist S. Brunson Campbell, who studied briefly with Scott Joplin, remarked "It was in 1898 that fate introduced me to Negro ragtime."[81] Joseph Lamb, one of the few white composers to be ranked alongside ragtime artists such as Scott Joplin and James Scott, stated: "95% of the best rags were written by Negroes."[82] Ben Harney, a musician generally considered white but very likely only passing for white,[83] was credited with introducing ragtime to New York in 1896. But whatever his race, he insisted he was not rightly the father of ragtime but rather its "father by adoption."

Despite the fact that black musicians led the way, it should not surprise us that white ragtime composers managed to publish and be recognized earlier. For few of the Negro composers and interpreters imagined that the music they were playing—and playing with—had anything of value. And even if they had taken their pieces seriously enough to want to see them in print, only a minority of black music makers had any training in composing or notating music. A large percentage of them could not read music but played by ear, often picking up phrases of rival ragtime pianists. So even though ragtime master Scott Joplin (who had had musical training) insisted that his rags were to be played exactly as written, the non-reading black musicians "faked" his pieces and others they played. They elaborated and invented as they went along—in other words, improvised, enjoying themselves in the process. They could not have imagined that their music would actually be admired and adopted by serious musicians, exploited by commercial sponsors and savored by a large public.

Moreover, talented black ragtime interpreters rarely played a piece twice in a set way. If an entrepreneur wanted to produce a piano roll with a tune by a ragtime pianist/composer, he would invite the artist to play and would cut the roll on the spot. But that particular performance might be entirely different from the way the same musician had interpreted that very piece the day before. The great virtuoso Eubie Blake played his ragtime number "Ma" differently every night of the week. When he was invited to make a recording of it, he simply performed an on-the-spot version of it.[84] And Blake, by the way, did not learn how to set his compositions to paper until he decided to go to music school in his sixties.

Finally, although some early white rags were self-published, white ragtime musicians usually saw their pieces in print and distributed before black artists because they had a far greater entrée into the commercial world of Tin Pan Alley. Some black composers were successful thanks to publishers like John Stark or Tin Pan Alley's Edward B. Marks and the Witmark brothers, but for most, the road was paved with obstacles, if not inaccessible.

The greater visibility of whites in commercial ragtime has led some critics to view it as a bi-racial creation, the product of a collaboration between black and white composers of early ragtime.[85] Yet it was not a case of whites co-inventing that clearly African-American phenomenon. Admittedly, white staff arrangers of publishing houses scored numbers for black composers uninitiated into the mysteries of musical notation. And like Max Hoffman they provided rag choruses for black coon songs such as Hogan's "All Coons Look Alike to Me." However, beyond some noteworthy musical compositions by white musicians (notably Joseph Lamb) the most prominent function of whites was bringing ragtime to the public. They had the know-how and the means to popularize and commercialize it through sheet music publication, editing and production of piano rolls and general promotion.

The Sound of Ragtime

Ragtime, an early form of jazz, is more than its well-known honky-tonk rhythm. Critics have variously described other aspects, holding, for example, that it is designed to be written and is non-improvisational, that it has European musical sources, that its structure draws from the march and the French quadrille, that it adopts folk and commercial tunes or has strong connections with dancing.

Such explanations may be valid, but they diminish the fact that ragtime's most fundamental and recognizable feature is, in fact, its rhythm. That rhythm consists primarily in an irregular off-the-beat syncopation in the treble against a steady on-the-beat tempo in the bass. The irregular syncopation follows precisely the old pattern common to the spirituals and recreational songs of the slaves:

That pattern occurs in countless ragtime pieces, from turn-of-the-century cakewalks and early rudimentary rags by both black and white composers such as Krell's "Mississippi Rag (1897)" and Mills' "Rastus on Parade (1895)" to the later classic rags of Joplin and Lamb. Witness the following example from the white songwriter F.A. Mills "At a Georgia Campmeeting (1897).

With the later ragtime compositions, spontaneous off-the-beat improvisations of black music became codified techniques woven integrally into the musical fabric. And the syncopated patterns became increasingly irregular and complex. Examples from Scott Joplin's "The Entertainer" (1902) in 2/4 time illustrate this development. Not only is the music in the treble accented off the beat, but notes are anticipated or held beyond the time expected. Unlike the early rags, two halves of a measure may be linked, as in the third measure of the following example. Or in other cases a beat may extend from one bar to the next, as at the end of the first measure below, where C is held over for one and a sixteenth beat into the second measure.

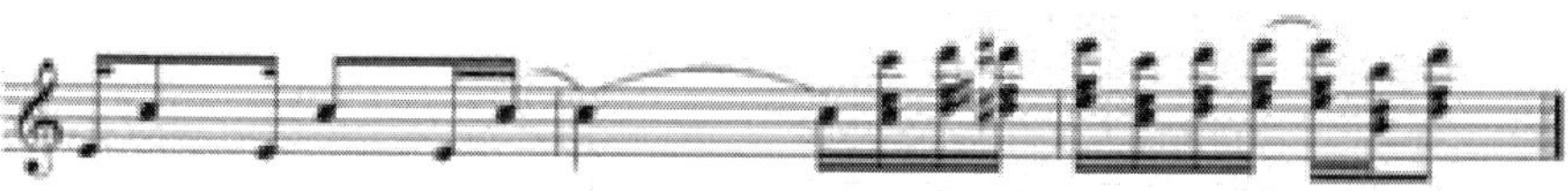

Such are the most recognizable patterns of classic ragtime. As opposed to most early pieces that called themselves "rags" but sounded more like ordinary one-step or two-step dances or marches, this is the sound we identify as true ragtime.

The invention of ragtime, like that of Dixieland jazz, had much to do with the vogue of marching bands and the adoption by blacks of the bands' musical instruments. Any so-called "European" influence on ragtime composers and pianists amounts to the fact that American march music—popular with whites and blacks alike—had its origins abroad, mainly in France's Napoleonic military bands.

Military marching ensembles flourished in the United States during the nineteenth century, and New Orleans, with its French background, had a goodly share of them. In the early 1800s, Francis (Frank) Johnson (1792-1844),[86] a talented Negro bandmaster and composer of marches, enjoyed great popularity there with an eclectic repertoire that included a number of his original compositions. Later, during the Civil War, a white leader, Patrick S. Gilmore, became Bandmaster of the

Union Forces and toured throughout the country. Then, from 1880 on, John Philip Sousa, newly named bandmaster of the United States Marine Corps, took the limelight as America's famed "March King." Sousa's music especially helped solidify the marriage of the structured white march and erratic black rhythms.

The story behind that marriage has been told countless times but bears repeating. To begin with, many post-Civil War Negroes joined clubs that had much in common with secret societies of West Africa. In New Orleans, for example, for a given fee, a club member could be assured of a fine burial (especially fine if he or she subscribed to several of these societies). And what could be more impressive than to have your society hire a real marching band to accompany your corpse to the cemetery and help commemorate your demise?

It was not the solemn march to the graveyard but the return from it that would have its impact on budding ragtime and jazz composers. For once the deceased had been duly interred, the band would follow the mournful tones of its hymns and stately marches with joyously syncopated black rhythms. For instance, on the way back, musicians might replace a dirge-like rendition of "Nearer My God to Thee" or "Flee As A Bird" with an upbeat, swinging version of "Down By The Riverside," "Didn't He Ramble?" or "When the Saints Go Marching In." Many a ragtime artist had heard as a child and fondly remembered the "hot" sounds of those back-from-the-funeral parades.

From the march ragtime adopted the structure of three or four different sections composed of sixteen measures each. Ragtime's introduction or "break" usually reduced the march's introduction from eight measures to four. But it held to the march's precise 2/4 (or at times 4/4) rhythm and steady "oompah" beat in the bass. In contrast with most of the old slave spirituals and with the blues which would follow, ragtime inherited the march's unremitting cheerfulness. As uncharacteristic as it may seem given the history and condition of African Americans, amid all the lively, playful pieces in black ragtime we find precious few melancholy strains.

The Elusive Origins of Ragtime

In dating the emergence of modern ragtime, most music historians hold to the 1890s period, and especially 1893, the year of Chicago's Columbian Exposition, when white musicians discovered black "jig" piano playing, and 1897, when the "Chicago Ragtime Sweepstakes" set off a race among composers of both races to submit rags for publication.

But did ragtime suddenly, magically, manifest itself in the 1890s, like some full grown Venus rising from the ocean? Was it mainly an offshoot of Sousa's marching music? Or had it been heard earlier? If we look closely at the history of ragtime, following its sound backwards in time, we discover one important truth. That is, ragtime did not generate spontaneously *ex nihil nihilo* at the end of the nineteenth century. It developed, instead, as a continuum, from farther back in time, its roots firmly entrenched in the African-American heritage.

According to ragtime composers and their contemporaries, ragtime music existed well before the nineties. When Eubie Blake practiced piano as a boy in the 1880s, much to his straitlaced mother's horror, he played ragtime pieces. And Blake described old-timers he had heard in his youth, pianists like Jesse Pickett and Big Head Wilbur, who had been playing that style for decades.[87] The talented black pianist Blind Boone also purportedly heard ragtime sounds as a boy in the 1870s,[88] that is, soon after Emancipation.[89]. Interestingly, when young Eubie Blake's mother protested, "Take that ragtime out of my house!" he was tempted to remind her that she herself had been singing exactly that sort of music in her church hymns.

Even before Emancipation, there were accounts of hot music in saloons and dance halls of the North. For instance, George Foster, in *New York by Gaslight* (1850) describes a trumpeter in Pete Williams' dance house emitting "red hot knitting needles" from his instrument, while the drummer "deals his blows . . . in all violation of the laws of rhythm."[90]

We cannot know exactly what such early black music sounded like, since no transcription of it appeared in contemporary sheet music or teaching manuals and since recordings on cylinders or disks had not yet been invented. That music would most probably not have been the exact equivalent of ragtime as we know it today. But more than likely it was based on the traditionally black off-the-beat syncopation illustrated above. And it probably contained characteristics of popular Negro banjo jigs with their emphasis on irregular stop time rhythms (see the first example, below).

Some writers have sought the origins of turn-of-the-century ragtime and later jazz in minstrel show music,[91] or the cakewalk[92]. However, if we look closely at those genres, we cannot credit them with having given birth to ragtime.

The minstrel show, as we have seen, generally maintained conservative sounds and rhythms. Although using some traditional black material, largely for atmosphere, it alternated white-style sentimental songs with bouncy but on-the-beat marches or two-steps, such as Dan Emmett's immortal "Dixie." An interesting exception to the traditional flavor of minstrelsy music could be found in the interpolation in the shows of Negro banjo jigs, for instance, Emmett's "Pea Patch Jig" and R. Meyers' "Sliding Jenny Jig."[93] In such tunes unexpected rests break up the rhythm, creating an irregular "stop time" off-the-beat tempo and a hint of pre-jazz syncopation.

Sliding Jenny Jig

Still, despite such examples, the minstrel show was not the most likely fountain of ragtime. Besides the fact that its music remained largely conservative, the "Negro jig" novelty numbers introduced in 1840s minstrelsy were usually performed on the banjo, and that instrument was not the most convincing conveyor of ragtime. A banjo could, and did, accommodate black syncopation. For by the time of minstrelsy, a fifth string had been added, stretched over a cigar box, producing "an African-like syncopation that had long been lacking in white music.[94] Yet the banjo, heard along with the customary fiddle and bones, produced what we would consider a hoe-down, rather than a jazzy, flavor. And though ragtime music would continue to be written for the banjo, the instrument could not in any sense render ragtime polyrhythms as sharply and effectively as would the piano. Unlike traditional African music makers who acquired expertise over years of apprenticeship, the average American banjo playing minstrel could not deliver several different rhythms simultaneously on his instrument. And the banjo itself did not allow even the expert player capacity enough for a rich development of polyrhythm and polyphony.

Piano keys, on the other hand, provided musicians with a wide musical range. The pianist enjoyed opportunities in both the treble and bass for constant innovation in interweaving melodies, playing with harmonies and creating fresh, new patterns of rhythm.

Ragtime, to be ragtime, needed the piano, and, until very late, the piano was not a standard feature of the minstrel show.

But although minstrelsy cannot be credited for spawning ragtime, a number of music historians continue to grant it that credit, pointing to the fact that the lively cakewalk played an important role in minstrel shows. That myth should and can be exploded—first by looking at the relationship between the cakewalk and minstrelsy, and then by considering the cakewalk itself.

It is a fact that cakewalks became prominently featured in minstrel shows, usually as the grand finale. But that did not occur until late in the nineteenth century. (Before that time minstrels had ended their productions with a lively "walkaround"[95]). By the time the cakewalk became an indispensable part of minstrel performances, the dance had already been making its appearance on stage in black variety shows and musical revues. In 1877, for example, comedians Harrigan and Hart featured a routine "Walking For Dat Cake" at the Théâtre Comique in New York, and in 1889 Sam Jack's *Creole Show,* also in New York, presented a cakewalk as its grand finale.

Minstrelsy did not generate the cakewalk but incorporated it when the genre was already developing into vaudeville and when the cakewalk had already become popular in dance halls and elsewhere. Furthermore, before the early 1900s, instead of introducing an off-the-beat ragtime style of syncopation in their cakewalks, minstrels generally held to the rhythm of traditional sounding marches or grand promenades. Minstrelsy would not infuse cakewalk performances with ragtime effects until ragtime became the rage in popular music.

As for the cakewalk itself, it had already existed on plantations in the slavery era. Performed by the slaves on special occasions, the dance was far more spontaneous and less structured than the later production numbers of late minstrelsy and musical revues or the end-of-the-century cakewalk events. In the slaves' cakewalk, allowed on special occasions, couples would dress up in the best finery obtainable and parade to music in the presence of their masters and invited guests. It was often their way of mocking the pompous airs of their masters, and they executed their take-offs with great exaggeration and high stepping. Edison's 1903 silent film, *Uncle Tom's Cabin,* portrays slaves celebrating Little Eva's return to the plantation with a cakewalk performed with high strutting steps, a type of a strutting that Arnold Shaw has likened to a drum majorette's prance.[96] In practice, plantation owners would present a cake to the most impressive pair among the performers.

But the rhythm of antebellum cakewalks undoubtedly bore little resemblance to ragtime. The earliest existent recordings of cakewalk music available today are mainly lively tunes in two-step tempo or traditional marches for the couples' promenading, occasionally with some syncopated banjo accompaniment.[97]

The cakewalk was resuscitated and became a craze in the 1890s, just before ragtime burst on the scene. The "Kullid Koons' Kake Walk," by white writer D. Emerson, appeared in sheet music as early as 1892. Like most cakewalks of that time and before, it contained little, if any hints of ragtime in it; rather, its march-like tempo had a customary, regular on-the-beat syncopation. Later, published cakewalks simply cohabitated with early ragtime pieces. A good many of them could be recognized by the familiar rhythm:

Then eventually, at the turn of the century, a number of cakewalks by black and white composers adopted a definite ragtime tempo (for example, "Fly You Blackbirds" from Brainard's 1899 *Ragtime Collection* or "Happy Jim" from Cole and Johnson's *In Dahomey* in 1903).

So clearly, the cakewalks did not engender ragtime music. Rather, they themselves became rags—or were simply labeled "rags"—in order to cash in on the new vogue.

Unraveling the Mystery: Concrete Evidence of the Early Genesis of Ragtime and Jazz

In tracing the origins of ragtime, we must reach much further back in time than Sousa's marches, late minstrelsy or the cakewalk craze. For the long road through the past inevitably—and unsurprisingly—leads us once again to the music of African-American slaves. In Chapter One we have already examined and offered examples of the pre-jazz polyrhythms found in that music. Those rhythms are well documented not only in slave song collections but also in antebellum scores for "Negro jigs" in early banjo teaching manuals, cited in the previous section.

Were such evidence not enough, researchers have available a number of sound recordings—particularly those of the Georgia Sea Islands produced by noted researcher Alan Lomax in the 1930s and in the sixties and seventies. Negro inhabitants of the islands, relatively isolated from white cultural influences, had preserved songs sung by their slave forebears. The off-the-beat syncopation, rhythmic hand clapping and grunts of work songs and field cries provide an obvious link between modern jazz and slave songs, both religious and secular.

One example from Lomax's collection, *Southern Journey,* shows a clear and constant relationship between the old songs and modern blues. Here are some recurring measures from "Row De Boat, Chile," taught to one of the singers by his slave grandfather:

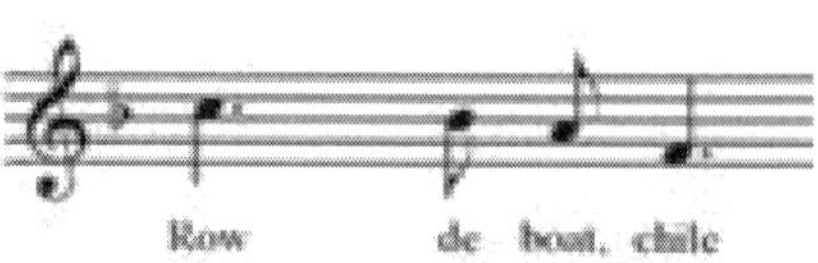

Above and beyond the patterns of repetition, later to be found in the blues, the song's melody is nearly identical to that of "Easy Rider (or "See See Rider") Blues," except for the latter's flatting of its "blue notes."

Finally, a most important proof of the strong connection between slave songs and modern jazz is found in the work of a prominent white American composer, writing as early as the 1840s. The compositions of Louis Moreau Gottschalk provide us with ample written evidence of a direct line running from the secular songs of New Orleans slaves and the jazz that would later absorb and transform the sounds of ragtime.

Gottschalk, a native of New Orleans, would achieve renown as a composer primarily for introducing into concert piano music off-the-beat rhythms that prefigured jazz. They were precisely the rhythms of slaves of his era and city of origin. Like other white Louisiana Creoles, Gottschalk's maternal grandparents had fled to New Orleans from Haiti after the island's slave uprisings of 1791. Born in 1829 and living on Rampart Street just a stone's throw from Congo Square, as a young boy he may have seen and heard the singing and dancing of slaves there.[98] But even if not, he was obviously familiar with the songs popular among New Orleans' Negroes, and could well have heard them sung by his Creole grandmother or his black slave nurse, Sally.

Afro-Caribbean[99] rhythms such as the *bamboula, calinda* and *counjaille,* accompanied by such instruments as drums and banjo, provided inspiration for pieces like his "Bamboula" and "Banjo" (which Gottschalk called "Danses des Nègres"). Gottschalk's compositions patently echoed the rhythms of popular songs and dances of black New Orleans of his time. A well-known New Orleans slave song, "Musieu Bainjo,"[100] offers the same irregular syncopations, later to be found in cakewalks and early rags.

This was the very tempo found in spirituals such as "Hold Out Yo' Light," "Somebody Knocking at Yo' Do'" and "Gwine to Shout All Over God's Heaven," an off-the-beat tempo fostered by the slaves' polyrhythmic interplay of call-and-response singing and clapping over a steady "bass" of foot stomping.

If added proof were needed that such proto-ragtime rhythms existed in slave times, Gottschalk amply supplies it in his 1844 composition, "Bamboula," a piece based primarily on the Creole folk song "Quand patate la cuite na va mangé li!" (When the potato's cooked, don't eat it up!). The song was performed in New Orleans to a Negro dance called *bamboula*—from the African drum of the same name. Gottschalk's composition clearly illustrates the syncopation heard in the *bamboula* and other Afro-Caribbean songs and dances of New Orleans.

A Lost Generation?

When music historians describe the African-American musical heritage, they logically begin with the slave songs, chronicling them up to 1865 and the end of the Civil War. Then, if they go on to include ragtime music, they will invariably skip a few decades and start with the 1890s, that is, around the time of ragtime's discovery and its adoption by whites. Between the two eras, however, they seem to have drawn a blank. There would appear to be a hiatus in black popular music during those post-bellum years, with little or nothing happening until the miracle of ragtime at the tail end of the century.

What did happen between 1865 and 1893? Did the black rhythms disappear? Or go underground?

To some extent they may have been relegated to the back closet. For, as critics have pointed out, many newly liberated Negroes of the post-war period, eager to become absorbed into the American mainstream, shunned the sort of music identified with slavery. Indeed, then and for years afterwards, a good number of African Americans with social or economic aspirations avoided the "taint" of ragged music or the blues. However, despite that trend, it is highly unlikely that most African Americans of the time would have completely cast off or forgotten their characteristic off-the-beat syncopation—and then suddenly reinvented it at the end of the century. On the contrary, free blacks continued perpetuating those rhythms, singing, swaying and tapping in church, playing or dancing in the streets, saloons or cabarets, patting juba, improvising and cultivating their unusual polyrhythms on musical instruments.

A number of observers have testified to such a perpetuation of black syncopated rhythms and improvisation in song and dance during the generation that followed the Civil War. Sidney Lanier, a musician, poet and literary critic of the time, described the patting of an African-American farmhand who executed a "quite complex successions of rhythm, not hesitating to syncopate, to change the rhythmic accent for a moment, or to indulge in other highly-specialized variations of the current rhythms . . ."[101] And Lanier offered one example of erratic juba rhythms in 1874-5, explaining it as an effect "produced by omitting the stroke, of foot or of hand, which the hearer expects to fall on the accented note."[102] He transcribed it thus.[103]

An even more telling example of post-Civil War Negro music, furnished by Lanier in 1875, clearly contains the future ragtime effects illustrated above in the pieces of Scott Joplin (for instance, holding a beat over to the following measure).

Lanier, commenting on that example, wrote,

> Observe the syncopations marked in this air. They are characteristic of negro [*sic*] music. I have heard negroes change a well-known melody by adroitly syncopating it in this way, so as to give it a bizarre effect scarcely imaginable; and nothing illustrates the negro's natural gifts in the way of keeping a difficult tempo more clearly than his perfect execution of airs thus transformed from simple to complex accentuations . . . Thus the negro shows that he does not like the ordinary accentuations nor the ordinary cadences of tunes.[104]

Other proofs of the continuation of black rhythms and improvisation in singing, dancing and patting abound (see, for instance, Dena Epstein's *Sinful Tunes and Spirituals,* Chapters Eight and Fifteen). But most clearly and directly connected with the development of ragtime was the post-war sound of "jig piano" and/or ragtime piano music.[105]

Pianos, so important in the history and development of ragtime, had become increasingly popular since the Civil War. Their price had dropped due to assembly line methods, the introduction of cheaper materials and the manufacture of the streamlined, affordable upright, invented in 1800. In 1866 alone, for example, 25,000 new pianos entered American homes. The nearly simultaneous timing of Emancipation and the prevalence of the upright piano could not have been more opportune; many musically talented African Americans quickly transferred their skills to that instrument.

Strengthening the connection between black musicians and the piano was the fact that the black rural areas, or ghettoes, were often located near or within the Tenderloin districts. There any self-respecting brothel with the means had its piano and at least one "professor" to entertain the clientele night and day with a wide variety of music that included a good dose of animated, low-down playing. Certainly, some lively form of syncopated "jig piano music" could be heard those days in bordellos and saloons.

In view of all this, clearly, the post-war generation did not stifle the sounds of traditional black music. However, modern chroniclers, lacking the hard evidence of published scores or recordings, have had relatively little information to go on and have understandably glossed over that period. In the case of black instrumental music, scholars have only been able to hint[106] at its development and evolution prior to the ragtime vogue. Russell Sanjek offers more details on that subject than most. According to Sanjek,

> In the post-Civil War years, black music involving embellished and syncopated melody lines, played against the 'slow drag' of parade music, was developed in Midwestern saloons, wine rooms, and brothels. Its creators were side-street and back-alley musicians who played their 'jig' or 'rag' interpretations of familiar songs, schottisches, quadrilles, and marches on pianos and with small bands.[107]

Such an explanation, while helpful, is only the tip of the iceberg, and we can but guess at the prevalence, the practice and actual sounds of black instrumental music of the post-war decades. What is indisputable, however, is the continuing, uninterrupted presence of that unusual and improvisational syncopation lying within the very soul of African-American musicians, a syncopation present at least since the time of the spirituals.[108] Willie "the Lion" Smith, for one, understood this truth: "All the different forms [of jazz]," he wrote, "can be traced back to Negro church music, and the Negroes have worshiped God for centuries, whether they lived in Africa, the southern United States, or in the New York City area."[109]

It is clearly a case of a musical continuum, one that centers primarily on a particular rhythm—a black rhythm enduring through slavery, minstrelsy and generations beyond. After the Civil War it continued to flourish in "jig banjo," "jig piano" and "jig dance," becoming further developed and enriched in bordellos, saloons and dance halls of black ghettos. Until it burst on the American and international scenes as "ragtime" and, later, "jazz."

A Traffic in Influence

Historically, the influence of white music on blacks and black music on whites may be seen as a perpetual trade-off, with the two races constantly adopting musical elements from one another. Starting with the slave era, as we have seen, the captured Africans, removed from their native culture, would have had little to build on musically if not for the white legacy. So they turned to the accepted white religious and folk music, to the popular European dances and marches and to European instruments such as the violin and, later, the piano, brass and woodwinds. Then eventually, the slaves melded white music with their own African heritage and managed to create their unique black sound.

When the unusual sound struck white entertainers as a potential meal ticket, they quickly commercialized and "whitened" it, offering it to the public it in the pseudo-southern setting of the minstrel show. Then no sooner had the war ended when emancipated blacks became minstrels themselves, imitating whites imitating them.

The black sound survived nonetheless, in African-American church services and recreational activities. It reached white music lovers in the more polished revivals of spirituals by the Fisk singers and other Negro college groups. It was captured, developed and perpetuated in dance, on the banjo and, above all, on the piano. Then once again the eternal boomerang went into motion with the white discovery of off-the-beat Negro ragtime piano in the

1890s. At which time white composers and entrepreneurs were quick to step in once more, often out of genuine admiration—and also from an urge to cash in on the new fad.

So whites in the music field immediately became involved, some of them recording, publishing and promoting the black music. Others quickly began to write their own music in the black genre and/or to provide rag arrangements for black artists with no skills in musical notation. Tin Pan Alley capitalized on the new vogue by spawning a whole stream of commercial songs passed off as "rags."[110] And white entrepreneurs produced ragtime in variety, vaudeville and other areas of musical theater (which employed only a minority of black artists).

The multiple boomerang brought with it a certain give and take, providing examples of collaboration and cooperation between the races: a practical, if imperfect, symbiotic relationship. On the other hand, it also could serve as a perpetual source of rivalry, obstruction and frustration. For to black musicians, the effect of "sharing" the musical scene with whites in the field must have felt at times very much akin to the master-slave system of antebellum days; the white promoter clearly sat in the driver's seat.

But without those white promoters and entrepreneurs, without a Gottschalk to imitate and perpetuate the sounds of slave music, without enlightened and dedicated whites like the indefatigable Alan Lomax, Harold Courlander and others bent on preserving the black heritage for posterity—and, yes, without a patently commercial Tin Pan Alley—white America and the world might never have discovered and savored the extraordinary sounds of African-American music.

Notes

80 The word denotes a frequent vying or showing off among peers, with one musician trying to outdo another.

81 "The Ragtime Kid," article printed in Hasse, p. 149.

82 Hasse, p. 244.

83 Pianist James P. Johnson maintained that Harney was black. Willie "the Lion" Smith referred to "the great Negro ragtime originator Ben

Harney" (p. 54). Russell Sanjek assumes he was an African American who "passed " (Vol. II, p. 291). But white or black, he could not be credited with having fathered ragtime, which had undoubtedly been around for years before its discovery and baptism at the turn of the century. Harney's "Mr. Johnson, Turn Me Loose," was the first true rag to become a national hit.

84 Documentation for the LP *Eubie Blake.* Early Rare Recordings.

85 A "racially ambiguous commodity," according to Jasen and Tichenor, p. 1.

86 See Chaper X for information concerning Johnson's dance band.

87 See Al Rose, *Eubie Blake,* p. 104.

88 See Jack Batterson, *Blind Boone,* p. 31.

89 This should not surprise us, since sounds and rhythms that appear to be modern innovations have often been traced to a distant past. The eight-to-the-bar "boogie-woogie" played in the 1920s, 1930s and 1940s, was the very same rhythm heard in "walking bass" used by Eubie Blake in his 1899 "Charleston Rag." And it would surface again in more recent music such as rock and roll.

90 Foster, p. 142.

91 The author traces the seeds of jazz to" a few dozen banjo tunes which have the flavor of the plantation." *Dan Emmett and the Rise of Early Negro Minstrelsy,* p. 213.

92 ". . . the cakewalk craze, which led directly and logically to the rise of ragtime as a popular cult." *The Art of Ragtime,* p. 113.

93 Reproduced in Hans Nathan's Dan Emmett and the Rise of Early Negro Minstrelsy.

94 Sanjek, Vol. II, p. 169.

95 A newspaper review of 9/10/72 mentions a "walkaround" in a Callender's Georgia Minstrels performance (*The Ghost Walks,* p. 19). Not before 1894 does *The Ghost Walks*—a thorough history of black stage shows—make mention of a cakewalk performed on a minstrel program.

96 *Black Popular Music in America,* p. 44.

97 Hear, for example, the cakewalks of the CD *I'll Dance Till the Sun Breaks Through.*

98 Gottschalk was born in 1829. The Congo Square events may not have continued on a regular basis after 1935-36.

[99] During his career Gottschalk journeyed to the Caribbean, where he would hear such rhythms and incorporate them in his works.

[100] *Slave Songs of the United States,* p. 113.

[101] *Science of English Verse,* pp. 186-87.

[102] *Ibid,* p. 189.

[103] *Ibid.*

[104] *Florida,* p. 30.

[105] See the paragraph about Eubie Blake in the sub-section" The Elusive Origins of Ragtime," *infra,* this chapter.

[106] For example, writers such as Southern, Kmen, Ward and Burns do mention the probability of pre-ragtime activity during the post-Civil War generation.

[107] Vol. II, p. 290.

[108] One example, the experience of a tourist in a barbershop may help drive that point home. The man relates how a Negro barber's assistant rhythmically brushes him off after his haircut: "With what facility he moves his supple wrist and makes the down-driving broom play over your back the most complicated tunes . . . beating time all the while with his foot, with precision . . ." Related in Khem, p. 237.

[109] *Music on My Mind,* p. 3.

[110] The phrase "passed off" is used advisedly here. A famous example of Tin Pan Alley ragtime without a rag beat is Irving Berlin's classic "Alexander's Ragtime Band."

4

WHITE WOMEN IN POPULAR SONG (1900-1929)

BLUSHING ROSES OF TIN PAN ALLEY

In the early twentieth century Tin Pan Alley[111] composers presented a standard and standardized image of white womanhood in their songs. And at the very same time African-American songwriters were painting an utterly different picture of the black female in theirs. If we tried to understand black and white women of the period strictly on the evidence of those songs, they would strike us as creatures from two separate planets. For the images of females found in the music of the two races could not have been more dissimilar.

Most strikingly, black women of ragtime and, especially, the blues, were pictured as sexually freer and described far more realistically than white women of song. Eventually, in the latter half of the century, that freer view of a down-to-earth and earthy black woman would have an impact on white popular music. But in the early decades—and, indeed, for decades afterwards—any such impact could penetrate only so far. In white popular songs the female image would remain fundamentally proper, essentially conservative.

1920s

By the time of the roaring twenties, understandably, that had to change, and jazz age white songsters of Tin Pan Alley would portray their females quite differently than their predecessors of the early 1900s. After all, a jazz age vamp could hardly be described in terms suited to her straight-laced great-aunt of Victorian times. Yet her image remained far more staid and oldfashioned than one might expect in an age known for its free-spirited sophistication. Even in those progressive times, lyrics relating to white women had little of the frank and uninhibited approach of those describing the African-American female.

To understand how songs about white women could never match the freer, more realistic portrayal of women in black popular music, let us look first at the former's role in society. In many ways it was a radically changing role but, nonetheless, restricted by a traditional conservatism.

Freedom and the White Female

Even before she shed her corset, as early as the last decades of the nineteenth century, white American woman had started on a road to increasing power and freedom. In retrospect, we can now see that her gains were not sudden and dramatic but gradual and cumulative, her journey a slow and uneven one. Much has been written about the events that helped propel her towards liberation. Among the most important ones were the following four changes:

1. The invention of labor saving devices such as the carpet sweeper, electric light, vacuum cleaner, plumbing with hot and cold running water, washing machine, and other innovations which greatly eased the average housewife's days of drudgery.
2. A greater mobility thanks to technological advances, notably the railroad. The "iron horse" most often carried married or unmarried women to urban areas and, frequently, from a house to a less spacious apartment, hastening the breakup of large extended families. Then later, the automobile would completely change the dating system, taking it out of the parent-supervised parlor and—especially with the

invention of the closed car—encouraging greater sexual freedom.

3. New developments which transported women into a world formerly reserved for men only. For example, the typewriter became a largely female domain and brought women into offices where they worked in close proximity with male bosses and colleagues. And many a department store opened up possibilities for females, who made their way there as vendors, buyers, even managers.
4. A major political advance: American women obtained the national vote in 1919.

Many more factors contributed to the progress and increasing freedom of white women: the economic boom of the early 1900s; the greater accessibility of advanced education; World War I and women's entrance into jobs vacated by servicemen; the movies which opened up new and exciting vistas; the theories of Freud, construed by many as a guide to sexual liberty; the pioneering of birth control by Margaret Sanger. These were among the important milestones marking the way to a more independent and liberal way of life for the female sex.

By the dawn of the 1920s woman's freedom seemed out of bounds to dismayed moralists. The vogue of close contact dancing was bad enough. But prohibition, besides promoting crime, encouraged women to accompany men into dark and smoky saloons for bouts of drinking and revelry.

Women's fashions reflected the increased liberalization. They also reflected a strong, widespread impulse to break out of the old, stifling Victorian constraints. As early as the turn of the century, dresses had exchanged their wasp-waisted, high-collared look for a softer S-shaped form. By the 1910s chic women sported Paul Poiret's slim-lined "Hellenic" style draped gowns, replacing their whalebone corsets with less constraining undergarments. Tennis, swimming and other sports demanded freedom of movement; divided skirts, inspired by bicycle riders, had their day, and bathing suits became skimpier and skimpier. And from the start of the century on, hemlines rose relentlessly, inch by inch, until the final shock, when bare knees of high kicking flappers flashed out over rolled silk stockings.

The Other Side of the Coin

In the 1900s, white women had come a long way, but they still had far to go. Their legal status had improved since pre-Civil War days, when females could neither testify in court, nor hold title to property, establish businesses or sign papers as witnesses. Yet in the early decades of the twentieth century one-quarter of the United States still denied married women the right to their own property, one-third allowed them no claim to their own earnings (even if their husbands did not work), and four-fifths of the states denied them an equal share in the guardianship of their children. Divorce laws held to a double standard in adultery cases, judging a straying woman harshly but imposing no penalties on an unfaithful husband.

Although increasing numbers of females were entering the job market, their pay scale remained inferior to men's. Meanwhile, on the political scene, the struggle for suffrage was a long and arduous one, stretching out over decades from the mid-nineteenth century. Some states, notably western and southwestern ones, had given women the vote even before the Civil War, but universal suffrage became a reality only after WorldWar I.

For a free-spirited white woman of the early twentieth century, such political, legal and economic obstacles were irksome enough. But even worse for many was the moral philosophy that lay behind them. Experts of the day, following the precepts of Nietzsche and Darwin, preached that society should not allow women independence, even higher education, since they were weak creatures—weaker than men both physically and mentally. Their true sphere? Domestic duties and motherhood. Their role? To tame their husbands and spread their sweetness and respectability throughout society. Restrictive laws had been invented ostensibly to protect women, since, as the reasoning went, they were merely grown-up children.

Small wonder then that in popular songs of the time white lyricists of Tin Pan Alley pictured women as adorable little girls.

The Sweet Little Girl of Song

From the popular songs produced in the early decades of the century, one might assume that all adult white women were vertically challenged. 1904 alone featured the diminutive child image in: "My Little Chick," "My Pretty Little Kick-a-poo," "Little Miss No-One From No-Where," "Since Little Dolly Dimples Made a Hit," "Dolly," "Good-Bye, Little Girl, Good-Bye" and in a reverse twist: "A Great Big Girl Like Me." Although the word "little" became less popular in songs of the 1910s, the label did not disappear. It still suited an era that idolized the child-like movie star Mary Pickford and had Broadway entertainers like Irene Franklin and Frances White performing baby talk routines in children's clothes. One of the most popular songs of 1912 was entitled "Be My Little Baby Bumble Bee." And even in the twenties, the hit Charleston number, "Has Anybody Seen My Gal?" describes a flapper with turned down hose, but measures her at only five feet two.

Just as a little girl of the day was expected to smile and be well behaved, the grown child-woman that men extolled in love songs was unvaryingly sweet. A handful of song titles from the turn of the century on illustrate the fact: "Sweet Rosie O'Grady" (1896), "Ida, Sweet as Apple Cider" and "Sweet Adeline" (1903), "Sweet Genevieve" (1906), "Sweetest Gal in Town" (1908), "Sweet Suzanne" and "Sweet Kitty Bellaire" (1910). The saccharine label made its way all the way through the twenties, with songs like "Sweet Georgia Brown" (1925), "Sweet Sue" and "Sweet Lorraine" (1928).

In singing the praises of their sweet and petite lady loves, the songsters perpetually transformed their love objects into flowers. The huge musical bouquet includes titles like "My Irish Daisy," "My Jersey Lily," "My Japanese Cherry Blossom" and "My Sunflower Sue." But above all, the cherished rose of ancient classical poets identified countless women of popular song, from "Ma Blushin' Rosie," of 1900 to Roses of the Rio Grande, Spain and Madrid in the twenties.

Any specifics describing these women followed the lead of a fourteenth-century Petrarch. All physical details confined themselves infallibly to red lips, naturally blonde hair and—unsurprisingly—eyes of blue. "Blue" would probably have been favored in any case, since it rhymed with "true." It also described clothing worn by the loved one, the most famous example being "Alice Blue Gown[112] ("In My Sweet Little Alice Blue Gown") from the 1919 show *Irene*.

How far could a man go in wooing one of these paragons? He could kiss and he could hug or cuddle her, but intimacy inevitably stopped at chaste embraces. Early on, the innocent lovemaking might be called "sparking," "kitchie-koo" or "coochie-coo," but songs of the first two decades most often adopted the verb "spoon," for a convenient rhyming with "moon" and "June." When you heard a phrase like "We'll fool around" ("By the Beautiful Sea," 1914), the most you would imagine was a jolly old splash-and-tickle brand of fun, as in "You Splash Me and I'll Splash You" (1907). Only rarely did a Tin Pan Alley number contain anything more suggestive, a notable exception being "You can go as far as you like with me in my merry Oldsmobile" (1905).

All this courting fun inevitably took place out of doors in some romantic locale. In actuality, especially before the 1920s and the closed automobile, most any wooing occurred inside the home, right in the young lady's family parlor and near the watchful eyes of her parents. Yet in countless ballads of the early 1900s couples spooned under the moon, in some country lane, by a stream or at the seashore. Although one can hardly imagine a winter hiatus on kissing and hugging, Nora Bayes and Jack Norworth would lament that "snow time ain't no time to sit outside and spoon" ("Shine on Harvest Moon," 1908), and songsters continued to schedule their love scenes in the "good old summertime."

Despite meteorological constraints, lyricists were inventive in finding all sorts of venues for courtship. The well-known bicycle built for two ("Daisy Bell," 1892) might not seem conducive to smooching, but in "Row, Row, Row" (1912), an amorous oarsman managed to steal kisses between strokes. In "He'd Have to Get Under—Get Out and Get Under" (1913), a couple in an automobile hugged and kissed between the times the young swain had to get out and fix the old jalopy. Yet even more adventurous writers situated their spooning in new-fangled airplanes. After the Wright Brothers' successful launching of the Kitty Hawk, 1903 produced such songs of aerial romance as "Come, Josephine in

My Flying Machine," "Come Take a Trip in My Airship" and "Up, Up, Up in My Aeroplane."

All this in a spirit of good, clean fun.

Naughty But Nice

In popular love songs aimed at a white audience, the male, quite naturally, took the aggressive role; he did the inviting and the pursuing. As for the women, the most these well brought up creatures could contribute to the courtship was encouragement, in the guise of flirtatiousness.

Songs of female coquetry abounded, especially in the early century. One of the best known and most durable of them all was "Oh, Tell Me, Pretty Maiden," from the 1900 musical show *Floradora*. If one took a serious look at the number, it would boggle the mind to fathom where the writer drew the line between propriety and downright shamelessness. Six beautiful young women, the "Floradora Girls," are confronted by six unknown males, doubtless while walking in the park. The men begin with the famous line, "Are there any more at home like you?" as the women coyly twirl their parasols. Rather than turn up their noses and walk away, the ladies reply, "There are a few, kind sir," quickly adding that the ones at home are, however, "simple maids and proper too." The men, no doubt with a bird-in-the-hand outlook, decide to forget about simple and proper girls somewhere else and walk with their present parasol twirling company.

Taking the scene literally, one might ask: 1) What are these virgin maidens thinking of, talking to and walking with total strangers? 2) Although the phrase "Are there any more at home like you?" was undoubtedly a popular compliment of the day, why, in the song, do the gentlemen insist on satisfying their curiosity about other women? 3) When the maidens reply that the girls at home are pretty "but simple maids and proper," does the "but" imply that they themselves are neither?

But of course one could not take such a number literally or be shocked by its implications. Contemporaries were too entranced by the charm of the scene and by the pretty song to think of the flirtation as anything but innocent.

In short time, however, innocent flirtation did not quite suffice for popular music. Although the concepts of sweetness, respectability and sexual limits still kept Tin Pan Alley songs virtuous, at the same time the word "naughty" incessantly came to the fore. "I Want to Be Naughty Too" and "Naughty Eyes" of 1908, "The Aero Naughty Girls of 1909" and "Naughty Marietta" of 1911 were followed by numerous other songs of naughtiness in women—though technically chaste maidens, we must assume.

The idea of naughtiness might seem to contradict the accepted standard of female respectability. But in fact it was not a contradiction but a compromise. Earlier, in the mid-nineteenth century there had been no grey area between a virgin and a downright whore; a woman was either the one or the other. That tenet prevailed even in the post-Victorian years of the early twentieth century. But the changing times demanded at least a bit more boldness in viewing and depicting women. As a solution, as Judith Papachristou has explained in *Myth America,* society settled on a mid-point between the pedestal and the brothel, arriving at "a quasi-sexuality . . . characterized by teasing and suggestiveness."[113]

At times, particularly in the musical theater, suggestiveness could become blatantly sensual. It is true that before the turn of the century, vaudeville had cleansed itself of its lascivious ladies in silk tights, who were now mainly relegated to burlesque houses. But as of 1907, an entrepreneur like Florenz Ziegfeld managed to display dancers and singers in varying degrees of semi-nudity, while touting his shows with the high-minded, if unconvincing, pseudo-esthetic: "A National Institution Glorifying the American Girl." Around that same time, movies were becoming so risqué that Hollywood was forced into self-censorship. Even the distinguished Metropolitan Opera House caused a scandal when, in 1907, police raided it after hearing about the sexy dance of the seven veils executed in the opera *Salome.*

Despite such scandalous displays, popular songs of white Tin Pan Alley, geared to a mass market, remained well behaved and above suspicion. In accordance with the accepted rules of the game, sex stayed in the closet and the love object was permitted only a certain degree of flirtatiousness or naughtiness. In a sense, the naughty behavior was really an affirmation of the moral standard. Just as taking the name of the Lord in vain challenges—and therefore acknowledges—the idea of a Supreme Deity, female roguishness of white song was a titillating game of challenging the standard concept of female morality without ever contesting it or overstepping its limits.

A telling example of Tin Pan Alley's compromise between naughtiness and propriety in females is "Ta-ra-ra-boom-de-ay." That song first became popular in the 1890s in a lavish Saint Louis brothel specializing in octoroon ladies of pleasure imported from New Orleans. A bawdy number, it was sung boisterously in that setting by the hefty African-American chanteuse, Mama Lou, who may have been one of the earliest female blues singers. White lyricists cleansed the song of its sexual message, making it fit for the delicate ears of London and New York society. In its final version, the words perfectly suited the acceptably naughty-but-nice standards of the time:

> A smart and stylish girl you see, belle of good society;
> Not too strict, but rather free . . .
> I'd like it known and understood, tho' free as the air, I'm never rude—
> I'm not too bad and not too good.
> Ta-ra-ra-boom de-ay . . .

So Tin Pan Alley's girl of song, though no shrinking violet, continued in her role as a flower in the garden of respectability. Lest there be any doubt about that, the songs made it clear that any apparent boldness on her part was only one step toward the main goal of both suitor and suitee: marriage. Proposals abounded in popular ballads, from the early century, with "Daisy Bell" ("give me your answer, do") on through the twenties. Even when a man had just encountered a woman on a trolley or strolling through the park, before the end of the song he might well ask for her hand.

In the 1920s, magazines like *Ladies Home Journal* and *McCalls* and the curricula of women's colleges increasingly stressed marriage and domesticity rather than professional work as a woman's true career. Popular songs did not run counter to the trend, and the musical proposals continued. In "Margie"

(1920), Eddie Cantor gives this reminder to the girl of the title: "Don't forget your promise to me/ I have bought the wedding ring and everything . . ." And in "Tea for Two" (1925), a lover paints a cozy picture of marriage to his sweetheart. He pictures his wife-to-be upon his knee as they both take tea, presumably without spilling, and he specifies their future roles in line with traditional protocol—he being the breadwinner, she the cook and chief bottle washer.

> Day will break and we will wake, and you will bake a sugar cake
> For me to take, for all the boys to see.

The flapper of the twenties did nothing to change the picture. Musicals might feature a cigarette smoking Charleston dancer shocking her parents with impertinent slang like "none of your beeswax" *(No, No, Nanette,* 1925), Listeners might smile at the rakish advice in the 1928 song, "Button Up Your Overcoat" ("Get to bed by three;" "Keep away from college boys when you're on a spree"). But nothing in the realm of popular songs shows a fashionable, nubile white woman breaking any of the established moral and social boundaries or desiring any future life outside of marriage.

In fact, the white woman of popular song remained essentially as she started out: conservative and coy, socially and morally respectable and—despite her tendency to kick up her heels now and then—sweet, petite and adorable.

Notes

[111] The name applies to the downtown Manhattan district of popular music publishing houses in operation from around 1905 on. The phrase, by extension, denotes the music marketed by those publishers.

[112] Inspired by the blue color worn by Theodore Roosevelt's daughter Alice.

[113] P. 114.

5

THE AFRICAN AMERICAN FEMALE (1900-1929)

THE BLACK VENUS OF THE BLUES

Introduction: The Problem of the Blues

The sound of the blues, like the sound of ragtime, was ever present in the many forms that jazz would take throughout the years. At first glance the alliance between ragtime and the blues may seem an unlikely one. For the blues originated as a natural, vocal outpouring of the soul. Sung by itinerant Negro banjo or guitar strummers, they stood in contrast to the clever, intricate and lively instrumentals of ragtime artists. Yet familiar patterns of blues writers and singers would be appropriated by ragtime musicians and incorporated into compositions both mellow and joyful.

The blues as blues would not truly find their public until the 1920s, with the great popularity of "race records" by female blues singers such as Mamie Smith, Ma Rainey and Bessie Smith. These would be distributed primarily to an African-American market.[114] When white musicians and entrepreneurs discovered that a genre called "blues" had arrived on the scene, they, naturally, sought ways of cashing in on the vogue[115] but with myriad songs labeled "blues" that usually bore little resemble the real article.

For the white public would never have accepted the blues as sung by the black, largely female, artists. Black ragtime had been an entirely different case. Far more feasible and far more inviting to try to imitate (or at least ride on the coattails of) that music with its exciting, exuberant rhythms. But the blues themselves posed problems, the most obvious one being their lyrics and the messages contained within, messages which could never find favor with the general public. In fact, the lyrics of the actual blues would have been thoroughly offensive to the ears of a white majority, attuned to tamer Tin Pan Alley songs.

The main obstacle to white adoption of the blues as blues was their view of women and love. Tin Pan Alley had its own views on those subjects, and they were nearly the mirror opposite of the black conception. The sharply contrasting images of women and their love lives produced by Tin Pan Alley on the one hand and by the blues on the other are central to an understanding of the black and white contributions to American popular song. So having examined descriptions of white women in song in the first two decades of the twentieth century, let us look at her African-American musical counterpart during the same time span.

The African-American Female

In song and in actuality the African-American woman of the early twentieth century differed radically from her white counterpart. If they seemed as creatures from two different planets it is because, in reality, they were. Although they inhabited the same cities at the same time, although their paths may have crossed, the two races of females, necessarily, remained light years apart.

While middle class white womanhood was edging toward new social and political freedoms, the African-American female—aground at the lowest level of society—underwent an entirely different fate. Emancipation from slavery had briefly held out a promise of freedom and progress for southern Negroes. But the gains they made immediately after the Civil War were short lived. The southern states imposed severe restrictions on their "uppity" ex-slaves, the Ku Klux Klan made its onslaughts, black males lost their presence in Congress and the Senate and much of their voting power. Segregated, ghettoized, deprived of a future, the women and men remained socially and economically at the bottom of the ladder.

A ray of hope beamed from the North. Before 1900, over ninety percent of all African Americans still remained in the South, often as sharecroppers on or near the same plantations where they had served as slaves, or they moved to large southern cities, hoping for more lucrative work. However, with the outbreak of World War I and the resulting dearth of manpower, black male laborers could find jobs in heavy industry up north. Moreover, the war had imposed a hiatus on European immigration, so African Americans moving to big cities would have less competition from the foreign born white-skinned workers. So they would be able, theoretically, to contribute more of a livelihood to their families.

In the winter of 1917, Robert Abbott, the editor of the black newspaper, *The Chicago Defender,* sent this rallying message to southerners, "If you can freeze to death in the north and be free, why freeze to death in the south and be a slave?"[116] Many heeded such advice, and from the turn of the century on, large cities like Chicago and Detroit doubled or tripled their Negro population each decade.

African-American females migrated northward in droves, often with their families but at times by themselves. They left with battered suitcases or carrying their possessions rolled in bed sheets. Some who couldn't pay the train fare, hopped freight trains with their men or walked along railroad ties. After arriving, the majority of women worked as menials—as domestic servants, laundresses, cooks, scrubwomen—and occasionally as factory hands, Only a very small minority managed to step into professional work, such as teaching in African-American urban schools or nursing.

Living in black ghettos, often in shacks or overcrowded tenements, a large percentage of these women found themselves on their own. Husbands who may have accompanied them to northern cities often discovered that despite opportunities created by the war, available jobs were mainly catch-as-catch-can. They might find brief stints as day laborers on occasional construction projects or other such jobs, rather than the more permanent and coveted positions of Pullman porter or hotel doorman. So a large number of those men moved on to other cities or returned southward to their former work in cotton or tobacco fields—leaving their transplanted women and children to fend for themselves. Meanwhile, many women with children were obliged to work long hours outside their home for white employers and their families.

The fragility of the black female's marriage and family life was not a new phenomenon. Indeed, it dated back to antebellum times, when slaves were deprived of legal marriage bonds, when parents and children no longer formed part of an extended family system as in African communities but, worse, could be torn apart at any moment, as masters sold individual members to distant locales. And slave societies in America had become essentially matriarchal in nature. But the lack of a strong and stable family system was now compounded by urbanization, discrimination and poverty.

The lot of a black female was not always unremittingly bleak. She could count on some support from her church, her local black community or a few social service institutions. In spite of hardships, she was more her own person than in the South. More dramatically, up North, the economic situation of some women improved. Still, such compensations could be seen as scattered oases in the vast desert of the black female's daily struggle.

Looking at the general picture, it is not surprising to note that, following the established pattern, white men had the highest income, and that white women came next in the scale (usually single women, since a far smaller percentage of white married women supplemented their husbands' income or confessed to doing so). Black males earned far less than whites, while, predictably, black females found themselves at the bottom of the ladder.

Obviously, skin color played an all-important role. An ambitious African-American woman might train to become an expert secretary-typist, but few, if any, offices of the time would hire her, and certainly not as a receptionist. To have anyone but a white-skinned girl visible to the public would have been unthinkable. The same held true for almost any areas beyond the menial ones.

Except . . . .

The World of Black Entertainment

A female of color with talent and ambition could aspire to success—even fame—as a singer, dancer or pianist in ragtime and, in the 1920s especially, the blues. Exceptionally, entertainment was one area where the shade of her skin did not automatically bar her from work in the public arena. For since the turn of the century, black musical talent had become a salable commodity all over the country. Black theaters and cabarets were mushrooming,[117] black fans were enthusiastic and the whites who comprised many an audience could not help but admire the artistry, energy and originality of the performers, both male and female.

The road to stardom was no easy one, but at least a person of color had access to it. Witness the fact that around 1915, of all professional blacks, a large majority were show people, actors and musicians (followed at a distance by teachers—mostly female—and an all-male clergy).

The field of music and entertainment was not only an accessible avenue for African Americans but a logical one as well. After all, from the earliest times of slavery, music had figured as an intimate part of the Negro experience. Later, certain black musicians and composers, such as Scott Joplin, James Reese Europe and Will Marion Cook would enrich the popular music field with their classical training in Europe and America. Significantly, New York's National Conservatory of Music opened its doors to blacks from its inception, in 1885. But more important for most African-American musicians was the popular stage of late minstrelsy and black vaudeville, the medicine show the cabaret or dive, places where they could strut their stuff night after night before paying customers.

African-American women of talent, as well as black males, seized the opportunity to be seen, heard and possibly earn money and fame as musical entertainers. The promise of money especially had to be a lure. In 1910, if they found a job in a touring vaudeville company, they could earn up to $50 a week. Compare that against the eight to ten dollars per week paid to domestic help at the time!

And so outside the sphere of the homes, schools or churches where they had practiced and developed their skills, they set out to try their luck in musical entertainment. Some made it into T.O.B.A. (the Theatre Owners Booking Agency, a white owned black vaudeville circuit, established in 1909), performing in tents or local black theaters. Others were lucky enough to be featured in the big Harlem nightclubs or even in Broadway shows like Williams and Walker's *In Dahomey* (1903), Cole and Johnson's *The Red Moon* (1909) or Sissle and Blake's 1921 blockbuster *Shuffle Along*.

A far larger number of women, however, wound up as singers and pianists in cabarets, cheap saloons and brothels. Like their male counterparts, they found that route the easiest to break into, since, for one thing, in the early 1900s no employment offices or unions would accommodate blacks. Successful blues singers like Victoria Spivey and Alberta Hunter began their careers playing and singing in bordellos as mere teenagers, while Edith Wilson started hers by sneaking out of her house to do a small-time gig at age thirteen. At times the customers' tips could offset a pittance of a salary—or none at all.

As their careers progressed into the 1920s, the songs they sang, in nightclubs, cabarets, dives or, if "discovered," in recording studios, would increasingly reflect the plight of the black female attempting to survive in a hostile world. A female whose main, if not sole, antidote to misery was physical love.

* * *

Considering the troubled history of the ghettoized African-American female, it is understandable that her description in Negro popular ballads should differ radically from that of the sweet and respectable white girl of song. As a class, black females could never hope to become as rich, as educated—or as respected—as white women. And from the end of the nineteenth century through the 1920s, the social and moral standards set for the middle class white woman—standards that we have seen reflected in the songs of Tin Pan Alley—had no relevance for the working class black female of the time. They are quite naturally absent from songs that portray her.

Instead, in black song, the darling little girl of Tin Pan Alley is replaced by Woman. The important musical medium to convey her dark image would not be the standard and tame Tin Pan Alley ballad but the soulful in-your-face blues.

Creating the Blues

Chronologically, the blues did not "follow" rags, since blacks had been playing and singing them (at least in rudimentary form) well before ragtime made its impact on the American musical scene, possibly as early as the 1870s, toward the end of the Reconstruction period. However, the blues were not commonly called "blues" until the twentieth century. Emanating from the backwoods of Kentucky, Alabama, Georgia, the Mississippi delta (whence came Charlie Patton, Son House and Muddy Waters) and other southern regions, they may have started as simple and haunting isolated phrases of the slaves' field hollers. Developing into musical laments, they could be heard in railroads, prisons and on the road. They began taking a common, more or less definitive form in the 1910s, then found popularity and peaked especially during the 1920s, when black female recording artists became the most prominent exponents of the genre.

Unlike the blues, ragtime was essentially an instrumental phenomenon. It did not need words at all. In fact, when Tin Pan Alley writers insisted on lyrics for songs that they stylishly called "rags," those products commonly possessed only faint echoes of true ragtime. The glory days of ragtime were its piano days, and ragtime also flourished in the instrumental sounds of New Orleans bands. The blues, on the contrary, needed words. They were, after all, a *cri de coeur,* developed, like the spirituals, out of the need to express feelings, to tell it "like it is."

While ragtime demonstrates intricate interweavings of rhythm and melody, the form of the blues remains simple and unsophisticated. The melody, words and structure of the blues hark back to the old slave songs.[118] Like the slave songs, most blues will begin by repeating identical lines of verse, then follow with a different one.

Spiritual:

Hold out yo'light, you heav'n boun' so'dier,
Hold out yo' light, you heav'n boun' so'dier,
Let yo' light shine aroun' de world.

Blues:

Woke up this morning, feeling sad and blue,
Woke up this morning, feeling sad and blue
Don't have nobody to tell my troubles to.

The blues eventually developed their characteristic twelve-bar structure consisting usually of three-line stanzas with four bars to each line. While the spirituals might repeat the first line more than once, the blues have generally held to one repetition and tend to rhyme the third line with the preceding repeated ones.

Additionally, one of the most familiar aspects of the blues is the "blue note," the flatting of the third or seventh (occasionally the fifth) note of the scale, to impart a minor, melancholy aura to the melody.

As for the subject matter of the blues, the same looseness and open-endedness found in the spirituals obtain throughout. For example, a song may start off with a description of some event in the singer's life, then switch unpredictably to his or her sexual desire or need for a drink. Moreover, as with composers of spirituals, blues artists feel free to borrow and incorporate lines, even whole passages, from other well-known songs of the genre. Yet, when performed, such "defects" somehow iron themselves out, and a good blues, like a good spiritual, will have the impact of a totality.

Critics have justly called the blues a secular form of spiritual. Like many slave songs they are highly personal in nature and have a feeling of spontaneity. Like the spirituals (and early black church music), the blues incorporated moaning and groaning and long drawn out "m-m-m" sounds. In contrast to the spirituals, however, very few blues concern themselves with religion. Instead most of them deal with down-to-earth realities experienced by many disempowered African Americans after slavery and Reconstruction: poverty, sex, drugs and drink, jail, cruelty and violence. And unlike the spirituals, which hold out hope for the oppressed, the realities of the blues remain bleak, fostering an atmosphere of sadness and despondency in the songs.

Although commentators on the blues, including black blues writer W.C. Handy,[119] have found a certain hope, even "joyousness" in the blues, it would be difficult to prove through a meticulous study of the songs that they are not overwhelmingly sad. The case is different with the joyous instrumental blues of New Orleans ensembles in the 1910s or the lively jazz band music of later years. For such orchestras enjoyed transforming blues melodies and structure into upbeat, swinging numbers. However, the songs and singing styles of itinerant blues singers and recording blues artists of the twenties have precious little truck with joy and hope. To quote poet Langston Hughes, the blues "are a long ways removed from the expectancy and faith of the Spirituals . . . Blues are sad songs sung to the most despondent rhythm in the world."[120]

The evidence of both lyrics and music leave not the slightest doubt. The blues are unremittingly "blue."

Black Venus of the Blues

She is a different kind of woman, unique and unfamiliar to most white musicians and white listeners. The African-American woman portrayed in the blues of the 1920s—songs created by male and female black writers and geared to black listeners—bears little or no resemblance to Tin Pan Alley's stereotypical white love object.

To begin with, the black woman of the blues does not have to be short, does not have to dress in size six petite. Indeed, she can be any size at all. In his "Bad Luck Blues" Blind Lemon Jefferson sings of a woman only "five feet from the ground," while in "Deceitful Brown Skin Blues" he confides,

> I got a brown 'cross town
> Taller'n a sycamore tree.

Very frequently she is seen, by men and by herself,[121] as "Big Mama," as in Blind Lemon's "heavy-hipped mama," whose "meat shakes on the bone" ("Deceitful Brown Skin Blues"). Often a woman blues writer will refer to herself as "your mama." And although at times she may call her man "papa," she is most certainly not his "little girl."

Lyrics portraying black females employ a more varied palette than the white portraits, limited largely to blond hair and blue eyes. The skin color itself ranges from black to "chocolate," "brown sugar" and "high yeller." As for dress, in blues of the twenties, as in the earlier ragtime number, " There'll Be a Hot Time in the Old Town Tonight," a female might well appear in red. "When I die," says Arthur "Big Boy" Crudup in "Death Valley Blues," "Tell all the women please come dressed in red." Red dresses, silks, satins and feathers, all reminiscent of the brothel, adorned many a black woman of song. But the most decorative frosting on the cake—unthinkable in white song—was a visible gold tooth or two, a most luxurious and enviable commodity in a black female of the day:

> You got a long black woman
> With gold teeth in her face. (Bertha Lee in "Mind Reader Blues")

> Now I got a brown skin girl
> With her front tooth crowned with gold. (Tommy McLennon in "Brown Skin Girl")

As for the character of the black female featured in blues, a sweet little flower she definitely is not. There is nothing shy or modest about her. In fact, she can be not only assertive but downright aggressive. Witness the lyrics of Alberta Hunter's "Downhearted Blues.[122]

> Got the world in a jug, stopper right here in my hand,
> And if you want it, sweet papa, you got to come under
> my command.

Sippie Wallace may sound subservient at one point in her "Mighty Tight Woman," when she says "I can be your sweet woman, also be yo' slave," but such "slavery" should be construed largely in a sexual context. In any case, she quickly follows that statement with more assertive ones:

> If you're a married man, you ain't got no business
> here . . .
> I might make your wife shed tears,
> 'Cause I'm a mighty tight woman, and there is nothing
> that I fear.

Sister Harris' stance is even more truculent, and by a long shot. In her 1923 blues "Don't Mess With Me," when a man she doesn't care for makes a pass at her, she stands up to him in a most unladylike (read: violent) way:

> I've got a razor that's got a nasty blade.
> Just pass on, circus, I've seen your parade,
> 'Cause I done picked the ground where your body's
> gonna be found.

For Bessie Smith, Victoria Spivey, Edith Wilson, Ma Rainey and others, guns and razors are the weapons of choice. According to Bessie Smith's "Black Mountain Blues,"

> Lord, I'm bound for Black Mountain,
> Me and my razor and my gun.
> I'm gonna shoot him if he stands still
> And cut him if he run.

Such violence aside, perhaps the song that best sums up the favorite stance of female blues singers and writers is Ida Cox's "Wild Women Don't Have the Blues."

> Go home and put my man out if he don't treat me right,
> Wild women don't worry, wild women don't have the blues.

These examples should make it obvious that the coyness and flirtatiousness found in Tin Pan Alley's white women could have no place in the black woman's repertoire. Such coquettish ploys are predicated on respectability, and, as we see, women of the blues have nothing to do with respectability. In fact, like Sister Harris they may boast of being "bad" in the sense of tough, able to defend themselves.

Rather than the subtleties of a demure coyness, they offer directness, reality and outright sexuality. Certainly, male blues singers and composers lay a heavy emphasis on sex. But they may also include themes like lack of money, gambling or jail. For women, sexuality is the principal preoccupation, identifying them nearly completely (*fornico ergo sum*). It is the heart and soul of their song.

Nearly every one of their blues is laden with sexual imagery and transparently sexual double entendres. Victoria Spivey's "Organ Grinder Blues" have nothing to do with a street musician, but, instead, they contain a blunt message.

> Grind it north, grind it east and west,
> When you grind it slow I like it best.

And Bessie Smith and Ma Rainey's "Don't Fish in My Sea" preaches:

> If you don't like my ocean, don't fish in my sea.
> Stay out of my valley and let my mountain be.

Other images evoking the sexual act include "shimmying," "barrelhousing" and driving or riding. "Easy rider," or "see-see rider," frequent phrases in the blues, most often refer to a woman's sexual partner, who might, in some cases, double as her pimp. If she has someone else on the side, that man may be seen as "another mule kicking in [her] stall."

In the vast majority of cases, however, the sexual symbolism relates to items of food. "Jelly," "jelly roll," "stew meat," " sweet potato" "peach tree" and "cabbage patch" are but a few labels referring either to body parts or the sexual act itself. And although phallic symbols are mainly the province of male blues singers, the women were known to employ them as well. Witness the lines of "Need a Little Sugar in My Bowl" or "Copulating Blues"[123]:

> I need a little sugar in my bowl,
> I need a little hot dog between my roll.

The perpetual emphasis on sex in women's blues leaves few holds barred. At times the composer-singers draw us into the realm of out-and-out prostitution. Ma Rainey's "Hustlin' Blues," Memphis Minnie's "Hustlin' Woman Blues," Lil Johnson's "Scuffling Woman's Blues," Chippie Hill's "Street Walker Blues," and other songs of their ilk remind us that, like the tango of Buenos Aires, one of the richest breeding grounds of the blues was the brothel. The black entertainers, men and women alike, had real contact with saloons and houses located in vice districts of Atlanta's Decatur Street, Memphis' Beale Street, New Orleans' "Storyville" or "Tenderloin" and their Harlem equivalents. Those songsters knew the score.

Their insistence on sex and the sexual act, unthinkable, of course, in the songs of Tin Pan Alley, was a given in the subculture of the blues. In a sense, sex represented many a black woman's lifeline, for, lacking even the tentative family structure of slavery, she had virtually nothing else to speak of. The system of a black family ruled by its white owner had now been replaced by a technical emancipation of slaves—but minus the stable male presence of a husband or "massa."

In addition, generally the modern black woman still had little or no access to a good education and professional or social standing. So naturally, she had no understanding of, or need for, the Victorian morality that kept a white woman chaste in order to make a fine match approved by parents and society. Without the resources and without the background that might have afforded her a sense of self and self-worth, she remained, instead, mired in a life of drudgery and, all too often, poverty and misery.

Sex was the closest she could get to happiness and, unlike booze, it was free—or, at the very least—affordable. So the female blues singer would sing of her sweet "rider," or "chauffeur," and no matter how cruelly he treated her, she would still crave his presence in her bedroom. In fact, her biggest complaint in song related to his abandoning her bed.

So Bessie Smith would lament in "Empty Bed Blues"[124]:

> I woke up this morning with an awful achin' head.
> My new man had left me just a room and a empty bed.

And Lil Johnson, in "You'll Never Miss your Jelly (Til Your Jellyroller's Gone)":

> I woke up this morning with the blues all 'round my bed.
> I felt just like somebody in my family was dead . . .
> My sweet man went away . . .

In the blues, when a man so abandons his woman, she tells us, first, that "he done her wrong," secondly, that she is in despair, and, lastly, what she needs to do about it.

She may be hopeful about his return and declare "He'll come back" or "I'll get him back."

Often, however, she adopts, with a certain bravado, an I-don't-care-because-I-don't-need-him attitude. In that vein the wronged woman may well declare there are other lovers out there, and he'll be sorry when she finds herself one." In "Farewell Daddy Blues," Ma Rainey's last line is: "When you look for your mama, she's gone with the farewell blues." In "Fare Thee Well, Mama's Gone, Good-Bye," by Peter Bocage and A.J. Piron, Clara Smith sings

> I'm going to get me a daddy, one who treats me right,
> Comes home and sleeps every night.

Quite a few rejected women dream of escaping, taking a train somewhere, anywhere else. Some aim to seek a lover out and get him back; some simply want to make a man regret his cruelty; others just yearn to get away from the scene of their misery. And by traveling to another locale—like Sippie Wallace, in "Every Dog Has His Day" or Bessie Jackson, in "Tired As I Can Be"—they might possibly find somebody better than the current faithless lover.[125]

Life's realities, however, made such dreams of escape idle threats or empty speculations. Black males, living a more itinerant existence, moving from place to place in hopes of a job or greater happiness, were far more likely to travel elsewhere. In Clara Smith's "Freight Train Blues," we learn that, to get her man off her mind, she decided to hop a freight train, but the brakeman wouldn't let her on. She concludes:

> When a woman gets the blues, she goes to her room
> and hides.
> When a man gets the blues, he catches a freight train
> and rides.

As Daphne Duval Harrison has pointed out, "Leaving a mistreating 'daddy' was easier sung about than achieved."[126]

And so, in the blues, the abandoned or abused woman finds other recourses, other outlets for her sadness and resentment. She may, for example, turn anger and frustration inward in a self-destructive way, seeking oblivion in liquor, at times winding up in jail. Or even contemplating suicide, like Sara Martin in "Death Sting Me Blues" or Bessie Smith in P. Fuller's "I'd Rather Be Dead and Buried in My Grave" and G. Brooks' "Dying By the Hour."

In the majority of cases, however, the wronged woman aims her anger directly at the man who left her. When that happens, no holds are barred; she is nothing less than lethal. Her weapon of choice may be a pistol "as long as my right arm," ("Sinful Blues" and "Wicked Blues"), a butcher knife ("Mistreatin' Daddy") or both gun and blade, as Ma Rainey suggested in "Black Mountain Blues ("I'm gonna shoot him if he stands still and cut him if he run"). Although Victoria Spivey, in "Blood Hound Blues," tells of administering poison to her abusive lover, most commonly the blues singers will stick to their guns, razors or knives.

As outrageous as this violence might appear to a general public, black audiences—certainly the female component—savored such lawless acts of revenge against abusive lovers. In theaters or tent shows, one could hear many a female shouting approval of the singer's threats, at times coming out with the spontaneous "Aymen!" of church meetings or "Say it sister!" In addition, record companies exploited such vengeful violence in sensational ads like the Columbia Records squib "Wow—but Bessie Smith spills fire and fury in 'Hateful Blues" or "Bloodthirsty woman confesses!" in OKeh Records' blurb for Victoria Spivey's "Dope Head Blues."[127]

Such murderous aggression may exist only in the rejected woman's imagination, but like her other solutions—hope, spite and impossible dreams of escape—it provides a catharsis for writer, singer and listener. Certainly, the blues themselves represent a catharsis and perhaps the main and only viable one. Like their male counterparts, no matter what happens to these women, they can continue "just singing the blues." That way they can articulate their individual pain, transforming it into art through the personal, down-to-earth and earthy music of their own people.

It is interesting that in the blues of the 1920s, in songs that so realistically addressed problems confronting African Americans marginalized in a big city, one would be hard pressed to find any direct allusions to the obvious truth that lay behind nearly all those problems. That is, skin color. Was the subject too painful or shameful to articulate? Would mentioning it have been too outright rebellious on the part of a people only recently out of slavery? Was it not allowed?[128]

Whatever the case, when Bessie Smith wrote "Poor Man's Blues," she confined her protests to economic, not racial realities. In that song she beseeched those more fortunate to "Open up [their] heart and mind." But she addressed her plea to "mister rich man," not "mister white man." We find only one major exception to that rule of silence, and in a commercial rather than a blues context. That is, in "What Did I Do To Be So Black and Blue?" from Fats Waller's and Andy Razaf"s *Hot Chocolates of 1929*. However, Razaf wrote that number most unwillingly and avoided making it a song of protest.[129]

So although the blues of that time frankly addressed almost all the major problems experienced by blacks, that one important matter of skin color remained under wraps.

* * *

If the flesh-and-blood black woman of the twenties shared little common ground with her white female counterpart, the same clearly held true for the songs of the two races. While the blues dealt with the harsh realities of black existence, white writers and performers of the time sang another tune entirely. As author Nat Shapiro put it, writing of white Tin Pan Alley: "The popular songs of the 1920's had only the most remote connection with reality."[130]

In contrast with the blues, a great percentage of white Tin Pan Alley numbers of the decade were resolutely optimistic. Witness such song titles as "I'm Sitting on Top of the World," "I'm in Love Again," "The Best Things in Life are Free," "Let a Smile Be Your Umbrella," "When You're Smiling," "Look For the Silver Lining" or assurances that the bluebird of happiness is waiting for you "Back In Your Own Back Yard."

Yet in spite of these great dissimilarities, it should not surprise us that when the black blues recordings of the twenties made their impact, white popular music speedily "adopted" the genre, with Tin Pan Alley writers grinding out song after song with "blues" in the titles. Of course this was usually true in name only. The classic "Birth of the Blues" of 1926 and the melancholy ballad "Am I Blue?" of 1929 bear little resemblance to the black genre in structure, melody and feeling.

Even Mercer's and Arlen's riveting "Blues in the Night" (1941), while beautifully capturing the atmosphere of the blues, cannot truly be called "blues." The piece is far more sophisticated than the traditional Negro blues (its driving beat was actually more suited to striptease numbers of the day). Although the music maintains segments of the blues twelve-bar patterns, it is far more melodic and varied than the music of the blues. Arlen's presentation lies more in the tradition of Handy's commercial "St. Louis Blues"[131] than the blues of guitar strumming backwoods singers or the female blues recording artists discussed here. As for the lyrics, they do evoke the Negro blues in phrases like "My mama done tol' me" and in the "whooee" of a distant train whistle. Yet they are carefully crafted—much too carefully to resemble blues lyrics. They are on the one hand more poetic:

> "The evenin' breeze'll start the trees to cryin' and the
> moon'll hide its light
> When you get the blues in the night."

And, on the other hand, they have far more sophistication in their perpetual internal rhymes and their phrases:

> "Take my word, the mocking' bird'll sing the saddest
> kind of song.
> He knows things are wrong, and he's right."

Finally, "Blues in the Night" is externalized: it tells a story and creates an atmosphere rather than delivering the direct "I feel" message of a genuine blues.

Although many other Tin Pan Alley writers would write songs about having the blues and many songs they called "blues," they could not allow themselves to recreate or imitate the authentic Negro blues. In the first place, the blues patterns did not conform to customary 32-bar, AABA[132] Tin Pan Alley pattern of songwriting. (It is true that Arlen ventured outside that pattern in "Blues in the Night" but he did not cast the song in a true blues form).

Far more importantly, however, it would have been professional suicide even to hint at the true substance of blues lyrics: their emphasis on sexuality, violence and suffering. Only a few southern white country singers of the twenties and thirties—artists like Jimmy Rodgers or Jimmie Davis—incorporated black themes and styles into their repertoire. But the overwhelming majority of white mainstream musicians most certainly did not. In the white context the blues would become standardized, romanticized, charming and even fun. In short, whitewashed.

In their original black context, they remained a cry of anguish.

Notes

114 See the section on race records in Chapter Seven, *infra.*

115 In its issue of August 2, 1923 (Vol 71, No. 11), *Variety Magazine* held that "The white publishers are getting onto this and entering many, many 'blues' in the market." But the statement referred to commercial songs of Sophie Tucker and others that did not follow the blues patterns developed by black musicians.

116 *Chicago Defender,* Feb. 24. (Vol. xiii, no. 8, p. 1). Abbott's point of departure was an article from the Macon, Georgia, *Telegraph* about an African American who had actually frozen to death in that region.

117 See the following chapter.

118 See, for example, the comparison between the field holler "Hey, Rufus" and the blues "See-See Rider," end of previous chapter.

119 In "The Heart of the Blues."

120 *Opportunity Magazine*. August, 1926, p. 258, quoted in Berry, *Langston Hughes, a Biography*, pp. 77-78.

121 A good number of female blues singers wrote their own songs, although some used material of black male writers such as Perry Bradford, Clarence Williams, Spencer Williams, Thomas E. Dorsey and others.

122 Composed with Lovie Austin.

123 By Clarence Williams, D. Small and T. Bryman.

124 By J.C. Johnson.

125 Sippie Wallace plans to go up country, because she wants another man "to take me on my night time stroll." Bessie Jackson will go back down south to her "used-to-be."

126 P. 90.

[127] OKeh Records' blurbs. Many of these appeared in advertisements in the *Chicago Defender* newspapers of the twenties. For excellent illustrations, see Harrison's *Black Pearls.*

[128] Angela Davis writes that she heard an account of Bessie Smith once singing, "All my life I've been making it/All my life white folks have been taking it." and suggests that may have gone unrecorded because of white censorship. P. 95.

[129] See end of Chapter Seven, *infra.*

[130] *Popular Music,* Vol. 5, p. 19.

[131] See my discussion of Handy in Chapter Seven, subsection "Lyrics and Composers: Going the White Route?"

[132] That is four consecutive parts to a song, each section composed of eight measures. The first half of a song consists of two eight-measure parts with an identical melody (A). That is followed by a release or "bridge" of eight measures with a different melody (B). The last eight bars revert to the original melody (A).

6

BREAKING IN

MUSICAL COMEDY FROM THE TURN OF THE CENTURY TO THE DEPRESSION

From the start of the twentieth century to the Great Depression and beyond, the interactions of black and white popular music would continue unabated. White entertainers maintained their practice of adopting the latest innovations of black musicians. And, as in the past, white entrepreneurs continued to encourage, sponsor and, at times, exploit those musicians. Meanwhile—the other side of the coin—many black composers and performers were, necessarily, setting their sights on white audiences. While enriching popular music with their own inventiveness, they would continually keep in mind the exigencies of white musical tradition and taste.

The American musical stage, with its long history of dealings between the races in popular entertainment, is a prime example of such black and white musical interaction,

The Business of Show Business

There was a time—the late nineteenth century to be precise—when it seemed that nothing could prevent talented black musicians from making their way in a field traditionally dominated by whites.[133] Black composers and performers had already gained experience and visibility on the American stage in the highly popular minstrel shows. Now they were ready to challenge white musicians on more sophisticated white territory: musical comedy. Circumstances warranted such a move. To explain briefly:

In the late nineteenth century, most black minstrels had been merely eking out an existence, still touring and performing but struggling against the competition of increasingly lavish productions by the better financed white companies. In any case, minstrelsy itself was already giving way to the newer vogue of vaudeville. Certainly, with African-American actors presenting the public with "the real thing," whites had less reason to continue donning burnt cork and perpetuating their pseudo-darky travesties. So rather than attempt to keep minstrelsy alive, from the 1880s on, many whites in the business abandoned the genre for the more popular vaudeville stage. With the blossoming of white vaudeville and variety shows, white operetta and the evolving genre of white musical comedy, minstrelsy was increasingly seen as a specialized and archaic curiosity, as served up by (mainly white) touring companies.

But in any case, minstrelsy—although somehow surviving through the 1920s—could not have remained in vogue forever. Both black and white minstrels shows had already changed radically by the end of the nineteenth century. The "olio" segment of songs, dances and skits had expanded more and more into vaudeville type routines, with acrobats, ventriloquists and magicians joining the standard comedians and song-and-dance men. Before the turn of the century, the shows even came to include female performers, previously unseen on the minstrel stage.

Some black musicians and entertainers of the time managed to make ends meet by performing in circuses, tent shows, medicine shows and carnivals. The more experienced and ambitious among them tried their hand at vaudeville. However, that arena, controlled naturally by whites, usually allotted only one short segment per show to black talent. Significantly, at the approach of the new century, some enterprising blacks decided to write and perform their own shows, that is, to compete with white composers, performers and music entrepreneurs in that popular white genre, American musical comedy.

Against all odds, they succeeded. And in so doing they proved to audiences that they were far more than Mssrs. Tambo, Bones or Interlocutor.

One of the first black musical ventures to break from the minstrel show template and challenge white musical theater on its own ground was Sam T. Jack's *Creole Show* (1889). Although Sam Jack himself was white, his all-black production introduced composers and performers who would have a huge impact on Negro musical theater—future stars such as Bob Cole, Billy Johnson and Sam Lucas and his wife. The scaffolding of minstrelsy was still in evidence in the production. However, unlike standard minstrelsy, the *Creole Show* abandoned blackface entirely and, moreover, included a chorus line of sixteen women—an innovation that would be adopted by black and white musical productions of the future. Rather than the familiar final walkaround of minstrel shows, the grand finale featured a lively cakewalk by dancers Johnson and Dean.

Like the *Creole Show,* other white-run black musicals ventured outside the confines of the traditional minstrel show while still maintaining some patterns of minstrelsy. Such transitional productions include *The Octoroons,* produced by white entrepreneur John Isham in 1895, and Isham's *Oriental America* of 1896, the first all-Negro show to play Broadway. Among the most popular of such shows were those of touring companies, such as the *Black Patti Troubadours,* starring "the Black Patti," Sissieretta Jones. That company, also under white management, retained the skeleton of the minstrel show format but at the same time emphasized Jones' operatic talents and featured singing and dancing by both male and female performers. Then at the turn of the century, two of the most prominent white-run road shows doffed the minstrel mask completely, making forays into vaudeville and proto-musical comedy. These were *In Old Kentucky* and *The Smart Set,* both touring from around 1900. Although simply song, dance and comedy revues built on the flimsiest of plots, they were, nonetheless, a start.

However, a big breakthrough had occurred on the New York stage somewhat earlier, in 1898. That summer New York audiences witnessed two landmark black-run musicals, *A Trip to Coontown* and *Clorindy, the Origin of the Cakewalk. Clorindy,* organized and produced by actor-writer-composer Robert Cole and his partner Billy Johnson, has been considered the first all-black musical comedy. For it abandoned both minstrelsy and vaudeville, having characters and an actual story line in the tradition of European operettas. The second groundbreaker, Will Marion Cook's, *Clorindy,* was a musical sketch with lyrics by poet Paul Laurence Dunbar and showcasing dancer-comedian Ernest Hogan. Even more than Hogan's comic gifts, the dancing in the show gave New Yorkers a foretaste of black musical comedy to appear in the twenties.

As the titles of such shows indicate, they were characterized and promoted as stereotypical darky fare. Obviously, if the one entrée to fame and success for black musical entertainers was self-mockery, those musicians had no recourse but to exploit the tried-and-true darky image.

Some critics have pointed to a form of subversive protest within the demeaning framework. Errol Hill and James Hatch, for example, have seen Bob Cole's use of whiteface makeup in his clown character, Willie, as "what may seem a gesture of defiance."[134] David Krasner cited the song "No Coons Allowed" from Cole's *Trip to Coontown* as an indictment, "an underlying critique of America's racism," and concluded: "For African Americans, 'signifying' or parodying racism became an important means of communicating resistance."[135]

Yet these musicals were not actual works of protest or resistance, for success, not protest was the aim. Any conceivable critique of the white establishment remained not only "underlying" but, in fact, buried within the lively humor, exaggeration and clowning of the actors. Much as earlier, any possible criticism of the white "massa" had been buried, or disguised, in the slaves' comically exaggerated cakewalk. All done in high spirits and all for a laugh.

So when a musical like Will Marion Cook's *Jes' Lak White Folks* portrayed vain attempts on the part of Negroes to be like rich whites, it was neither a plea for equality nor indictment of white society with its exclusiveness and snobbery. Rather, it mocked the ridiculousness of blacks who tried to ape that society. The show's ambitious character, Pompous, was no rebel or breaker of barriers. He was simply a latter-day counterpart of Molière's hilarious "bourgeois gentleman," a commoner who clumsily attempted to rise above his station by imitating the airs of a French nobleman. Or, closer to home, he could be seen as a direct descendant of minstrelsy's foppish Zip Coon or Jim Dandy. The explicit point of such a ploy was not to incite or raise consciousness but simply to get as much laughter as possible from the audience—and, of course an ample take at the box office.

As for the references to segregation in Cole's "No Coons Allowed," it might surprise us that such a song was sung before white audiences. It told the story of a black man wanting to take "his Lulu gal" to a fine restaurant but seeing a sign excluding them. Going to the courthouse to protest such injustice, he encounters the very same sign there, "No Coons Allowed." As Krasner points out, that song appeared shortly after the Supreme Court declared segregation legal.[136] But such harsh realities notwithstanding, there was little, if anything, that could be seen as incendiary or revolutionary in the number and nothing to disconcert an audience or detract from its amusement. For the words sung and the performance of the piece were once again, parodic and comical, in other words, safe.

In his writings on wit and humor Freud makes the point that oppressed minorities have always used jokes about their plight as a way of exorcising pain. One is reminded of the old Negro ditty about a black and white man gambling. The black wins but is too "skered" to pick his winnings up. Similarly, Bert Williams would soon be singing his "Jonah Man" song, a wry tale of everything-happens-to-me. In the shows of Cole and Cook, the difficulties of living in a white world come across not as rebellion but as customary everything-happens-to-us war stories of the Negroes.

Both *Clorindy* and *Coontown* were written and produced by African Americans and featured an all-Negro cast. Both made it to the stage without white sponsorship. The same held true for a whole succession of early twentieth-century black musicals by Cook, and others by Robert Cole in collaboration with J. Rosamond Johnson and his brother, the writer and future NAACP activist James Weldon Johnson.

Among the most notable of the early black musicals written by Cook were *Jes' Like White Folks* (1899), *In Dahomey* (1903), the first major black musical on Broadway, *Abyssinia* (1906) and *Bandanna Land* (1909), the last two produced by and starring the great comic Bert Williams and his partner, George Walker, and featuring Walker's singer/dancer wife, Ada (later "Aida") Overton. Such all-Negro shows with their talented performers, their high-paced dancing, their dusky humor and introduction to the stage of the new syncopated rhythms,[137] achieved popularity and success with both black and white audiences.

Generally, black musicals produced by whites had an easier time of it, for productions undertaken exclusively by black entrepreneur-musicians might encounter a whole variety of obstacles. Especially when it came to touring in southern locales where performers had to contend with discomfort, deprivation and, at times terrorization at the hands of bigoted bystanders. Still, the North, while comparatively civilized in attitude, was hardly a Mecca for black-run shows. Prior to forming his own company, for instance, Bob Cole had had major difficulties with a white manager when he stood his ground over an adequate salary and ownership of his own music. Because of that—and because of racial discrimination on the part of some theater managers in New York—when Cole set out to produce *A Trip to Coontown* on his own, he faced a virtual boycott that made his staging of the show close to impossible. The first performances took place in seedy out-of-the-way theaters where the cast had to make do with costumes and props left over from other shows. After a series of successes on tour in the United States and Canada, however, *Coontown* returned to New York, enjoying better theaters and a three-year run.

By the end of the first decade of the twentieth century, the vogue of black musicals on the New York stage began to wane. In fact, critics have noted[138] a decline that lasted from around 1909 to the twenties. Some have attributed this to competition from the new dance bands or movies, others to an intensification of white prejudice or to audiences weary of the black formula. Whatever the case, after Cole and the Johnson brothers *Shoo-Fly Regiment* (1907) and their *Red Moon* (1909) the African-American presence on the New York musical stage diminished.

One notable exception should be mentioned, a truly bright spot on the black musical comedy scene during the 1910s: It was *The Darktown Follies,* written by J. Leubrie Hill, Will Vodery and Alex Rogers. The show, earlier entitled *My Friend From Kentucky,* was produced in 1913 at Harlem's Lafayette Theater; other versions of it appeared later in various locales. The dancing especially, executed by the finest of black talent, astounded white audiences, for it was far superior to anything seen on Broadway. In one memorable sequence, "At the Ball," the whole cast circled counterclockwise, singing and shuffling in line in front of the footlights and behind the scenes, as in an old-fashioned ring shout. Florenz Ziegfeld was so impressed he purchased the routine for his *Follies of 1914*—but without using any members of the highly talented black cast or giving credit to J. Leubrie Hill and his co-writers or cast members who coached his dancers.

Outside of *The Darktown Follies,* Negro musical comedy became relatively rare on the New York stage during the 1910s. The dearth of black shows may have been triggered in large part by the illness and death of major black performers, for 1910 alone marked the fatal illness of three important musical comedy figures: Bob Cole, Bert Williams' partner, George Walker, and writer-entertainer Ernest Hogan. Creating even more of a void in black theater, that year the brilliant but partnerless Williams left black show business, joining the all-white Ziegfeld Follies, where he would remain for nearly a decade.

But if New York stages were not featuring black performers, New York was not the world. During that same period, 1909 to 1920, black musical theater enjoyed an active life, even flourished, elsewhere, especially in the South and Southwest. Although, at the turn of the twentieth century a mere handful of black owned theaters—most of them honky-tonk operations—gave performances in those regions, by 1909, 112 Negro theaters were presenting all-Negro touring companies and their musical revues regularly to African-American audiences there. By the twenties, in fact, nearly every good-sized southern city had its own black-owned theater. And a few cities had black newspapers (the Indianapolis *Freeman,* for example) that occasionally featured reviews of the shows coming through.

Among the most active early African-American pioneers of black-owned theater were Pat Chappelle, owner and manager of the Rabbit's Foot Company and other theaters in the Tampa area, Robert Motts, organizer and proprietor of Chicago's Pekin theater and Sherman H. Dudley, a theater entrepreneur who began his career as an actor in minstrelsy and vaudeville.

For a while, in the early 1900s, Motts presented not only musical comedy to his audiences, but legitimate theater, enacted by his resident Pekin Stock Company. Although the stock company eventually folded, musical comedy at the Pekin drew large African-American audiences. Inspired by the example of Mott's success, other entrepreneurs of color backed the construction of black-owned theaters in cities with a large enough Negro population.

As for Dudley, he was able to realize his very practical dream of a whole circuit of black theaters in America. In January of 1912 the Indianapolis *Freeman* published a letter in which Dudley proposed that African Americans of vision lease already existent theaters in key American cities. These were white-owned houses that had formerly featured melodramas, or "pistol dramas" which had now gone out of style, so that the premises were on the market and up for grabs.[139] Around this same time Dudley himself bought several theaters in Washington, D.C., and with other entrepreneurs answering his call, by 1916, his black theater circuit included over twenty-eight houses in the South, East and Midwest.

What prompted this sudden and dramatic burgeoning of local black theaters? Undoubtedly the most crucial single factor was the fact that potential African-American audiences had no easy access to the popular black musical shows. In the South, people of color were totally excluded from black or white shows in most white establishments. And in large cities, as in the North, white theaters willing to accommodate blacks remained "separate but equal," in other words, segregated.

So when New York's popular black musicals toured their areas, a large population of southern blacks were barred from seeing those shows, while others chose not to view them under the segregated system.

Whether in the North or South, most of the segregated houses followed the time honored custom of nineteenth-century white churches, relegating black patrons to a separate section of a hall, often to the rear or side. In a large enough theater, they might be confined to the third balcony, or "nigger heaven." The segregation took place even in tent shows or in popular medicine shows, where quack doctors hyping panaceas from their wagons, attracted audiences by presenting musical entertainment. In such performances, black attendees were customarily restricted to benches or makeshift seating at the very back.

In this same spirit of separate-but-equal opportunity, during the 1920s white owners of theaters geared to African-American theatergoers regularly offered a second performance of a black show at midnight for an exclusively white audience. This was a regular practice of the Theater Owners Booking Association[140] in its southern circuit, labeled a "midnight frolic" or "revel." But northern theaters engaged in the custom as well, and it suited not only white theatergoers but also white actors who raced from the final curtain of their own shows to see what the black casts were doing. (Earlier in the century, New York's Bijou Theater set aside certain nights for blacks to attend a show using the whole hall, "even the boxes."[141])

Such solutions may have appeared practical, even fair, to the white theater owners, but the policies of segregation had a demeaning effect on black clients. In New York in the 1920s and thirties, for example, even if a black patron offered to pay up to twice the price of admission in order to have an orchestra or parquet seat, he or she would likely be informed that the tickets had been sold out—no matter that the customer had arrived well in advance of the show. And a Harlem theater such as the Lafayette (which later became the Apollo) insisted that its black audiences—even its well known black performers—enter by a back door located on the next street over. Such practices would continue well into the 1930s and, in some instances, even later.

From these facts alone—and also the fact that black musicals could easily attract African-American audiences if allowed to—it was clear that a need existed. A need for theaters accessible to blacks, owned, managed and staffed—in short, controlled—by blacks, theaters in which black audiences could feel completely welcome watching artists and entertainers of color perform their shows onstage.

In filling that need, in creating their own venues, black entrepreneurs like Dudley, Motts and Chappelle were unconsciously following the pattern already set by nineteenth-century Negro churchgoers who left the white houses of worship to found their own, more familial and welcoming, churches.

Discovering the Gold Mine

After the first successes of Cook and of Cole and Johnson, it took very little time for white entrepreneurs to understand that they could easily cash in on the popular new formula of black shows. A potentially lucrative, untapped consumer group was out there, ready for the taking: goodly numbers of African Americans who would pay to see and hear talented performers of their own race. So, unsurprisingly, Robert Motts had no sooner opened his Pekin Theater when white-owned theaters in Chicago followed suit by engaging black shows in their own houses. That follow-the-leader trend would continue even stronger in the 1920s, the same decade that witnessed the rise of the black female blues singers.

One of the most visible examples of white entrepreneurs capitalizing on black show business was the Theatre Owners Booking Agency (TOBA), a white agency founded around 1909 by F.A. Barrasso. That organization engaged Negro talent to perform for Negro audiences, mainly in the South.

The original TOBA Circuit distributed shows in around forty theaters, theaters almost exclusively owned and run by white entrepreneurs and managers. The black performers hired on the Circuit usually worked under less than satisfactory conditions, were underpaid and, at times, treated shabbily or dishonestly by a number of managers and producers. But TOBA at least, provided them with work and the opportunity to be seen and heard. A less than satisfactory but workable symbiotic relationship.

The Circuit was reorganized in 1920-21 by the black theater impresario, Sherman Dudley, who began by featuring the female blues singers of the twenties. The system came to include over eighty theaters in cities and towns of the South, Southwest and Midwest. This second incarnation of TOBA started out under a more just and reasonable administration. Still, with such a complex operation and with the bottom line the main or sole criterion, all was not ideal. On the bright side, some theaters, the Roosevelt in Cincinnati, for example, did provide decent, modern facilities for the musicians. And a number of theater managers on the Circuit dealt fairly with them. However, mainly because of the stringent contract that still left performers at the mercy of the white owners and managers, it was often said that the acronym TOBA stood for "Tough On Black Asses."

The gold mine exploited by white-owned theaters and TOBA became increasingly attractive to white entrepreneurs—in fact, irresistible—in the wake of 1921. For that year the black musical *Shuffle Along* truly opened their eyes and prompted them to action.

Shuffle Along

After 1910 and the virtual disappearance of black shows on the New York stage, suddenly, miraculously, an exciting musical comedy written, directed and produced by blacks took the city by storm. The opening date: Monday, May 23, 1921. The place: the 63rd Street Music Hall. It was hardly the Shubert Theater but at least it could be said that *Shuffle Along* had made it to Broadway. Ragtime pianist and composer Eubie Blake wrote the music, and his partner, singer-actor-songwriter Noble Sissle, contributed the lyrics. The book was by Flournoy Miller and Aubrey Lyles, formerly resident writers and performers at the Pekin Theatre and now stars of the *Shuffle Along* cast.

Before opening in New York, the show had faced miserable conditions on tour and, lacking real support, verged on bankruptcy. Still, directors and cast persevered, and they somehow managed to open in the City. The 63rd Street Music Hall, one of the few possible venues available to black players, was in reality simply a lecture hall in which a proscenium and other theatrical amenities had yet to be installed. If these were not obstacles enough, that year Broadway provided enormous competition, with the *Ziegfeld Frolics,* the popular musical *Sally,* starring Marilyn Miller, and such celebrities as Ed Wynn and George M. Cohan treading the boards, all in more likely theaters.

Newspaper critics were slow in taking note, but the public came flocking to the event. Finally, after an excruciating wait for critical recognition, favorable reviews began to appear. More importantly, audiences both black and white, were swept away by the show. It ran for 504 performances, achieving higher quality with every passing week and ultimately grossing close to a million dollars.

According to Stanley Green, "Little money was spent on costumes or scenery, but white audiences were happy to travel a bit north of the theatre district to enjoy the show's earthy humor, fast pacing, spirited dancing, and infectious rhythms."[142] Without a doubt, the most "infectious" of its songs was "I'm Just Wild About Harry," a classic which Blake had originally devised as a waltz but transformed into 2/4 time when singer Lottie Gee insisted that a waltz was too romantic for a black show and that she could only perform it in a bouncier one-step rhythm.

Harlem Renaissance writer Langston Hughes saw *Shuffle Along* countless times; in fact, he claimed he chose Columbia University over an education in Switzerland so he could experience that show. For Hughes, *Shuffle Along* marked the true beginning of the Harlem Renaissance. "It just gave the proper push—that pre-Charleston kick—to [the] Negro vogue of the twenties that spread to books, African sculpture, music, and dancing."[143]

In a similar spirit, author Barry Singer wrote:

> From its frantic pace to its jazzy melodies, from its sassy chorus girls with their bobbed haircuts to its

> essence as an expression of contemporary black culture cleverly tailored for white Broadway consumption . . . . *Shuffle Along* theatrically ushered in the Roaring Twenties . . . Here was a show that, in its incorporation of black dance, black music and black performance style, was destined to provide American musical theater with many of its most familiar twentieth-century conventions.[144]

Ground had already been broken for black musicals with Cook, Cole, the Johnsons, Williams and Walker. But that was over a decade earlier, when both black and white musical comedy remained in a relative state of infancy. Those 1898 black shows had seemed interestingly new, with their rhythmic, rudimentary touches of ragtime syncopation, but they were musically unmemorable. By 1921, however, George M. Cohan had set his breezy pace, while Victor Herbert, Franz Lehar and Jerome Kern had infused popular song with highly lyrical melodies. Blake, a gifted musician though relatively untutored at the time, had extensive experience in ragtime and jazz and a facility for invention. He was able to meld the sounds and flair of white musical comedy with those of African-American jazz. His own performance in the show[145] was nothing less than brilliant.

Finally, ensuring the quality of *Shuffle Along* as a musical landmark was a highly talented cast,[146] which included showstopping singer Florence Mills (who replaced female lead Gertrude Saunders)[147] and a competent orchestra featuring violinist, Hall Johnson, a former member of James Reese Europe's orchestra and future director of the Hall Johnson Choir.

Other all-black musicals attempted to ride on the success of *Shuffle Along*. But like that show they encountered obstacle after obstacle. Broadway was loath to take a chance on such "novelties." If a theater did consider booking a Negro musical, it had to be after the season, that is when lack of air conditioning would make audiences scarce. *Strut Miss Lizzie,* which opened shortly afterward, in 1922, fell deep in debt to its white managers, then tried its luck uptown. But despite considerable talent, the show soon folded.

Nonetheless, such roadblocks did not stop the flood of black musicals, which would continue, usually under white sponsorship, well into the thirties. Also appearing in 1922, were the *Plantation Revue,* produced by white Lew Leslie, and the greatest black hit of the year, *Liza*. Brimful of musical talent, it was the first black show to make it to Broadway during the regular theater season. Although *Liza* introduced the Charleston dance for the first time on stage, it was Miller and Lyles' *Runnin' Wild* of 1923 that really popularized the dance, as performed to the irresistible music of James P. Johnson's famous "Charleston."

The Harlem Scene

The influx of African Americans into Harlem began in earnest during the 1910s. Many of them came from the "Tenderloin" district of Manhattan's west side, as Harlem's white residents, largely Irish and Jewish, fled in droves. White landlords demanded exorbitant rents of the newcomers, far more than what the whites had paid. Often a two-room apartment rented for as much as the entire house would have earned before being divided up into small units for black tenants. As a result, rental fees swallowed most of the income of African-American tenement dwellers—income most commonly earned from any low level, low paying jobs they managed to scrounge up. Thus the popular custom of rent parties in the small apartments.

Rent parties flourished as a Harlem institution from around 1914 to the end of Prohibition in the early thirties. They took place mainly on Saturday night or Thursday, when live-in maids had the night off. But they could be held any night of the week, that is any time before the first of the month, when a landlord might put your furniture on the street if you couldn't meet the rent. Handwritten flyers or cards printed by the roaming Wayside Printer with his "pushcart press" could be passed out to friends at the poolroom or on the street. Guests might be charged a fee of ten to fifty cents apiece, then pay extra for homemade beer or liquor and a kitchen meal of pig's feet, ham-hocks, boiled cabbage and the like. They would dance all night long, sometimes well into the following morning, to the sound of Harlem jazz musicians who earned a dollar or more from the door receipts. These hired entertainers were drawn from among the unemployed or professionals looking for extra cash. They often included the very top Harlem musicians, for example, pianists such as James P. Johnson, Willie "the Lion" Smith or Fats Waller.

There was no dearth of available talent, for Harlem had a lively musical scene, especially during the Prohibition twenties and in the thirties. Outside of the ubiquitous rent parties, music could be heard in numerous night spots and cabarets above 132nd Street and in theaters catering to an African-American clientele. Moreover, besides accommodating a large number of black bands and jazz ensembles, Harlem was New York's primary locus for black musical shows.

Cabarets such as the Cotton Club[148], Connie's Inn[149] and Ed Small's Paradise[150] nightly presented lively musical revues. The 1929 black musical *Hot Feet* had its start in Connie's Inn before moving to Broadway, and Fats Waller and Andy Razaf's *Hot Chocolates of 1929* was originally entitled "Connie's Hot Chocolates," since it was also produced by Connie Immerman, the owner of Connie's Inn. Before writing songs for Broadway shows, white songwriters Jimmy McHugh and Dorothy Fields had been providing Cotton Club revues with much of their musical material. White music entrepreneur, Lew Leslie, had directed those revues before bringing black talent to Broadway.

A number of the Harlem nightclubs had black owners and managers, for example, the Mexico, Brownie's Basement and assorted cellar clubs featuring hot jazz along Harlem's "Jungle Alley" on West 133rd Street. The best known of them was Ed Small's Paradise (opened in October of 1925). Located in a spacious basement, it was racially integrated, featured the jazz music of Charlie Johnson's orchestra and waiters who danced the Charleston while serving Chinese food and bootleg liquor to the customers. (This was, after all the Prohibition era, and shady bootleggers found a handy outlet for their illegal hooch in the Harlem nightclubs.)

But the most famous of the nightclubs, the Cotton Club and Connie's Inn, were in the hands of white owners, some of them notorious gangsters.[151] Although the owner of Connie's Inn, Connie

Immerman, could not be termed a gangster (he had formerly run a more or less legitimate Harlem delicatessen), his family had taken the bootlegging route since the early days of Prohibition, and Immerman himself eventually wound up operating his Inn with the backing of the notorious Dutch Schultz.

As for the well remembered Cotton Club of Duke Ellington, Fletcher Henderson and Cab Calloway fame, to call it a "shady" enterprise would be a rank understatement.

It's creator, backer and behind-the-scenes manager was the ruthless gangster Owney Madden. In 1923, Madden took over and refurbished the old Douglas movie house at 142nd Street and Lenox Avenue, turning it into a nightclub and a medium for vending his bootlegged hooch. Former heavyweight champion, Jack Johnson, fronted the operation until 1929, when he sold out to a syndicate run by "Big Frenchy" DeMange, a violent parolee and bootlegger.

Cab Calloway described the Club as follows:

> The waiters were dressed in red tuxedos, like butlers in a southern mansion, and the tables were covered with red-and-white gingham tablecloths. There were huge cut-crystal chandeliers, and the whole set was like the sleepy-time-down-South during slavery . . . I suppose the idea was to make whites who came to the club feel like they were being catered to and entertained by black slaves.[152]

The Cotton Club's format was modeled after Connie's Inn, offering black musical revues with "high yaller" or "cotton-colored" chorus girls. However, unlike Connie's Inn, where Immerman had his revues created by black writers and composers, the Cotton Club's shows were written by whites. And that nightclub was by far the most prestigious venue for musicals in Harlem. For opening night performances only the *crème de la crème* could get reservations. The local African-American community would gather in droves to watch the celebrities on their way in. Both these nightclubs admitted only white audiences[153]—downtown aficionados of black music and a host of adventure seeking "slummers." While a number of black Harlemites resented the white intrusion—and their own exclusion—the black entertainers in the clubs had no objections to the sea of white faces. After all, their careers and their livelihood depended on the system.[154]

Like the nightclubs of the twenties and thirties, Harlem theaters would fall largely into white hands. Attempts by Harlem blacks to open their own theaters for musical comedy—unlike the successful ventures of southern entrepreneurs like Mott or Dudley—were short lived. For Harlem itself remained virtually under white control. In fact, at the time, less than twenty percent of all Harlem business was under black ownership.

Up until 1914 or so, African-American Harlemites could only attend specifically black theaters. Just two existed there, the Lincoln and the Crescent, both on 135th Street,[155] although white entrepreneurs would eventually purchase and control them. The better known white owned Lafayette Theatre had begun offering black musical productions to African-American audiences in the 1910s, using the standard system of segregation. That system continued to apply in the twenties and thirties.

After the huge 1921 success of *Shuffle Along,* white theater owners and managers in Harlem, men like Frank Schiffman and Leo Brecher, became more and more involved in producing black shows. Schiffman took over key Harlem theaters during the 1920s, including the Lafayette and the Alhambra, presenting black musicals to both African-American and white audiences—still on a separate or segregated basis.

There were obvious financial advantages for whites to jump on the bandwagon. In the first place, black performers would necessarily accept far less money than their white counterparts. Secondly, black musicals meant guaranteed audiences: African Americans would turn out *en masse* for the shows, and downtown whites, hearing of their success, would flock to see them. So throughout the twenties, indisputably the golden age of black musicals, and well into the thirties, white entrepreneurs took over. In fact, by the early thirties they were producing nearly all the black shows on Broadway. And they were grinding out increasingly lavish productions of black musical entertainment in Harlem. New stages opened up to accommodate the shows there, stages in houses such as the Alhambra and the famous and enduring Apollo. Such theaters operated under the aegis of whites such as Milton Gosdorfer, Leo Brecher and—most notably—Frank Schiffman.

Schiffman's name has been mainly connected with Harlem's Apollo theater, which he (and later his son) ran for many years. He was a shrewd businessman and often a tough boss. Still, if only for reasons of practicality, he devoted himself to promoting top-notch black musical talent within the context of the Harlem community and to drawing large African-American audiences to his shows. In so doing he created a legend out of the Apollo Theater.

The Durable Stereotype

Well into the 1930s, the watermelon eating, chicken stealing darky of nineteenth-century minstrelsy clung like an albatross to black composers and performers of musical comedy. A good number of those involved or interested in black theater protested against the insulting caricatures and called for change. Sylvester Russell, for one, a correspondent for the black *Indianapolis Freeman,* wrote articles in 1904 and 1907, urging that both whites and blacks eliminate the words "nigger" and "coon" from their songs and, indeed, from their thinking.[156] Bob Cole, who, himself, had composed and produced the show entitled *A Trip to Coontown* in 1898, later insisted that the coon image be eradicated.

As for the black entertainers themselves, Bert Williams and his partner, George Walker were often singled out by blacks for perpetuating the stereotype. Williams was, in fact, highly sensitive to and saddened by the racial discrimination he experienced,[157] but in order to break into show business, he had blackened up his already dark skin and called his act "Two Real Coons," claiming that he and Walker were thereby distinguishing themselves from the white imitators. When criticized for keeping darkydom alive in show business and for not using models like certain blacks at Oxford and Yale, Williams explained[158] that he and his partner were in a bind. For black audiences wanted to see black entertainers perform as whites and white audiences wanted just the reverse. Their solution was to portray familiar characters drawn from the masses.

Williams' fare did, at times, break from the coon mold to convey the tribulations of Everyman. Still, on stage, he never abandoned the burnt cork that masked his light skin, nor his shuffling darky persona—nor the Negro dialect which the West Indies born Williams had had to learn as a foreign idiom.

In actuality, in the first decade of the twentieth century, when such as Russell and Cole were protesting the coon image, the fad of coon songs had already been dying out. Ragtime songs by blacks and whites used the word and the caricature less and less, while black musical shows were becoming more and more sophisticated. But in spite of these facts, black musical comedy could not truly rid itself of the darky stereotype. For that is precisely what white audiences wanted to see and what white theater critics would accept.

In 1908, for example, a reviewer of the New York *Dramatic Mirror* could not understand why the producers of Cole and Johnson's *Bandanna Land* permitted the cast to wear straight hair. He conceded, however, that in any case ". . . it really does not matter, [since] the singing of the straight-haired chorus is just as vigorous as it would be with the kinks."[159] Examples of other similar reviews abound, and a good number of them would sound shockingly insulting to modern day readers.

A 1909 review in *Variety* gave this critique of the sister team, Desmond and Bailey: "They sing rather well together, but there is not enough of the 'coon shouting to keep things lively."[160]

Another 1909 *Variety* review faulted the song-and-dance team, Johnson and Dean, for venturing to include Hungarian and English music in their show, on the grounds that "Their forte is singing 'coon[161] songs and dancing." And in 1910, a Dallas article describing a performance of the Black Patti Company shared those sentiments, holding that "A nigger that is willing to come right out and be pure nigger . . . can be quite the funniest thing going."

Over a decade later, in a review of the show *Put and Take,* critic Jack Lait was clearly dismayed that black performers were dressing and acting like white ones. They should not attempt to compete with whites, he opined. They may think they are as good but the fact remains that they are "different"; therefore they ought to be "distinct—indigenous." Rather than dressing up, the men should have worn plantation jumpers. And the girls "should have been fancifly [sic] dressed as picks [pickaninnies], Zulus, cannibals, or cotton pickers." Lait concluded: "There wasn't enough Colored stuff in the show."[162]

In most white reviews the writers recognized the quality of the black shows, with their side-splitting comedy and, especially, their high-paced and energetic dancing. Nevertheless, what had attracted them to the black shows in the first place was their exotic "blackness" and, of course, their funny, quaint images of slow, shuffling Jim Crows or Sambos and comically fatuous Zip Coons, exaggerated dandies unsuccessfully aping their white "superiors." To step outside the framework of such holdovers from minstrelsy was to risk losing the much needed support of white audiences.

Naturally, talented black composers and performers longed to show they could to do more than repeat patterns of the past. Ada Overton Walker, for one, decried the fact that black shows could not present love scenes, that white audiences would not accept romantic themes in a black context.[163] Not until 1921 and *Shuffle Along* did romance play any real role in a black show—and even that inclusion had been risky to venture. (The principals of the show, wary of a negative white reaction to the love interest in the musical, were greatly relieved that neither audiences nor critics objected to it.)

But that bit of romance notwithstanding, as late as 1930s, the darky stereotype would continue to characterize black musicals.

If a musical comedy did not center on the South, on pickaninnies, watermelons and dancing on the delta, it found other ways of satisfying the demand for a black "atmosphere" in black shows. Writers and producers set the scene in exotic African venues such as Abyssinia or Zanzibar. Actors masqueraded as *café au lait* Indians or Asians. And in the late twenties and early thirties, although the old darky of minstrelsy had all but faded away, musicals continued to advertise their Negritude in titles such as "Blackberries," "Blackbirds," "Ebony Scandals," "Ubangi Club Follies" and, yes, in 1933, good old "Plantation Follies."

Ironically, a *New York Sun* review of *Blackbirds of 1928,* despite its rave notice, complained of the stereotypical style of the show, "odd vagaries which the white mind has fixed as the traditional expression of the colored genius."[164] In a later *New York Sun* article reviewing a 1930 *Blackbirds*, Richard Lockridge wrote:

> It would be interesting to discover, and quietly murder, the man who first convinced Negro comedians that the way to be comic is browning black faces. You take a Negro, who is apt to have naturally certain qualities which the white race cannot acquire, and black him up. You lay on his dialect with a trowel . . . You make him, in short a bad imitation of what was not a very good imitation in the first place.[165]

It would seem that reviewers had to have it both ways. By the end of the decade the stereotype had obviously become tiring. Yet what alternative was there for a black show to make good commercially?

Small wonder then that talented African American artists felt trapped and frustrated. To survive and succeed, they were condemned, despite their preferences and better judgment, to an endless repetition of the old successful formula. That is, unless they imitated whites just as whites were imitating them.

Notes

133 The first glimmerings of that trend occurred early on, even before the Civil War. From the 1840s into the seventies a free black family from Connecticut, the Luca family, went on tour, singing and, at times, using a semi-circular minstrel type format in performances.

134 P. 156.

135 P. 35.

136 Pp. 34-37. Segregation was legalized in 1896.

137 *In Dahomey,* for example, included several cakewalks and a certain amount of off-the-beat syncopation in songs like "Swing Along." Five years earlier, *Clorindy* was, according to James Weldon Johnson, the

first show to introduce raggy off-the-beat rhythms (*Black Manhattan,* p. 103), but the score of the musical has, unfortunately, not been preserved.

138 See, for instance, Riis, *More Than Just Minstrel Shows,* p. 55; Singer, *Black and Blue,* p. 79-80; Sampson, *The Ghost Walks,* pp. 532-533.

139 A copy of Dudley's letter of 1/20/12 may be found in *Blacks in Blackface,* p. 42.

140 See the following section.

141 From a review in the *New York Telegraph* of 9/20/01, quoted in *The Ghost Walks,* p. 237.

142 *Broadway Musicals,* p. 34.

143 *The Big Sea,* pp. 223-224.

144 *Black and Blue,* p. 80.

145 Recorded on the LP *Shuffle Along.*

146 Josephine Baker, of later Paris fame, was hired for the dancing chorus while the show was on tour.

147 Mills, a performer of great charm, had a high reedy voice. Saunders, whose performance, unlike Mills' was preserved on record, sings in a high register but manages to inject sexy sounds in her soprano. Her "Daddy, Won't you Please Come Home?" with strings of "da-da-da-da-daddy . . ." anticipates Mary Martin's 1930s sexy baby-talk style in "My Heart Belongs to Daddy,"

148 Lenox Avenue at 142nd Street.

149 Basement next to the Lafayette Theatre, at 7th Avenue and 131st Street.

150 7th Avenue, between 134th and 135th Street.

151 Not all the gangsterism was restricted to whites, of course. For a small-scale example, black "five-percenters extorted $5,000 a week from Harlem's Apollo Theatre under threat of disrupting the shows unless paid off.

152 *Of Minnie the Moocher and Me,* p. 88.

153 Rumor had it that W.C. Handy was not allowed into the Cotton Club on a night they played his "St. Louis Blues." There were only a few exceptions to the Club's rule of segregation: dancer Bill Robinson and singer Ethel Waters managed to get tables for their African-American friends. And Connie Immerman, in time, admitted black patrons for midnight shows.

[154] In the filmed documentary *The Cotton Club,* when Cab Calloway and other Cotton Club entertainers were asked if it didn't bother them not to have only whites in their audience, they seemed surprised, then explained that they were, after all, entertainers and delighted to be playing for any audience.

[155] The better known of the two, the Lincoln, had an all-black stock company in the early 1900s.

[156] The text of Russell's articles may be found on pp. 314-317 and 407-408 of *The Ghost Walks.*

[157] In an oft-quoted remark, W.C. Fields said, "Bert Williams was the funniest man I ever saw and the saddest man I ever knew."

[158] See Appendix C for William's letter to Albert Ross. *Variety Magazine.* Vol. IX, No. 1, 12/14/07, p. 30.

[159] Cited in *Blacks in Blackface,* p. 131.

[160] Vol. XIII, No. 7, Jan. 23, 1909. Coon was sometimes used with an apostrophe since some people thought the word derived from "racoon."

[161] Vol. XVI, No. 4, Oct. 2, 1909, p. 17.

[162] *Variety.* Vol. LXIV, No. 1, p. 17, Aug. 26, 1921.

[163] See her letter of 10/6/06 to the Indianapolis *Freeman,* reprinted in *The Ghost Walks,* p. 371-372.

[164] From an undated clipping in the Harvard Theater Collection. Stamped April 13, 1926. This review, like others, gives special praise to headliner Florence Mills with her "thin bright voice and her infinite gusto."

[165] October 23, 1923 issue.

7

CROSSING OVER

SINGERS AND SONGWRITERS

LeRoi Jones," referring to the relationship between black and white popular music, described it as "a picture within a picture within a picture."[166] His image is an apt one, for, as we have seen, from the start black musicians appropriated characteristics of white music and, melding their own cultural heritage with that music, transformed it into an original African-American genre. Then immediately on discovering the black musical style, whites in the business copied it. Whereupon black artists, little daunted, set about imitating whites imitating blacks. This perpetual picture-within-a-picture phenomenon would continue in multiple configurations throughout the development of twentieth-century jazz and dance band music.

Musical crossovers—imitations of black musicians by whites and vice versa—escalated as the twentieth century progressed. From the 1910s through the early forties, with the flourishing of syncopated dance music and the rise of the big band era, more and more talented white musicians could be heard reproducing the sounds of black jazz. And for their part, during that same period black musicians were continually adopting popular styles developed by white ones.

Because of the accelerated crossovers, the lines between black and white music would begin to fade, becoming, at times, even undistinguishable. For example, in the twenties and thirties certain white instrumentalists like Jack Teagarden and Mugsy Spanier had so captured the black sounds that it would have been difficult, if not impossible, to identify their race simply by hearing them on an unidentified jazz recording.[167] Moreover, some recording sessions of those decades—unlike the customarily segregated public band performances—included black jazz performers with white bands and, although rare at the time, some whites in black ensembles.

This increased blurring of lines in black and white instrumental music would also occur in the realms of singing and songwriting in America. As with the bands, for singers and composers the process was gradual one and far from smooth. Let us examine that process, describing first how white vocalists adopted an African-American style at some point in their careers.

Doing the Black Thing

At the turn of the twentieth century, white singers in vaudeville, burlesque and on Broadway were belting out current coon songs—many of them by African-American composers—in black dialect. Among the most famous of the white "coon shouters" were women such as the Broadway stars May Irwin[168] and Marie Cahill. As early as 1896, May Irwin sang Ernest Hogan's "All Coons Look Alike To Me" and, somewhat later, the equally stereotypical "Mr. Johnson Turn Me Loose" by Ben Harney. In the 1910s, Nora Bayes, Elsie Janis and Stella Mayhew performed numbers with such titles as "Come Along, My Mandy," "De Devilin' Tune" and "Savannah" (in which Mayhew rendered such unmemorable phrases as "Dem niggers can certainly dance"). By that time Irving Berlin had been infusing his compositions with a ragtime beat, and the white popular song world had caught onto the contagious rhythms. One notable example: Nora Bayes and Jack Norworth customarily ended their duets with a smooth and engaging reprise of the song's melody arranged in ragtime.

Were such imitations on the part of white singers not enough, a good number of those singers—long after minstrelsy's heyday—were still blacking up. Al Jolson is a notorious case of a white appearing in blackface even into the thirties. But more surprisingly, some white female singers, even famous ones, blacked up as well. Sophie Tucker and Fanny Brice smeared their faces with burnt cork and black greasepaint early in their careers. Necessarily so, because, like Al Jolson[169] and Eddie Cantor, they were unromantic figures, neither handsome nor alluring. Without physical appeal, one of the surest and safest ways of breaking into show business was going the black route. Sophie Tucker learned that fact early in her career, when, at her first major audition, she heard the manager say she had to blacken up since she was "too big and ugly."[170]

But whether in blackface or not, many singers who did not qualify as dashing Irish tenors or lovely dewy-eyed sopranos adopted a semi-black style, often making an unconvincing stab at a Negro dialect. On occasion, they used songs by African-American composers. Such was the case, for example, of Fanny Brice, who introduced "Lovey Joe" by black writers Will Marion Cook and Joe Jordan, in the *Ziegfeld Follies of 1910.* More notably, Sophie Tucker, on the insistence of her black maid and friend, Mollie Elkins, took a chance on black songwriter, Shelton Brooks, and was ever grateful for the decision, since Brooks' song, "Some of These Days," helped propel her to fame in 1911. The trend, however, was to use black-tinged numbers from white composers of Tin Pan Alley, since, as we shall see, whites clearly had a corner on the song market.

How far could a Caucasian female singer go in imitating her African-American counterparts? On stage or in recordings, few, if any, would dare follow black singers like Ma Rainey or Victoria Spivey into the explicitly sexual terrain of the blues. Among the well known white singers, Sophie Tucker—who was not a blues singer, although she has been so labeled at times—probably came the closest to the earthy sexuality of the black blues singers. She achieved that in great part by seasoning her numbers with innuendos and suggestive movements. And closer to the

Black Venus of the Blues than the Sweet Little Girl of Tin Pan Alley, Sophie was nobody's baby—but everybody's Red Hot Mamma. The words of her theme song even emphasized her far-from-sylph-like figure: "You're gonna miss your big fat mamma some of these days."

Still, despite her gusto and her broad hints of naughtiness and her bawdiness, even Sophie Tucker did not overstep the established limits for white singers. For example, in "Some of These Days" the singer specifies that her unfaithful lover is going to miss her "huggin'" and "kissin'"—but most certainly not her "jelly roll"!

During the 1920s white singers with a varied repertoire would, at times, include black sounding songs as novelty numbers. Blossom Seeley delivered her honky-tonk "Yes Sir, That's My Baby"—pronounced "yes suh, that's mah baby"—and Ruth Etting, known primarily for her sweet and romantic ballads, included in her repertoire some black tinged songs like "Everybody Loves My Baby, but My Baby Don't Love Nobody But Me." As for the males of that time, Al Jolson is, without doubt, the most glaring example of a white trying to sound like an African American. One has only to picture him in blackface, on his knees, hands outstretched to audience, and nasally, schmaltzily, belting out white Buddy De Sylva's "My Mammy."

The use of black themes and music by white singers became less pronounced, more subtle, during the 1920s and thirties. The old novelty black-oriented numbers began to sound trite, as songwriters grew more sophisticated and as America entered its golden age of popular song. So red hot mammas, Mandys and mammies were out. Instead, another, different, aspect of black song was having an effect on some white vocalists. It was the sound of the blues. Of course, as we have seen, white female singers could not adopt the actual texts of Negro blues. Neither would they imitate the often harsh or raspy groans of blues recording artists. And they did not follow the twelve-bar blues format but, rather, held to the standard thirty-two measures of Tin Pan Alley numbers. However, the singers could, and did, take on some of the lushness and lilt of the blues. Such qualities were present occasionally in bluesy overtones of Ruth Etting (although standard sweet renditions seemed most suited to Etting's blonde prettiness).

The singing styles of Connee Boswell and—to a great extent, Mildred Bailey—were more obviously tinged with a blues tonality. Connee Boswell, a native of New Orleans, began her career in a trio with her sisters, Martha and Helvetia (Vet): the famous Boswell Sisters. They had started out as instrumentalists playing classical pieces. But taken with the music of their black family servants, they oriented themselves toward a style of smooth black jazz[171] singing, easy on the ears of a general public. The Boswell Sisters would soon inspire a spate of other singing trios or quartets, including black groups like the Mills Brothers and the Ink Spots. And in one more black-to-white-to-black musical boomerang, Connee herself came to influence the styling of black vocalist Ella Fitzgerald.

Among other white female vocalists evoking the black blues style in the late twenties and thirties were a number of well-known "torch singers." Libby Holman, for example, who sang her melancholy "Moanin' Low," on Broadway in 1929[172] in the setting of a Harlem tenement. And Helen Morgan also projected an intimate blues feeling,[173] although her voice had a higher register than Holman's. Morgan, often perched atop a Steinway, regaled audiences with can't-help-loving-that-guy songs, such as "My Bill" (a Gershwin number first sung in 1927 by Morgan as Julie, a mulatto passing for white, in Jerome Kern's *Showboat*).

And there was Mildred Bailey. White with a mother of American Indian stock, Bailey was very close to black musical culture and to black musicians of her day. And despite a fairly thin voice, her singing had the feel of the blues, evoking Bessie Smith or Ethel Waters. She was often billed as the "rockin' chair lady" for her rendering of Hoagy Carmichael's "Old Rocking Chair's Got Me," a song which pictured an old Negro in his cabin, awaiting judgment day. With Bailey, the black connection was so strong that people were often surprised, hearing her on radio, to discover she was not an African American[174]

As for white male singers, one of the most popular among them, Bing Crosby, was tempted by black jazz singing but took a surer path to national success. Deeply influenced by Armstrong's phrasing and a great fan of Ethel Waters and other black artists, Crosby started his career in jazz singing as a member of The

Rhythm Boys, featured with Paul Whiteman's band. However, thanks to the microphone and radio, which permitted a more intimate style than the previous belting-out of the vaudeville stage, he abandoned jazz and conquered America with his sweet, smooth, listenable style of "crooning."

Some other white males preferred a style closer to the black music they admired. That was true of Hoagy Carmichael's singing as well as his songwriting (discussed below), both flavored with Negro nuances. While not imitating a Negro dialect, Hoagy lazily drawled a repertoire of black-tinged songs. As did trombonist and vocalist Jack Teagarden, who grew up amid blacks and had a great fondness for the spirituals.

And a number of white male vocalists tried obviously to sound as black as possible. Some of them succeeded: Louis Prima is a case in point. Born on the edge of Storyville, he was a great admirer of King Oliver and an inveterate imitator of Louis Armstrong. And Prima's "Basin Street Blues," recorded with Pee Wee Russell in 1935, is one of several numbers in which he seemed bent on out-Callowaying Cab Calloway. Around the same time, white Tony Pastor was modeling himself after Louis Armstrong with gutteral vocalizings in numbers such as Artie Shaw's 1938 recording of "Indian Love Call."

Doing the White Thing

If white singers copied black ones, it made eminent sense for black vocalists to return the compliment. And many of them did. Once again, this was partly out of sincere admiration but also, to a great extent, for reasons of expediency. After all, white singers had a far easier path to success, so why not follow in their footsteps and copy their formulas?

Back in the early 1900s, even if black singers did not set out intentionally to imitate whites, some promoter or other would often engineer that connection, having a black artist piggyback on the reputation of a white one. For instance, from 1896 through the late 1920s, Sissieretta Jones starred in her black vaudeville touring company, The Black Patti Troubadours. A singer of operatic and popular songs, Jones was labeled "The Black Patti" to indicate to all that her talent was equal to that of the famous white operatic soprano, Adelina Patti. Similarly, early in the century, Susie Anderson of McAdoos Georgia Minstrels was called "The Black Melba," just as, in legitimate theater, actor W. A. Seymour had the epithet, "The Black Booth." Such a practice survived well into the twenties. In that era Ida Cox won the title of "The Sepia Mae West," and brassy blues singer Sarah Martin, copying a white singer—who had earlier copied the black style—billed herself as "The Colored Sophie Tucker." Then, in one more about-face of the same ilk, Ethel Waters became touted as "The Ebony Nora Bayes."

The twenties, however, provided a sort of oasis in which black vocalists—eventually males as well as females—could truly "sing black"; they could cultivate part of their own heritage, the blues, and get handsomely paid for it as well. For that was the decade of a rash of successful blues recordings or "race records"[175] launched by women like Mamie, Bessie and Clara Smith (all unrelated) and joined by such men as Blind Lemon Jefferson, Blind Blake, Charlie Patton, Son House, Mississippi John Hurt and others.

But before the spate of blues recordings, that is, before it became stylish and economically viable for black singers to use native black material, many of them had been delivering a far less authentic type of music. This was more common with the female singers. For male blues artists discovered by field scouts of the record industry had more likely spent their time strumming and singing traditional style blues in backwoods areas of the South. On the other hand, a large percentage of the women had been working as professional entertainers; their repertoire consisted not of homespun blues but, mainly, of assorted vaudeville, minstrel or musical comedy numbers by writers such as Cole or Blake. Theirs was not necessarily a white repertoire but the sort of variety show or cabaret fare that whites (and blacks) expected of black entertainers of the time.

Some, like Victoria Spivey, Lucille Hegamin, Alberta Hunter, Mamie Smith and Edith Wilson, recycled into the blues once the recording trend began, although their former material had been eclectic, standard and commercial. In fact, Mamie Smith's breakthrough in the blues recordings of the twenties, started not with an actual blues song but with a standard Tin Pan Alley type ballad by Perry Bradford, "That Kind of Love." Then later, when the "race record" oasis dried up, at the approach of the Depression, some singers associated with the black blues had a hard time of it. Bessie Smith, for example, tried, without success, to save her career with a broader, commercial fare. Others of talent, less firmly associated with the blues—or just plain luckier—were able to survive into the thirties.[176] Some managed by falling back on their stage or cabaret experience and taking a more generic, less authentically black, route.

Indeed, during the thirties and early forties, when white singers like Peggy Lee and Lee Wiley were sounding more and more like black ones, well-known black female vocalists were sounding less and less black. Because those singers, hearing echoes of their native sounds as reproduced and/or modified by some white stars, were impressed and often influenced by them. Ethel Waters, for example, who was never limited to blues singing, appreciated and absorbed some of Nora Bayes' style,[177] just as newcomer Ella Fitzgerald modeled herself to some extent after Connee Boswell. True, Ella was greatly influenced by Louis Armstrong's phrasing (as were so many other vocalists), and true, she perfected a black jazz medium in becoming the "Queen of Scat." But given her perfect enunciation and delivery, it would be as hard for the uninitiated to guess her color from her singing, as in the case of white Mildred Bailey.

So in the thirties there occurred a progressive "whitening" of the style of black female singers. Unlike the blues shouters of the twenties, black female vocalists of the following decade did not say "cain't" or "mah po' man." Even Billie Holiday (long associated with the blues[178] but a self-styled jazz singer rather than a purveyor of blues), and, later, Sarah Vaughan, demonstrated only a faint inflection of traditional black speech and vocal quality. And beyond a few numbers such as Holiday's "Strange Fruit" and "God Bless The Child," their repertoires consisted mainly of standard white songs. Indeed, in 1937, Maxine Sullivan, won fame by singing—with impeccable enunciation—a jazzed version of the Scotch ballad "Loch Lomond" with white bandleader Claude Thornhill.

Unlike these female entertainers, the well-known African-American male singers tended to project a deeply black sound. A Leadbelly was always a Leadbelly, singing the same way with the same fare until he stopped singing. Louis Armstrong was always Louis Armstrong, with his dialect impervious to knife cutting, his slurring and mispronunciation of words and his garbled syntax. Always Louis even when he blithely took on a cabaret song like Edith Piaf's "La Vie en Rose" (including the title in French!).

The brilliant blues singer Jimmy Rushing, whose voice has been likened to "gravel stirred in a jar of molasses,"[179] might have presented a different pattern. For unlike Armstrong, Leadbelly and many backwoods blues singers, Rushing had acquired higher education, having attended Wilberforce University. But his delivery of the blues remained authentically, stunningly black, even though his pronunciation was a careful compromise between refined speech and the traditional African-American dialect. As Ralph Ellison explained:

> Jimmy has always shown a concern for the correctness of language, and out of the tension between the traditional folk pronunciation and his training in school, he has worked out a flexibility of enunciation and a rhythmic agility with words . . .[180]

So in contrast to black female songsters discussed here, those male singers and many others of the time did not "whiten up" their vocals. Exceptions could be heard, however, particularly around the 1940s, when the Mills Brothers recorded their hugely popular "Paper Doll" (1943),[181] a frothy Tin Pan Alley number presented in a completely assimilated style.[182] And a far more striking case of a black singer adopting the white model is found in the performances of Billy Eckstine. For although Eckstine—not only a singer but a trumpeter and bandleader as well—was deeply involved in black jazz and bop music, and although he hired avant-gardists like Dizzy Gillespie and Charlie Parker in his band, his singing was in an absolutely standard white mode graced by a flawless diction. His was an unusual example of a handsome African-American artist who became popular among whites not as a black stylist but as a singer of romantic ballads, such as "Skylark," introduced in the early forties.

Not many black male singers of the time followed Eckstine in conspicuously crossing over into the white style. However, as we have seen, by the end of the thirties and around the time of the Second World War, the sounds of black and white female vocalists were beginning to sound interchangeable.

Lyricists and Composers: Going the Black Route

For generations after Emancipation, well into the 1940s, white musicians continued writing songs in a black mode. The style of that musical cross-dressing changed through the years, ultimately abandoning the heavy humor, thick dialect and blatant stereotyping of minstrelsy, coon songs and the blackface clichés of early vaudeville. By the twenties and thirties there emerged a group of white songwriters genuinely interested in and truly familiar with black song and its heritage, going back to the spirituals. Writers who also were able to capture the feel of black music naturally and effectively.

Hoagy Carmichael was one of the finest of the lot. Both a composer and a lyricist—although he often collaborated with other lyricists—he could be seen in various Hollywood films, playing piano in shirt sleeves at some honky-tonk bar, while singing one of his own compositions. Although Carmichael early learned piano from his mother, it was black pianist, Reginald Du Valle, who instructed him in jazz playing and taught him the rudiments of improvisation. He was influenced by his friend Bix Beiderbecke, and, like Beiderbecke, Teagarden and other white musicians, had been inspired by sounds of black music emanating from riverboats shuttling between New Orleans and Chicago. And like so many others, he could not help but be influenced by Louis Armstrong.

Quite naturally, the black connections transferred to his songwriting and became a constant presence there. We have only to consider a few of his song titles: "Riverboat Shuffle," "Georgia On My Mind," "Washboard Blues" and other southern flavored, folksy numbers that alternate with his more sophisticated fare. As for his aforementioned "Old Rockin' Chair," Richard Sudhalter believes it could have been inspired by a Negress, "Black Granny Campbell."[183]

Lyricist and jazz singer Johnny Mercer, a southerner from Savannah, often wrote in the rural style of Hoagy Carmichael (the two did collaborate at times), though his songwriting was eclectic and often worldly. His output in the black vein included a number of train songs and a 1939 recording of "Sent For You Yesterday And Here You Come Today," patterned after Jimmy Rushing's version of the bluesy number, recorded earlier with Count Basie. He also wrote black inflected novelty songs such as "Ac-cent-tchu-ate The Positive," set to Harold Arlen's music in 1944. Later, in the 1950s, he would furnish words in a "hip" black argot for Duke Ellington's "Satin Doll." And among Mercer's most memorable black style lyrics are those he wrote for Richard Arlen's classic, "Blues In The Night," one of the finest and most popular songs of the day.

Arlen himself, whose output included scores for Broadway musicals and music for *The Wizard of Oz*, also fitted smoothly into the black musical mode. Early in his career he had familiarized himself with the arrangements of Fletcher Henderson and other black jazz musicians. He also studied blues recordings—the "race records" of the twenties—and patterned his own music after them[184] Certainly, his 1943 classic (written with Mercer) "One For My Baby," although in Tin Pan Alley format, has all the flavor of the blues.

In the early thirties, Harold Arlen wrote for eight revues presented by the Cotton Club. Furnishing music for the black stars of the show came naturally to the composer.. Referring to Arlen's work at the Club, William Zinsser opined: "He had absorbed the idioms of African-American jazz by hanging out in Harlem clubs with George Gershwin, and he fused those rhythms with the Jewish[185] melancholy that was his birthright."[186]

Arlen's friend George Gershwin not only provided Tin Pan Alley, Broadway and Hollywood with a host of popular songs, but was, unlike his songwriting peers, a serious composer of extended musical works as well. His connections with black popular music and jazz were forged early in life. Like Harold Arlen, Brooklyn born Gershwin was familiar with Harlem, having spent part of his boyhood there. At seven years of age he listened to the famous black bandleader James Reese Europe performing on 134th Street, and later, as a young man, he met Eubie Blake and was on familiar terms with Harlem pianists James P. Johnson and Willie "the Lion" Smith.

Ironically, despite Gershwin's knowledge of and immersion in black musical culture, his greatest seller, composed when he was around twenty years old, was the pseudo-black number "Swanee," sung by Al Jolson in 1919. Such commercial pandering aside, Gershwin's absorption of black culture would later bear fruit with the 1935 folk opera, *Porgy and Bess* (lyrics by DuBose Heyward[187] and Gershwin's brother, Ira).

Equally important as the Gershwins' use of African-American themes, was George Gershwin's appropriation of African-American rhythms. Ever present throughout his work, they provide a base not only for such popular songs as "Fascinating Rhythm" and "I Got Rhythm" but also for more ambitious pieces such as his rhapsodies and concertos.

The numbers of white songwriters adopting and adapting the black musical heritage are legion. In fact, almost all, outside of Romberg and other writers of European-style operettas, demonstrated at least traces of it at some point or other in their work. A few, like Gershwin, managed to create something of importance with that heritage. Jerome Kern did so with his groundbreaking *Showboat,* which presented songs like "Ol' Man River" and "Can't Help Lovin' That Man" in the context of a coherent story—a rarity on the musical stage of the time—while addressing such social problems as miscegenation and racial prejudice.

Other white songwriters capitalized on black music and culture strictly for purposes of stylish entertainment. Among the most talented of the lot were Buddy DeSylva and Dorothy Fields, who was already writing fine lyrics in her early twenties. The two were hired by Lew Leslie to write the first Cotton Club shows. They brought their talents to Leslie's Broadway revue *Blackbirds of 1928,* which was billed as "A Distinctive and Unique Entertainment with an All-Star Cast of 100 Colored Artists."[188] The production was good and the writers competent. Still a cloud hovers over the musical because of one particular song, a song largely responsible for making the show a success.

It appears that the number "I Can't Give You Anything But Love," which became a great hit, may have been written by Fats Waller and Andy Razaf. Those writers, often down and out, would sell their songs, usually for a mere pittance. At times they peddled them to other black songsters and more often to white ones. According to Barry Singer, author of the book *Black and Blue,* soon after the show a rumor circulated that "I Can't Give You Anything But Love," had, in fact, recently changed hands, having been sold in the office of black publisher Irving C. Mills—a place where Jimmy McHugh often hung out.

Neither Fats Waller nor Razaf ever revealed whether they themselves were the ones who had written and sold the hit song. However, in a *New York Post* profile of Waller, he was quoted as having sold a song during the twenties for $500 (an appreciable sum considering most of such song deals), only to see it used in a musical comedy and become a best seller, gaining the new "writer" $17,000. As for Razaf, he was rarely heard complaining of such misadventures, but apparently, while terminally ill in the hospital, when someone asked him what his favorite song was, he replied "I Can't Give You Anything But Love."[189]

Certainly, the appropriation of black themes and musical innovations by white songwriters had its negative side. That aspect is cogently described by Barry Singer, who states:

> Many white composers like Gershwin were penetrating Harlem nightlife at this time, to the innermost low-down dives, in their passion for black music. And lyricists like Dorothy Fields, Ted Koehler, even the young Lorenz Hart and Ira Gershwin, though at a greater physical distance, studied closely the slangy, impudent lyric argot of black music.
>
> This attention was enormously flattering to Harlem's black songwriters . . . Yet inherent in this studious attention were the seeds of usurpation . . . Thus, when

> in time Gershwin, Arlen, McHugh, Koehler, and Fields at last mastered music and lyric writing in the black style, they inevitably, however, unintentionally, begat the disenfranchisement of the very black music makers whom they venerated . . . [190]

Lyrics and Composers: Going the White Route?

Odd as it might seem, black songwriters had the edge on white ones when it came to writing in both genres, black and white. For they were able to compose and publish not only the old typical black coon songs but numbers in the white style of Tin Pan Alley as well. Unlike the black stage show performers, who could not copy their white counterparts without offending white audiences, black songwriters, working invisibly behind the scenes, could produce music and words of any color. On the other hand, white Tin Pan Alley musicians were necessarily more limited when it came to appropriating black song. They could go only so far in imitating African-American composers and lyricists in an earthy genre like the blues. And their adaptations of ragtime or jazz to popular song were generally commercialized and watered down versions of the real thing.

Yet, quite naturally, white composers and lyricists had greater success using patterns and motifs of black popular music than vice versa. For, like Daniel Emmett or Stephen Foster in the days of early minstrelsy, they possessed the means and the opportunities. Unsurprisingly, they had solid control of the stage and music publishing and would soon be running the radio and the recording industry.

So black songwriters had a much more difficult time making their mark by reversing the tables and using the style or material of standard white songs. It was hard enough trying to earn a living with stereotypical coon songs. But even after generations of freedom, to break through with a product that portrayed and targeted not blacks exclusively but all humanity would appear daunting, if not impossible. .

In the 1920s and 1930s, another obstacle stood in the way of black writers. wishing to reach a general public, specifically the white public with its buying power. That obstacle was the increasing sophistication of white urban Americans during the twenties and the development of an American intellectual elite. Such trends would affect the business of writing songs. For the black population, deprived of so many educational and cultural opportunities, could hardly keep pace with the white intelligentsia, many of whom were well known writers, artists, journalists and critics.

On the one hand you had a white group benefiting from the prosperity of the twenties, many gravitating to Ivy League schools, doing a European Grand Tour and discovering the cultural world and manners of the continent. You had, from the start of the twenties until the Depression years, the "Algonquin Round Table," with its brilliant and biting conversationalists lunching daily at New York's Algonquin hotel: people such as Dorothy Parker, Franklin P. Adams Robert Benchley, Alexander Woollcott, George S. Kaufman[191] and Edna Ferber. And, above all, you had wit, a clever wit that would soon color the songs of white Tin Pan Alley.

Now consider the black musicians. The African heritage was an oral one; the ancestors of African Americans had not come from milieus enriched by universities. Then as slaves in America, many had been discouraged from reading or even forbidden such a pursuit. With Emancipation, a good number of former slaves and their children made enormous strides in quick time, but such gains were soon be closed to them. Later, at the turn of the twentieth century, even a good education, if available, would not guarantee African Americans a chance at a job with a living wage.

The field of popular music, at least, presented opportunities for ambitious African Americans. And to write coon songs or the blues, little or no instruction was needed. Although an appreciable number of black musicians had acquired higher education and a solid cultural background, for most songwriters education and training beyond a certain minimum would have meant time wasted.

As for wit, it was never really part of their mode. They could spoof and satirize, as had their forebears, but theirs was primarily a humor born of pain. Besides, wit usually requires a certain amount of worldliness. The worldliness of a Cole Porter, for example, who, in his "I Get A Kick Out Of You" appears to have experienced everything glamorous to be found in high society. So much so that he has wound up world weary, jaded: been there, done that. So why bother to have champagne, sniff cocaine, see castles in Spain or go up in a plane? For, as he says with his multiple internal rhymes: "Riding up high with some guy in the sky is my idea of nothing to do . . ." Now, it's possible that the black music makers had, indeed, sampled cocaine or more likely, reefers,[192] but weary of champagne? Tired of flying in a plane? Fed up with castles in Spain? Such unlikely ideas might remind us of Bert Williams in the 1910s, dressed on stage as a down-and-out tramp and singing with wry humor, "I'm Tired of Eating in The Restaurants."[193]

So if it had been difficult in the past for black songwriters to join white ones in reaching a general public, the gap became even greater in the twenties and thirties, as white popular song rose above its homespun traditions, and well designed melodies were matched by charming cleverly rhymed phrases. In 1925 Lorenz Hart was penning lyrics like "We'll Have Manhattan, the Bronx and Staten Island too," and later, "Wild again, beguiled again, a wimpering, simpering child again."[194] And Dorothy Fields would write in 1935,[195] "You never gave the orchids I sent a glance/No, you like cactus plants. This is a fine romance."

With such lyricists on the scene, and with giants of American popular music like that master of melody, Jerome Kern, and the prolific and enduring composer/lyricist, Irving Berlin, black songwriters faced fierce competition and a long road ahead. Not even a Harlem Renaissance of the twenties, spurred on by white intellectuals, could help close the gap between black ambition and white success by encouraging and abetting African-American songwriters. For the black Renaissance focused mainly on serious writers and artists, and popular songwriting, hardly considered a "serious" genre, was not in the loop.

How did black songwriters cope with such problems? A W. C. Handy could cope very well indeed by capitalizing on one important area of the black heritage, the blues. Canny as well as talented, unlike other African-American songwriters, Handy was paid royalties. In fact, one composition earned him $25,000 in royalties every year for forty years: "St. Louis Blues," published in 1914. Handy's case was exceptional, of course. But he knew how to mine a wealth of black musical material and serve it up to a general public, a white public, in a palatable, exciting way.

"St. Louis Blues" is smoothly crafted, with variety and contrast in rhythm and melody. The sections, each of them hauntingly beautiful, are unified by the driving melancholy of the bluesy sound. But the word is "bluesy," since the only part resembling the real blues is the beginning:

> I hate to see that evenin' sun go down (repeated once)
> 'Cause my baby, he done left this town
> Feelin' tomorrow like I feel today" (repeated once)
> Gonna pack my bag and make my getaway.[196]

Now that part, despite its likeness to the blues, contains, even in the first two short phrases, clues that the song was written for the general public of the time. In the first place, the man who left is "my baby" of Tin Pan Alley, rather than the "Sweet Papa" or "Rider" of the blues as sung in the country or recorded later in the city blues of the twenties. But the type of rhyme—and more so, the subsequent five-letter rhyme of "rings" and "strings" tells us that the song has been manufactured by a relatively literate person (in this case, Handy himself) someone very different from a Blind Lemon Jefferson or a Bessie Smith.

The lyrics—like the lyrics to almost all of Handy's songs, whether written by others or by him—have the consonant rhyme, the sort of "educated" rhyme that graced the phrases of contemporary white songs. In a consonant rhyme a writer always matches the last consonant or consonants of a syllable, as in "door" and "floor." In the case of a Lorenz Hart, a Cole Porter or other sophisticated white writers who came to the fore in the twenties and thirties, that type of "perfect" rhyme would occur with multiple syllables. For example, Hart's "Manhattan/Staten" or, elsewhere "greenery/scenery."[197]

In the blues, however, as in the spirituals, we most find a much simpler, more rudimentary form of rhyme, of the "assonant" type, where the rhyming syllables' vowels are similar but the final consonants do not match.[198] Example: "more" and "gone." Or "bones" and "home." Sometimes, in traditional African-American song, the rhyming syllables do not match as spelled because of the Negro dialect, which tends to drop final consonants entirely. For instance, a blues rhyme might consist of "door" and "roll," because the two words, although ending differently as spelled, would likely be pronounced "do" and "ro."

But beyond Handy's polished rhyme schemes, his themes and the style of his lyrics are thoroughly commercialized to please a contemporary public. His "Beale Street Blues" (1917). for which Handy himself wrote the lyrics, are nothing less than worldly. "The seven wonders of the world I have seen/And many are the places I have been"—such a concept was precisely on a par with white, classically trained Vernon Duke's words nearly two decades later: "I've been around the world in a plane/ I've settled revolutions in Spain" (from "I Can't Get Started," written in 1936). And for further commercial viability, Handy wrote a goodly number of nostalgia songs, of the sort popular with the public for decades, with words such as "'Way down South where the Blues began . . ." or "Down South, in Nature's own garden/ Where hearts never harden . . ."[199]

That nostalgic take-me-back-to-old-wherever plea, standard in the output of white Tin Pan Alley, would be exploited by other black songwriters. For example, it is exactly the gimmick songwriter Spencer Williams would use in 1928 in his famous "Basin Street Blues," with its idealized description of a southern "land of dreams" where everyone is equal and happy. But somehow, one wouldn't expect such commerciality on the part of the self-proclaimed "Father of the Blues," W. C. Handy. Still, by so "whitening" his blues and introducing them to the American public, Handy succeeded in making that public aware of the blues as a genre. His publications, commercial or not, were undoubtedly instrumental in launching the blues in the twenties and bringing them into the mainstream of American music.

Other black songwriters set their sights even more directly on white Tin Pan Alley, writing songs—ballads of love or upbeat numbers—having no relation to southern themes or traditional black song styles. Such attempts at crossing over could be found as early as the late nineteenth century, with Gussie Davis, considered one of the most successful black songwriters of Tin Pan Alley. Davis—whose race was generally unknown to performers of his songs—composed a spate of sweet waltzes and sentimental ballads "to please the ladies."[200]

Later, the prolific songwriting team of Cole and J. Rosamond Johnson, pioneers of black musical shows, like Davis, wrote music geared to the white taste. Johnson, for one, wanted to get as far as possible away from the coon song image and write songs with a large potential market, for example, romantic numbers, "giving both sexes an opportunity to vent their sentiments decorously."[201] And so the pair did, composing early twentieth century songs such as "The Maiden With The Dreamy Eyes" and writing music and lyrics for white Broadway revues. All the while continuing to manufacture the stereotypical black fare that Johnson objected to, sung to white audiences by white coon shouters like May Irwin.

Then, in the twenties, black songwriters continued that practice, alternating black flavored numbers with romantic ballads in Tin Pan Alley style but often cultivating a more authentic black music as well: ragtime or the blues. Eubie Blake and Noble Sissle, for example, are among the best known of these songwriting multiple-headers. They wrote and performed numerous rags which alternated with black hued ditties—and, frequently, with standard white style love songs. For example, the love interest introduced into *Shuffle Along*—a first in black musical comedy—demanded a romantic ballad. So the pair provided it in "Love Will Find A Way," which, despite the cast's fears, was well received by white audiences. (A much greater hit, however, was their rousing, catchy "I'm Just Wild About Harry," a piece that could have been written by George M. Cohan.) And nine years later, Blake would compose, with lyricist Andy Razaf, one of the most beautiful love ballads in American popular song: "Memories of You" (*Blackbirds of 1930*).

Pianist/composer James P. Johnson was known for his test piano piece "Carolina Shout" and "The Charleston," featured in the 1923 musical *Runnin' Wild*. In addition to composing numerous jazz pieces, Johnson also created sweet ballads like "Old Fashioned Love" from the same show and "If I Could Be With You One Hour Tonight" (1926). Lyricist Henry Creamer, who collaborated on the last number, wrote, with partner, Turner Layton, songs for black shows and, like Shelton Brooks, also furnished numbers to white singers like Sophie Tucker and Nora Bayes.

High, perhaps highest on the list of black writers targeting a white public in the twenties and thirties was the team of composer Fats Waller and lyricist Andrea Razaf. Waller's name is justifiably famous, his talent indisputable. Razaf ranked among the most competent black lyricists of his time but is of far lesser renown than Waller, his name unfamiliar to the general public of today.[202] Of course, Waller had a great deal to offer, as a superb composer of popular melodies, a pianist, singer and entertainer (who constantly mugged for his audiences). Razaf, however, was, for all intents and purposes, strictly a lyricist. Waller's talents as a composer and vendor of popular music were at least equal to those of most of his white contemporaries. How did Razaf measure up to the white lyricists of his time?

Andrea Razaf, a high school dropout[203] became a versifier, or "rhymer," as he would say, and, from his early years, he applied the craft to popular songwriting. Much of his early writing appears a bit labored. Whether or not he was familiar with the sophisticated rhymes of Cole Porter, Ira Gershwin, Lorenz Hart or Howard Dietz, his own rhyme scheme remained extremely simple, as he matched "town" with "brown" or "symphony" with "harmony." And verbally, he played it rather safe, never taking such chances as Cole Porter did in writing "It's delightful, it's de-lovely." His partnership with Fats Waller seems to have been an inspiration to him. The two worked well together and Razaf's uncomplicated lyrics blended beautifully with a lilting song like Waller's "Ain't Misbehavin.'"

> No one to talk with, all by myself,
> No one to walk with, but I'm happy on the shelf . . . [204]
>
> Or "Honeysuckle Rose:"
>
> Don't buy sugar, you just have to touch my cup,
> You're my sugar, it's sweet when you stir it up.[205]

With that same simplicity Razaf was later able to fit words beautifully and smoothly with Eubie Blake's love ballad, "Memories of You."[206]

Over the following years, Razaf was in demand by black and white musicians for his knack of writing sprightly lyrics for jazz and swing numbers. So, although he was not in a category with the worldly white phrasemakers of song, he became quite at home in his own genre, and highly competent at it as well.

Were the Waller/Razaf musical numbers black or white? Although many Waller tunes had the sounds of black jazz, most of his songs clearly followed the established patterns of white Tin Pan Alley. As for lyricist Razaf, he did write bawdy blues numbers such as "My Handy Man" (with James P. Johnson, 1928), and his "Honeysuckle Rose" contained risqué double meanings. However, the songs he wrote for a general public were overwhelmingly, respectably white. For example, the very idea of the title phrase "Ain't Misbehavin'" is completely foreign to the black blues. It assures us that the singer is remaining faithful, saving his love for his inamorata—and, according to the lyrics, happy about it to boot!

Even "Black and Blue" ("What Did I Do to Be So Black and Blue?"), from the same show as "Ain't Misbehavin" (*Hot Chocolates of 1929*), contained nothing which would ruffle white audiences, in spite of its talk of skin color. Razaf would never have written a song about color in the first place had he not been literally pinned against the wall and forced at gunpoint to do so by gangster Dutch Schulz,[207] a backer of the show. But in writing it, he couched the issue of racial prejudice in a semi-humorous context. That is, instead of making the song a complaint about white discrimination, he pictured a girl unhappy with black men going after lighter skinned girls ("Brown and yellers all have fellers/ Gentlemen prefer them light"). And Razaf introduced lines intended to get a chuckle rather than a tear, keeping the number apolitical—at least on the surface.[208]

* * *

As we have seen, racial crossovers marked the paths of vocalists and songwriters alike, and in both cases there occurred a sort of melding or blending of black and white styles. At first glance it might seem that black singers and writers had the advantage over white ones, since they could cultivate their own music and white music as well. Whereas their white Tin Pan Alley counterparts could imitate the black musical style only up to a point and had to avoid entirely the earthy realism of the blues. However, when it came to the bottom line, that is, gaining access to a large public and reaping rewards of fame and success, the scales tipped, as one might expect, in favor of the white musicians.

Crossing over was one thing; breaking in, another. How far were the black songwriters and lyricists able to go?

Notes

166 *Blues People,* p. 110. Jones was referencing the Quaker Oats cereal box of his day, showing a Quaker woman holding a cereal box which pictured the same woman holding an identical box, and so on.

167 According to a frequently cited anecdote , trumpeter Roy Eldridge claimed he could always recognize the race of an unidentified player on a record. But when music critic Leonard Feather put him to the test, Eldridge did not fare well in his guesses.

168 Whose "Bully Song" was discussed in Chapter Two in the section on coon songs.

169 Jolson, unlike the others mentioned here, actually preferred to appear in blackface.

170 *Some of These Days,* p. 33.

171 Gunther Schuller, in *The Swing Era,* describes Connee's approach as a black singing style with "a black-influenced jazz diction." P. 642n.

172 In *The Little Show* by Arthur Schwartz and Howard Dietz.

173 Such intimacy of style was encouraged by the increasing use of the electric microphone and the vogue of small cabarets and nightclubs featuring vocalists.

174 See the internet squib on Mildred Bailey on Multiracial.org.

175 Discussed in the following chapter.

176 Adelaide Hall, of *Shuffle Along* fame, is an outstanding example of a black who survived into the thirties with a black sound. In the twenties and thirties she was hired by Duke Ellington—who generally preferred doing instrumentals sans vocals—and provided a growling, wordless soprano sound that served as a sort of obbligato to his music. An extraordinary "instrumental" adaptation of black scat singing.

177 According to Gary Giddons, "Waters adapted white theatrical styles to a black image." *Visions of Jazz,* pp. 52-53.

178 For example, her Hollywood biography of 1972 was titled *Lady Sings the Blues.*

179 Merod, "Singing in the Shower: Ralph Ellison and the Blues." La Folia.com online musical review.

180 *Shadow and Act,* p. 246.

181 Six million copies sold.

182 In the same era, however, the equally popular Ink Spots included in their sweet renderings, the deep voice of bass singer Orville Jones intoning "honey chile" phrases in comedic black vaudevillian tradition.

183 *Stardust Melody,* p. 128.

184 See Melnick, p. 51.

185 A great number of songwriters were Jewish, as were many white singers who blackened up (Sophie Tucker, Fanny Brice, Eddie Cantor, Al Jolson and a very large number of blackfaced minstrels who preceded them). Among the Jewish writers active before World War II one can name Jerome Kern, Irving Berlin, Oscar Hammerstein, the Gershwins, E.Y. ("Yip") Harburg, Harold Arlen, Lorenz Hart, Kurt Weill, Arthur Schwartz, Howard Dietz, Frank Loesser and Dorothy Fields. As we shall see later, the phenomenon was repeated with show business entrepreneurs. The world of popular music was open to Jews, and many were able to break into it.

186 P. 60.

187 Heyward wrote the 1925 novel, *Porgy,* on which the musical was based and also did the book for the show.

188 Green, S., *Broadway Musicals,* p. 63.

189 Singer, p. 211-212. It is possible, however, that if DeSylva and Fields took the song in question, they made some alterations. In particular the lyrics of their published song have a more polished rhyme sceme, flow and structure than those of most of Razaf's songwriting.

190 *Ibid.*, p. 141.

191 Who directed and wrote the libretto for several Broadway musicals.

192 Marijuana was also referred to as "muggles" at the time, a fact undoubtedly unbeknownst to J. K. Rowling.

193 This discussion should not imply that black musicians were unsophisticated. To the contrary, many were. Certainly, few musicians, black or white, could match the elegance of a Duke Ellington. But Ellington was not a lyricist, and the worldly style of white lyricists could hardly be matched by black songwriters without the wherewithal to acquire a similar polish in society.

194 "Bewitched, Bothered and Bewildered" from *Pal Joey,* 1940.

195 For Kern's music in the film *Swingtime* with Fred Astaire and Ginger Rogers.

196 This is followed by a section in tango rhythm ("Got the St. Louis blues, just as blue as I can be"), since, as Handy often said, the tango was very popular at the time.

197 "In a mountain greenery/where God paints the scenery . . . While you love your lover, let/Blue skies be your coverlet" from "Mountain Greenery" (*Garrick Gaieties of 1926*).

198 In his account of a 1832 visit to a Maryland plantation, James Hungerford noted, "When [the slaves] do attempt to rhyme they frequently take more than poetic license, being satisfied—when they cannot do better—if the vowel-sounds at the ends of the lines agree." P. 184.

199 *A Treasury of the Blues,* p.158 ff.

200 Sanjek, *American Popular Music and Its Business,* Vol II, p. 283.

201 *Ibid.*

202 Originally named Andrea Razapkeriefo, Razaf was, by all accounts, born to royalty on his father's side.. His father was a native of Madagascar and nephew of the hereditary queen of the island. His maternal grandfather, a freed slave, practiced law and spent time in the United States Diplomatic Service.

203 According to Barry Singer, he had been a "promising student" but left high school because his mother wanted him to work and help support the two of them. See p. 29.

204 From *Hot Chocolates of 1929.*

205 Published in 1929.

[206] From *Blackbirds of 1930.*

[207] See Singer, pp. 216-218.

[208] In fact, according to Singer (*ibid*), when Edith Wilson sang such lines as "My only sin is in my skin," a hush fell over the audience. At the end of the song, after a silent pause, they stood and applauded. "Black and Blue" has, in more recent times, been construed as a protest song. It was presented as such in the oft-staged *Ain't Misbehavin'; the Fats Waller Musical Show* of the 1990s and early 2000s.

8

QUEST FOR A PUBLIC

RACE RECORDS AND THE TIN PAN ALLEY MARKET

Early in the 1920s, an impressive number of black performers and composers became players in the arena of American popular music. A major breakthrough, it happened most dramatically in recording studios. That it happened at all was a sheer miracle. For if Sophie Tucker, scheduled to record, had not chanced to take ill at the last minute, if the African-American songwriter Perry Bradford had used a little less persistence with studio managers, if the black singer who replaced Tucker had not been a woman, and a good looking one, and if she, Mamie Smith, hadn't sung a blues at her second session, the 1920s success of recorded black musicians might have remained a vain dream.

Before Mamie Smith cut her first record, the typical music of African Americans, ragtime and blues, went largely unrecorded. Not completely, for singers of color had been heard earlier on cylinder[209] and disk, and some black bands had made records early in the century. And ragtime rhythms had been reproduced on disk in the 1910s, notably by James Reese Europe's marching band before and after World War I.[210] But the first important and successful record to render the sounds of black jazz was performed by a white combo, the Original Dixieland Jazz Band (1917). As for the blues, they were conspicuously absent in recording studios of the time.

Then in February 14, 1920, General Phonograph's OKeh Record Company, at Perry Bradford's urging, produced Mamie Smith's first record. It consisted of two ordinary pop songs written by Bradford: "You Can't Keep a Good Man Down" and "That Thing Called Love." The record sold well enough to warrant another studio session with Smith, and in August of the same year she obliged with the groundbreaking "Crazy Blues." To call it a hit would be a rank understatement; in only a few weeks, over 75,000 copies of the record were sold in Harlem alone. Then, in no time at all, black newspapers started advertising the sale of "Race Records" featuring Mamie Smith and, soon, other blues songstresses. It was a trend that would last for nearly a decade.

Companies like Columbia, Paramount and OKeh vied with each other in copying the successful formula of a female vocalist belting out the blues with a jazzy backup combo (or sometimes just a piano accompaniment). They had suddenly discovered an untapped, unexpectedly large, new consumer group.[211] They had identified a whole population of African Americans who would flock to record stores[212] to buy up the music they thrived on—black music, their music, rendered by performers they could identify with.

So the companies sought and found vocalists to compete with Mamie Smith, singers like Alberta Hunter, Victoria Spivey, Sara Martin, Clara Smith and, the greatest of them, Bessie Smith.[213] They sent Negro agents to the South to scout out new talent to promote. Not content to let the white companies corner the market, the Black Swan Record Company, founded and run by Harry Pace in 1921, billed its product as "The Only Genuine Colored Record Company. Others Are Only Passing for Colored."[214] Black Swan enjoyed two years of success thanks especially to its talented star, Ethel Waters, before succumbing to competition from radio and other competitors[215].

It is interesting that females, rather than traditional guitar playing male blues singers, dominated the race recording craze until the end of the 1920s. In fact, many of these women (e.g.:

Alberta Hunter, Sara Martin and Mamie Smith herself) were originally not really blues artists but eclectic singers, with a repertoire that included commercial popular songs familiar to variety and vaudeville. Unlike the undisputedly authentic "Mother of the Blues," Ma Rainey—who would also be recorded in the twenties—they simply recycled themselves into blues singing because of the new demand. In fact, "Crazy Blues" sung by Mamie Smith was more in the line of a standard commercial number than a real blues.

The recording companies did not overlook male singers, and some, like Blind Lemon Jefferson, Blind Blake and "Papa" Charles Jackson, had their day in the studios, especially in the second half of the decade. But despite the occasional male blues or novelty singer and male quartets, and notwithstanding recordings of preacher's sermons and performances by gospel choirs, the competing record companies perpetuated their original, winning formula of a lead female blues singer with backup. One does not quarrel with success.

To the black public—especially in the hinterlands—the women spelled glamour when they came touring in live performances. Mamie Smith, Bessie Smith, even the supremely homely Ma Rainey, would take to the stage in bespangled satin gowns, feathers billowing in their hair and sporting a plethora of real or fake diamonds. Females in the audience could admire that glamour and, at the same time, could identify personally with the message of daily heartache in the blues as sung by their idols.

The record companies, assuming that only Negroes would have any interest in this new genre, targeted the black population exclusively. In the North, they restricted their advertising to black newspapers. As a result, during the twenties, most northerners remained completely unaware of the recorded blues singers. In the South, however, where blacks and whites lived in much closer proximity, whites heard the new music and a good number of them became, themselves, part of the "race market."

The term "race records" was first used in advertising by OKeh Records, in 1923. Although the label may sound demeaning to us today, at the time it was not considered discriminatory or debasing at all. On the contrary, newspapers such as the *Chicago*

Defender made proud use of "the Race" in their articles. According to Ronald Foreman, ". . . the nation's Negro citizens found both comfort and support in [such] references to a commonality of black people."[216]

While the race record industry thrust black singers and their blues into the limelight, financially, it had its downs as well as ups. The white record companies, as well as the ephemeral Black Swan, faced severe competition from the new vogue of radio, which offered musical entertainment entirely free. In 1923, for example, Columbia Records teetered on the brink of bankruptcy. However, Columbia was undoubtedly saved by its launching that year of a race record series featuring the great talent of Bessie Smith. And profits from race records helped keep other companies afloat as well.

For a while, at least. For even before the Depression, in 1927, "talkies" burst on the scene with Al Jolson in *The Jazz Singer.* Radio increasingly took over the nation's listeners, often regaling them with the sound of exciting new jazz bands. All of this spelled decreased profits for the record companies. But with the crash of 1929 and the population's drastically diminished purchasing power, the companies—and, of course, the race record industry itself—were hit hard.

By 1930 the halcyon days of race record blues had become a thing of the past.

An Eye on Tin Pan Alley

After the triumphs of black musical comedy in the first decade of the twentieth century, the presence of African Americans in popular music became relatively scarce both on the stage and in the song publishing business. The 1910s, however, saw some hopeful signs for black music composers. In 1914, for example, W.C. Handy's "St Louis Blues" took New York, and especially Harlem, by storm. And that same year the newly formed American Society of Composers, Authors, and Publishers (ASCAP) included six black composers in its group of 170.

During World War I, however, relatively few black compositions came to light. Instead, in 1917 and 1918, Tin Pan Alley unleashed a plethora of patriotic songs mainly by white composers, and over a third of those published had a direct connection to the war. These musical flag wavers were largely promoted by the War Department, which, in an effort to rev up enthusiasm for an unpopular war, had thrown its support behind Tin Pan Alley, decreeing that popular music was an essential part of the war effort. Clearly, at that time, the irreverent black sounds of low-down blues and ragtime had a far less potential for the song market than stirring martial rhythms or sentimental ballads about faraway soldiers and the girls—or dear old mothers—they left behind.

Then after the war and especially during the 1920s, prospects for black songwriters took an upswing. After the triumph of *Shuffle Along* and the rise of race records, increasing numbers of songs by black composers appeared in sheet music publications. Despite the fact that most of those composers (Irving Jones, for example) were grinding out coon songs, it would seem as though some progress was at last being made by African Americans in the white dominated song publishing field.

In the long run this did not turn out to be the case. For the impact on the publishing business would in no way compare with the brilliant black presence in show business and the decade-long success of race records. In the last analysis, throughout the twenties and thirties, black forays into white Tin Pan Alley would remain, as before, sporadic and ephemeral.

It was unfortunate but inevitable. In the first place, authentic Negro songs like the blues of race records, although often censored before a final recording, were still far too earthy for the "respectable" white market targeted by Tin Pan Alley publishers. Secondly, the white composers themselves were quick to absorb the black sounds of jazz and blues and dress them in familiar Tin Pan Alley patterns that had proved commercially viable. So why bother with the black originators?

Moreover, white lyricists, with a tradition of literacy behind them, had a huge leg up on the black minority and were, as we have seen, becoming increasingly sophisticated in their concepts, structure and rhymes. Although some such songwriters found themselves at least partially dependent on their Negro counterparts, the majority could do very nicely, indeed, on their own and had no need for competition from black musicians.

Besides—and above all—it was precisely the white majority that controlled the music publishing business.

Consequently, ambitious black musicians with education and experience did what some had already done and what others would continue to do. They formed their own companies. The first African-American music publisher to set up office in New York was Richard C. McPherson (professional name: Cecil Mack), who founded the Gotham-Attucks Music Company in the first decade of the 1900s. McPherson had studied at the University of Pennsylvania and had briefly attended the university's medical school before turning to music in order to make ends meet. His Gotham-Attucks company published works of the major figures of early black musical comedy (including Cole and Johnson, Cook, Williams and Walker) and sundry other Negro composers.

The next important African-American music publishing enterprise in operation was the Pace and Handy Company, organized in 1918 by partners Harry Pace and W. C. Handy. Prior to their collaboration, Pace had been a professor of Greek and Latin at Lincoln University, a black college in Missouri, while Handy had been writing and teaching music in Memphis. Before Pace set up the Black Swan Recording Company in 1921, he went into partnership with the not-yet-famous composer of "St. Louis Blues" to start a music publishing business. Originally working from Memphis' Beale Street, in 1918 they moved to New York and an office on Broadway. The specialty of their company was publication of the blues. Needless to say, the most numerous and popular of their musical publications came courtesy of the self-styled "Father of the Blues" himself, W. C. Handy.

Not long after Pace and Handy set up their New York publishing firm, Will Vodery and Bert Williams followed suit. Much has, justifiably, been said about Williams but undoubtedly not enough about Vodery, a man of many gifts. Pianist, army band organizer, songwriter, orchestra leader in musical comedy, activist, arranger (*Shuffle Along,* revues for the Ziegfeld Follies)—that list of his talents is hardly inclusive. In his youth, Vodery had won a scholarship to the University of Pennsylvania, organized an orchestra there and studied piano and violin with a prominent music teacher. During World War I, after forming and directing an award-winning black regiment band, he was offered a scholarship to the Paris Conservatory of Music. Obviously, like his fellow publishers, R. C. McPherson, Pace and Handy and Bert Williams, Vodery had at his disposal rich cultural resources and a superior talent.

Pace and Handy and Williams and Vodery located their offices in the Gaiety Theatre Building on Broadway near 46th Street. Joining them in the same building was a third music publisher, Perry Bradford, the songwriter who had introduced Mamie Smith to OKeh Records. From what is known of Bradford, he was not on a scale with his fellow publishers. Outside of purportedly introducing the "Black Bottom" to the American public and beyond his coup in helping to launch race records, the sometimes songwriter appears to have been a hustler and a not-too-trustworthy operator. Still, savory or not, Bradford did promote his fellow African Americans in the publishing field.

Other African Americans, Clarence Williams, for example, founded music publishing companies in the twenties. However, since starting one's own company was most certainly a risky business, and since the white publishers virtually monopolized the field, the majority of Negro songwriters necessarily placed their hopes in the established white firms. They would haunt Tin Pan Alley offices daily, cajoling the bosses, joking around, pounding out their new tunes on the office uprights. Some among the most talented and ambitious could count themselves successful. For example, when early black musicals like *In Dahomey* or *Bandanna Land* made a splash on the New York scene, firms such as Edward Marks and Witmark and Sons published songs by Cole and Johnson, Will Marion Cook, Ernest Hogan and others among the luminaries of the new black music.

Then in the twenties, following the example of the profitable race record industry, a number of white publishers found that it made economic sense to set up their own "race" subsidiaries. In 1923 Irving Berlin established his Rainbow Music subsidiary, directed by black songwriters Porter Grainger and Bob Ricketts. That same year another white enterprise, the Jack Mills Publishing

Company, introduced its own subsidiary, tapping the talents of black songwriters such as Will Vodery, Spencer Williams, Shelton Brooks and James P. Johnson. The E. B. Marks company instituted its "African Opera Series of Blues," and publishing firms such as Shapiro, Bernstein and Company, the Skidmore Music Company and Joe Davis followed suit.

The black-owned publishing companies and the "race" subsidiaries of white firms helped greatly in promoting black popular music. But they could go only so far in achieving real progress. In actuality, many black songwriters, including some of the most talented, wound up with very little to show for the songs they sold. In spite of the Copyright Act of 1909, in spite of ASCAP and notwithstanding the fact that many black composers held publishing contracts, they were really not protected.

For example, while a white musician could generally be assured of royalties, an African American, grateful to receive recognition and remuneration, was most often paid outright, with any royalty clause struck from his or her contract. This would happen to composer Shelton Brooks and countless others (as to singers Bessie Smith and Billie Holiday). When a royalty clause did apply to a composer's contract, according to James Reese Europe, "A white man would receive from six to twelve times the royalty"[217] of a black composer.

Lyricist Andy Razaf was one songwriter who did receive royalties, when managed by white publisher Joe Davis in his "race" subsidiary, Triangle Publishing. In an unusual move, Davis, at the very start of their collaboration, even handed Razaf an advance against future royalties. Just as astonishingly, he offered Razaf working space in his back office (customarily occupied by white composers) and asked him to close up shop after him—an evidence of trust that deeply moved Razaf. It is true that a contract with Davis greatly favored Davis himself, and from a modern perspective the publisher might be seen as having unfairly exploited Razaf and his partner, Fats Waller. But for black composers, any publishing contract was a boon. Afforded the longed for opportunity of breaking into Tin Pan Alley, they did not look at the fine print or quibble with clauses.

Even for songwriters of quality like Waller and Razaf, contracts and steady work did not come easily, so they had to scrounge a living as best they could. The alternative for many black songwriters, including Razaf, was to find work as elevator operators, janitors, and in sundry other low level jobs. But at the same time, hope against hope, they kept on writing songs. Very commonly, a black composer in need of cash for food, rent or booze would sell this or that song outright for a few bucks to a publisher—even to another songwriter. Such was the case of Waller and Razaf who, when broke, as they often were, gave up ownership of certain songs in order to survive. Waller, for example, might pick up $50 for—a song, and when really down on his heels, as little as five dollars—only to spend it on liquor in some all-night bar. (The fact that he and his fellow songwriters might sell the same number to several takers at various times did not quite even the score.)

Seedier stories abound. Edward Marks tells how, in the early 1900s, a group of white song hawkers known as "the cuff boys" "used to haunt the colored clubrooms for the special purpose of scrounging songs."[218] Marks also confides that a certain African-American songwriter, having lost track of all the musical pieces he had ground out, probably lost more than he had sold. And according to black bandleader Sam Wooding, when a Tin Pan Alley songwriter of the twenties hit a snag in his composition, he might go and "get one of those spades to come" and fix it. Wooding adds that some of the white composers "fresh off the boat" and unskilled at their craft, would call in Razaf to straighten out the lyrics and Luckey Roberts or Shelton Brooks to fix the music.[219] Small wonder that a false and slanderous rumor circulated concerning the prolific and gifted Irving Berlin—the legend that he kept "a colored boy in his closet" to help him compose his songs.

In fact, white publishers and recording entrepreneurs were not alone in taking advantage of black songwriters, for some of the worst treatment meted out came from blacks in the business. Perry Bradford was notorious for stealing and taking credit and profit from other black songwriters' material[220] or paying them just a few dollars for their work. Clarence Williams had a reputation for doing the same and being downright unscrupulous in his operations. According to Danny Barker,[221] Mayo Williams, in charge of black recording artists at Decca, managed to take an unduly large cut from money due his fellow African Americans. And the list does not end there.

One example of exploitation of black artists by black entrepreneurs is Clarence William's unscrupulousness in managing Bessie Smith's career. Williams was taking 50% of Bessie's earnings, and he made more money on her first recording than she did. When she realized to what extent he was cheating her, Bessie, after storming into his office and covering him with abuse, signed a contract with white Frank Walker of Columbia For Walker, the man who had originally sent Williams to bring Bessie up North, offered Bessie far more favorable terms (the fact that he himself struck out the royalty clause did not seem to matter.)

But if black businessmen could prove at least as ruthless as white ones, the fact remained that, whether in publishing, show business or recording, white entrepreneurs were in the majority and in control. So exploitation of Negro artists by whites would necessarily overshadow examples of unfair treatment by their African-American counterparts.

Obviously, in the business of popular music, the Negro composer encountered crags and snags galore on the so-called road to success. Was it possible to make any real headway?

Notes

209 As early as the 1880s.

210 Brian Rust lists "Too Much Mustard" and "Down Home Rag" in recordings of 1913 (Vol. I). Europe's last ragtime records, including "Clarinet Marmalade" and "Jazzola" were made for Pathé in 1919.

211 Although literacy in the African-American population had steadily increased, that group was far less likely than whites to buy printed sheet music, and they certainly had fewer pianos at home. Phonograph records were a far more accessible medium for black listeners.

[212] Initially the disks were available through record stores in black communities, mainly in cities like New York, Detroit, Cleveland or Milwaukee. But they soon had distribution in a thriving mail order business.

[213] None of the Smith singers were related to each other.

[214] *Blues People*, p. 129. In the June 2, 1923, issue of the *Chicago Defender*, Pace called his company the "Only bona fide Racial company making talking machine records. All stockholders are colored, all artists are colored, all employees are colored." Reprinted in *Blacks in Blackface,* p. 52.

[215] Other black-owned record companies followed but would not achieve great success until the formation of Berry Gordy's Motown Company in the 50s.

[216] See his doctoral thesis, *Jazz and Race Records,* p. 92 *ff.*

[217] *New York Tribune* interview of November 22, 1914, printed in Badger, p. 121.

[218] *Op. cit,* p. 93.

[219] Quoted in Melnick, pp. 34-35.

[220] Although, as mentioned, a national copyright law had been in effect since 1909, that did not prevent songwriters, many of them black, from taking someone else's composition, possibly altering the words, renaming it and taking the credit. It also did not prevent them from the practice of selling the same song to several publishers.

[221] *A Life in Jazz,* p. 153.

9

A ROCKY ROAD

BARRICADES AND BREAKTHROUGHS

Roadblocks and Land Mines

From the enactment of Jim Crow laws in the 1870s until well beyond the waning of the Ku Klux Klan and the end of World War II, black musicians came face to face with discrimination, daily insults and abasement.[222] Worse, a number of them risked mortal danger in the course of their careers.

This held true particularly in the South, where over a hundred lynchings of African Americans took place in 1900 alone. Although open aggression against black entertainers was relatively rare, harassment and racist crimes did occur in their midst.

Witness the example of Louis Wright, a 22-year-old trumpeter with the Georgia Minstrels. In February, 1902, in the town of New Madrid, Missouri, Wright's company was marching in a street parade to publicize an upcoming show. Snow had fallen and a group of white bystanders began pelting the musicians with snowballs. The marchers asked them to stop, but to no avail. At one point, Wright, incensed, cursed the fellow who was barraging him. The aggressors became so angry at the "nigger's" insult that that night, after the performance, they had him jailed on the false pretext that his company was armed and dangerous. The next day they took him from his cell and hanged him from a tree, where the his body remained for days until cut down and sent in a box to the young man's mother.[223]

Other incidents followed. In 1925, in Florida, a group of white men ordered a drummer on tour to teach their dates the Charleston. The drummer complied, and later the men beat him up and castrated him, fatally wounding him.[224] And less violent but debasing acts of aggression occurred throughout the years. Early in their career, entertainers Bert Williams and George Walker were walking along a southern road, when a group of white vigilantes forced them to strip and proceed on their way wearing burlap. Later, in 1921, after an argument between Mrs. Benbow of the all-Negro William Benbow Company, a large mob of Louisiana whites undressed and whipped a dozen or so members of the troupe.

Although such acts were not everyday occurrences in the music world, black skinned musicians could take no chances in a South where post-Civil War signs read "NIGGER READ AND RUN. IF YOU CAN'T READ RUN ANYHOW." Describing how performers coped while on tour in southern states, Henry Sampson wrote:

> It was a general practice for the male and female members of a company to dress in plain working clothes, frequently appearing as field hands or domestics. No flashy jewelry was worn, and the women took great care to conceal their attractiveness when moving about the town. Direct contact between performers and the town folk was minimized. Many black shows carried a white manager or business representative who would make all the necessary arrangements with the local theatre manager and the city officials before the arrival of the company.[225]

In a 1910 newspaper article, Salem Tutt Whitney explained how his Smart Set company handled a stint in the highly segregated town of Rogers, Texas, where Negroes were blocked from attending the local theater, even with black entertainers on the bill.

> . . . word reached us before we got there that things would be anything but pleasant for us if we played there. But those kind[s] of things never worry our [white] manager. However, on our arrival, we were pleasantly surprised to hear that the entire police force (one six-foot ranger) had been reserved to insure our protection . . .
>
> Notwithstanding the above facts, the members of the company took no chance on any ways obstreperous or flashy in their appearance.

Whitney goes on to describe how the performers appeared on stage dressed as ordinary cotton pickers, domestics or Texas rangers and kept a low profile in the town. He concludes:

> One would never think that there was more than $3000 worth of diamonds possessed by [the cast], to say nothing of the sealskin coats and costly hats, etc., among the ladies, and the deportment among the ladies has been 100% perfect, or we never would have covered the territory we have, with absolutely no trouble."[226]

With segregation legal in the South, any presumed transgressions might lead to arrest and time in jail. In southern cities and towns, companies of black musicians could run into trouble with the law if they happened to have any white performers in their midst. Certainly, the discovery of a white woman in a cast of black men could spell deep trouble, given the usual sexual implications. But even within all-female groups, no racial intermingling was tolerated, so any white woman in a show or band had to attempt to pass for black. Such stringent attitudes could make the simplest acts—going to the ladies' room, registering at a check-in counter—major headaches.

Similar problems continued to beset musicians touring the South throughout the thirties and well beyond. David Stowe cites the case of drunken well-heeled white dance hall clients of the thirties attacking band musicians, ". . . taking advantage of a law that allowed a white to assault a black for a $300 fine."

Even the top black stars and their entourage were subjected to discrimination and danger. Stowe states that "members of the Calloway band playing in Fort Lauderdale in the thirties required a police escort to leave the stand for water during intermission" and notes that "fraternizing with whites on or off the bandstand, even when initiated by whites, was especially taboo"[227]

Trouble for African-American musicians was not confined to the South. On the evening of August 15, 1900, three days after a black Tenderloin pimp stabbed a New York policeman to death, crowds of angry whites rioted in the streets. Apparently encouraged by police, the rioters pursued and mercilessly beat any Negroes they could find on Manhattan's west side. Among the many innocent victims of their wrath were the well-known black songwriter-composer Ernest Hogan and Bert Williams' stage partner, George Walker—purposely singled out because they were well known, identifiable and performing nearby.

Hogan and Walker had previously experienced enough racist insults in the South to last them a lifetime. But their treatment that night in the "enlightened" North was nothing less than violent. Walker was pulled off a streetcar and pursued by a huge crowd armed with clubs and stones. Fleeing down Broadway, he somehow managed to escape and hide in a cellar[228] until daybreak. That same night, Ernest Hogan, similarly chased by a mob, wound up so badly injured he was forced to leave the cast of Cook and Dunbar's *Jes' Lak White Folks.*

A less blatant but more durable and far-reaching form of northern discrimination targeted black entertainers explicitly. This was the work of the "White Rats," an association of white theater activists organized in 1900 to prevent the booking of black performers on the major vaudeville circuits. The obstacles this questionable group put in the path of artists of color was a factor in deciding a number of the latter to give up entirely or to seek a career abroad.

Later, during the thirties, Billie Holiday endured insult after insult in northern areas, for instance, having to enter her hotel through the back door, being obliged to darken her complexion with grease paint (she looked too white to sing with black orchestra members) or being restricted to a maid's role in a Hollywood film.

And—a more egregious example—while Holiday was on tour in Detroit, a white trumpet player was beaten unconscious and kicked in the mouth for having a drink with her.

North or South—though in the South especially—the obstacles confronting African-American entertainers on tour were legion. Barred from white hotels, in many towns they found few, if any, places to stay and precious few cafés or restaurants to welcome them. If lucky, they might secure a lodging in a small "colored rooming house" or hotel. More times than not they would be housed by a local Negro family contacted in advance. Less fortunate travelers might attempt to sleep nights in unheated theaters or railroad stations and eat packaged snacks on a hit-or-miss basis. And since whiskey was easier to come by than nourishing food, many performers became addicted to the bottle. Attempting to bathe or wash up in public toilet could be a highly tricky business. More urgent bodily functions posed even greater problems. For as Danny Barker put it, ". . . the segregation laws did not allow black backsides to sit on the same toilet as white backsides." So, male or female, "You hit the bushes on the highway."[229]

For well-known stars or the few top bands that could afford it, a private bus or railroad car solved many problems. It provided them with a "hotel" that housed their whole staff, instruments and equipment, while transporting them from town to town for tent and stage shows. A group unto themselves, in such a conveyance they avoided any extensive dealings with townspeople, could eat, sleep, rehearse and relax. A bus—or even better—a comfortable and roomy private train—vastly simplified the performers' lives—and also saved them money on hotels and restaurants.

Such was the case with singer Bessie Smith and company in the 1920s (and later Duke Ellington and Cab Calloway). Bessie's private railroad car, custom made by the Southern Iron and Equipment Company, was 78-feet long. As her biographer Chris Albertson put it,

> . . . the magnificent bright-yellow car with its green lettering became familiar—you knew when the Empress was in town . . . the car was large enough to carry the entire show. It had seven staterooms—each

> one comfortably sleeping four—kitchen, bathroom with hot and cold running water, and a lower level accommodating as many as thirty-five people . . . a room in the rear housed the canvas [tent], along with cases of soft drinks, Crackerjacks, peanuts, and other items were sold by Bessie's crew doubling as vendors . . . Food was prepared in the car's galley, often by Bessie herself . . . [230]

Even affording such fine private transportation did not ensure security on tour, since railroads frequently refused to carry private cars of black entertainers. A breakthrough occurred in 1925, when the United States Interstate Commerce Commission ruled that railroad companies could no longer draw the color line when it came to private cars. Yet with one obstacle out of the way, many others remained.

Whether on tour or working a specific area, whether in the North or South, the musician of color had to cope with some manner of insult or injustice every day of the year. The most illustrious among them were barred from eating in decent restaurants—often having to perform on an empty stomach. And they could not ride in a hotel elevator (unless employed to run it). In 1933, lyricist Andy Razaf of "Ain't Misbehavin'" fame, en route to a Station WGN broadcast at Chicago's Drake Hotel, had to ride up there in the only conveyance available to blacks—the freight elevator. Even an artist with the stature of W.C. Handy underwent demeaning experiences. In fact, it has been said[231] that he was turned away from the Cotton Club on a night his own music was featured there.

The great musical comedy star, Bert Williams—whose reactions to such discrimination were philosophical and wry rather than bitter and angry—told an unfortunate personal tale of such discrimination. Plagued with poor blood circulation, he sought treatment at a black-owned sanatorium in West Baden, Indiana. There they provided him with a bicycle for outdoor exercise. One day, while out riding, he was stopped by the local sheriff who, seeing a black skinned man with a bike, asked "Where'd ya steal it at?" Refusing to accept Williams' explanation, the sheriff confiscated the bicycle, obliging Williams to walk all the way back to the sanatorium.[232]

An oft-cited incident originally told by Eddie Cantor, who worked alongside Williams at the Ziegfeld Follies, shows how the black comedian countered prejudice with humor. One night Williams invited Cantor to go with him for a drink at a bar known to refuse to serve dark skinned patrons. When Williams ordered a gin, the surly bartender announced that it would be $50 per glass. So he promptly took out a $500 bill and said, "Give me ten of them."[233]

As sweet, generous and benign as Bert Williams was in his relationships with others, and as humorous as he could be in countering prejudicial slights, such affronts affected him deeply. Small wonder that W.C. Fields said of him "Bert Williams was the funniest man I ever saw and the saddest man I ever knew."[234]

A good percentage of the black musicians plagued by racial prejudice were well educated, a number of them offspring and descendants of Negroes who had made a mark in politics and education during the Reconstruction era. To cite just a few, Bob Cole was a graduate of Atlanta University. Will Marion Cook, the son of a law professor at Howard University, studied music at Oberlin Conservatory and the Hochschule in Berlin and graduated from the National Conservatory of Music, having learned composition there under Dvorák. James Rosemond Johnson, brother of the noted James Weldon Johnson (trained at the New England Conservatory of Music). Entertainer Abbie Mitchell, reversing the common order of black musicians gravitating from classical music to jazz, left musical comedy to learn the workings of music and harmony. She studied music for two years in Paris and later taught it at the Tuskegee Institute in Alabama. Later, Fletcher Henderson, a college graduate, went to New York planning to do post-graduate research in chemistry, but, infatuated with jazz—and doubtless aware of lack of opportunities for black chemists—he abandoned his studies for a career in music and became a renowned bandleader.

Many of these people were highly ambitious, and one is struck by the great percentage of them who left their initial training in classical music and other professions for the perpetual ups and downs of a career in popular music. A good many of them, like W.C. Handy, were simply overwhelmingly attracted to the blues, ragtime and jazz. Nothing else could satisfy them, no other training or experience was relevant.

Others, however, men like Will Marion Cook, would have preferred, at least at the start, a career in more "serious" professions. But at some point they had to acknowledge that their chances of real success in the white professional world were relatively slim. In contrast, opportunities for talented black musical entertainers were far more numerous and accessible. Although they usually earned much less than white musicians and were restricted to backbreaking road trips, with enough talent they could at least find jobs. As Paul Robeson put it: "A Negro lawyer could only go so high, no matter how good he was. On the stage, it was different. Only the sky, I felt, could be my roof."[235]

It is understandable that a good number of black entertainers emigrated or spent as much time as possible overseas. In Europe, in Australia or New Zealand, they were most often treated as human beings and not excluded as creatures of color. The talented among them were appreciated, often accepted in high society. Neither Josephine Baker—for whom France was "home"—nor Ethel Waters ever received an invitation from President Harding or Calvin Coolidge, but in Europe they sang for royalty. And the long-suffering comic, Bert Williams, became a strong favorite of the King of England.

As for the United States, Williams, musing on the fact that, despite all his honors and public acclaim there, he was "Jim Crowed generally," commented, "I am just wondering. I would like to know when (my prediction) the ultimate changes come, if the new human beings will believe such persons as I am writing about actually lived?"[236], [237]

Some Breakthroughs

Racial discrimination in the popular music world did not go unopposed. In fact, a good number of African-American musicians refused to accept the system passively but spoke out and organized in protest. Unfortunately they might as well have been trying to reinvent the wheel. After all, would be activists among black musicians had no prior system of protest or power structure to call up and use as a template. They possessed neither political clout nor economic resources. So their attempts at opposition were, in the main, impromptu, sporadic and often quixotic.

In the 1890s, Bob Cole, incensed at the low pay and poor working conditions available to black entertainers, issued a "Colored Actor's Declaration of Independence." His was a brave statement that nonetheless fell largely on deaf ears. Somewhat more effective eventually were a series of clubs and benevolent organizations organized by and for black musicians in the first decades of the twentieth century. One of the first, the "Colored Actor's Beneficial Association," appeared on the scene in 1905 through the efforts of Williams and Walker, Cole and Johnson, Ernest Hogan, Billy Kersands and Abbie Mitchell. Short-lived, it was superseded by a more successful organization, "The Frogs" (1908 to the mid-twenties). Founded in Harlem by some of the above musicians, and including orchestra leader James Reese Europe, the society aimed, among other things, to build a collection of black theater archives and to raise money for needy African-American entertainers..

Europe himself—who would later become known as musical director for dancers Irene and Vernon Castle—founded the most famous of the black musicians' unions: the Clef Club (1910-24). A chartered organization, it served primarily as a booking agency for dance orchestras. It provided a way of dignifying the work of blacks in popular music and of providing those of talent with a steady source of work and income.

A more casual, informal resource for black musicians, the Marshall Hotel on New York's West 53rd Street, offered a meeting place for aspiring artists. Some of them lived at the Marshall; others haunted the hotel bar in hopes of getting engagements through contacts there.

Such limited solutions as these—clubs, benevolent societies, meeting places and hangouts—represented stop-gap measures at best, providing jobs, contacts and, at times, a certain sense of self for the Negro musician. But they could open only so many doors to the world of popular music. For greater access to that world, the black musician would have to depend on his oft-time imitators and rivals: white musicians and entrepreneurs.

White Knights?

The whites who helped promote African Americans and their music might well be accused (as they eventually were) of having something to gain from their contributions. For the majority of them were in the music business rather than the business of philanthropy. Still, many of them were anxious to better conditions for black musicians and did their best to bolster and assist those they knew personally and professionally.

Jacob Schiffman, owner of the Apollo Theater, has already been cited[238] for his involvement in Harlem's black community. Unlike the mainly white Cotton Club, his Apollo Theater had a predominantly black staff, including its stage manager, band conductor and musical director, technical designer and sound technician. And Schiffman himself contributed to funding the NAACP in its early stages.

Julius Witmark, of Witmark and Sons song publishers, was one of the first entrepreneurs to print and promote the music of early black composers. (It was the Witmarks who published the music of William Marion Cook's 1898 landmark show *Clorindy or the Origin of the Cake Walk.*) A founding member of ASCAP, Witmark successfully proposed Sissle and Blake for membership, which permitted them—exceptionally—to earn royalties from their music.

Edward B. Marks, another known name in the business, published compositions of black musical innovators such as Cole and Johnson, Cook, Hogan and other of their contemporaries. Marks proudly commented on the subject: "And so our young publishing firm witnessed and fostered the first mass invasion of the amusement world by colored America."[239]

John Hammond, a producer for Columbia records and at times a controversial figure, was early drawn to the work of talented black musicians. "Talented" is the operative word here, for Hammond prided himself on his ability to scent out those of the highest quality, such as Fletcher Henderson, Bessie Smith and Count Basie. Those whom he admired but did not discover on his own, he promoted in every way he could.

Hammond has been faulted on several counts, for example, his criticism of Duke Ellington's "Black, Brown and Beige," which Hammond deemed pretentious and not on a level with Ellington's other work; his signing of Bessie Smith to a contract with no royalties; his mistaken account of Bessie's alleged "bleeding to death" for lack of white medical care, his making a profit from black musicians though himself a scion of a wealthy family.[240]

Yet Hammond was sincerely and deeply committed to improving the lot of black musicians and of African Americans in general. In the thirties, he raised funds for the defense of the "Scottsboro Boys," nine young southern Negroes who had been wrongly accused of raping two white women. He joined the board of the NAACP in 1937 and continued to work for African-American causes throughout his life. Concerning his active commitment to racial justice, Hammond explained, "Usually my involvement in political and social activism resulted from my love for jazz and the people I met who shared that enthusiasm."[241]

A very large percentage of the "white knights" who promoted African-American musicians and their cause were Jewish. Two realities lay behind that fact. Firstly, as it has often been said, the Jews had also been victims, a minority oppressed for centuries, and because of this, many of them empathized with African Americans and supported their cause. But secondly, the music field, like the cinema, was visibly dominated by Jews. So if help and support were to come from anywhere, it would, in all mathematical likelihood, emerge from the great number of Jewish entrepreneurs, composers and entertainers in the field.

Theater owners such as the Shuberts, Klaw and Erlanger and various of the white Harlem theater entrepreneurs; composers like Victor Herbert, Rodgers and Hammerstein, Irving Berlin, George Gershwin, Harold Arlen; entertainers such as Al Jolson, Eddie Cantor, Sophie Tucker and countless others dating from white minstrelsy to the present—the list of Jews in the music field appears endless.

Unsurprisingly, out of this number, Jews who supported black artists were—like their Christian counterparts or more so—accused of exploitation of blacks.[242] In some cases this was certainly true. But in many others Jews, even those profiting financially from black talent, did much to help them overcome traditional obstacles and gain a sense of self-respect. Said Duke Ellington of his Jewish agent, Irving Mills, "He broke down so many darned barriers for Negro musicians you couldn't count them."[243]

And Louis Armstrong's words about his agent, Joe Glaser were: "God bless his soul. He was the greatest for me and all the spades that he handled."[244] Glaser, despite his shady private life, did accomplish much in the desegregation of live and recorded jazz ensembles. Armstrong only spoke of Glaser with love and even dedicated some memoirs written late in life to Glaser, signing: "His boy and disciple who loved him dearly."[245]

As damning as the accusations of financial exploitation were allegations that whites, Jews in particular, appropriated the creation of blacks, thereby depriving them of their black heritage.[246] Some truth lies behind the claim, for, after all, black music was there, attractive, exciting, begging to be imitated, adapted and used. So we find Victor Herbert translating the black heritage into his *Showboat,* Gershwin celebrating and immortalizing it in his own *Porgy and Bess,* Arlen providing music for Harlem's Cotton Club and composing songs for Hollywood's version of the black musical *Cabin in the Sky,* Berlin commercializing black music in his rags and pseudo rags and Cantor, Jolson and Tucker frankly imitating black singers.

But appropriation or not, there are many examples from among the white admirers of black music—Jews and non-Jews alike—who went out of their way to provide public and personal support for the less fortunate blacks who had contributed so much musically. It would be an exaggeration to attribute to all those whites the idealistic motives credited—justifiably—to philanthropist Julius Rosenwald: ". . . honor, the obligations of great wealth, abhorrence of bigotry . . ."[247] Yet, on the evidence, the motives that lay behind their support were diverse, in some cases idealistic, and did not stem completely from a what's-in-it-for-me mentality.

In the latter part of the 1930s a promise of progress for the Negro musician appeared in the form of the Federal Theatre Project (1935-1939), an offshoot of Roosevelt's Works Progress Administration (WPA). The FTP's Negro Theatre Project established black units in around twenty-three American cities. Although the FTP was geared primarily to drama, it also benefited a number of musicians, notably in such productions as *The Hot Mikado* and *Carmen Jones.*

But this was a promise and by no means a solution. The African American in American popular music could not interpret it as light at the end of the tunnel. For the rock laden road continued to stretch far ahead, endless and unrelieved, in a monotonously familiar pattern of *déjà vu.*

Notes

222 Of course such affronts did not magically end in the forties or even the fifties, but the period in question was more generally and openly discriminatory.

223 Incident reported in *The Ghost Walks,* pp. 246-7.

224 Incident reported in *Blacks in Blackface,* p. 29, and in *Night People,* p. 44.

225 *The Ghost Walks,* p. 198.

226 *Ibid.,* pp. 543-4.

227 *Swing Changes,* p. 126. Dempsey Travis noted that as late as 1962, "at the height of the civil rights movement, Louis Armstrong and his integrated All Stars were prohibited from playing in New Orleans, his home town, and many other cities below the Mason-Dixon Line." (*The Louis Armstrong Odyssey,* p. 168).

228 Accounts of this event vary. According to a report in the *New York Journal* (9/01-00), cited in *The Ghost Walks,* pp. 221-2, police intervened to protect both Hogan and Walker, and both men wound up in the Marlborough Hotel. A description in the more recent biography of Bert Williams, *Nobody,* mentions neither the police nor the Marlborough Hotel (see pp. 54-5), although the two men

were indisputably victims of the riot. And other accounts allege police participation in abetting the attackers.

229 *A Life in Jazz,* p. 166.

230 *Bessie,* pp. 94-5.

231 See, for example Lewis, *When Harlem was in Vogue,* p. 209.

232 See *Nobody,* p. 141.

233 *Ibid,*, p. 133.

234 *Ibid,* p. 132.

235 Quoted in *Showtime at the Apollo,* p. 24.

236 *Ibid,* p. 138.

237 The hoped for "changes" had certainly not materialized in 1939, when famous contralto Marian Anderson—constantly plagued by racism—was prevented by the Daughters of the American Revolution from performing in Constitution Hall in Washington, D.C. The situation prompted Eleanor Roosevelt to resign from the D.A.R. and to invite Marian Anderson to sing on the steps of the Lincoln Memorial Easter of that year.

238 See Chapter Six, *supra.*

239 *They All Sang,* p. 100.

240 Frank Kofsky, was one of Hammond's most vehement critics on the subject of the latter's business dealings with black artists (see Chapter Fourteen for more about Kofsky).

241 *John Hammond on Record,* p. 91.

242 Concerning such accusations see Lees, *Cats of Any Color,* p. 195.

243 *Duke Ellington Reader,* p. 106.

244 Cited in Bergreen, *Louis Armstrong, an Extravagant Life,* p. 409.

245 *Ibid.*

246 One of the most severe criticisms of Jewish adoption of black music has come from a Jew himself, author Jeffrey Melnick (see *A Right to Sing the Blues*), some of whose commentary may strike a reader as oddly anti-Semitic.

247 *When Harlem Was in Vogue,* p. 101.

10

STARTING UP

THE EARLY JAZZ DANCE BANDS

The European Legacy of Black Jazz

There is no question that jazz was a black phenomenon generated by black musicians. Nevertheless, the sounds of jazz drew not only on the African-American heritage but—as in the case of the spirituals—on white European music as well. That music would continue to influence the shape and trajectory of American jazz throughout the course of the twentieth century.

Many of the most creative of African-American musicians, from the days of Cole and Johnson through the big band era and beyond, had extensive training and experience in European musical structures and techniques. To cite just a few: William Grant Still, whom Gunther Schuller called "the dean of black classical composers,"[248] studied with avant-garde composer Edgard Varèse and others, besides training at the New England Conservatory of Music. Erskine Tate, who led the pit orchestra in Chicago's Vendome Theatre in the twenties, was college educated and conservatory trained, and the musicians in his band all read music and had a hand in composing it. Stride pianist James P. Johnson wrote symphonic pieces and a one-act opera. Fats Waller, who learned organ in church as a boy, had grounding in traditional European counterpoint and, besides his extensive jazz and popular composing, ventured, at times, into classical areas. Bandleaders Jimmy Lunceford and Andy Kirk both acquired classical training, studying with Wilberforce Whiteman (Paul Whiteman's father). Arranger Don Redman, a music major in college and recipient of two conservatory degrees, capitalized on his classical background, emphasizing harmony in his orchestrations. The list goes on.

William H. Youngren, in discussing traits of white European music in jazz, has pointed out that black jazz, like traditional European music, is tonal, set in a major or minor key, and, like eighteenth-century classical music, it employs "chord progressions that determine a melody's changing relation to the key of the piece."[249] Echoes of centuries old musical styles and, most importantly, an emphasis on melody and harmony, were absorbed into the fabric of African-American jazz.

Further strengthening the white musical influence on black jazz was the use of European musical instruments. In New Orleans, since the American Revolution and through the early decades of the nineteenth century, marching musicians in French Napoleonic military bands and players in Spanish, German, Italian, Irish and Swiss militia companies could be heard sounding fifes, drums and various brass instruments. Horns introduced in the South by itinerant Mexican performers became available cheaply to black musicians at the end of the Civil War, when relegated to pawnshops by musicians of the erstwhile Confederate Army bands.[250] Later, around the time of the Spanish-American War of 1898, the Mexican and other military brass bands playing in New Orleans had contact with local black musicians and a considerable impact on them.

Brasses, woodwinds and eventually the piano—so important in the development of black ragtime—such instruments had been designed to synchronize with the chordal and melodic progressions of classical European music.

Continuing the white-to-black trajectory, Souza's example, particularly, inspired the formation of brass bands, both white and black, enjoying popularity in the city from the 1880s on. And from the turn of the twentieth century on, black bands would capitalize on the music of Tin Pan Alley, incorporating the structural, melodic and harmonic patterns that characterized the popular music of white America. Finally, as we shall see, the twentieth-century black bands would absorb—and often improve on—techniques of arranging used by leading white orchestras.

But despite its use of European structures, techniques and instruments, African—American music was unlike anything that European or American whites had previously known. The unusual off-beat syncopations, the brilliant improvisations, the sounds of blues and ragtime—and, most dramatically, the dynamic drive of the ensembles—combined to make black band music an original American creation.

Let us look back briefly at the evolution of black bands, focusing mainly on the all-important dance bands.

A Brief History of Black Dance Bands

American instrumental bands, whether black or white, have had a variety of functions over the years. For the public's listening pleasure, nineteenth-century ensembles offered light, popular musical entertainment at private functions, in hotels and restaurants or outdoor concerts in public parks. More excitingly, following the white example, they often served as marching units, parading through the streets on special occasions. The most memorable of such events were the black funeral parades of New Orleans, with their solemn march to the grave, then, following the drummer's roll, their joyous return, with a ragging and improvising of favorite spirituals and marches. (A "second line" of admirers, including small children, followed, irresistibly drawn by the driving sounds of the band's march back from the cemetery.)

But rather than limiting themselves to "listening music," the bands generally functioned as dance orchestras as well, playing in dance halls, cabarets, on river boats or at public and private balls. For such occasions they might consist of six to eight players, creating a typical ensemble of violin or mandolin, guitar, cornet or trumpet, clarinet, trombone, bass and drum.

As for Negro dance bands specifically, a number of them could be found in Tenderloin saloons, most often associated with prostitution and gambling. In 1850, George Foster's *New York by Gaslight*[251] described a combo at Pete William's Dance House in the city's red light district. Consisting of a violin, trumpet and bass drum, it accompanied dancers with wildly hot rhythms. After the Civil War especially, similar small black dance ensembles played not only in the Northeast but in areas such as San Francisco's Barbary Coast, a district rife with saloons and gambling houses, or on the south side of Chicago, in New Orleans' French Quarter and elsewhere. Such small units often limited themselves to violin, banjo and string bass, until the 1870s and eighties, when the use of horns increased. And after 1910 the piano, that perfect medium for ragtime rhythms, would become a common feature of dance bands both small and large.

At the higher end of the scale, as far back as the early 1800s, black dance orchestras were making their presence known at the creamiest levels of society. Over a century before dance ensembles became known as "swing bands," a free Negro of Philadelphia, Francis ("Frank") Johnson[252] was conducting an orchestra for fashionable dances of the region's white elite. Besides composing music, playing several instruments and leading a marching woodwind band, Johnson organized a string ensemble that played at balls and "assemblies" of old Philadelphia society and at exclusive dances in Saratoga Springs. His orchestra mainly accompanied contemporary quadrilles, reels and other figure dances for which he acted as caller. Significantly, on a concert tour of Europe, Johnson met Johann Strauss I and brought Strauss' waltzes, along with the European tradition of the cotillion, back to America. For years Johnson's highly popular orchestra continued to play for dances in cities and towns all along the east coast.[253]

In Johnson's day a number of white ensembles sliced off a share of the society dance market. They were following a pattern set in Europe, where society dance orchestras were organized early in the nineteenth century during the Congress of Vienna (1812-22). There, the orchestra of Joseph Lanner, an Austrian violinist and entrepreneur, and Lanner's spin-off orchestra led by Johann Strauss I inspired a host of such dance ensembles.

But in the United States, although dance bands were not the exclusive province of African-American musicians, Negro orchestras predominated. Following on Johnson's heels, from the 1880s until World War I, black dance bands continued to be featured primarily at society dances, most notably in the Northeast between Washington and Boston.[254]

Until the turn of the century, Negro society dance orchestras did not publicly offer the black music that would blossom into ragtime. Their musical fare, like that of their white counterparts, consisted of accompaniment for dances, such as quadrilles, waltzes, schottisches, polkas or martial two-steps, like Sousa's "Washington Post," and a variety of sweet or novelty American popular songs. But in the 1910s, around the time of World War I, black dance bands, whether geared to high society or the Tenderloin, would increasingly feature the jazzy syncopations that accompanied ragtime dances sweeping the country at the time.

James Reese Europe was the first important black dance orchestra leader to move in that direction, prefiguring the jazz and swing bands to come. Larger than life, Europe caught public attention for his role as bandleader of the World War I heroic all-black 369th Infantry Regiment of the American Expeditionary Force (the "Hellfighters' Band"). But even before that, Europe had become a musical celebrity, largely thanks to his association with dancers Irene and Vernon Castle, beginning in 1913.

It might surprise us that in the non-integrated society of that time, the gifted, lily white Castles—the toast of New York's moneyed elite—chose to link their career with that of a Negro bandleader (who had not yet achieved fame with his World War I regiment). For James Reese Europe was the ebony-skinned son of an ex-slave who had entered the black middle class. Yet the collaboration of the Castles and Jim Europe was a very logical one.

That collaboration did not arise out of some bold democratic gesture on the couple's part. Rather, it had behind it a long tradition of black musicians playing for upper-crust whites. It harked back not only to Frank Johnson and the black society bands of the late nineteenth century, but, even earlier, to musical slaves entertaining at their masters' grand balls. As for Jim Europe, by the time he met the Castles, he had organized concerts of black music in Carnegie Hall and had already created his Clef Club and Tempo Club, successful booking agencies for black bands performing at society dances. And Europe and his orchestras already had entrée into the circles of Mrs. John Wanamaker, Mrs. Stuyvesant Fish and other members of New York's famous Four Hundred.

Interestingly, many in that society labored under the assumption that their Negro entertainers could not read music but, supposedly, like so many of their forebears, played completely spontaneously. A propos of their stereotyping, Eubie Blake said:

> Now this is the truth. Europe's orchestra was filled with readin' *sharks.* That cornet player, Russell Smith! If a fly landed on the music he'd *play* it, see, like *that.* But we weren't supposed to read music! . . . [so] I'd get all the latest Broadway music from the publisher, and we'd learn the tunes and rehearse 'em until we had 'em all down pat.

Then, as Blake explained, they would play from memory, without any sheets of music, at these social events, always leaving room for a little improvisation, or "faking." And, according to Blake, their white listeners would say, "Isn't it wonderful how these untrained, primitive musicians can pick up all the latest songs instantly without being able to read music?" Blake commented ingenuously, "That William Grant Still who played oboe with us—I wonder if he could read music when he was arrangin' for Paul Whiteman."[255]

But undoubtedly more important to the Castles than the training and class of Europe's society orchestra was the fact that of all the bands they had been dancing to, Jim Europe's, more than any others, exactly suited their performance of the dances they were popularizing in America.

The year 1913 marked the start of a great dance craze in the United States, a craze that would be intensified by the performances and teachings of the Castles themselves. The most exciting—and controversial—dances of the 1910s were inspired by the favorites of Negro dancers of San Francisco's Barbary Coast. Their names evoked a sort of musical zoo: the "turkey trot," the "grizzly bear," the "bunny hug" and so on, reminiscent of the old slave dances involving animals, such as turkeys, 'possums or buzzards[256],[257] In cabarets and dives such numbers were seen executed by couples in close contact, often with sensual, grinding movements of the "slow drag," popular in the South. It was a style that evoked nineteenth-century Afro-Caribbean belly-rub dancing and the grinding motions of traditional dances on the west coast of Africa.

The Castles' aim was to adapt the modern ragtime genre—along with Argentina's sensuous tango (also originating from Negro rhythms)—to the taste of high society. They replaced the awkwardness of Barbary Coast turkey trots and the sexuality of its close hugs with smoothly elegant dancing—all the while keeping a certain sense of fun and humor. For this, Europe's lively, polished renditions were perfect. And, additionally, Europe, often along with Ford Dabney and Noble Sissle, composed new dance numbers, one-steps such as "The Castle Walk" and most notably, a series of fox trots, a dance genre that would become increasingly popular in America.

James Europe's dance music, while not properly in the realm of modern jazz, could definitely swing. It provided the new syncopated dances with an infectious beat. In other words, the dances inspired his music and his music inspired dancing. This cross-fertilization of dance and music, an age old phenomenon, would apply to the various permutations of jazz throughout the years. Writer Jeff Taylor has said that the dance fashions contemporary with Europe and the Castles "set the stage for the intricate relationship between jazz and dance that would remain for the first fifty years of its history."[258] In fact, that relationship, which already had a long history, would endure well beyond that half century.[259]

New Orleans and the Early Black Jazz Band

Years before jazz was actually called "jazz,"[260] black musicians had organized bands performing music containing all the elements of that genre. It is only natural that the most important of the black pre-jazz ensembles originated in the South, where slavery and Negro musical entertainment had gone hand in hand.

The most fertile breeding ground of black jazz-oriented band music was lively New Orleans, a multi-national, cosmopolitan city with a rich musical tradition (supporting as many as three opera companies in the nineteenth century). New Orleans did not invent American jazz single-handedly and out of whole cloth, since the main substance of that music, ragtime and the blues, had been developing in Missouri, Kansas, New York and other areas as well. The music of ragtime composer Scott Joplin, blues maker W.C. Handy and talented musicians of other regions traveled the Mississippi route to New Orleans. And New Orleans musicians themselves toured in other southern cities already familiar with the syncopated sounds. Nonetheless, even if New Orleans could not take full credit for the invention of those sounds, it contributed far more than any other city, to the creation of the American jazz idiom.

In retrospect, it appears inevitable that New Orleans was such a fount of black musical creativity. That city had an extraordinarily high percentage of free people of color before the Civil War. The population of freed slaves had tripled between 1777 and 1791, under Spanish rule, then doubled in next decade or so. By the early nineteenth century, free blacks made up between one third and one half of the population of New Orleans. They, along with blacks in bondage—notably slaves who worked in the city and enjoyed nearly the same liberty as their free brethren—would greatly enrich the city's already strong musical heritage.

For black music was a fact of life in New Orleans well before Emancipation. As it has often been said, New Orleans' Catholic French and Spanish heritage had fostered a greater permissiveness towards the singing and dancing of the slaves than could be found in most southern towns, steeped in an Anglo-Saxon Protestant culture. And as noted above,[261] even after the Louisiana Purchase of 1803, African-American music continued thriving in the city under the Protestant whites, who allowed the continuance of Negro singing and dancing in Congo Square until 1835-36 and possibly for a period up to ten years later.

Descendants of the slaves would perpetuate that musical tradition. They did so in the context of a most unusual demographic structure, a caste system that made of New Orleans not a bi-racial community but largely a tri-racial one. There was the white population, located in various districts according to means, profession, nationality or happenstance. There were the dark-skinned former slaves or free blacks, most of whom were living on streets uptown (and who by the turn of the twentieth century would constitute the largest black minority in North America). And thirdly, there were the light-skinned Creoles, products of intermarriage,[262] who mainly resided in downtown areas.

The Creoles, who considered themselves—and were long considered—far above the ordinary uptown blacks, often gravitated to "serious" music, even forming their own philharmonic society in the 1830s and a Creole orchestra in the 1870s. On the other hand, less favored, or less pretentious, uptown black musicians[263] cultivated an earthier style, a style closer to their familiar spirituals and to the blues. But the dichotomy between the two castes and their brands of music, was not to last.

As for New Orleans whites, their role in music cannot be underestimated. From early on they played in orchestras, at dances and functions, in street parades and elsewhere. By the turn of the twentieth century, white ensembles like "Papa" Jack Laine's Reliance Band of New Orleans—which included, at times, light-skinned Negroes and Creoles—offered lively renditions of popular tunes of the day at park bandstands, in dance halls or from advertising wagons.

But the Negro musicians played a far more important and innovative role on the band scene. Building on their heritage of syncopated church music, on ragtime and on the blues, early twentieth-century ensembles were producing a rough version of what would later be known as "New Orleans" jazz." A bandleader might run through the melody with a cornet player, who would then take the lead, with the others, generally non-readers, filling in as best they could around the melody. There would be few, if any, solos, and when the leader wanted the music hot, no one took a rest but all pitched in with great gusto. By 1910, some of these New Orleans bands were emitting increasingly hot and jazzy music, often freewheeling rags or lowdown "gut bucket" blues.

That sort of music was generally out of bounds for the average self-respecting white musician who might aim at "worthier" goals such as classical genres or, at the very least, sweet versions of popular songs in hotels, restaurants and private functions. Although, in swinging New Orleans, whites could not help but be drawn to the lively syncopated style—and some, like Papa Laine or George Brunies, cultivated it—performing that music was, to a great extent, frowned on. As George Morrison put it, "For a white boy to beat a drum and play for a living was a disgrace. [His family] would disown him. They wanted nothing but the colored man to play for them."[264,265]

On the other hand, black musicians on the uptown side of Canal Street, even those from conservative families condoning only religious or classical music, could seldom resist the allure of the jazzier sounds within earshot. For ragtime could be heard not only in dives, cabarets and brothels along with the blues but out in the streets, everywhere. Performers and would-be performers uptown seized the musical (and financial) opportunities available to them, playing not only sweet music for upscale dances but ragtime as well. Then, thanks to their steady work and take home pay, the scruples of moral minded parents often gave way to acceptance and even a grudging admiration.

When it came to the middle class downtown Creoles, many had extensive musical training and reading skills and considered themselves too respectable for hot syncopated music and the seedy venues in which it was so often played. However, in the late 1890s they became legally segregated from whites and forced into black ghettos. Deprived of their former trades and clienteles (many had earned a respectable living as skilled artisans or shopkeepers), they had little recourse. A number of them set aside their music reading skills and joined their darker brethren winging it in gigs around town, while still working at daytime jobs.

It is highly likely that these relatively more sophisticated and trained downtown Creole "readers," steeped in European harmonies, helped color or tame the more spontaneous and rougher attack of uptown improvisers. Don Marquis bears that idea out in pointing to Manuel Perez, an important downtown Creole musician, and the uptown mulatto virtuoso, Buddy Bolden, stating "Perez was responsible for refining many of Bolden's ideas on the cornet, and he helped combine the best of Bolden with the Creole music so that by 1910 elemental jazz was on its way to becoming classic jazz."[266] Although exact details of how such cases of fusion came about are unknown to us today, the interaction between uptown and downtown musicians undoubtedly contributed greatly to the shaping of modern jazz.

In New Orleans a rudimentary form of jazz could be heard well before the twentieth century and decades before Jim Europe introduced a ragtime beat into his concerts. There were, of course, the city's parading brass ensembles, incorporating raggy rhythms in their marches and improvising. Technically, that practice amounted to an adaptation of piano ragtime to band instruments, with the rhythm instruments carrying the ragtime piano's left-hand bass, while brasses or woodwinds sang out the right-hand treble melodies. But in the context of New Orleans street bands, the ragging did not derive from a formal or conscious technique. It was spontaneous. A way of having fun by replacing standard tempo of a march with the familiar black off-the-beat rhythms—or "faking" when a musician could not read music.

One of the very first New Orleanians to adapt the raggy music of the brass bands to a dance ensemble was the legendary Charles "Buddy" Bolden (1868-1931). "King" Bolden, a much admired band leader starting in 1895, reigned for little more than a half decade, since he achieved fame in New Orleans around 1900, became irascible and given to fits of depression in 1906, was diagnosed with schizophrenia and spent the rest of his life, from 1907 on, in a mental institution. Yet he was, and still remains, a legend—and for other more important reasons than the oft-quoted fact that his cornet could be heard "for miles around." With a six-piece ensemble[267] and a repertoire including Scott Joplin rags or themes from well known marches, spirituals, blues and popular sheet music of the day, Bolden produced an irresistible sound, overshadowing his rivals and gaining enduring renown.

No recordings exist to give us a clear idea of what Bolden's music actually sounded like.[268] According to accounts of his contemporaries, it largely depended on his audience. He could, and did, play numbers to accompany waltzes, quadrilles, the two-step and other standard dances of the time and was capable of delivering a sweet, soft sound. As for his contribution to the realm of jazz, although he developed ragtime rhythms, he also liked to play a "rough" and "low-down" slow drag kind of blues, some of them, like "Buddy Bolden's Blues" or "Funky Butt," verging on the crude or obscene.

Bolden's band music was undoubtedly not a polished product and certainly a far cry from the conservative and more manicured tones of his Creole contemporary, John Robichaux. For unlike such musicians, although Bolden and some of his band could read music, they preferred to play by ear, and they worked out their arrangements themselves in practice sessions. These were apparently "head" arrangements, that is, arrangements devised informally by Bolden or band members on an *ad hoc* basis and partially memorized. But it was Bolden's own playing that captured audiences of the day. By all accounts it amounted to a driving force.[269] More importantly for jazz history, Bolden has often been pointed out as the man who "started it all." Certainly, his emphasis on the earthy blues in a ragtime repertoire helped open the way for and fuel the development of twentieth-century jazz.

The sound of fledgling jazz bands had evolved considerably in Bolden's time, not only because of musical innovations and steadily changing styles but also because of new developments in the choice of instruments. The homespun tuba, a popular feature of marching bands, was replaced in the early 1900s by the more sophisticated double bass. The sweet tones of violins gave way increasingly to the more aggressive horns and percussion. However, since many New Orleans bands were multi-functional and marched in parades, the piano did not feature in early ensembles and only became a standard fixture of bands in the 1910s. And not until around 1916[270] would the saxophone introduce its mellow sound and begin to double with—or take the place of—the brighter clarinet that wove birdlike obbligatos over the basic melody.

Brasses took on an increasingly prominent role, with the cornet (more and more frequently replaced by the trumpet) animating the music. From Bolden's day on the brasses provided a compelling tone and opportunities for interaction, improvisation and inventiveness. Not to mention gimmicks. For Freddie Keppard, King Oliver and other instrumentalists would make ample use of bathroom plunger heads, cups or water glasses as mutes, throat growls and their tongues—to achieve moaning, wailing and growling and "dirty" or "jungle" effects.[271] Musicians vied with each other to create a hotter and hotter sound. Anything was possible.

One must not imagine, however, that all black bands were constantly belting out hot and jazzy sounds. Some never attempted it. And as for hot bands like Bolden's, Keppard's or Oliver's, they, like others, could and did adapt to a more "legit" ambience, playing solemn marches in parades to the graveyard or waltzes and sweet popular music at Tulane proms.

Storyville: Myth and Reality

Legend would have it that jazz was born in the Storyville section of New Orleans. In the last decades of the twentieth century critics began to challenge that assumption.[272] It is undoubtedly a simplistic one—yet perhaps not totally inaccurate. Before discussing the truth and fallacy of the Storyville-cum-cradle-of-jazz cliché, let us consider the area itself.

In 1897 town alderman Sidney Story sponsored an ordinance restricting prostitution to one area of New Orleans. And achieved thereby a dubious immortality, unwittingly lending his name to the city's newly created Tenderloin. For, although New Orleanians referred to the area as "the District," the press dubbed it "Storyville" (despite Story's indignant protests).

The measure had been long in coming. In New Orleans—a port town controlled by the Mafia for over two decades following 1869—prostitution had run rampant all over town, steadily accompanied by bribes to gangsters and police along with knifings, shootings and various other assorted acts of mayhem. Limiting prostitution to one specific region was intended to have—and, indeed, did have—the effect of diminishing crime in the city.

In the "District" one found brothels of every ilk, from one-room "cribs," where a woman might charge less than fifty cents to a dollar, to more costly, well appointed "palaces." The latter type, run by the likes of Lulu White, "Countess" Willie Piazza or Gypsy Shaefer, were glowingly described in newspaper advertisements and in the *Blue Book,* a guide to Storyville's sporting houses. In such establishments ladies of the night, often octoroons, purveyed pleasure expensively, albeit hastily, to their white patrons. And only whites had legal access to any of Storyville's rooms or houses of assignation.

Where there were brothels there were very often musicians. Quite naturally, these were black musicians, and, generally speaking, pianists, or "professors," whose tinkling created the right atmosphere to loosen up patrons (and possibly mask noises from upstairs). Upscale houses engaged the finest of New Orleans piano players, men such as Tony Jackson or Jelly Roll Morton. Although unsalaried, such "ivory ticklers" had little to complain of. For their music inspired not only lavish rounds of champagne on the part of clients but also heavy tips for the "professor."

How did the New Orleans bands fit into this picture? A pianist alone provided all the music necessary for the ambiance of a bordello, and most such places could hardly accommodate a loud, six- or seven-piece ensemble (Mahogany Hall appears to have been one exception). Yet famous New Orleans band musicians and leaders did work often in Storyville, for the District housed, along with its brothels, an assortment of cabarets, saloons and dance halls such as Club 25, Pete Lala's, the Funky Butt and the Frenchman's, in addition to restaurants featuring dance music. Although most of New Orleans musicians may have worked outside the District,[273] it would be hard to agree with the contention that "the majority of black musicians of outstanding ability in New Orleans never worked so much as a single night in Storyville."[274] Bands playing in District venues were not only very common but among the best and most admired in New Orleans.

Storyville bands included Joe "King" Oliver's, mainly at Pete Lala's Café, Freddy Keppard's, most often at the Tuxedo, Kid Ory's at Lala's and Club 25 and Manuel Perez at Joe Rice's Café. Among the noted musicians featured in Storyville bands were clarinetists Sidney Bechet, Johnny Dodds and George Baquet, pianist and entrepreneur, Clarence Williams,[275] trombonist Zue

Robertson and the future bandleader, Luis Russell. As for Louis Armstrong, he was too young to be performing in Storyville in the 1910s, but during the early 20s, before joining Joe Oliver in Chicago, he could be found playing at Tom Anderson's Saloon on the District's North Rampart Street. Here you have some of the most renowned and influential of New Orleans musicians, those who would carry New Orleans music to Chicago, New York and other big cities. Local jazz celebrities who did not operate regularly in Storyville—Buddy Bolden and Bunk Johnson, for example—led bands there on occasion.

So if, technically, jazz was not born in Storyville, New Orleans jazz most certainly came into flower there through the artistry of its most brilliant local exponents.

White Jazz in New Orleans

How did white musicians figure in the New Orleans scene? If jazz sounds interested them at all, they had to be well aware of the black performers there and their exciting music. For in uptown New Orleans, blacks and whites lived in close proximity, with a white musician housed perhaps not more than a door or two away from a black one. As a boy, Larry Shields, future clarinetist of Chicago's white Original Dixieland Jazz Band, lived just two houses away from Buddy Bolden on First Street. And Leon Roppolo,[276] who would become clarinetist and a key figure of the white New Orleans Rhythm Kings, resided on Adams Street, only one or two doors away from the topflight black bass player, Pops Foster. Roppolo, as a youth, had early contact with Negro jazz in his father's Negro saloon, where he would hound black clarinet players to "teach him some licks."[277]

White teenage and pre-teen music lovers were known to find any kind of pretext to get close to a Storyville dive in hopes of hearing—and possibly even meeting—the great cornetist, Joe Oliver.[278] Ambitious young white musicians haunted the District, youngsters who would become, according to Al Rose, an "entire generation of great white Dixieland stars,"[279] including future members of the Original Dixieland Jazz Band and the New Orleans Rhythm Kings.

Throughout New Orleans passersby could witness black funeral parades and hear Negro music in parks, at Lake Pontchartrain and on riverboats. Well-heeled whites were known to join black patrons of Storyville's Frenchman's Saloon and assorted other dives to hear ragtime or blues by Negro musicians.[280] And any wayward white husband sneaking out to a Storyville brothel could not avoid catching the rhythmic strains of black music hammered out on an upright or even a Steinway grand piano.

Inevitably and immediately, white jazz ensembles sprang up in the city, some of them with players formerly in "Papa" Jack Laine's Reliance Band. Like the black bands these white units would typically consist of a "front line" which included cornet, clarinet, trombone—at times a violin—backed by a rhythm section generally composed of string bass and guitar. Exploiting the sounds of Oliver and Keppard, the white groups were active in the New Orleans scene, sometimes working alongside black ones. However, they provided little threat to the highly popular black ensembles; according to bassist Pops Foster, they got almost all the jobs.[281] Some white players would eventually achieve prominence, but not until migrating northward and forming bands in Chicago.

It was there, as we shall see, that key figures in black New Orleans jazz would migrate—musicians such as King Oliver (to be followed later by his protégé, Louis Armstrong), Sidney Bechet, Freddie Keppard, Kid Ory, Johnny and his brother, Warren "Baby" Dodds, Honoré Dutrey, Manuel Perez and "Papa" Celestin. And it was there that white musicians would capitalize on the black New Orleans ragtime sound, giving it new labels: "Dixieland" and that public relations buzzword: "jazz."[282]

The Nationalization of Black Jazz

It was a case of musical miscegenation. The black sounds of ragtime had early been discovered by white musicians as they wended their way from St. Louis and Sedalia to Chicago, Nashville, Detroit, Kansas City, Philadelphia and New York. Those sounds, appropriated by white players, composers and entrepreneurs, quickly filtered into the music of Tin Pan Alley.

In the 1910s, especially from World War I on, white clones of early black bands playing ragtime and blues were proliferating and becoming increasingly active. This was happening not only in New Orleans and Chicago but in many other cities throughout America.

The increased activity of whites in black music came about for a variety of reasons. For one thing, like the crusaders and itinerant merchants of the Middle Ages, black musicians ventured far from their original bases. Following the big fairs, taking the river boat and railroad routes, satisfying their wanderlust, on tour or seeking new jobs, they brought their music to a wide segment of audiences, both black and white.

But even if the black musicians themselves did not travel, their syncopated music did. From the time of the first published turn-of-the-century rags, ragtime sheet music was disseminated throughout the country. So in any home with access to a piano someone could become familiar with the latest in black music. Naturally, those who could afford such a luxury were mainly white. Then, in the latter part of the 1910s, when white groups from New Orleans began calling their ragtime music "Dixieland jazz" and making records of it, audiences for the black inspired music greatly increased from coast to coast. Indeed, it was largely through the recordings of these white imitators that the black sounds (which we shall now refer to as "jazz") would truly begin to infiltrate into the mainstream of American popular music.

In the past many critics have assigned an exact starting date for the diaspora of New Orleans black jazz: 1917. For that year the U.S. Navy closed down Storyville and its red light establishments in an effort to protect its sailors from vice. Tradition would have it that the closing of the District prompted the emigration and dispersal of black jazz from New Orleans to northern cities, to coasts east and west, primarily up the Mississippi River to Chicago.

But in fact, as more recent writers have pointed out, not all important jazz musicians left New Orleans in 1917, and not all émigrés headed straight for Chicago. Freddie Keppard, for example, migrated first to the West Coast before 1917; Buddy Petit, a trumpet luminary and style setter (though, unfortunately, unrecorded) tried the West Coast briefly but returned to home base; King Oliver did not pull up stakes until 1918 and Louis Armstrong not until 1922, when Oliver invited him to join his band at Chicago's Lincoln Gardens.

Besides, the sounds of New Orleans musicians had already traveled well beyond the city at least from the early years of the century. Pianist Tony Jackson, had played in Chicago in 1906 and Jelly Roll Morton two years later. Certainly, the nomadic Jelly Roll had been heard in many areas outside of New Orleans since early on—in Biloxi, Mississippi, Chicago, Memphis, Los Angeles and, apparently, as many cities as work and women were to be found. And, the reverse of the coin, in those early years, musicians from all over the South traveled to New Orleans for the races and could be heard playing piano at places such as Pete Lala's.[283]

Finally, although 1917 was, indeed, an important date for black jazz,[284] the closing of Storyville that year was not solely responsible for New Orleans' jazz exodus. For that city had been in an economic slump all throughout the 1910s, and musicians were often hard pressed to find enough work there. Tales of already successful black bands in the North, notably, in Chicago, were constantly luring them to greener pastures.

Chicago, "where more railroads began and terminated than anywhere else"[285] and where the African-American population was fast increasing,[286] provided a rich venue for them. For one thing, black rag rhythms ("jig music") had undoubtedly been heard in that city before their breakthrough at the time of the Chicago Exposition of 1893. And some Negro dance bands were playing syncopated music there prior to the 1910s, well before the arrival of New Orleans' King Oliver and his contingent. Moreover, like New Orleans, like Kansas City, Memphis and New York's Harlem, Chicago was no tight-laced lady. Mobsters played a large role there, and, as in those other cities, the bootlegging that accompanied Prohibition spelled profits for numerous clubs, cabarets, joints and jukes—consequently, for jazz.

With conditions so propitious for black jazz bands, New Orleans musicians already established there were quick to urge their compatriots to come join them.

Joseph "King" Oliver (1885-1938) answered the call. He became part of the Chicago dance scene around 1919 and formed his Creole Jazz Band there in 1920. It was one of the most impressive groups of its kind, featuring brilliant musicianship and combining patterns of the blues with the verve and drive of energetic ragtime rhythms. With Oliver's hiring of his protégé, Louis Armstrong, in 1922, the Oliver band became a legend.

Listening to early recordings of Oliver today, despite the problems of the early acoustic system and a style that initially may strike us as archaic, his music, especially on replay, amply proves itself. It has variety, contrast of rhythm and melody and a beat that definitely swings. It is collective, ensemble playing, leaving little room for virtuoso solo improvisations. But amid the felicitous intertwining of all the instruments in the group, each part can be clearly distinguished and each has its own personality. Gunther Schiller most aptly sums up Oliver's early music in his description of its "joy, warmth of expression . . . its polyphonic complexity, its easy, relaxed swing . . . its lovely instrumental textures, and its discipline and logic."[287]

Unlike the big bands to come, Oliver's men did not depend on professional written arrangements. Yet one cannot assume that the players simply ad-libbed together to create music all of a piece. Oliver knew where he wanted his band to go, and he had musicians who knew how to get there. Their pieces were well rehearsed and more or less worked out by Oliver in advance of performance. Listeners might marvel at the apparent spontaneity of improvised duets by Oliver and Armstrong. But as Armstrong would later explain,[288] during a break the leader would lean over to him and move the valves of his horn, so that the young man would know how to fit his own music in. Moreover, Armstrong, the great improviser-to-be, did not let loose in free-swinging solos of any length while with Oliver but remained modestly content to play alongside his mentor in the role of second cornetist.

Most importantly, the emphasis was on disciplined teamwork. Oliver's group created an ensemble sound unmatched at the time. It was not, however, an exact duplication of his New Orleans product. For in the course of the Chicago years, Oliver's music, which had sounded less polished in New Orleans—with even a fluff or sour note here and there[289]—became smoother and more structured, adapting itself to the ears of more sophisticated audiences.

Although New Orleans players did not introduce jazz to Chicago, Oliver's band captured the city with its New Orleans ensemble style and certainly enriched and influenced existent music already there. And in Chicago as elsewhere the first black jazz style that white musicians would begin imitating and promoting in earnest was precisely that of Oliver and his contemporary New Orleanians.

The huge impact of King Oliver's band at Lincoln Gardens on aspiring white jazz musicians cannot be underestimated. Time and again white instrumentalists have testified to the importance of their trips to the south side to hear Oliver and his brilliant young trumpeter, Louis Armstrong. Members of the white New Orleans Rhythm Kings, Bix Beiderbecke, Benny Goodman and his brother Harry, the group calling themselves the "Austin City High School Gang"—Bud Freeman, Dave Tough, Frank Teschmacher, Jimmy McPartland—and others went nightly to take in the strains and rhythms of the groundbreaking virtuosos. Earlier, when the band played at Chicago's Dreamland Café, according to pianist Lil Hardin Armstrong, ". . . they'd line up ten deep . . . mostly white fellows . . . in front of that stand."[290] "They" included Hoagy Carmichael, Muggsy Spanier, Eddie Condon, George Wettling, to name only a few.

Oliver and his musicians, were, of course, constantly aware of the hangers-on and viewed them with mixed feelings. Seeing white musicians taking notes on their shirt cuffs (a practice that has been testified to again and again), they might attempt to camouflage their techniques in order not to be copied by what they termed "the alligators." But when it came to young admirers like Beiderbecke, Freeman or Spanier, they, in particular Louis Armstrong, were welcoming and helpful, even letting the neophytes sit in with them after hours. Recalling visits made by these aspirants, Louis' agent, Joe Glaser said, "I used to let them in free. Hell, they were kids and never had any money."

These white admirers of black jazz were not unaware of white jazz music. In fact, a number of them had discovered New Orleans jazz not through Oliver but, like Bix Beiderbecke, through available recordings of white ensembles imitating the black sounds. That is, primarily recordings of the Original Dixieland Jazz Band and the New Orleans Rhythm Kings, (see the following section). Novice players like the Austin High Gang cut their musical teeth on the NORK's records, slowing each section down until they had mastered it note for note. But a trip to Lincoln Gardens to hear King Oliver, especially after Armstrong had joined him, was a trip to a musical Mecca and joy to the ears. And it provided, at the same time, an education for the curious and aspiring neophyte.

So understandably, many an ambitious white lad scarcely out of knee pants would make his way to Lincoln Gardens in those days. As Bud Freeman tells it:

> The big, black doorman weighed about 350 pounds, and every time he saw us he would say, 'I see you boys are here for your lessons tonight.' He knew.[291]

White Ensembles On the Move

A white band playing New Orleans jazz (then generally known as ragtime) was first heard in Chicago in 1915, when Tom Brown and his ensemble began performing at Lamb's Café. Hyping themselves as a "Dixieland Jazz Band," they didn't last very long as a unit but prompted a host of white imitators. They were not, by the way, the first to use the word "jazz" in connection with the syncopated sounds of the South, for the term "jazz music" had been used earlier, at least since 1913 and probably before that.[292]

Two years later, in 1917, a white group from New Orleans calling itself "The Original Dixieland Jazz (or "Jass") Band" made history by cutting the first jazz record of music labeled jazz.[293] Unlike the New Orleans Rhythm Kings, a later white combo, the ODJB did not acknowledge its debt to black New Orleans musicians. However, their sound and their musical selections—delivered at a dizzying tempo[294]—were clearly the province of New Orleans and its Negro syncopators.[295] Headed by Nick La Rocca, who had played cornet with "Papa" Jack Laine's Reliance Brass Band, the ODJB had emigrated to Chicago in 1916. The following year, thanks to their highly popular performances at Reisenweber's Restaurant in New York, they were invited to make records for Columbia and Victor. Their most famous cut, "Livery Stable Blues," was a standard novelty number sprinkled with horse whinnies (a staple of New Orleans black cornetists) for comic effect.

So a white band was the first to record "Dixieland jazz" the name white musicians gave the New Orleans sound. Interestingly—and ironically—the talented New Orleans black cornetist, Freddie Keppard (who had already played jazz on the New York vaudeville stage) had been invited to make a record earlier. Had he accepted, the first recording of New Orleans jazz need not have been a white imitation. Keppard, however, declined the invitation, for fear, as his contemporaries claimed,[296] that his style and techniques might be copied if heard on record.

And an even greater irony: not only whites but many black listeners and players heard the ground-breaking African-American syncopations for the first time on recordings of white musicians. They would inspire players, both black and white, to make a career in the realm of Dixieland jazz.

The ODJB's recordings do not fare well when judged against those of other groups recorded shortly afterwards, and the group, frankly, did not compare with other bands, black or white, cutting records just a few years later. Granted, the recording process before 1925 put musicians at a great disadvantage. It was an "acoustic" or "mechanical" method (as distinguished from the later "electric" method, employing microphones). The "acoustic" system obliged players to face and direct their sounds at a big horn, either individually or in a group. Often, the recording studio had to be kept very warm, even in summer, in order to keep the wax soft enough for the recording stylus to etch into the disk. Band members, recording separately, had difficulty hearing each other. And they could generally not use regular drums, which would have knocked the stylus out of its groove in the wax (although one can hear some drumming by Tony Spargo on the ODJB recordings). Instead, bands often had to use wood blocks or other inferior substitutes for the drums that provided rhythm and drove the music in live performances.

Such facts may explain part of the ODJB's recording problems, although other groups, such as the New Orleans Rhythm Kings and King Oliver's Creole Jazz Band, faced much the same sort of obstacles in the early twenties but projected a superior quality and smoothness. In assessing the ODJB, critic Rudi Blesh gives them rather mediocre grades. Damning the group with faint praise, he opines. "While the playing of the ODJB does not equal the fine Negro playing of classic jazz, or even that of the more average bands . . . it must be considered a form of jazz."[297]

Other white bands were quick to ride on the success of the ODJB with similar five-piece ensembles, for example New York groups like Jimmy Durante's Original New Orleans Jazz Band[298] and Earl Fuller's Famous Jazz Band, which included future bandleader Ted Lewis. Then, in August of 1922, The New Orleans Rhythm Kings (NORK), a white jazz ensemble originating in New Orleans, recorded for the Gennett label.[299] This young group, headed by trumpeter Paul Mares and including clarinetist Leon Roppolo, trombonist George Brunies, pianists Elmer Schoebel and Mel Stitzel and drummer Ben Pollack, had been playing at Chicago's Friar's Club before the Gennett engagement. Their music, like that of the ODJB, clearly echoed the sounds of King Oliver and other black New Orleanians. As Mares would modestly explain later with: "We did our best to copy the colored music we'd heard at home. We did the best we could, but naturally we couldn't play real colored style."[300] Still, a comparison of the NORK's version of "Livery Stable Blues" with the original recording by the ODJB, shows the latter group superior, doing more polished ensemble work in keeping with the style King Oliver had been developing in Chicago and at times demonstrating a greater smoothness than Oliver.

The first African-American group to record was Kid Ory with "Ory's Original Creole Band" performing "Ory's Creole Trombone" in June, 1922. Edward "Kid" Ory (1886-1975) had led one of New Orleans' most popular bands from 1912 to 1919, before moving on to California. Although Ory recorded before the NORK did that same year, his record company, Nordskog of Santa Monica, provided such poor distribution that his music was virtually lost to the public. So it was only in March of 1923, when King Oliver first brought his band into the Gennett Studios of Richmond, Indiana, that a black jazz ensemble would be truly heard on disk. (Oliver's records with Gennett, OKeh and Columbia that year are considered among the finest of the genre. But contemporaries of Oliver were disappointed, finding little of the excitement and drive the band exuded in live performances.)

1923 was the year recording companies began issuing jazz records in earnest. And in July of that year the NORK made one of the first racially integrated records,[301] recorded with Gennett and featuring Jelly Roll Morton.[302] From that time, and through the second half of the 1920s, when electric recording provided a much higher fidelity than the old acoustic method, jazz ensembles, both black and white ones, came to mass attention via records.

Jelly Roll

In the framework of black and white musical relationships, Ferdinand Joseph Le Menthe, better known as "Jelly Roll" Morton (1885-1941) is an anomaly. He did not invent a particular style or musical gimmick that could be easily copied by whites or blacks (although he claimed to have been the inventor of jazz). Instead, his main contribution to both races—and to posterity—was his own superior talent as composer-arranger and pianist. One of the most important figures in the annals of jazz, Morton was the first musician in the new medium to put his compositions to paper, and many of those compositions, full of variety and rhythmic imagination, were brilliant and ground-breaking. Rooted in the ragtime tradition, Morton could execute rag rhythms with verve and precision. But his greatest legacy to the realm of jazz undoubtedly lay in his blending of ragtime and the blues. Jason and Jones analyze that blend thusly.

> In shifting the feel of ragtime from the brisk 2/4 to the looser 4/4, he removed the stiffness from his ragtime playing. He took the traditional three-chord harmonies of the blues and gave them an array of colors. Any good jazz player varies his effects, but Morton built variations into his composition as well as his performances.[303]

In his personal, seemingly effortless, modern sounding combination of sparkling ragtime and lowdown "gut bucket" blues, Morton accomplished what no one else had done, creating in the process a suave, sensual and sophisticated sound that would weave its way into modern jazz music.

It would be difficult to assign Jelly Roll Morton a clear role in the history of black and white musical interplay. And equally difficult to assess where he stood personally vis-à-vis white musicians and whites in general. In retrospect, he seemed to have glossed over whatever racial problems he and his black contemporaries may have faced. Still, the following facts are not without interest.

Morton was a light-skinned Creole. Proud of his French background, which he described in retrospect as far more upper crust than it was, he made a point, as did other fair-complected New Orleans Creoles, of pointing out that this or that other musician was dark in color. Twice married, he wed extremely light-skinned women, the first of whom spent her life passing as white. Morton did seem completely at home in Storyville dives and brothels—even proud of the times spent pounding the piano in that milieu. But most often the brothel in question was a high-class "palace," with upscale furnishings and chandeliers, where the handsome and gifted Morton could be pampered and shown off to advantage.

As for the whites around him, Morton worked well with and gave credit to those he admired, for example, members of Chicago's white New Orleans Rhythm Kings. And he did not appear to harbor any particular animosity toward his Caucasian contemporaries. In fact, most of his racial slurs were aimed at darker members of his own race. However, during his career he became increasingly aware that the white imitators were moving in fast on the jazz scene, and that fact gave him pause. Between 1930 and 1933, frustrated by a lack of cooperation or sense of discipline from his players who were unwilling or unable to follow his notated arrangements, he told them:

> You cannot play around, just because you think you're so great. I'm telling you those white boys are not playing corny any more. They're coming up right along. I hear

> them playing my tunes. They're getting the *idea* of how to play hot. Once they get it, they're going to use it. Then they're gonna sell *you* for five cents a dozen. If I ask you now to go out on a gig, it's thirty-five or forty dollars for the night. But it won't be long till you'll be around the club, standing on the corner, with your instruments under your arm and glad to get a five-dollar job.[304]

Morton's lecture had little to do with racial consciousness-raising but pinpointed a very practical reality. For in the heart of the Depression, the white "shadows" of black jazz bands were looming larger and larger and, as he foresaw, acquiring ever greater skills with which to rival the best black ensembles. Following the example of bands such as the ODJB and the NORK, other white groups had emerged, including the New York ensembles mentioned above, Chicago's Austin Five (the Austin High School Gang) and the Ohio based Wolverines, headed by Bix Beiderbecke.

Beiderbecke's name alone should provide proof enough that Jelly Roll Morton's prediction of serious white competition was far from an idle warning. The handwriting was on the wall.

Notes

248 *The Swing Era,* p. 703n.

249 "The European Roots of Afro-American Jazz," *Oxford Companion to Jazz,* p. 19.

250 According to Al Rose, Dave Perkins, a black New Orleanian who played with Papa Laine's white band, bought up a good number of such instruments when the Mexican military band left theirs behind after playing at the 1884-85 World's Fair. *I Remember Jazz,* p. 15.

251 See Chapter Three, *infra.*

252 *Ibid.*

253 According to an 1839 article in the *Detroit Free Press,* "As a composer or musician [Johnson] stands without rival in the States." Cited in Sanjek, Vol. II, p. 216.

254 A number of notables among nineteenth-century black society bandleaders are cited by Eileen Southern in *The Music of Black*

Americans. Among them are Peter O'Fake of Newark, N.J., Sy Gilliat and George Walker of Richmond, Virginia, and "Old Man" Finney of Detroit, Michigan. See pp. 340-341.

255 *Eubie Blake,* p. 59.

256 As in the "buzzard's lope." Animal dances had also been traditional in Africa.

257 Other animal dances popular in the early 1910s were the "mule walk," "eagle rock" and "fish tail."

258 "The Early Origins of Jazz," *Oxford Companion,* p. 45.

259 See Chapter Fifteen for a more detailed discussion of that relationship.

260 The label became popular around 1916-17, as we shall see.

261 See Chapter One, *infra,* p. xx.

262 Often combining African with French, Spanish or Haitian ancestry.

263 Very probably, there were exceptions to this commonly accepted distinction between the cultures of uptown blacks and downtown Creoles of color. But from what can be gleaned from chronicles and published interviews, that dichotomy may be accepted as a general rule.

264 From Morrison's interview with Schuller, *Early Jazz,* p. 363.

265 The prejudice against white gentlemen playing dance music had a long tradition. Dena Epstein wrote: "During the eighteenth century, neither gentleman amateurs nor professional musicians played for dancing or other casual entertainments. Only servants could." P. 112.

266 P. 85.

267 Bolden on cornet, along with clarinet, trombone, guitar, double bass and drums.

268 In 1942, Bunk Johnson, armed with brand new dentures for playing, did attempt to recreate the Bolden sound on records. But there has been enough controversy surrounding his revival of the past to make one hesitate to accept the re-creation as completely accurate.

269 According to his sister-in-law, Dora Bass, Buddy "broke his heart when he played." Cited in Marquis, p. 99.

270 Before that, stock arrangements for dance bands did not include parts for saxophones; a saxophonist would have to use the arrangement provided for cello.

271 Jim Europe called such sounds (achieved also by pinching the mouthpiece of wind instruments while blowing hard) "a racial characteristic." See *The Music of Black Americans,* p. 365.

272 Chapter Seven of Al Rose's informative *Storyville,* for example, demystifies in detail the theory that Storyville gave birth to jazz music.

273 According to Pops Foster's account, p. 37.

274 *Ibid,* p. 106. In fact, this book itself includes a good deal of data supporting the fact that many important jazz bands played the District.

275 A nephew of Storyville madam, Lulu White, Williams actually lived a few years in her brothel, Mahogany Hall.

276 Sometimes misspelled "Rappolo."

277 Interview with Jack Weber in *Hear Me Talkin' to Ya,* pp. 58-59.

278 See, for example, Dr. Edmond Souchon's charming account of his sneaking into Storyville as a lad with another ten-year-old. Disguised as newspaper boys, they hid nightly in the off-limits "district" in order to hear and ultimately exchange a few words with their idol, Joe Oliver. Related in *Reading Jazz,* p. 339.

279 *Storyville,* p. 122

280 Jelly Roll Morton, in his interviews with Alan Lomax, included in the book *Mr. Jelly Roll,* insisted (with some exaggeration no doubt): "There was no such thing as segregation at all in that section—in fact nowhere in New Orleans at that time," p. 19.

281 Foster, P. 61.

282 The word, taken from black slang, appears to have signified the sexual act (like rock and roll later). But it had been used in a variety of ways, and, undoubtedly, black musicians could be heard saying "Play that jazz." They did not, however, use "jazz" generally to identify their music.

283 See Clarence Williams' account of his early years in New Orleans in *Hear Me Talkin' To Ya,* p. 13.

284 See the discussion, below, of the recording of the Original Dixieland Jazz Band that year.

285 Sanjec, Vol. II, p. 291.

286 It had already doubled between 1890 and 1900. In 1910 the black population was well over 40,000, larger than most major black

communities in the South, including Nashville, Tennessee, and Charleston, South Carolina.

287 *Early Jazz,* p. 77.

288 *Hear Me Talkin' To Ya,* p. 104.

289 See Dr. Souchon's account in *Reading Jazz,* p. 346.

290 *Hear Me Talkin' To Ya,* p. 115.

291 *Crazeology,* p. 6.

292 See Stoddard, p. 193.

293 Black ragtime had already been recorded by bands both black and white. For example, the United States Marine Band made recordings of Joplin's "Maple Leaf Rag" in 1906. James Reese Europe's band, recorded by Victor in 1914, included ragtime inflected pieces in an orchestral format. But the ODJB was the first to record music in the ensemble style characteristic of the New Orleans black bands.

294 Perhaps because of recording exigencies and the need to get a piece on a disk accommodating only a minimal number of minutes.

295 As Gunther Schuller has noted (*Early Jazz*, p. 176n), it would have been highly unlikely that growing up in New Orleans La Rocca had not been exposed to the sounds of Storyville's greats, such as Bunk Johnson, King Oliver, Freddie Keppard *et al*. This view is confirmed by La Rocca's contemporaries. Bud Scott, for one, referred to the ODJB as "young white kids in New Orleans trying to copy our music" (*Classic Jazz*, p, 40). And Preston Jackson noted that La Rocca's band "used to hang around Joe Oliver and got a lot of ideas from his [band]" (*Hear Me Talkin' To Ya,* p. 42). Yet La Rocca went so far as insisting that Negro jazz was a fiction and that whites started the whole business.

La Rocca also vigorously claimed authorship of pieces of unknown origin, long played by black musicians, *e.g.,* "Tiger Rag" and "Livery Stable Blues" (formerly called "Barnyard Blues"), pieces which he was quick to copyright.

296 Sidney Bechet disputed that explanation, holding that Keppard had felt recording would turn their music into a business, thereby ruining it. See Bechet's autobiography *Treat it Gentle,* p. 112.

297 *Shining Trumpets,* p. 202.

298 Before becoming a famous comedian, Durante played piano. In forming this band, he sent away for New Orleans musicians such as the light-skinned Creole, George Bacquet.

299 That same year the Original Memphis Five, a group of mainly northern whites, also recorded, but the NORK's recordings were far better known and appreciated.

300 *Jazz Masters of New Orleans,* p. 128.

301 The author of an internet squib points out that critics are wrong in deeming it the first, since it was preceded in 1918 by the recording debut of Durante's band (which included Baquet, a Creole of color) and adds that Negro pianist/composer Clarence Williams recorded with a white group in 1921. See www.geocities.com/infrogmation/norkhist.html.

302 Gennett had a strong affiliation with the Ku Klux Klan. The NORK introduced the light-skinned Jelly Roll to Gennett personnel as "Cuban."

303 *Black Bottom Stomp,* p. 136.

304 *Mr. Jelly Roll,* p. 217.

11

BIG BANDS

THE BLACK PACE SETTERS

Introduction: The White Challenge

In the 1920s and 1930s white bands were becoming ever larger, ever more competent and ever more popular as they adopted jazz sounds that had once been the province of African Americans. In fact, certain white instrumentalists and leaders such as Bix Beiderbecke and Frankie Trumbauer (to be followed later by Jack Teagarden, Benny Goodman and others) were starting to produce the sounds of top-quality jazz, lacking only the authentic skin color.

It would not have seemed surprising in the least had the groundbreaking black musicians protested the white appropriation of the black sounds. Yet, even when the Depression hit America, narrowing the margin of opportunity for African-American musicians, complaints of an artistic takeover were not being voiced, at least not publicly. Not until the late thirties and early forties, after big band swing had become an increasingly white phenomenon, did black musicians and the black media truly sit up and take notice.

How can we explain such silence vis-à-vis a discernible encroachment by white musicians on traditional black artistic territory? For one thing, even in the twenties and early thirties, few African-American musicians imagined that they were creating a valuable "Art"[305] or manufacturing sounds that would become America's main contribution to world music. Their evolving syncopations were either a means of getting bread- or booze—on the table, a way of supplementing whatever day jobs they had, great fun and entertainment, a source of pride in outplaying or "cutting" the next guy, or simply a personal necessity.

Bearing this out, in the 1970s, recalling a rag he had composed, Eubie Blake confided, "It ain't until modern times that I ever really looked at it as a piece of music."[306] And near the end of his career Louis Armstrong would say to Earl Hines, "We didn't know we were making history, did we?"[307] The truth is that beyond the thoughtful analyses of a handful of astute critics,[308] the word "art" rarely figured in references to pre-swing jazz.[309]

Besides, even if African Americans had considered their music a valuable commodity, the white appropriation might have posed no real threat to them, given their past musical history. For since early times, whenever white musicians took over African-American musical inventions, the black creators had always managed to come up with solutions for survival. As we have seen, if whites pretended to be Negro minstrels, Negro entertainers could go one better by presenting their own "genuine" minstrelsy. If white vaudeville made black minstrelsy obsolete, blacks could counter with a new vogue: ragtime. And if white pianists decided to copy black ragtime piano, their occasional competition gave black musicians no cause for alarm; ragtime piano remained largely the province of African Americans. As for blues singing, that intrinsically Negro genre could not truly be appropriated by whites but, like ragtime, was only suggested or "whitened" in Tin Pan Alley transformations. In those areas, although black musicians might feel the weight of white economic control, culturally they were not disenfranchised.

In fact, many black musicians of the pre-swing era appeared quite tolerant and accepting of their white competitors. Some, undoubtedly, were flattered by the avid interest in black music demonstrated by white admirers. And a number of them were quick to pay tribute to white musicians of quality and acknowledge their expertise. Jelly Roll Morton, for instance, claimed that George Brunies of the NORK played the best trombone he had heard.

Trumpeter Rex Stewart recounted how the Fletcher Henderson band, convinced it was unbeatable, was amazed when Jean Goldkette's white unit "cut" them at Roseland Ballroom in 1927. He freely admitted, however, that Henderson's men had, indeed, been outplayed by their white rivals. Later, in an April, 1931, recording of "Singin' The Blues," Stewart, who held Bix Beiderbecke in reverence, faithfully kept to Beiderbecke's previous rendition of the solo.[310] (And, as we shall see, a good number of black musicians would wind up emulating their white emulators.)

But the tolerance and good will of black musicians toward their white imitators would be severely tried after 1935, once "swing" had become a national byword and an international vogue. For then, the balance of musical power would lie squarely in the hands of white musicians—or "ofays," as labelled by many blacks—and their entrepreneurs. Small wonder that many African-American musicians would come to experience a frustrated sense of entitlement.[311]

Meanwhile, however, during the twenties and thirties, black bands continued to provide the country with its most exciting music, little knowing to what extent they were contributing to the history of American music.

Black Jazz Before the Twenties

Today many critics draw a strong line between ragtime and jazz. But in fact, when the label "jazz" came in vogue at the time of World War I, it did not signal the introduction of a new genre. Instead, people were simply applying a modern, catchy word to what had previously been known as "ragtime" or "syncopated music." In fact, even as late as 1922, Rex Stewart called "Livery Stable Blues" (touted as jazz by the Original Dixieland Jazz Band) a ragtime piece, and he considered his own music "ragtime trumpet," which, "over the years, acquired names like 'get-off horn,' 'swing,' 'hot,' 'bop' . . ."[312]. Generally speaking, one could say that jazz was ragtime as it had evolved through the years, along with its ever-present counterpart, the blues.

Moreover, although we mainly associate ragtime with an old-fashioned honky-tonk bounce, at the start of the twentieth century, that music had already contained the sounds and feeling of our modern jazz. This is true of some compositions of that early master of ragtime, Scott Joplin—his "Solace," for instance. Although billed as a tango, the song's lazy interplay of rhythms and its recurring sustained blue note produce a smooth bluesy sound more typical of the thirties. An even more telling example is found in the music of pianist/composer Eubie Blake, who, with naturalness and ease, substituted a flowing, more sophisticated style for the old windshield-wiper ragtime regularity. As far back as 1899 Blake was varying the sound of his rags with a boogie-woogie bass—that is, decades before "boogie woogie" became a fashionable term for that jazz beat ("We called it a 'walking bass'," he said[313]).

Jelly Roll Morton claimed to have invented jazz in 1902. As improbable as that may seem,[314] many of his compositions had all the markings of modern jazz. Outside of his raggy rags and piano "fingerbreakers," he composed and performed blue-tinged, sensual pieces, using contrapuntal figures and a great variety of rhythms in the bass. His playing undoubtedly had the sound and swing of the jazz we know well before his first publication, "Jelly Roll Blues" in 1915.

In New York in the early 1910s, a sophisticated "Harlem stride piano" style was under way; instead of the trite honky-tonk sounds so often associated with ragtime music, stride pianists had developed a full, rich bass, great variety and unexpected melodic and rhythmic effects.[315] In New York and Baltimore players such as James P. Johnson, Eubie Blake, Willie "the Lion" Smith and Luckey Roberts were, according to Gunther Schuller, "in the vanguard of the Eastern jazz movement by virtue of their harmonic sophistication and increased technical virtuosity."[316]

As for the black jazz bands, their music was certainly in evidence at the very least a decade before the christening of jazz. Reb Spikes a sax player with Sid LeProtti's jazz band on the Barbary Coast, said that in 1907 they could have called their ragtime music "jazz."[317] And when he returned there in 1914 the style that had previously been called "ragtime" was then finally dubbed "jazz."

Add to that the fact that, although ragtime was supposed to be played (according to Joplin) exactly as written, non-reading black musicians of the ragtime era were said to "fake it." That is, they played around with a piece they had heard and worked jazz improvisations on the chords, whether they could identify those chords or simply "feel" them. For example, Sidney Bechet a confirmed non-reader, was improvising on the clarinet as a child, before 1910. He would not stay with his first teacher, George Baquet, because "what [Baquet] played wasn't really Jazz . . . he stuck real close to the line . . . straight out how it was written."[318] In the early twentieth century, a pianist like Jelly Roll Morton was improvising expertly, while the irrepressible Eubie Blake never played the same piece the same way twice.

In view of all this, it is clear that the New Orleans bands did not suddenly introduce a new music, jazz, to the nation. Those bands, with their particular instrumentation, their emphasis on a 4/4 tempo and their exciting style, did have the strongest impact on the development of jazz nationally.[319] But they were not its originators. As Eric Hobsawm put it, "All black America was ready to burst out into one form or another of the jazz idiom . . . at most new Orleans accelerated whatever tendencies toward jazz existed locally."[320]

Jazz has been a continuum, evolving throughout the years and throughout the country, metamorphosing into sundry forms and acquiring a variety of names. Even the relatively unspontaneous styles of swing heard in the late thirties and forties should rightly be included in the rubric of jazz.

Black Bands in the Pre-Swing Era (1920-1935)

Black jazz bands had early become ubiquitous, sounding out their rhythms on the East and West Coasts of the United States, in the South and Midwest. They flourished most notoriously in ports and in gangster-ruled areas. There, prostitution, gambling and illicit drinking in Prohibition years spawned speakeasies and provided ample opportunities for black jazz in myriad clubs, dives and dance halls.

Chicago was undoubtedly the most famous of jazz milieus of the twenties. With its considerable African-American population, its infusion of musicians from New Orleans and elsewhere and its gangland bootlegging, it hosted hundreds of ballrooms and clubs featuring jazz, particularly on the south side. Next in importance came Kansas City, Missouri. Ruled by gangster Tom Prendergast and local mobsters, Kansas City was home to a great number of black jazz ensembles, most notably the Benny Moten Orchestra and those of Andy Kirk, Harlan Leonard and Jay McShann. On the West Coast, Les Hite led one of Los Angeles' best known orchestras, which, at one time, would include trumpeter Dizzy Gillespie. In addition to such focal points of African-American jazz, a good number of other "territory" black jazz bands could be heard in areas throughout the country.

Many of the most prominent among the musicians in those territories would eventually gravitate to New York. This was strikingly true of Chicago, where opportunities for so many jazz musicians clustered there diminished in the late twenties. By that time, New York, with its increasing radio and recording opportunities and its visible stamp of recognition, had emerged as the Mecca of the jazz music business.

Whatever the locale, jazz venues of the time differed in organization and mode of operation. Some places, such as Baron Wilkins' Exclusive Club in Harlem and the Dreamland of Los Angeles, did business under black ownership. A good number of them, however, like Harlem's Connie's Inn, had white owners who often hired black managers to oversee the day-to-day operations. As for the clientele, certain of the ballrooms and clubs—Chicago's Royal Gardens, for instance (which had reopened in 1922 under the name "Lincoln Gardens")—geared themselves almost exclusively to African Americans. On the other hand, others, like Chicago's south side Sunset Café, were quick to welcome white visitors—and the increased income they produced. Thus the abundance in the twenties and thirties of the so-called "black-and-tans."

The black-and-tans offered entertainment by black musicians, and had black waiters and staff, but unlike Harlem's Cotton Club, which catered almost exclusively to whites, their clientele consisted of both African Americans and white visitors—whom their Negro hosts blithely referred to as "slummers."[321] In some black-and-tans white clients might have an area to themselves, while in others they felt free to mingle with the blacks there, at times dancing with them as well. During the twenties and early thirties, eager white dancers and jazz fans mixed nightly with blacks in well-known ballrooms such as Harlem's Savoy. And also in Chicago's Grand Terrace Ballroom, where, according to bandleader Earl Hines, "The audiences were mixed. Segregation never crossed anyone's mind."[322]

Unsurprisingly, however, segregation did cross people's mind, even on the jazz scene, and therefore not all jazz band venues were of the black-and-tan variety. So when a well-known black nightclub or ballroom did not attract or invite white patrons, it sometimes featured a "midnight ramble" or "frolic."[323] That is, after a regular performance for its black clientele, a club would raise prices high and open its doors to white visitors. Very often these were white musicians eager to hear—and sometimes jam with—the black jazz maestros after their own gigs had ended for the night.[324]

Until the late twenties, black jazz bands continued to be featured in prestigious venues such as the Moulin Rouge in Chicago and the Waldorf Astoria in New York, establishments catering to an exclusively white clientele. And throughout the thirties, radio audiences could hear Duke Ellington or Cab Calloway broadcasting from the Cotton Club, Chick Webb from the Savoy, Fletcher Henderson from the Club Alabam in Times Square (later from Roseland and Connie's Inn) or Earl Hines from Chicago's Grand Terrace Ballroom. For when radio was new, stations in search of cheap or free programming were wiring into prominent nightclubs and ballrooms and broadcasting live music from bands, including the better-known black ones.[325] (Any lack of payment to the orchestras was offset by free publicity over the airwaves.)

The engagement of black bands in upscale white owned nightclubs and ballrooms was short lived, however. Later, in the thirties, places such as New York's Waldorf Astoria, Roseland Ballroom and other downtown night spots would replace Negro orchestras with white ones. At that time only a chosen few among the highly talented (e.g., Duke Ellington and Louis Armstrong) would penetrate society's inner sanctum or feature in Hollywood films.

Black and White Bands: a Formula for Bigness

If we trace the history of well-known dance bands of the twenties and thirties, we find that virtually all of them steadily increased in size over the years. They may have started out with five or six pieces, adding a couple more every so often and reaching ten or twelve by the end of the twenties. In fact, if successful enough to survive into the forties, they could wind up, like Duke Ellington, with eighteen members distributed among brasses, reeds and a rhythm section consisting of drum, bass and piano.

Such increases may be attributed in large part to the strong popularity of ballroom dancing. For the dancers filling the ballrooms appreciated a smooth, full and lush sound for fox trots and waltzes and a bright, driving one for the lindy or "jitterbugging," as swing dancing was often called then. In any case, larger and larger ensembles became a must after 1935. Even King Oliver and other early New Orleans bands had to take on more musicians or risk fading out of the picture entirely.

With the greater number of instruments, bands began to depend increasingly on written arrangements, rather than attempt to wing it with the "head" arrangement used in small New Orleans combos of yore—that is, a general, unwritten idea of how to proceed, dreamed up by one or more band members and rehearsed until it more or less worked. Head arrangements continued to be used, but now, more and more, musicians would have to conform in the main to a written score or risk pandemonium. Consequently, they would be expected to read music.[326] They would also become part of a system which demanded increasing structure and discipline under the direction of a leader who, to keep a large band on track, was often autocratic. As for musical creativity, arrangers did allow greater space than in the past for individual solo flights by various instrumentalists, so people could hear a "hot" musician do his bit. However, any one player's improvisational contribution had to be limited to one or two solo breaks, assigned to this or that section of a set arrangement.

Arrangements had actually been used for years, usually "stock" arrangements, rather uncreative systems stocked by music publishers, such as Carl Fisher, and sold to dance orchestras of seven to ten pieces. Black bands as well as whites depended on them in the early twenties. But soon the standard stock arrangements would no longer suffice. Bands grew ever larger, listening audiences were becoming more and more sophisticated and improved recording techniques demanded greater professionalism and originality. The arranger—the competent arranger—was becoming as essential as the director of a Broadway play. Only in rare cases (as with Louis Armstrong) could the talent of a particular musician compensate for a banal arrangement.

While gifted white musicians created many fine scores for big bands, black musicians held sway in the field of arranging. One of the first and most important among them, Don Redman, is known principally for providing Fletcher Henderson with scores that would propel Henderson to the forefront of big band jazz. But soon other black musicians like Henderson himself, his brother Horace and the likes of Benny Carter, Andy Gibson, Edgar Sampson, Billy Strayhorn and Sy Oliver would create brilliant arrangements for big bands, both black and white. It was, in fact, Fletcher Henderson's scores that opened the way for Benny Goodman's phenomenal success. And in short time the gifted Mary Lou Williams would contribute excellent scores to bandleaders of both races, such as Benny Goodman, Earl Hines, Duke Ellington, Louis Armstrong, Tommy Dorsey and others.

The black ensembles cannot be credited with having invented the original formula for big band arrangements. That distinction may be attributed principally to Ferde Grofé, a white classically trained musician and noted composer. In the 1910s Grofé, undoubtedly, taking his cue from concert and military bands, began arranging dance music by grouping the instruments in separate units or "choirs" in harmony with one another. He alternated solo playing with polyphony and, importantly, granted a major role to saxophones. After 1916,[327] on the heels of Grofé's innovations, most dance orchestras began to consider saxophones a must and either added saxophone players or had their clarinetists double on sax.

Parenthetically, this late, seemingly hasty, introduction of the saxophone in bands may surprise us, especially since the sax would become so intimately connected with jazz and dance bands through the ensuing years. But earlier, the saxophone had not been a component of New Orleans jazz, since the New Orleans pioneers restricted themselves more or less to instruments used by nineteenth-century marching bands. And, further, the sax was not invented until close to the middle of the nineteenth century.[328] Played first in classical music, then taken up by vaudeville, the instrument was a long time in becoming part of the dance band scene.

Moreover, since whites were the first to adopt the saxophone in dance bands, the trained and more experienced white performers of the early twenties were often technically superior to aspiring African-American saxists. The latter, however, would not only close the gap but would advance beyond their white contemporaries in the realm of jazz. (Two cases in point: the brilliant improvisations of Sidney Bechet on soprano sax and the extraordinarily rich contributions of tenor saxist Coleman Hawkins.)

A white bandleader, Art Hickman, was one of the earliest to use saxophones. Hickman formed his first orchestra in San Francisco in 1913 with just six pieces, then acquired others through the years. Using Grofé as arranger and capitalizing on Grofé's formula of instrumental sections (and adding saxophones in 1919), Hickman was undoubtedly the first well-known leader to employ the new sectional type of arrangement that would come to characterize big band music.

Soon an up-and-coming Paul Whiteman would also use Grofé as his arranger, once again according to the concept of instrumental "choruses" in harmony, granting a special importance to the reed section. Indeed, it was Grofé who created the orchestral or "symphonic" sound that Whiteman was so proud of and who was greatly responsible for the white bandleader's overwhelming success.

So while black ensembles were continuing to break new paths in jazz, a white arranger and white dance bands of the 1910s and early twenties had provided a very practical model, a musical template, which would be used by bands of both races. As black and white dance orchestras both increased in size, they would depend more and more on competent arrangers and bandleaders to give the formula life and energy.

Although whites may have provided a practical musical template, when it came to creativity, the black bands were clearly the pace setters, once again developing an original sound out of a tried-and-true recipe. Most prominent among the jazz band pioneers was Fletcher Henderson. Henderson and his musicians would go well beyond standard formulas, creating an irresistible musical dynamic that would evolve into swing.

Fletcher Henderson and His Big Band

In the early twenties, before Fletcher Henderson started out as an orchestra leader, black dance ensembles in New York did not generally include jazz in their repertoire and were not known for their swinging beat. In fact, most of them followed the bland, commercial lead of an Art Hickman or Paul Whiteman. Although pianists like James P. Johnson and Eubie Blake had been creating jazz rhythms, and although small combos had their late night jam and "cutting" sessions, the larger black dance bands catered to their mainly white ballroom clients with standard two-steps, waltzes and tangos, along with tame ragtime rhythms, as heard in the orchestras of Ford Dabney, Will Marion Cook, Wilbur Sweatman or George Morrison.[329] Further militating against a jazz sound was the fact that popular bands tended to feature large banjo and violin sections rather than emphasize the interplay of brasses, reeds and percussion.

Fletcher Henderson, who formed his own orchestra in 1923, started out, like others, with a conservative sound, but in view of the public's increasing demand for exciting jazz music, he soon began to inject his dance music with a new vitality. In those days, black dance bands with players who could read music usually depended, like their white counterparts, on uninventive stock arrangements modeled on patterns set by Grofé. Henderson, too, used stock arrangements, but thanks greatly to his arranger Don Redman,[330] they became increasingly modified, varied and rhythmically more sophisticated and jazz oriented. Instrumental parts were added, transitions inserted, new, original endings substituted and substantial room made for improvisational jazz solos. By the end of the twenties, Henderson and his band were making far less use of stock scores or modifying them to a great degree and depending on their own head arrangements, with heavy input from Fletcher himself and his brother Horace.[331]

Ballroom dancers, radio listeners and record buyers of the twenties and thirties had come to appreciate hot sounds in dance orchestras. So improvisational solos throughout a piece became a must.[332] Fletcher Henderson made it his business to choose the finest of jazz instrumentalists for each section of his band. And besides insisting that his players be able to read musical scores, he expected them to be not only outstanding soloists but competent ensemble players as well. Artists such as Coleman Hawkins on tenor sax, Jimmy Harrison on trombone, Rex Stewart on cornet, Roy Eldridge on trumpet and Sid Catlett on drums provided superior grist for the mill.

Importantly, during 1924-25, Henderson, who had unsuccessfully tried to persuade Louis Armstrong to join the band, was able, finally, to bring the young trumpet player on board. Armstrong's short stint with Henderson afforded him greater visibility and the opportunity to hone his improvisational skills.[333] At the same time, his luminous groundbreaking improvisations, his innovative phraseology, his driving yet nuanced style had a considerable impact on arranger Don Redman and on Henderson himself. With arrangements that increasingly bore Armstrong's influence, the Henderson band moved rapidly in the direction of a swing idiom.

With Armstrong's arrival, big band music had to change. Although the neophyte Armstrong had felt challenged at the start by the professionalism of Henderson's band, after he began to play with them, they themselves would be challenged. His superior tone, his varied style, his ease, his timing, his daring but sure improvisations were original and unmatchable. With such a phenomenon, there had to be greater room for solo work and a greater propensity for swing. After Armstrong's stint with them, Henderson's band, like other bands of the time, could only evolve. As Rex Stewart explained, "The ensemble performers were no longer stilted and static, but rather free-flowing and as impelling as the improvisational solos."[334] Putting it more succinctly, Danny Barker, describing the post-Armstrong sound of the band, said that it "pulsed."[335]

So using Grofé's basic structure but infusing it now with a strong jazz feeling, or "pulse," Fletcher Henderson developed an ensemble deemed the best hot band in America—a band now considered the foremost pioneer of swing.

Unfortunately, the recorded music of the Fletcher Henderson orchestra rarely captures the hard driving, exciting sound described by his contemporaries. A good many of the pieces, even some from the early thirties, when his style had become more sophisticated, sound banal or plodding on disk. Some of the failure may be due to the fact that Henderson was often less prepared and careful than other bands when it came to recording. He and his players were undoubtedly also spiked by a live audience and possibly lost enthusiasm in a recording studio. Moreover, the time constraints of recording left them little opportunity to launch into their improvisational solos. But in fact, Henderson's work, recorded or live, was not always inspired. Indeed, at times—for example, after the great loss of Redman as an arranger[336]—it appeared to flounder. Throughout a series of ups and downs, the leader hit his stride particularly in the late twenties and the mid-thirties. Any jazz enthusiast hearing his later versions of pieces like "King Porter Stomp" or "Christopher Columbus" cannot but be carried along by Henderson's music, his animated call-and-response sections (often a three clarinet ensemble alternating with the brass) and, above all, his irresistible rhythm and drive. In other words, his swing.

The pieces just cited, like others in his repertoire, may be recognized as music that helped make the reputation of a white bandleader: Benny Goodman, touted as the "King of Swing." For such scores did wind up as Goodman property. The fact is that Fletcher, try as he might, could not continue to make it on his own. In winter of 1934 he was finally obliged to break up his band and sell his arrangements to earn money.

The Henderson orchestra, arguably the most advanced of bands, and certainly one of the most exciting, had an enthusiastic, if limited, following. Although his name was not a household word, fans of his radio broadcasts, dancers at Roseland Ballroom and a good number of jazz aficionados followed his music avidly. And his band felt confident of its superiority. Further, at least in the 1920s, during a period of post-war prosperity, Henderson did not have to struggle to find bookings or eke out a living.

His good fortune was not to last. Fairly easygoing and short on a sense of responsibility, after losing his Roseland job in the late twenties, he had to contend with an increasing lack of bookings to cover the band's salaries. And unlike Benny Goodman, Tommy Dorsey or Glenn Miller, he lacked the character and soul of a perfectionist. At times his players might show up at gigs and recording sessions; unfortunately, at others they either didn't appear or arrived hours late.

Other factors added to the weight of his ultimate failure. In 1928 he came out of an automobile accident with a broken collarbone, eventually leading to paralysis of his left side. After the accident, according to his colleagues, he appeared less sanguine and less interested in business matters. Add to that John Hammond's theory that Fletcher's awareness of the color bar dulled his ambition, making him "his own worst enemy."[337]

Certain important realities of the time played a strong role in Henderson's downslide. The main reality being that for a black band to succeed, it needed strong white backing. When Henderson started out, in the twenties, large booking agencies like William Morris or Music Corporation of America (MCA) did not take on Negro bands as clients. But at some point, especially in the thirties, he might have connected with any number of good booking agents, who could have kept him in business and in the public eye. In the twenties, Henderson had been riding the crest and was perhaps too complacent about it. He did use some agents for bookings but throughout most of his career, bookings and promotion were organized and carried out by his wife Leora. That do-it-yourself solution worked in the twenties but was highly unsuited to the following decade with its system of large white booking agencies.

An up-to-date white leader, Benny Goodman, would later succeed where Henderson failed. As Frank Driggs wrote, "Fletcher Henderson's band was excellent but Benny Goodman was . . . supported by a powerful booking agency, network radio programs, and a recording firm that could properly promote him . . ."[338 339]

One may well be reminded of a crass piece of advice about managers given by a New Orleans bouncer to Louis Armstrong: "Be sure and get yourself a white man that will put his hand on your shoulder and say, 'This is my nigger.'"[340] (Armstrong eventually took that advice and in May of 1935 hired a white agent—bootlegger, pimp and rapist—Joe Glaser. Despite Glaser's murky reputation, Louis never regretted his decision.)

Unfortunately, when agents did try to book Henderson they often found him and his band unreliable, with sometimes as few as fifty percent of them showing up for a recording engagement. Small wonder that with such absence of discipline and lack of backing, Fletcher Henderson and his band earned far less than their white contemporaries—even taking into consideration the fact that black bands customarily earned less than white ones. (Don Redman, for example, received only $25 per arrangement while with Henderson. But Paul Whiteman commissioned twenty arrangements from Redman—at $100 apiece!)

The going had become so difficult for Henderson, that in the winter of 1934 he was obliged to break up his band. It was at that point that John Hammond intervened, hitting on a solution whereby Henderson became staff arranger for Benny Goodman. In retrospect this may appear like one more example of racist exploitation, to wit: "Superb black bandleader relegated to the wings by white impresario while providing fledgling white leader with arrangements leading to the latter's fame and fortune." But that was not an accurate statement of the case.

John Hammond,[341] the scion of a wealthy family, was a champion of racial justice and a lover of African-American music. He had a fine ear for quality in black jazz musicians and while a producer for England's Columbia records he discovered, recorded and promoted top artists like Bessie Smith and Count Basie. He had become an ardent Fletcher Henderson fan. Early in the thirties, when Fletcher's career was about to collapse, Hammond obtained bookings for him and in 1932 produced what was to be one of Fletcher's greatest recording sessions.

Hammond, who also admired Benny Goodman, helped the young white bandleader form his first permanent band, in 1934. Up to that time Goodman had been torn between achieving high quality jazz or settling on the sort of commercial musical "fix" that would earn him quick money. Hammond's influence on Benny Goodman changed the quality of his music for the better, and Hammond's introduction of Henderson's arrangements got Goodman's band off the ground. On the other hand, at the same time, Henderson's providing Benny Goodman with his arrangements assured his own financial security. So Hammond undoubtedly considered that interracial marriage brokering as a win-win situation. (Yet, in 1961, Hammond would state: "[Fletcher] made great recordings of his own compositions which sold a minimal number, only to have the same tunes and arrangements cut by Benny Goodman with astronomical sales"[342]).

Henderson left Benny Goodman in 1935 to start up another orchestra. After a series of triumphs and failures he went back to arranging for Benny Goodman in the late thirties and again in 1945. Until the early 1950s he sporadically attempted various comebacks, sometimes even experimenting with a sweet sound à la Guy Lombardo, but returning now and then to the task of injecting Goodman's band with the Henderson vitality. Of this appropriation of black talent by an ambitious white orchestra leader, Gunther Schuller has written,

> Herein, then, lay the uncanny amalgam of success that precipitated the Swing Era: spicing up familiar commercial, popular material with a Harlem-oriented musical seasoning and selling it via a white band for a white musical/commercial audience."

And, bearing out John Hammond's view, Schuller adds,

> . . . in a number of instances Goodman took over, virtually intact, the identical arrangements Henderson had already previously recorded and performed for years. With Henderson these performances remained relatively unnoticed . . . with Goodman they became world hits.[343]

It was a fact of life. White jazz bands not only had entrée to ballrooms and big hotels but, with the blessings of media such as radio and recordings, they reached vast audiences. And, as usual, white entrepreneurs held the power and purse strings.

Other Pioneers

Although Fletcher Henderson was undoubtedly the most important progenitor of swing music, other black dance orchestras of twenties and early thirties were developing their own jazz styles, further contributing to the sound that led to swing. Most of the bandleaders had formerly worked as instrumentalists in other groups before venturing out on their own (Erskine Hawkins is a notable exception, having started his musical career as a leader).

Like Henderson, the majority of these bands did not set out with a hot sound but gradually worked their way to it.

McKinney's Cotton Pickers, organized by drummer William McKinney, began as a territory band in Springfield, Ohio, in 1923, the same year the Henderson band started performing. The band grew larger, acquiring a number of fine musicians, and in 1924 gave a command performance for the Prince of Wales at White Sulfur Springs, the famous West Virginia resort. It soon acquired gifted musician/arrangers John Nesbitt and Don Redman (who left Fletcher Henderson in 1927). The fortunes of the McKinney orchestra began to rise in 1926, when the white bandleader Jean Goldkette, organizer of a string of Goldkette orchestras, invited them to play at Detroit's Graystone (or Greystone) ballroom. Thanks to Goldkette's contacts, the band, which took the name "Cotton Pickers" in 1927, was able to record with RCA Victor and other companies.

The McKinney experience, while different from Fletcher Henderson's, has in common with it a leitmotif that will continue to run throughout this chapter: white backing for black bands. With both leaders, as with many others, white sponsorship was needed to keep them financially stable.

Two important contemporaries of McKinney, both based in Chicago, were Erskine Tate, performing at the Vendome Theater (before migrating to New York's Savoy and Cotton Club) and Earl "Fatha" Hines at the Grand Terrace Ballroom. In the second half of the 1920s these black bands were generating a kind of swing that pre-dated and often surpassed the swing of white bands of a decade later. If proof were needed, one has only to listen to Tate's 1926 superb recording of "Static Strut," featuring Louis Armstrong and the pianist Teddy Weatherford.[344]

As for Hines, despite extensive classical training, like so many other African-American musicians, he wound up choosing jazz as a surer route to financial success. Hines is known today more as a brilliant and inventive pianist than as a bandleader. Yet much of his energy went into fronting and leading dance bands in Chicago venues, principally the Grand Terrace Ballroom, with its Mafia "protection."[345] Hines' bands, like others of the day, became larger over time. They also developed an increasingly swinging style, and like the orchestras of Henderson, McKinney, Tate and so many other black groups, their sound antedated that of Goodman, the officially crowned "King of Swing."

Although starting out in the 1920s, and despite rough going in the mid-thirties, Hines' bandleading career extended to the forties, by which time he had been featuring such artists as singers Billy Eckstine and Sarah Vaughan and instrumentalists Dizzy Gillespie and Charlie Parker, who would both help move jazz into the realm of be-bop and beyond.

McKinney, Tate and Hines ranked among the most prominent of black bands outside of New York City. But New York had become the major center for dance bands, and a number of black groups there vied with Fletcher Henderson on that terrain.

Chick Webb's orchestra was deemed, with reason, one of the hottest of New York bands. It took several years for them to reach that level and achieve popularity. Leading his own band in 1926, at the age of seventeen, Webb experienced a series of ups and downs—the downs often attributable to naiveté and a trusting nature. Again, a white sponsor, agent Moe Gale, made success possible by opening the right doors.

Engaged as the resident band of Harlem's Savoy Ballroom in 1933, Webb's orchestra continued a tradition started there in the late 1920s: the Battle of the Bands. Fletcher Henderson, Fess Williams, Duke Ellington, Cab Calloway and others would appear after hours to challenge Webb in cutting contests, and he gave them severe competition. In fact, in 1937, when popular Benny Goodman went to the Savoy to do battle with him, Chick Webb won the day, hands down. He had created a fine band, a disciplined ensemble with aptly chosen top-of-the-line musicians. But it was undoubtedly thanks to the Webb vitality that the band won that night—a vitality created in large part by his percussion section and his own unbeatable command of the drums.

Chick Webb did not, of course, only perform jazz, since he played for a clientele that also wanted an appropriate beat for smooth dancing. Webb provided it with a lilting tempo and romantic melodies. Clearly, however, his forte was music that expressed his magnificent sense of swing and drive.

Webb's greatest commercial success came after hiring soon-to-be-famous singer Ella Fitzgerald (although he took her on with the greatest reluctance, since young Ella was far from the raving beauty most would deem suitable for fronting a band). While Webb's early recordings with Ella as vocalist included stunning jazz performances by his band, her popular sweet Tin Pan Alley ballads and novelty numbers ultimately took over the spotlight[346] and inevitably diluted the quality of the instrumental sound. Such was the case as well with Hines, McKinney, Andy Kirk and others who had to remain economically viable in the mid- to late thirties, when vocalists became an important, indeed, necessary feature of big bands. But listening to recordings of Webb from the early to mid-thirties, even shortly after Ella joined him, one is struck by the richness, the multi-textured variety, complexity, depth and energetic swing of his music.

Cab Calloway was, and is still, known for his showmanship, his gyrations in front of a band and, above all, for his chanting of "Minnie the Moocher," with its "heigh-dee-heigh-dee-heigh" and "ho-dee-ho-dee-ho"—phrases which became household words among both blacks and whites.[347] But although Calloway was primarily an entertainer and a fronter for an experienced ensemble (the Missourians), he did oversee the hiring of competent musicians who gave the band quality and an increasingly driving swing beat.

When Calloway first arrived in New York from the Mid-West in the late twenties, he had been playing with a group called the Alabamians. Their music consisted of old-time numbers and banal novelty tunes, mixed with a bit of passé Dixieland. They were totally crushed in Harlem playing opposite Cecil Scott's band at the Savoy, for as Calloway put it, "Those guys played gut-bucket-stomping, gutsy New York jazz."[348] After that he moved fast, leaving the Alabamians and taking over the Savoy's house band, the Missourians. By the late thirties and early forties the group included such players as sax players Chu Berry and Ben Webster, trumpeters Jonah Jones and Dizzie Gillespie and drummer Cozy Cole.

Calloway replaced Duke Ellington at the Cotton Club in 1931, and though he played there only three years, his name has been associated with the big Harlem nightclub ever since. Playing to the nightclub's white-only audiences, he was enormously successful there, and between the Cotton Club gig, subsequent theater engagements, recordings and profits from a corporation he had set up, his huge receipts enabled him to hire players such as those named above. In the midst of the Depression, while only in his twenties, Calloway was riding high indeed. Hired by Lucky Strike to do a radio show, he was the first African-American entertainer to break the national network racial barrier.

Of course, Calloway's unusual showmanship and appeal had attracted white backing, and without that backing such a level of success and strong financial base would not have been likely.

Jimmy Lunceford, who replaced Cab Calloway at the Cotton Club in 1934, led one of the most popular of New York bands, and like Calloway's, his unit achieved a high quality jazz sound over the years. Lunceford, like Andy Kirk, had had classical training as a youth in Denver with Wilberforce Whiteman (Paul Whiteman's father), on a variety of brass and woodwind instruments. He later studied at and graduated from Fisk University, where he would become Assistant Professor of Music, and at the City College of New York. He took as the nucleus of his first band a number of Fisk graduates, some of whom he had coached during a stint as Athletic Director at Manassa High School.

"Musicianship" and "discipline" are words that Lunceford's contemporaries have often used to describe his technique as a leader and to explain the high quality ensemble performances of his band. But much of that success may be attributed to fine arrangements, notably those of trumpeter Sy Oliver. Oliver's scores were highly danceable, featuring the "Lunceford two-beat," described by Paul Simon as a "light, loping, swing." Adding to Lunceford's popularity as a bandleader was his showmanship. For example, before Glenn Miller appropriated the gimmick, Lunceford had his band raise their derby hats, bobbing them up and down to the rhythm of a particular section of music.

Lunceford, despite losing some of his top men,[349] continued swinging into the forties (he died in 1947). But given the economics and politics of the music world, the high quality of a black band did not ensure its success. As might be expected, well-placed whites were instrumental in furthering Lunceford's career. For instance, white publisher, Irving Mills, engineered recording engagements for the band. Of course Mills took a sizeable cut from such engagements, as was his wont. And in order to get his firm's music recorded and on the air, Mills made sure that Lunceford used one of his own arrangers. So the band recorded white arranger Will Hudson's scores, including "White Heat" and "Jazznocracy," complex fast numbers untypical of Sy Oliver's more relaxed style. But a far more telling example of the white connection was revealed in the forties, toward the end of Lunceford's career, when the band learned that they were actually owned not by Lunceford but by white agent Harold Oxley, who was paying even Lunceford a salary.

Other black bands of the twenties and thirties were prominent in the evolution of jazz to swing. Some of them, functioning as "territory bands," played outside the New York or Chicago area. Such was the case of Andy Kirk and his Kansas City "Clouds of Joy." Like other black bands, Kirk's began with stock arrangements but by 1930 had acquired good scores from professional arrangers. The orchestra had many admirers and achieved a certain renown in its time. But despite the fact that Kirk, like Lunceford, had had solid training under Wilberforce Whiteman, he lacked the discipline of a Lunceford, and his career as bandleader would reach a series of considerable lows as well as highs.

One of Kirk's best moves was hiring, in the late twenties, the extremely talented pianist/arranger Mary Lou Williams—immortalized by their number "The Lady Who Swings the Band." For she was, indeed, largely responsible for their swing. John Hammond gave Mary Lou good support, but the band's more important white "angel" was agent Joe Glaser, who booked them into a Cleveland ballroom where they could broadcast over a national hook-up in a program featuring a top sports commentator of the day. Commented Mary Lou Williams, "What power and money can do!"

Among the most influential bands in the Midwest were Walter Page's Blue Devils of Oklahoma City and Kansas City's Bennie Moten's band. The Blue Devils started out in 1926, four years later than Moten's group. Its one recording, "Blue Devil Blues" (1929), a lowdown blues number, is testimony enough that the band had unusual quality and swing. This was due to a great extent to fine jazz musicians like Oran "Hot Lips" Page on trumpet, Bill Basie on piano and blues vocalist Jimmy Rushing. However, that memorable band not only fell victim to the Depression but in no time was raided by rival Bennie Moten, who appropriated "Hot

Lips" Page, Rushing, Basie (later to be christened "Count") and the disenfranchised Walter Page himself on double bass.

As for Moten, although starting out in 1922 with an old-fashioned ragtime beat, he eventually—thanks largely to his forays into Page's outfit in the early thirties—wound up leading one of the nation's finest swing orchestras. Later Basie's own band would follow Moten's lead, in emphasizing the blues. But Moten's impact on swing ran deeper than his passion for the blues. As Marshall Stearns has explained:

> The Moten band raised the riff[350] to a fine—and even improvised—art, while retaining the blazing solo work of top jazzmen, and frequently combined the best of both . . . the over-all goal was always a more flowing, driving rhythm, with which even the riffs were never allowed to interfere. With the same goal in mind, the guitar was substituted for the banjo, and the string-bass began to 'walk,' or play melodic figures instead of pounding away at one or two notes. All of these innovations of the 1932 Moten band became standard five or six years later.[351]

In New York City, ranking among the most popular black bands were Cecil Scott and his Bright Boys at the Savoy and Roseland; Charlie Johnson, whose blue sounds could be heard at Small's Paradise;[352] Luis Russell, who helped create the modern swing sound by substituting the string bass for the tuba and whose fine band often backed Louis Armstrong; Teddy Hill heard broadcasting from the Savoy Ballroom (and later to be involved in bop music); Willie Bryant, dubbed "The Mayor of Harlem," whose various ensembles at the Savoy and elsewhere featured top New York instrumentalists.

A more famous jazz figure, William "Count" Basie, was born in New Jersey in 1904 and began his career a few years later than most of the black bandleaders discussed here. In 1928, stranded in Kansas City while playing piano gigs, he remained there with Walter Page's Blue Devils, the ill-fated band with the unforgettably hot sound. With Moten's raid on the Blue Devils, Basie, along with and other members of the group, joined the Moten orchestra. Then, in the mid-thirties, after Moten's death and the breakup of his orchestra, Basie formed his own nine-piece unit featuring musicians of the Moten group, including the endurable former bandleader and bassist, Walter Page

Certainly, Basie's has been among the most admired and respected of the swinging black bands. His orchestra acquired that distinction although Basie himself was neither a strict perfectionist nor a disciplinarian. He and his group put less stress on precision ensemble work than Jimmy Lunceford and others. In fact, they sounded fairly loose at times. Rather than depend on fine arrangers, Basie and his band often devised "head" arrangements with a more spontaneous feel to them. According to Billie Holiday, who sang with the band in the late thirties, here is how, typically, Basie's arrangements would take shape.

> The cats would come in. Somebody would hum a tune. Then someone else would play it over on the piano once or twice. Then someone would set up a riff a ba-deep, a ba-dop. Then Daddy Basie would two-finger it a little. And then things would start to happen . . . [353]

As haphazard as such a procedure—or lack of procedure—may seem, the end result could be impressive. For lending the band a special vitality was its rhythm section, consisting of drummer Jo Jones, bassist Walter Page, guitarist Freddie Green and, of course, Basie himself on the piano. And the Basie orchestra also included such choice Blue Devils alumni as trumpeter Oran "Hot Lips" Page, vocalist Jimmy Rushing and Lester Young on the sax. What with Basie's blues background as pianist with the Page and Moten bands, blues always remained a top priority with him, and few bands could match his rendering of them.

Enter the white connection. In 1935, John Hammond, on the road in Chicago, happened to be turning the dial of his car radio to the far end and reached a small station, W9XBY, transmitting from Kansas City over a police-call wavelength. What he caught was Count Basie and his band broadcasting from the Reno Club, a rather seedy K.C. dive. The rest is history. The story, told many times over, is that Hammond, blown away by the band, contacted agent Willard Alexander of Music Corporation of America (MCA).

Alexander left New York and caught Basie's performance at the Reno Club. He found the band a bit rough around the edges but exciting, and he signed them up. Naturally that meant important bookings and recording dates for Basie and company.

The Count Basie orchestra remained strong, continuing even after Basie's death in 1984. Given the odds favoring white musicians, whether the band could have had such a long career without white backing seems dubious. In any case it still survives at this writing, a "ghost band," under the leadership of Grover Mitchell, and includes several instrumentalists who played under Basie himself.

The two greatest names in the history of black bands of the era are indisputably Duke Ellington and Louis Armstrong. Armstrong, however, cannot be truly counted as a bandleader, for unlike Ellington and other big names considered here, he did not assemble and direct a specific orchestra known under his name. Rather, he hired various bands to back him up. Even if his acts were billed as "Louis Armstrong and His Orchestra," the ensembles had been selected *ad hoc* to set off his formidable skills.

Ellington, however, was an orchestra leader *par excellence,* possessed of talent, taste and organizational know-how. Most importantly, besides his skills as a leader and superb pianist, Ellington wrote—or had a hand in writing and arranging—the music played by his band. The fact that he developed his compositions with specific orchestra members in mind contributed to the quality of their overall performance. And the musical creations themselves had depth, richness and beauty enough to ensure Ellington's reputation as the foremost composer in American jazz history.

His success owed little to any formal training. Rather, he had acquired his musical knowledge on a hit-or-miss basis. Early on, a conservatory-trained pianist took young Ellington under his wing and taught him to read music. After that, a high school teacher took an interest in him and gave him the fundamentals of harmony. As for his jazz education, he claimed he learned from hearing people whistling in the street or playing the syncopated music in black pool halls and dives. The highlight of his early "education" in jazz piano was a 1921 piano roll by James P. Johnson. Day after day a friend slowed his player piano mechanism down so that Ellington could see each note of Johnson's "Carolina Shout" as the keys went down and up, until, finally, he could imitate the piece perfectly.[354]

In his early teens Ellington not only played in dance bands but successfully organized and hired out his own units. Although he was adept in art, he apparently turned down a scholarship to Pratt Institute when in high school. It was certainly true that the dance music world offered an aspiring and talented African American far greater opportunity and remuneration than most other fields. But in any case, like so many others, Ellington could not resist the call of black jazz, a medium he would often refer to as "the music of my people."

He began to make a name for himself in his native city, Washington, D.C., but would rise to fame only after 1923, when he took a likelier route to success, New York City. Starting as a pianist with Elmer Snowden's "Washingtonians," he took over the band after Snowden left and in no time at all was showered with such rave reviews as "the hottest band this side of the equator."[355] Agent Irving Mills heard the five-piece group at the Kentucky Club and immediately became Ellington's backer.

Besides taking forty-five percent of Ellington's profits and royalties, during his fourteen years as Ellington's booking agent, Mills would add his own name to most of the Duke's compositions. This was not unheard of; on the contrary, it appeared to be standard practice at the time. But of course, without that white backing, fame and fortune might have remained a dream. Mills secured record deals with Columbia and had Ellington's band booked at the Cotton Club (replacing King Oliver, who had declined the job) from 1927 to 1932. His career was launched. His Washingtonians, expanded to fourteen fine instrumentalists (including those masters of jungle growls, Bubber Miley and "Tricky Sam" Nanton) along with vocalists such as Ivie Anderson, traveled to Hollywood and won acclaim throughout the States and Europe. For decades, Duke Ellington would make history with his recordings, his live public performances and his own compositions.

As an orchestra leader, Ellington's apparently easy going, loose *modus operandi* in rehearsals would seem to belie the precision of his performances. According to trumpeter Rex Stewart, the Duke would arrive with some scraggly pieces of paper with a few of his notes. He might have some parts for saxes but nothing for sax player Johnny Hodges. So at one point Duke might say casually, "Hey, Rabbit [his nickname for Hodges], give me a long slow glissando against that progression" and then yell to Cootie Williams 'Hey Coots, you come in on the second bar in a subtle manner growling softly like a hungry little lion cub . . ."[356] And Ellington would not hesitate to change the structure of a score entirely from top to bottom, at the last moment. Yet the end result was, invariably, quality.

At the close of the thirties, when other leaders of big bands, both black and white, were nearing the end of the road, Duke Ellington's fortunes were on the rise. He exchanged agent Irving Mills for Willard Alexander, who had just left MCA to open a band department for the William Morris Agency. Alexander had far better contacts than Mills and immediately booked Ellington's band into prestigious places such as Boston's Ritz Carlton and Chicago's Hotel Sherman. And while retaining a number of long-term band members, Ellington added fine new talent such as bassist Jimmy Blanton, in 1939, and tenor sax Ben Webster, in 1940. But most important for Ellington was the start, in 1939, of his nearly three-decade association with pianist/arranger Billy Strayhorn. Strayhorn not only took over most of the daily work of arranging but he became, in effect, Ellington's co-composer and, indeed, is credited as composer of the band's theme song, "Take The A Train."

That Ellington himself was prolific and outstanding as a composer was no mean feat for an African-American artist of the big band era. As we have seen, unlike white bands, colored units could not spend weeks at a time in hotels while on the road; instead they most often had to undergo a continual series of back-breaking one-nighters here and there, finding food or rest on a catch-as-catch-can basis. Consequently, Ellington often had to compose and jot down his work hastily while traveling on the road. The phrase "ivory tower" had no relevance in such circumstances.

Besides facing such handicaps, creating music designed to accompany dancing would have posed a problem to any serious composer, black or white. As Ellington well knew, he had first of all to keep the dancers happy. For one thing, that meant providing a strict tempo for their foxtrots or jitterbugging. Moreover any dance number had normally to be built around the format of Tin Pan Alley 32-measure compositions. Along with introductions, reprises and codas, they comprised three-minute-or-so packages—a span just long enough not to bore a dancer with a given rhythm or partner. Although

Ellington claimed that his dancing public inspired him, he clearly yearned to create more than the standard ballroom product.

So he went on to compose longer concert pieces, such as "Reminiscing in Tempo" (1935) "Black, Brown and Beige," presented at Carnegie Hall in 1943. Such extended works contained elements of beauty but received mixed reviews from critics of the day.[357] As a composer, Ellington is primarily remembered now for his beautiful, more popular, dance compositions such as the sensuous "Mood Indigo" the leisurely syncopated "Satin Doll" or the exotic "Caravan." Like poets of yore, he was obliged to create his own musical "sonnets" working within a standard tight framework.

However, despite the exigencies of ballroom dancing, despite the fact that his music was tailored to—and sometimes shaped by—the talents of certain players and despite all the obstacles confronting an African-American composer on the move, there is no denying the quality of Ellington's music, its tone, its variety, its richness. Although the Duke was passed over for a Pulitzer Prize in 1965 (two members of the jury immediately quit in indignation), he has rightfully been honored by universities, American presidents (Johnson and Nixon) and dignitaries abroad. Musical expert Gunther Schuller, after analyzing Ellington's compositions, concludes: "In jazz he was a giant among giants . . . he may yet one day be recognized as one of the half-dozen greatest masters of our time."[358]

Ellington was much more than just a swing bandleader and, indeed, transcended any one particular trend or movement in jazz. In other words, he was Duke Ellington. Still he may be seen as an important pioneer of swing, for his dance music had a swinging flow and drive well before "swing" became known as such. And he contributed a greater richness and beauty to that music than most of his contemporaries and more than almost any of his successors. He also helped provide a label for the future vogue with his famous 1932 recording of "It Don't Mean a Thing (If It Ain't Got That Swing)."

So Duke Ellington, Basie, Moten and their black contemporaries were swinging in those decades, as their predecessors had been doing at least since the time of Jelly Roll Morton. Recordings make it amply clear to us today that the black bands of the twenties and thirties were already employing the rhythms and techniques of the music that would lead to a white phenomenon labeled "swing."

In that same time period, other black bands were, similarly, developing those pre-swing sounds, Unfortunately, many of them are relatively unknown today or completely lost to musical history. For as we have seen throughout this chapter, in order to achieve recognition, in fact, in order to survive, such bands needed much more than sheer talent. Their success—their very existence—depended, once again, on that key figure, the well-connected white entrepreneur.

* * *

In the second half of the thirties, the Swing Era was officially launched. During that time, white musicians would, directly or indirectly, incorporate techniques and sounds developed by the black bands. With an eye to the bottom line, white orchestra leaders would smooth, commercialize, package and publicize that music—and, of course, make capital of it.

Notes

305 In 1922, according to clarinetist Garvin Bushell, the Dodds Brothers, playing with King Oliver, did think of themselves as original creators, indeed, "artists." (See *Jazz Masters of New Orleans,* p. 90.) Such a stance, however, appears to have been rare.

306 Rose, *Eubie, p. 42.*

307 Cited in Hogsbawm, *The Jazz Scene,* p. 29.

308 The first "serious" reviews of jazz music began appearing in *Phonograph Monthly* in 1927, with conservatory trained critic R.D. Darrell describing the "sonority" and "tonal qualities" of Ellington's "Black and Tan Fantasy." See *The Ellington Reader,* p. 33 *ff.*

309 According to Charley Gerard, even after swing had taken over, ". . . back in the 1940s, claiming that [a black jazz musician] deserved to be treated as an artist was a revolutionary concept in the music business." *Jazz in Black and White,* p. 14.

310 Black sax player Benny Carter copied Frankie Trumbauer's solo in the same number back in the twenties. He later explained that he had found nobody else as interesting to listen to at that time (*Swing to Bop,* p. 34).

311 Examples of consciousness-raising vis-à-vis white appropriation of swing in the late thirties are cited in *Jazz: a History of he New York Scene,* p. 296. According to one article of that time, published in the black newspaper *The New Amersterdam:* ". . . the success of or best swing bands has been hurt by the scores of imitators that have sprung up among ofay musicians."

312 *Jazz Masters of the 1920s,* p. 48.

313 *The Eighty-Six Years of Eubie Blake.* Columbia LP. This was said à propos of his "Charleston Rag," an 1899 composition. Originally titled "Sounds of Africa" by Will Marion Cook, Blake later renamed his piece for the Charleston dance of the twenties.

314 Outside of the grandiloquent boast, he would have been only twelve at the time—unless, as some critics maintain, he was born in 1885 rather than 1890, as he himself claimed.

315 According to Jasen and Jones, "The hallmark of stride is the *alternation* of syncopations between the hands. The left hand is often relieved of its duty as a metronome, set free to jam with the right, to provide syncopated countermelodies, and to produce unexpected accents to contrast with those in the upper octaves. Stride literally doubles the possibilities for syncopations . . ." *Black Bottom, p. 72.*

316 *Early Jazz,* p. 255.

317 *Jazz on the Barbary Coast,* p. 78.

318 *Treat It Gentle,* p. 79.

319 James Lincoln Collier, in stressing the impact of New Orleans music, wrote "it is abundantly clear from business newspaper accounts that there was no jazz in New York until the New Orleans bands arrived, and the same is true of the West Coast." (*Jazz, the American Theme Song,* p. 202). That statement is correct in that nothing actually christened "jazz" was read about earlier in newspapers, but certainly, the sounds of unlabeled jazz were already present in those locales.

320 *The Jazz Scene,* p. 23.

321 According to sax player Reb Spikes, at Purcell's in San Francisco, the place was small, so ". . . we didn't have any special area for the tourists and slummers to sit in." *Jazz on the Barbary Coast,* p. 95.

322 Quoted in *Jazz; the American Theme Song,* p. 16.

323 As did the theaters described above in Chapter Six.

324 Where the "midnight ramble" format did not apply, some aspiring white musicians might still appear in night spots that catered to a black audience.

325 As we shall see in the following chapter, the white bands had a far more prominent national coverage on radio.

326 Some, like Bix Beiderbecke, could never meet that expectation. Sidney Bechet patently refused ever to learn to read music, convinced, like many other New Orleans players, that it would sap his originality and spontaneity. On the other hand, Louis Armstrong, who shared that belief, did eventually learn to read musical scores.

327 Dance bands had used saxophones before that date, around the time they became included in stock arrangements, but now began considering them a necessity.

328 By Adolphe Sax, a Belgian musician/inventor, who produced and performed on a bass saxophone in 1842, then went on to create other types of saxes in various keys.

329 Jeffrey Magee makes the point that the lack of jazz styling in black bands of the twenties was not a failure but a sign of cultural assimilation and proof that black musicians could succeed in a white musical sphere. See *The Uncrowned King of Swing,* p. 29 and *passim.*

330 Trained at the Boston Conservatory of Music and the Detroit Conservatory of Music.

331 They also made use of outside arrangers such as John Nesbitt, Benny Carter and white Bill Challis.

332 Not all soloists could "wing" it completely before an audience, and it would especially risky to attempt it in a recording studio. Rather than try to create a solo spontaneously, on the spot, musicians often practiced and set much or even all of it in advance.

333 The stint with Henderson also obliged Armstrong—who had earlier learned the rudiments of reading music with Fate Marable, but who preferred playing by ear—to decipher and execute a detailed, annotated arrangement.

334 *Jazz Masters of the Twenties,* pp. 22-23.

335 *A Life In Jazz,* p. 70.

336 Redman left in March of 1927 to become co-leader of the McKinney Cotton Pickers band.

337 Documentation for CDs, *The Fletcher Henderson Story,* p. 16.

338 *Ibid,* p. 46.

339 Additionally, Magee emphasizes the fact that the band members were not too happy about being "protected" by white agents and seemed particularly hostile to John Hammond, who was anxious to further Henderson's career. See p. 169.

[340] Bergreen, *Louis Armstrong, An Extravagant Life,* p. 376.

[341] Discussed earlier, in the last section of Chapter Nine.

[342] Documentation, *The Fletcher Henderson Story,* p. 16.

[343] *The Swing Era,* p. 9.

[344] On the 1977 LP *Sweet and Low Blues.*

[345] Al Capone was the most notorious among the Mafiosi there.

[346] As commercial as that may seem, it should be noted that before Ella, Webb's vocalist Chuck Richards, alternated between an aping of Louis Armstrong's singing and a sickly sweet crooning of corny songs (e.g.: "Why Should I Beg For Love?")

[347] Cab Calloway and his "heigh-de-heigh" have been recently featured on "Sesame Street." In 1932, his gyrations were filmed by the Fleischer brothers and transposed by designers into a "Betty Boop" cartoon. In the animated short Calloway wound up as a writhing walrus ghost backed by a hot band of skeletons.

[348] *Of Minnie the Moocher and Me,* p. 38.

[349] He replaced arranger Sy Oliver (lost to Tommy Dorsey) with the talented Gerald Wilson.

[350] Riff: a short improvisational jazz phrase, around two measures long, introduced in a number and often repeated or called back and forth by different instrumental sections.

[351] *The Story of Jazz,* pp. 204-5.

[352] A good example of the Johnson sound may be heard in a 1929 recording of "The Boy in The Boat," *Sweet and Low Blues* LP.

[353] *Lady Sings the Blues,* pp. 61-62.

[354] Ellington was not the only young musician to use that technique. Ethel Waters advised Fletcher Henderson to study Johnson's "Carolina Shout" in order to have more swing in his music. And that piano roll number would become known as a "test piece" for other aspiring jazz pianists such as Fats Waller.

[355] See *The Duke Ellington Reader,* p. 23 *ff.*

[356] Quoted in *Jazz Masters of the Thirties,* pp. 97-98.

[357] We shall treat John Hammond's negative criticism of "Reminiscing in Tempo" in Chapter Fourteen. More recently, however, Gunther Schuller found excellence in that same piece (see *The Swing Era,* p. 74 *ff*).

[358] *The Swing Era,* p. 157.

12

BIG BANDS

THE WHITE PRESENCE

The 1930s saw the rise of the white swing bands and their virtual takeover of American popular music. The thirties also brought with them economic catastrophe on the heels of the Wall Street Crash of 1929, a disaster which dealt its blows to the popular music business as to other industries of the day. Was there a direct cause-and-effect relationship between Depression economics and the rise of the white swing bands? Not entirely. Economic factors contributed greatly to their success. But so did the style and quality of the music produced by the white ensembles. And the racial caste system would play a very strong role in bringing white swing music to the forefront.

But before discussing the rise of the white swing orchestras, let us put the subject into perspective by examining the situation of African-American and white musicians during the years of the Depression.

Depression and The Big Bands, Black and White

Both black and white bands faced serious problems after the Crash of 1929. For one thing, they had each been greatly dependent on income from recordings, but the record industry was hit hard in the early thirties, particularly by competition from radio programs. In fact, record sales dropped from over 100 million in 1929 to as low as five or six million in 1933. Making matters worse, the burgeoning movie industry with its escapist films was drawing audiences away from jazz and dance venues. And the "talkies," a fact of life since Jolson's 1927 *Jazz Singer,* deprived many a silent film piano or organ accompanist of a job.

As might be expected, opportunities were even scarcer for African-American musicians than for white ones. Of course, many blacks could have said "What Depression? It's always been Depression for us." And in a number of ways that was true. For the lyrics of the blues provide ample testimony to the fact that even in the boom years of the 1920s, the black population remained at an inferior, often precarious, socio-economic level. Then, in the thirties, when the financial status of many whites took a dramatically steep drop, the blacks, of course, had less to lose. But lose they did, with the economic scale running its customary gamut—in descending order—from white males, to white females, to African-American males to African-American females at the nadir.

For black band players in the thirties the news was not all bad, and their situation would have its ups as well as its downs. On the down side, the repeal of Prohibition at the end of 1933 forced the closing of a good number of speakeasies throughout the nation, places which had provided African-American jazz musicians with employment opportunities. Further, in New York, after 1935 race riots in Harlem, uptown was considered unsafe[359] for the white clientele of such cabarets as Connie's Inn and the Cotton Club.

On a brighter note, however, Harlem's Savoy Ballroom and the Apollo Theater continued successfully to host black band music throughout the decade. Moreover, as with the white orchestras, the repeal of Prohibition saw the opening in many areas of the country of new cabarets and clubs for black players. And, as in the white arena, a number of cafés and ballrooms which had prospered as speakeasies became cheap dance halls with wall-to-wall couples swaying through the night. Such dance halls, whether catering to a white or black clientele, demanded live dance music (often with each frustratingly brief three-minute-or-less segment costing a customer his hard earned dime). In those venues and elsewhere, opportunities for African-American band players were available, even during the Depression years.

And significantly, in the second half of the thirties especially, jobs opened up for black band players in the downtown district of New York City. In 1933 Connie's Inn had already moved from Harlem to the Palais Royal at 200 West 48th Street, and the Cotton Club took over those premises in 1936. The most famous of the black jazz bands, Fletcher Henderson, Duke Ellington, Cab Calloway, had been playing downtown since the 1920s, but the trend in that direction increased in the late thirties. The Empire Ballroom, the Onyx Club, the Yacht Club, Nick's Tavern, the Diamond Horseshoe, the Kentucky Club and Café Society Downtown are but a few of the downtown spots hosting ensembles of Lionel Hampton, Count Basie, Benny Carter, Fats Waller and other black jazz musicians.

Some renowned ensembles, notably those of Ellington, Hines, Calloway and Basie, not only survived the Depression but even thrived in it. Usually with the backing of their white agents and sponsors, they continued recording and performing in public throughout the decade and often into the forties and fifties. What is more, in the latter part of the thirties, black musicians became increasingly known and appreciated by the general public. Somewhat ironically, that came about largely due to the success of white swing bands. For their increasing popularity spiked a lively interest in jazz in general. According to Al Hodes, "It was in the late thirties that the first knowledgeable audience for jazz was forming in the United States."[360] This new jazz audience would now become aware of the talented black jazz bands and their performers..

Previously, in the twenties and early thirties, the average listener could well have heard of stars like Armstrong, Ellington or Calloway but would not have had a clue about a Coleman Hawkins, a Cootie Williams or the bands of Earl Hines, Andy Kirk and Jimmy Lunceford. By the late thirties, however, a popular magazine such as *Esquire* was covering both black and white jazz recordings in every issue, while *Life* and other periodicals helped familiarize the public with the music of both races.

Encouraging this trend, record producer Milt Gabler, who ran the Commodore Music Shop in New York, pioneered the inclusion of names of individual performers featured on recordings by listing them himself and by convincing a number of record companies to follow suit. African-American as well as Caucasian musicians profited by such a move. But as far as black jazz was concerned, a greater means of promotion in the late thirties may well have been the creation of jazz clubs throughout America, a phenomenon which had actually begun in Europe, especially with Hughes Panassié's Hot Club de France. As David W. Stowe tells it, the American jazz clubs, along with middle class writers and critics associated with them (that is, former Ivy Leaguers à la John Hammond) ". . . did force Americans to confront the fact that a conspicuous portion of their popular culture was undeniably indebted to African Americans."[361]

And as a final note on the optimistic side, during the thirties, African-American musicians were increasingly included in prominent white swing bands. Artie Shaw, for example, was one of the first white bandleaders to feature a black singer (Billie Holiday) as lead vocalist. But the trend toward musical integration truly began with Benny Goodman. Prodded by John Hammond, Goodman not only recorded with black musicians but began including players such as Lionel Hampton and Teddy Wilson in small groups and presented Basie and other black star performers in his Carnegie Hall concert of 1938. Other white bands soon followed suit, recruiting and hiring the best black talent available.

All the pluses and all the gains mentioned here may appear to add up to a rosy future for African-American band musicians. That, unfortunately, is not a realistic reading of their situation. For white bands had striking advantages over black ones, a fact of life increasingly obvious from the mid-thirties and the advent of the Swing Era.

One of these advantages lay in filmmaking, for the film industry, with its escapist movies, was making money during the Depression when many other industries were fighting a losing battle. In the early thirties Hollywood was seen as the enemy, drawing away clientele from the jazz and dance bands. But musical films began to offer opportunities for glamorous orchestra leaders and their ensembles. "Glamorous," at the time, meant strictly the white bands and their leaders. Only the very top black entertainers took the spotlight in feature films, celebrities such as Louis Armstrong, Duke Ellington, Cab Calloway or dancer Bill Robinson. When dance orchestras came onstage during intermission at double features, again, pale-skinned players were the order of the day.

And white musicians had the edge in radio, an extremely rich resource for band music in the thirties. The radio industry, having developed from only one station in 1920, to nearly a thousand in 1927, greatly expanded its network in the early thirties. By 1934, mushrooming radio sets were providing entertainment in over 90% of American homes. So young stations hungry for programs that would appeal to their listeners—at little or no cost-filled a great percentage of their air time with live dance band music. As mentioned, such music was often piped directly from nightclubs and ballrooms and featured some of the top large black bands. But unsurprisingly, white bands had more numerous opportunities in radio and a far greater coverage nation wide.

It would seem logical that radio, with its entertainers invisible to the public, would not distinguish between black and white and would open opportunities to African-American musicians. Yet that did not happen. For the national networks, unwilling to risk losing their southern white listeners, reserved prime time for white bands only. Even the most talented of the black bands, such as Earl Hines and Count Basie, could be heard only on local late-night broadcasts, or "remotes."[362] There was, in fact, no way that African-American bands could dream of vying with white ones in the radio broadcasting arena. That world was virtually blocked to them.

The record industry offered more possibilities for black talent than radio. Although racial discrimination occurred in that area, recording studios interested in jazz and dance music accommodated players both black & white, and at times, racially mixed ensembles. Black artists, like their white counterparts, recorded frequently. Under contract with one record company, a Louis Armstrong or Fletcher Henderson, like a Bix Beiderbecke or a young Benny Goodman, would moonlight outside of their exclusive contracts, recording anonymously or under a variety of aliases, with sundry record companies. Many used *ad hoc* ensembles called by any name that occurred to them on the spot.

There was money to be made in the studios. For despite the fact that recording fell on hard times in the early thirties, the industry soon revived. For one thing records amassed a huge audience thanks to those favorite fixtures of the era, the juke boxes. The songs played on them at a nickel a pop were listened to, danced to, then often sought and bought in music stores for seventy-five cents apiece.

What is more, the recording industry received a great boost from its former rival, radio. Announcers hit on the idea of using records in lieu of live bands for musical entertainment. And so the disk jockey was born. Thanks to disks spun over the air, record stores were soon flooded with eager buyers. So radio turned out to be a boon rather than a bane for the recording business and recording artists in general.

But—the broken record drones on—especially for white recording artists.

Here, once again, we see a closing of the door to the black bands and a major leap ahead for the white ones. For the new records-on-radio phenomenon would largely favor whites. A case in point: one of the first examples of recorded band music on radio occurred in 1932, a time when the recording industry had hit rock bottom. That year Al Jarvis of Station KFWB in Los Angeles launched his program, "The World's Largest Make Believe Ballroom." Now Jarvis, as it happens, was great fan of Benny Goodman. (His promotion of Goodman recordings may have contributed to the bandleader's great success at Los Angeles' Palomar ballroom in 1935.) Jarvis gave air time to other swing orchestras as well. But the bands of a Fletcher Henderson or an Earl Hines had little or no air space in the world's largest virtual ballroom.

A bit later, in 1935, Martin Block, taking his cue from Al Jarvis instituted his own "Make Believe Ballroom," and he coined the phrase "disk jockey" to describe his role as record spinner and commentator. The program originated when, as staff announcer for station WNEW, he opted to fill up time spent awaiting news of Bruno Hauptmann's trial for his alleged kidnapping of Charles Lindbergh's son. Rather than keep live orchestras on hold, it seemed cheaper to play their records. With Block, as with Jarvis, white swing bands like Benny Goodman's and Artie Shaw's came prominently to the fore.

Whether recorded or live, the music heard on radio throughout the thirties was overwhelmingly that of the white bands. Tobacco companies such as Old Gold, Camel and Chesterfield, sponsored on their so-called "nicotine network" the big bands of Paul

Whiteman, Fred Waring, Tommy Dorsey, Artie Shaw, Glenn Miller, Horace Heidt, Kay Kyser, Harry James, the Casa Loma Orchestra and Larry Clinton, among other white ensembles. And on Lucky Strike tobacco's popular "Your Hit Parade," the lesser known white orchestras of Al Goodman, Mark Warnaw and Raymond Scott played music popularized by the big white swing bands.

Unsurprisingly, given the relative lack of radio promotion for black dance orchestras—and the fact that white bands were welcome in many more venues such as hotels, nightclubs and theaters—the general public had far less familiarity with the names and sounds of the black bands. So naturally, when it came to American popularity polls run by radio, newspapers and magazines, the white ensembles won hands down over highly talented black bands (even over Ellington's!), the very bands that had paved the way for the swing era.

So all in all, despite a good number of concrete gains for African-American musicians during the Depression years, the big white swing bands continued to dominate the field of American popular music. The magic key to success was, once again, power. That power would help make the names of talented and ambitious white musicians synonymous with the Swing Era.

The White Bands: Sound and Stereotype

White bands were already flourishing in America long before the triumph of swing. With ballroom dancing enjoying enormous popularity since World War I, a number of white dance orchestras had become household words in the twenties and early thirties. Promoted by top agencies, favored by radio, recordings and films and welcome in fashionable hotels, cabarets and restaurants, the dance ensembles of Art Hickman, Paul Whiteman, Ted Lewis, Meyer Davis,[363] Guy Lombardo, Ben Bernie, Fred Waring, Leo Reisman, Sammy Kay, Lester Lanin, Glen Gray, Jan Garber, Wayne King and the Coon-Sanders Nighthawks were darlings of the public.

What did these bands sound like? Although their styles varied, all of them maintained a marked 4/4 fox trot dance beat of pendulum regularity, alternating with oom-pah-pah waltzes and polkas. While many black bands thrived on blues and stomps, at times using unfamiliar head arrangements, the white ones kept to a standard, recognizable repertoire of Tin Pan Alley tunes. Rarely straying from the melody, their sections played mainly in unison, rather than polyphonically. They performed pieces usually of three-and-a-half-minutes duration (the normal time for recording on 78 r.p.m. disks), and often featured goodlooking vocalists. Their generally "sweet" ballads alternated with upbeat novelty numbers nearly always delivered in a ricky-ticky tempo and geared to a fast fox trot or one-step.

By 1927 it had become fashionable for these white groups to include jazz musicians and some jazz numbers in their repertoire. But few if any among them matched their black counterparts in freedom, depth and variety. Rare was the band that evinced traces of the driving hot sounds or the swing of a Jimmy Lunceford, a Luis Russell, a Cecil Scott or a Chick Webb. Those white orchestras that did venture into the jazz realm often substituted technique and a breakneck speed for style and feeling. The white performers might impress listeners with their training and precision but were not known for playing the relaxed and "low-down" music heard in black bands.[364] It would take years before some white orchestras such as Woody Herman's would truly absorb and render the sounds of black jazz. In the twenties and early thirties they seemed more at home with the strains of standard sweet and dependable music.

The sweetness and conservatism of such bands may best be understood in the context of their most visible clientele, the dancers. For unlike the freer style black dancers in dives of Harlem or San Francisco's Barbary Coast, the white patrons of stylish nightclubs and hotels were not about to perform a sensuous "slow drag" or a version of the "shim-sham-shimmy." Even the highly popular black Charleston of 1923 did not take over as a social dance for the general public but was most often performed as a bravura demonstration by leg flinging exhibitionists. And until the conquest of swing in mid-thirties, white dancing couples did not kick up their heels in imitation of the Savoy's African-American jitterbug acrobatics.

So there is a good deal of truth to the old stereotype that labels white band music of the time "sweet" and the black ones "hot." Yet to put the white band/black band picture in a truer light, certain disclaimers should be made on both sides of the equation.

For example, contrary to the stereotype, black bands did not always cultivate hot sounds. As we have seen, many of them started out imitating the successful formulas of white orchestras such as Art Hickman's or Paul Whiteman's. This was certainly the case of early ones such as groups led by violinist/bandleader George Morrison. Or those of clarinetist/leader Wilbur Sweatman, a contemporary of James Reese Europe. Sweatmen began his career in circus and concert bands, then only later capitalized on the ragtime vogue with his Ragtime and Jazz Band. As for the New Orleans black pioneers, their sound depended on their audiences, since they could play hot in Storyville dives or sweet at white society functions or Tulane proms.

Paradoxically, the black bands, evolving over the years, became both smoother and hotter. King Oliver developed a suaver, more polished sound that contrasted with his rougher attack of his New Orleans days. On the other hand, as noted, Fletcher Henderson acquired an increasingly swinging style, especially after experiencing Louis Armstrong's free and expressive improvisations. Fundamentally, however, both of these examples point in the same direction: a veering away from the honky-tonk ragtime beat toward the smoother, yet irresistibly driving sounds of swing.

Meanwhile, the white bands, like the black ones, did not always conform to their expected musical style, that is, the polite, commercial mode of sweet dance orchestras. As we shall see, Ben Pollack, a graduate of the New Orleans Rhythm Kings, preferred the jazz route, and commercial bandleaders like Jean Goldkette, Paul Whiteman and others flirted with jazz, even featuring the finest of jazz soloists in their performances.

The areas of black and white music appeared to be coming closer to one another—a phenomenon which we have already seen in the case of singers and songwriters. By the thirties Tin Pan Alley music increasingly adopted the flavor of black jazz, while black bands exploited more and more the tunes of Tin Pan Alley, adopting their standard 32-bar structure in lieu of a more open-ended jazz format. As Gunther Schuller stated, "As the jazz age approached and jazz styles narrowed down to a kind of early mainstream, the more polite bands became hotter and the hotter bands more polished."[365]

Nevertheless, in comparing recordings, we can still hear a major difference between the majority of white dance orchestras of the twenties and early thirties and the black dance bands discussed in the previous chapter. Although the white-is-sweet, black-is-hot stereotype does not apply a hundred percent of the time, it has a good deal of truth in it. For in point of fact, unlike their black counterparts, few white bands of the era would or could really swing.

Popular White Bands Before 1935

In the 1910s, with the ballroom dance craze sweeping America, white dance bands were rapidly springing up around the country. By 1924 over 900 dance bands, most of them white, provided work for some 7,200 musicians. Some of the best known among the early white ensembles were Art Hickman, Paul Specht, Ted Lewis, Ted Benson, Meyer Davis and Isham Jones, to be followed by Jean Goldkette, Glen Gray (heading the Casa Loma Band), Paul Whiteman, Sam Lanin, Horace Heidt, Ben Bernie, Kay Kyser, Leo Reisman and Guy Lombardo. A good number of such bandleaders formed agencies, hiring out various other groups bearing their names, whether they appeared personally or not. (A "Jean Goldkette Orchestra," for example, might not include Goldkette's top instrumentalists or Goldkette himself.)

Hickman's San Francisco based orchestra is seen today as the first important dance ensemble of the pre-war era. Hickman, as we have seen, collaborated with Ferde Grofé and was the first orchestra leaders to adopt Grofé's groundbreaking ideas for big band arrangements. In the context of their new approach, four different sections ("choral groups") of the band—brass, reeds, percussion and strings—played off of each other with countermelodies, a different melody for each section, rather than forming one harmonic ensemble as customary in the past.

At its inception, in 1913, Hickman's band consisted of a mere six pieces—piano, trumpet, trombone, drum and two banjos. Then in 1919, after stock arrangements and dance bands had begun to feature saxophones, he added two saxes to his ensemble. The new instruments proved to be a great asset, for they lent a richer sound to the ensemble. So Grofé and Hickman began introducing breaks in the music and filling them with choruses of saxophones.

The sounds of the Hickman orchestra could not truly qualify as jazz. Hickman himself had early been an aficionado of black Barbary Coast dives and had been convinced that, despite the liquor and cigar smoke and filth of those honky-tonks, "There is where all jazz originated."[366] Yet he himself hated to be labeled a jazz bandleader. He was, after all, playing for his dancing public. Therefore he would not want to be involved with that lowdown black music, in which the "true grace of Terpsichore was buried in the muck of sensuality."[367] So, as the leader of a commercial white dance band, he offered what was known as "sweet jazz," as opposed to the hot variety, in other words a basically un-jazzy jazz. Still, conservative or not, Hickman's innovative ideas, mainly those relating to the use of saxes, helped pave the way for the future swing bands in which the reeds would so often dialogue and contrast with the brass section.

Along with Hickman, Isham Jones may be seen as an important white precursor of the swing era. Jones began his career as bandleader/sax player in Chicago in 1919. Eventually known as a songwriter ("I'll See You In My Dreams," "It Had To Be You"), he started out by developing one of the finest dance orchestras of the twenties. An extremely well disciplined ensemble, it had a fuller sound and a greater rhythmic variety than most white bands of the time. It also had a greater feeling for jazz. The group was familiar with King Oliver, having heard his orchestra at Lincoln Gardens in the mid-twenties. It also included a number of jazz musicians, such as Pee Wee Erwin and the young Woody Herman, whose own later group, "Herman's First Herd" developed out of an offshoot of Jones' orchestra, "Isham Jones' Juniors."

But despite its jazz inflections, the style of the Isham Jones orchestra could not generally be termed "hot." His 1934 recording of "Blue Room," while neatly rendering its jazzy Fletcher Henderson arrangement, could not capture the swing of the good black bands of the early thirties—nor of a Goodman or a Jimmy Dorsey at the time of Jones' recording. Such observations, however, do not diminish the fact that the Isham Jones ensemble, one of the earliest white dance bands to venture into the realm of jazz, remained among the most competent and popular orchestras of its day.

The Jean Goldkette Orchestra stood well in the forefront of white big bands playing in the twenties and early thirties. A French native, classically trained, Goldkette was less a bandleader than an entrepreneur. For example, he took over and reorganized the well reputed black band, McKinney's Cotton Pickers, and he hired out various groups of musicians under his name. Meanwhile, his most noteworthy players performed in his "flagship" unit, the Victor Recording Orchestra, housed in Detroit's Graystone (sometimes spelled "Greystone") Ballroom, leased and managed by Goldkette.

Goldkette himself had little talent for jazz. Nevertheless he was well aware of the attraction that modern medium had for the listening and dancing public. In Chicago, he had heard King Oliver and other New Orleans musicians playing to enthusiastic audiences. To be in the swim, he formed a nucleus of fine jazz musicians, including, most memorably, sax player Frank Trumbauer, cornetist Bix Beiderbecke and future bandleaders Jimmy and Tommy Dorsey. With such a group it is understandable that Goldkette's contemporaries said the ensemble could really swing. Benny Goodman, for one, pronounced the Graystone band of 1927 "plenty good,"[368] and black trumpeter Rex Stewart deemed it "the first large white swinging orchestra in jazz history.[369]"

Unfortunately, judging from recordings, today we are left with little evidence that the Goldkette band did swing. Instead, the disks have a heavy dose of corny songs, inane vocals and novelty tunes with a whoop-de-doo, razz-ma-tazz beat.

From all accounts this non-jazz orientation of the Goldkette recordings may be blamed on the Victor management's belief that the public wanted to hear only polite, commercial music from white orchestras and hot sounds exclusively from black ones. This stereotypical view was held most notoriously by Victor's recording director, Eddie King, who pre-selected the Tin Pan Alley tunes Goldkette's band had to record, who refused to let them perform their Bill Challis jazz arrangements and who very much disliked the most likeable Bix Beiderbecke. Later, a Goldkette musician, Stanley "Doc" Ryker, would say of King, "I don't know why he hired the band at all. The stuff he didn't want, why that was our style."[370] Evidently, the group had to sneak in a bit of their type of music only after the official recording sessions with King had finished.

(Interestingly, Fletcher Henderson's band experienced the reverse side of such black/white stereotyping in recording. They were frustrated at not being allowed to record the waltzes and other sweet numbers that formed a good part of their repertoire at Roseland.[371])

Despite their obstacles in recording for Victor, the Goldkette band enjoyed the reputation of being the finest most modern dance band in the mid-west. Bolstered by that reputation and armed with their nucleus of first-rate jazz musicians, they headed for New York in 1926 to do battle with Fletcher Henderson's band at Roseland Ballroom. They had Trumbauer's competent direction and playing, they had a BixBeiderbecke in tow, they had rehearsed to a fare-thee-well and they aimed to give the battle everything they could deliver. Fletcher's musicians, however, had nary a concern. They had heard Goldkette's group was good, but they knew they themselves were the greatest.

Then, as Rex Stewart tells it in his humorous and engaging account of the event, the self-assurance of the Henderson band turned into dismay, amazement and, finally, a begrudging admiration. The "Johnny-come-lately white band from out in the sticks"[372] cut them overwhelmingly, remaining on the bandstand for encore after encore. According to Stewart, "They creamed us. Those little tight-assed white boys creamed us . . . I don't like admitting it, but I was in the band and we were whipped!"[373] How could that have happened? Stewart attributes the Goldkette victory to Bill Challis' imaginative arrangements, to their beat—what with Steve Brown's "slapping hell out of that bass fiddle"—to Trumbauer's inspiring musical leadership and to having the crowd with them because "they were new faces and blowing like mad."[374]

So obviously, the Goldkette band could and did rise to the occasion, and it is possible that, when playing for a receptive audience—rather than recording for a narrow-minded studio executive—they could shine in the realm of jazz. Unfortunately, if we consider the bulk of existent Goldkette recordings, it is difficult to imagine them consistently able to match a band like Henderson's, despite their fine arranger and great jazz musicians.

One cannot attribute Goldkette's lack of "hotness" entirely on Victor's stereotyping or having to record inane Tin Pan Alley numbers. For one thing, at Victor, the band recorded under directors other than Eddie King, directors who were far more sympathetic to jazz, especially after the Roseland triumph. And they did record jazz pieces (such as the Dixieland flavored "My Pretty Girl" or their oft praised "Clementine," featuring beautiful improvisational solo work by Bix Beiderbecke). Yet if we compare such 1927 recordings against 1925 and 1926 disks of Fletcher Henderson—for example, "Sugarfoot Stomp" or "Stampede,"[375] the Goldkette disks lag far behind. Yes, the musicians were apparently saddled with some corny tunes. But, certainly, Fletcher Henderson's band—or even Ben Pollack's—would have put a better spin on such songs as "I'm Looking Over a Four Leaf Clover." We are left, unfortunately, with little evidence that Goldkette's orchestra could approach the jazz quality or swing of a good black band of their time.

This relative lack of swing becomes obvious if we focus on Goldkette's 1927 recording of "I'm Gonna Meet My Sweetie Now" and Fletcher Henderson's "Variety Stomp" of the same year. Goldkette's piece has been considered a hot number, one that might possibly have been included in the battle of the bands described here.[376] It has exactly the same tempo as Henderson's "Variety Stomp." Yet the Henderson recording demonstrates a far greater variety and a hotness provided by elements such as Jimmy Harrison's trombone *glissandos,* Joe Smith's driving trumpet, Coleman Hawkins' sax and Henderson's lowdown, barrelhouse piano solos. Despite Goldkette's star musicians, his piece maintains a more regular rhythm and texture and has a more "polite" feel to it. Joe Venuti's jazz violin solos are competent enough, but somehow, a violin, any violin, usually sounds a bit corny and old-fashioned in the context of a jazz number.[377]

It is disappointing that we cannot know exactly how the two bands sounded live at Roseland. But whether or not Goldkette's band was able to produce a good level of jazz drive then or on other occasions, it must be generally credited for its fine musicianship and the fact that it launched great performers such as Frankie Trumbauer and Bix Beiderbecke.[378]

Starting out in 1927, the Casa Loma Orchestra, an offshoot of Jean Goldkette's band, became one of America's favorite dance bands, especially popular among college promgoers. From the standpoint of jazz, Casa Loma, like Goldkette's group, had the advantage of fine musicians and a highly competent jazz arranger—in their case, arranger Gene Gifford[379]—whose advanced and complex musical scores demanded great technical precision. With such assets, the Casa Lomans created a first: a white dance band that introduced lively instrumentals into their repertoire, pieces such as "The Casa Loma Stomp," "Black Jazz" and "The Maniac's Ball." Virtuoso numbers played with what critics have referred to as a "machinelike precision."[380]

Listening to those recordings today, one may well get the impression of a dizzying hurriedness, for they were performed at breakneck speed. Richard Sudhalter explains this hastiness by the fact that they were trying to outdo other bands.[381] Whatever the case, in such jazz pieces the band may have been hot but it did not swing. As for a slower number, such as Ellington's "Sophisticated Lady," the orchestra was simply not up to the challenge. Its 1933 recording of the classic now seems dated and banal, with its pronounced 4-4 beat and schmaltzy violin carrying the melody.

In spite of such deficiencies, the Casa Loma Orchestra, a skilled and energetic ensemble, can be credited as a pioneer in the realm of white big bands. Albert McCarthy sees the orchestra as an influential band, a transitional one, "providing a link between the dance orchestras who could turn out creditable hot performances and the swing groups of the Goodman and Dorsey variety." And he adds, "Whatever its failings—and the lack of a really good rhythm section was a perennial one—it deserves credit for its pioneering spirit and the technical expertise of its personnel."[382]

Generally speaking, the Casa Loma Orchestra, essentially a sweet band, was perfect for dancing. In its forays into the area of jazz, it inevitably lagged behind the black pre-swing era ensembles described in the previous chapter.

The same could be said of the majority of the big name white bands of the time, including the orchestra led by the self-dubbed "King of Jazz," Paul Whiteman. Whiteman had been classically trained under his father, Wilberforce Whiteman, who was horrified to see his own son drawn to popular commercial music. Conceivably because of a desire to reconcile his father's wishes with his own penchants, Whiteman set out to create what he termed "symphonic jazz." To that end, he created a large, smooth and disciplined unit, including a violin section, and he worked closely with Ferde Grofé, capitalizing on Grofé's now familiar idea of having the various instrumental sections, or "voices" alternate with one another. A symphonic approach but in the context of contemporary popular music.

But "King of Jazz"? Whiteman knew that jazz was the latest buzzword and that an infusion of jazz in his orchestra would ensure his popularity. But he himself confessed "I know as much abut real jazz as F. Scott Fitzgerald did about the Jazz Age."[383] He certainly did his homework, attempting—albeit unsuccessfully—to understand how jazz and jazz improvisation worked. He repeatedly checked out Fletcher Henderson's band, he listened to black bands in Harlem nightspots and he sent his musicians to learn what they could from Duke Ellington at the Kentucky Club (Ellington's men wryly termed them "spies"[384]).

Further, he engaged a number of fine jazz instrumentalists, taking over Goldkette's jazz stars in 1927, when the Goldkette band folded. He hired Trumbauer, Beiderbecke and the Dorsey Brothers and later added Jack Teagarden and Bunny Berigan. He took on Goldkette's arranger, Bill Challis and black arrangers Don Redman and William Grant Still. He would have eagerly hired the finest of African-American jazz musicians, if he had had any chance of surmounting the prejudices of the day.

In addition to adding jazz elements to his own orchestra, Whiteman consistently promoted jazz and jazz musicians such as Red Norvo, Mildred Bailey, Johnny Mercer and Hoagy Carmichael. And in an attempt to convince the American public to take jazz seriously, he organized a big concert tour, launched at New York's Aeolian Hall in 1924. The concert included a jazz retrospective, starting with ODJB fare, and it featured George Gershwin playing his "Rhapsody in Blue," a piece commissioned by Whiteman specifically for the event.

With so much of Whiteman's efforts pointing in the direction of jazz, one might have expected to hear a jazz inflected style of music and a conspicuous amount of drive or swing in his performances. *Au contraire.* Despite a good dose of impressive eight- or sixteen-bar solo breaks delivered by his star soloists, and despite a number of recordings that get off the ground now and then, the Whiteman "jazz" sound is a regular, pronounced 4/4 ricky-ticky, honky-tonk beat to the strains of large instrumental sections (including violins aplenty) playing in unison with an unremitting sameness. Whiteman's music, described by Barry Singer the as a "the milkiest, jazz-flavored . . . arrangements,"[385] would be imitated by many others, including the "milkiest" of them all, the vibrato laden Guy Lombardo.

Ironically, we can see Paul Whiteman taking the stage in the 1928 video, *Jazz Dance Ball,* and tearing up a sheet of paper as he enters. The paper, one may surmise, is a musical score. Whiteman shreds it before our eyes, to indicate grandly—and, one would hope, humorously—that his is a *bona fide* jazz outfit, determined to improvise rather than merely read an arrangement. But then he and his orchestra promptly launch into an arranged, well disciplined, commercially bland and completely Whitemanesque rendition of a popular Tin Pan Alley tune. Unfortunatcly for Whiteman's reputation, on the tape, that performance is immediately followed by a superb performance by Louis Armstrong!

In wanting to create "symphonic jazz," Whiteman subtracted both from symphonic music and from jazz. And although he claimed to have made " a lady of jazz," his lady swept jazz into the closet.

Nevertheless, given Whiteman's great commercial success, it is understandable that many white orchestras preferred to follow his formula rather than adhere to the more jazz oriented route of an Ellington, a Lunceford or a Henderson. A good number of them would depend on professional arrangers and competent jazz soloists to introduce, especially toward the end of a number, the requisite hot phrase or two. A few licks that would appeal to dancers and listeners—just so long as they did not truly distract from the smoothness and evenness of the dance music. Sweet, unchallengingly polite, cute at times with their Tin Pan Ally raggy numbers, the white bands, despite their individual styles, basically resembled one another.

An exception to the rule could be found at times in Ben Pollack's band. Pollack had played drums with the New Orleans Rhythm Kings in the early twenties, pounding out the black rhythms the NORK so admired. Then he started his first dance band in California around the middle of the decade. Unlike the white bands discussed here, Pollack's group did not go the "symphonic" route and did not depend on scores from professional arrangers but used in-house arrangements and/or developed lively "head" arrangements of their numbers. Some of those numbers were driven by a hot Dixieland beat.

Certainly, Pollack's approach—until late in his career, when he sought a more commercial route—had a greater jazz orientation and far freer improvisation than the average white dance band of his time. In fact, it has been considered the first large white band to play jazz music. Before Pollack formed his band, white jazz could usually be heard only in small ensembles like the ODJB or the NORK, while the larger white dance bands concentrated on more commercial fare. And Pollack himself was, according to Benny Goodman, "one of the first white men to play fine drums."[386]

Some of the top white musicians in American swing got their real start working in Pollack's band, for example: clarinetist Benny Goodman, trombonist Glenn Miller (who also provided Pollack with arrangements), trombonist and vocalist Jack Teagarden, cornetist Jimmy McPartland and later trumpeters Charlie Spivak, Harry James and Mugsy Spanier. The hot, swingng sound of jazz performers under Pollack's leadership comes through convincingly on such records as the 1927 "Waiting for Katie," arranged by Fud Livingston and featuring a fine Benny Goodman solo, or the lively "Two Tickets To Georgia," cut in 1933, with a vocal by Nappy Lamare (happily not by Pollack himself, who misguidedly fancied himself a singer).

Although uneven in output, Pollack's was one dance band that could do jazz. Though Pollack ultimately succumbed to mediocre renditions of commercial music, in its heyday his orchestra represented a striking exception to the white-sweet/black-hot stereotype of the twenties and early thirties.

Benny Goodman and the Swing Era

In the early thirties jazz seemed to lose its hold on the American public. The recording business had hit its slump in the throes of the Depression, but hot music had even less of a chance in that area than the sweet, commercial bands. The bland orchestras of a Jan Garber or a Guy Lombardo had a greater attraction for both record buyers and radio listeners during that bleak time. So understandably, many orchestra leaders, both black and white, had to sell out in order to survive. That is, rather than aim for the adventurous in their approach, they would give the public what it wanted, take the money and run. Even if that meant performing sweet and cute Tin Pan Alley tunes in a pedestrian but accessible style. Such, at the time, was the case of Earl Hines, The McKinney Cotton Pickers, Ben Pollack and many others.

And such—at least temporarily—was the case of Benny Goodman.

It did not start that way. As a pre-teenager in knee pants in his native city of Chicago, Goodman was already astounding listeners with his clarinet jazz improvisations on excursion boat runs and with the Austin High School Gang. A great fan of the NORK, the ODJB and Bix Beiderbecke, he was very familiar with King Oliver's Lincoln Gardens band as well and has acknowledged the influence of Oliver's clarinetists, Jimmy Noone and Johnny Dodds.[387] While still a boy, he would participate in nightly jam sessions with black musicians at Chicago's Three Deuces and was allowed to sit in occasionally with the Earl Hines band.

In 1925, when only sixteen, Goodman joined the Ben Pollack orchestra in California, where drummer Pollack encouraged the young clarinetist to join him in hot improvisations. When Pollack moved his group to New York in 1928, Goodman went with them. He soon was making literally hundreds of jazz recordings in the various studios. But he was clearly experiencing a certain ambivalence *vis-à-vis* jazz around that time, and especially at the start of the thirties, with the onset of the Depression. During that period he was also recording with commercial bands such as Sam Lanin, Ben Selvin, Meyer Davis and Ted Lewis. A good dose of his energies went into performing uninspired Tin Pan Alley sweet and novelty numbers.

It was a question of money, of course. Especially since Benny Goodman, having grown up in poverty, necessarily ranked money very high on his list of requisites. Yet he was torn, craving a career in the jazz he loved.

Once again, John Hammond appeared on the scene in the role of Prime Mover. The two met in 1933, a time when hot jazz, out of favor with the American public, was highly appreciated in France and England. Hammond, who was producing jazz recordings at Britain's Columbia Records, offered Benny a contract and opened important doors for him. At the same time he served as what has been termed Benny's "musical conscience."[388] Firstly, he steered his protégé away from his commercial endeavors and back into jazz. And secondly, he convinced Benny to collaborate with African-American jazz artists.

Benny was reluctant at first on the second count. Making recordings with black musicians was one thing. But hiring them in his own band? His first response to the idea was "I won't get another job in this town."[389] But little by little it happened, starting with small groups. He first included pianist Teddy Wilson in a trio and later added vibraphonist Lionel Hampton and would feature Basie and other black stars in his 1938 Carnegie Hall concert.

While such moves may seem like a compromise to us today, they were unusual at the time, truly a first. With Hammond cuing him from the wings each step of the way, Benny Goodman's hiring of African-American musicians undoubtedly opened the door for the desegregation of swing bands that would take place a few years down the road.

Benny formed his first big band in 1934. Thinking in terms of jazz at that point, he reasoned that few white bands outside of the Dorsey Brothers were playing hot music at the time, so he would start his own jazz-oriented contingent. He discovered, however, at an engagement at Billy Rose's Music Hall that year, that the patrons didn't know how to dance to the new, swinging music: the Lindy Hop and other forms of jitterbugging hadn't yet come downtown from Harlem. But that, too, would change.

The end of 1934 found Benny Goodman broadcasting nationally each week on *Let's Dance,* an engagement brokered by his agent Willard Alexander—who, himself, had a good deal of contact with Hammond. Goodman's jazz music followed two other sections of the program, a smooth and a Latin music hour, so on the East Coast he was only heard by listeners tuning in after midnight. (As we shall see, however, there was an up side to that inconvenient timing.)

Perhaps the most significant development at that moment was his collaboration with Fletcher Henderson. As indicated in the previous chapter, this was also the work of John Hammond, who knew that by giving Benny his arrangements and by writing for him on an ongoing basis, Fletcher could survive financially after the breakup of his band. On the other hand, he was well aware that Fletcher's arrangements would greatly contribute to Benny's musical credibility. On reflection, it would seem that Benny turned out to be the winner by far. As Ross Firestone put it, Fletcher's scores made him the "beneficiary of a dozen years of experimentation, development and gradual perfection of a style of big band arranging that was to give him the identity he needed."[390]

Immediate and dramatic proof of Fletcher's value to Benny was the 1935 triumph of the Goodman band at California's Palomar Ballroom, the event usually considered to have kicked off the Swing Era. To summarize briefly a story that has been told many times over: On the band's tour westward, they bombed repeatedly, and by the time they reached the Palomar, they had lost all hope of success. The Palomar engagement started badly, with the band playing conservatively to keep on the safe side, but the dancers showed little enthusiasm. Then finally, in desperation, someone (possibly Gene Krupa) suggested going whole hog and pulling out the Fletcher Henderson scores. So they did. Bingo. Enthusiastic listeners cheered, and the news of the band's success spread immediately.

And here is the happy ending to the Goodman band's short-lived, post-midnight *Let's Dance* broadcasts. Given the time difference in California, many of the Palomar patrons had probably heard them on the show, which would have reached them at an earlier, more feasible hour. But even if not, they could have had access to the voice of that Goodman fan, Al Jarvis, spinning his disks on Los Angeles' Station KFWB. That was the music they wanted to hear, and that is what the band, with its Fletcher Henderson's scores, ultimately delivered at the Palomar.

Triumph after triumph followed, including the band's overwhelming reception in 1937 at New York's Paramount Theater, where hundreds of teenagers played hooky from school to hear them.

So began the swing era, with it's titular "King," Benny Goodman.

That Thing Called Swing

Like the word "jazz" in 1917, the term "swing" of 1935, was a promoter's dream. The label undoubtedly helped spread and maintain the popularity of the Goodman sound and the sound of those white bands that followed him.

It was not a new term. In fact it dated at least as far back as 1907 with Jelly Roll Morton's composition "Georgia Swing." In 1908, Scott Joplin advised readers of his piano exercises to play them "slowly until you catch the swing."[391] So black musicians had used "swing" as a noun as well as a verb, indicating that a band or a number had to have drive, had to set feet a-tapping. But the most famous example of its nominal use before the Goodman adventure was Duke Ellington's 1932 "It Don't Mean a Thing (If It Ain't Got That Swing). Some writers have suggested the word "swing" caught on in the mid-thirties largely because the BBC promoted it after realizing at a rather late date that "jazz" had a sexual meaning and needed a more proper designation.

As for the sound itself, again, we must not imagine swing as the sudden, magical birth of a brand new musical invention with Benny Goodman's breakthrough of 1935. For, as we have seen, he had built to a great extent on the sound of black bands of the twenties and early thirties. Yet Goodman and the white swing bands that followed him did not simply take existent black jazz and hand it to the general public; such an assumption would be simplistic. Rather, they worked with the black rhythms and techniques, modified them and polished them to a fare-thee-well before delivering them to their dancers or recording them.

The black bands had already smoothed jazz greatly, undoubtedly influenced by white commercial bands. But the arrangers for big white swing bands smoothed and simplified the black sounds further, so that the vertical stomps and jumps of the past gave way to a more horizontal, lilting flow, even in fast numbers. Written arrangements of 32-bar Tin Pan Alley standards incorporated riffs, previously improvised "fillers," into set patterns. Rather than head arrangements or collaborative compositions, the bandleaders depended on detailed, carefully planned professional scores.

Swing arrangers did leave room in their numbers for improvised solo breaks by various band members. But such breaks were limited and usually predictable. The musical product had now become, as one critic put it, "clean, precise and magnificently technocratic."[392] Swing presented the public with a highly structured brand of music, a music repeatedly rehearsed and overseen by methodical, meticulous disciplinarians such as Benny Goodman, Tommy Dorsey and Glenn Miller.

Such structuring was necessary. "Bigger" had become synonymous with "better," and the ensembles had, in the latter half of the thirties, expanded to sixteen or eighteen pieces, sometimes even more. An every-man-for-himself type of improvisation would have spelled pandemonium. Thus the increasing importance of written arrangements and players who could read them. And thus the increased necessity for a strong leader. In the past, a leader could usually be any instrumentalist in the band; sometimes band members had even taken turns fronting an orchestra.

Now, a leader didn't even necessarily have to be a great player. More importantly, he had to be good-looking—for movies that began to feature him and for teenagers who loved to idolize him. Above all, he needed to have the requisite know-how. He had to select (or steal) the finest players and most creative arrangers. He had to keep his band on track. He had to make sure the final cut of a record had been rehearsed enough times to ensure airing of a perfect product, a guaranteed hit. And he had to know not only his music but public relations and business matters.

For business mattered more and more. For instance, in addition to the usual contacts with theater, nightclub and ballroom management, swing bands now had to reckon with the increased role of the media. As Peter Townsend said, "[Swing's] rise to prominence coincided with the consolidation across America of the commercial and technical infrastructure necessary to support it. It emerged in full force in the mid-1930s at a time when a small group of radio networks for the first time covered the entire country . . ."[393] Radio became ever more centralized, swallowing up important phonograph companies.

In targeting the radio networks, ambitious bandleaders looked to the ever powerful booking agencies. Through those agencies they would have access not only to radio but to the recording industry and to Hollywood studios—which would eventually buy up all the major music publishing companies. By the end of the twenties, the main booking concerns had amalgamated and controlled almost all access to such media.

Swing was nourished by the media and the media nourished itself on swing. By 1939, swing recordings accounted for a huge percentage of records sold in the United States.[394] The new craze served to intensify the American public's love of ballroom dancing and dance music and to make the dance scene ever more profitable economically. Scott DeVeaux, speaking of the swing era, said, "In a short time, dance music became astonishingly big business. Only a few years after the initial swing craze, dance orchestras generated nearly a hundred million annually, employing some thirty-two to forty thousand musicians, as well as another eight thousand managers, bookers, promoters and other support personnel."[395]

Small wonder that bandleaders had to know their business. Those among them who did know it and who well understood the exigencies of the bottom line, knew that the term "artistic freedom" could apply only up to a point, that their music could not be loose, freewheeling or daringly inventive but had to conform to a successful formula. Those who wanted to succeed aimed at fabricating "a standard product which they could sell through every medium to as many people in as many places as possible."[396]

Given the necessarily formulaic nature of much of big band white swing, its set written arrangements and its structured presentations, one might wonder how the bands could actually deliver a swinging sound. The fact is that the best ones could and did. Although all of them featured sweet romantic ballads in their repertoire, their swing music captivated America with its its melodic charm, its rhythmic impulse, its flow, its interplay of contrasting motifs and its ever interesting dynamics of *fortissimos* and *diminuendos.* Less challenging than much of the black jazz that preceded it, white swing could be called commercial in the sense that it was accessible and understandable to the general public. And the public savored that music precisely because—while capitalizing on the examples of a Henderson, an Ellington or a Lunceford—the bands imbued it with an irresistible drive, making it impossible not to dance or sway to it.

The Swing Era In High Gear

The Dorsey brothers, alto sax Jimmy and trombonist Tommy, had already organized a swing band by 1934, a year before Benny Goodman's bandleading exploits made him "King of Swing." Earlier, in the twenties, they had played in standard dance bands, usually with ordinary stock arrangements. Both brothers, however, had also had experience in jazz, occasionally soloing with Goldkette, Whiteman and various other bands, though Jimmy had a greater reputation in jazz and a more pronounced influence on his contemporaries.

We cannot know what the Dorseys' orchestra might have contributed to the swing era, since it soon broke up, on the heels of perpetual squabbling and violent arguments between the co-leading siblings. They went their separate ways, each forming his own band, with Tommy taking the limelight for a good period of time (Jimmy coming more into favor in later years). But Tommy himself, undoubtedly aware of his relative shortcomings as a jazz trombone improviser, took a "sweeter" route. Capitalizing on his great lyrical quality and billed as the "Sentimental Gentleman of Swing," he achieved popularity for romantic ballads like "Stardust" or his signature number "Getting Sentimental Over You." His place in the spotlight was also assured by his hit 1937 recording of "Marie," in which members of the band interspersed vocal riffs throughout the number (a technique appropriated from the black orchestra of Doc Wheeler, who, in turn, had copied it from Don Redman).

Anxious to be taken more seriously in the jazz realm, Tommy Dorsey added jazz drummer, Buddy Rich, to his band and shortly afterwards acquired the groundbreaking vocalist, Frank Sinatra, from Harry James' orchestra. But the most obvious improvement in his ensemble of the late thirties was his hiring of Sy Oliver, the gifted black arranger, trumpeter and singer in Jimmie Lunceford's orchestra.[397] Of this development Alyn Shipton has noted that Oliver found the Dorsey musicians good readers but with less of a sense of swing than the Lunceford group. Still, according to Shipton, the musical marriage achieved wonders: "To my mind, Oliver's success in remodeling [Tommy Dorsey's] band makes it one of the hidden secrets of the swing era, not adequately praised in the literature of jazz for its outstanding achievements."[398] In the same vein Gunther Schuller has said, "I have never encountered as dramatic an overnight impact on any orchestra by just one individual as in the case of Sy Oliver with Tommy Dorsey's orchestra."[399]

The African-American connection, seen here with Dorsey and more in evidence with Benny Goodman, did not play as great a role with other prominent swing bands of the late thirties. Exceptionally, Charlie Barnet was, along with Goodman, one of the first leaders to employ black musicians. He was deeply influenced by Ellington and Basie, was known for his jazz rhythms and his was the first white band to be billed at Harlem's Savoy Ballroom. However, the more famous among his swing contemporaries, leaders like Glenn Miller, Harry James and even Artie Shaw who led an interracial band in the forties, seemed to travel along a whiter way in the prime of the swing era.

This appears especially true of one of the most memorable of all white swing leaders, Glenn Miller. Although Miller admired Lunceford and Ellington and although, as a young man, he must have accompanied the Pollack band to hear Oliver and Armstrong on Chicago's south side, he appears to have whitewashed the African-American component both personally and professionally. That his Army Air Force Band remained all white during the war may be attributed to the notorious segregation in the Armed Forces (despite John Hammond's partially successful efforts to counter it). But given Miller's own history and apparent elitism, one might wonder whether he would ever have followed the example of other white leaders and welcomed black musicians to his band, had he survived the war. Idle and perhaps unfair speculation.

As for Miller's music, it was also whitewashed in the sense that black jazz had to be tamed and transformed into a product that would please a white general audience. That meant simplifying jazz polyphony and rhythms while keeping enough variety and contrast to hold listeners. It meant understanding Dixieland jazz but taming it so that potentially killer-diller numbers like "In The Mood" (taken from a formerly used pattern of black riffs) could be executed on the dance floor smoothly and without mishap. It meant further playing it safe by setting improvisations in stone, so that they were often repeated note for note each time with nothing left to chance. It meant alternating upbeat numbers with romantic ballads to dream on.

But most of all, along with all the orderly taming and the discipline, it meant creating and maintaining a beat, a lilt, a swing to send joy to the heart of dancers and set their feet in motion. Miller did achieve that magic. With his own, very recognizable reedy sound, he distilled black jazz into one of our smoothest incarnations of swing. White swing aimed at white dancers, white record buyers and white radio listeners. But irresistible all the same.[400]

With the white swing bands, the aim of the game most often amounted to a series of big commercial hits that would sell records in the millions. Trumpeter/leader Harry James, who knew his jazz but specialized in schmaltzy ballads, hit the jackpot in the early forties with "You Made Me Love You" and "Sleepy Lagoon." Artie Shaw scored with "Begin the Beguine," "Frenesí" and his theme song "Nightmare." Larry Clinton, leading one of the sweetest of swing bands, had his "Reverie" and "Deep Purple." Goodman's "Sing, Sing, Sing," Dorsey's "Getting Sentimental"—such hits, promoted on radio and in films, were the life blood of the business-minded white swing bandleaders.

* * *

The post-Goodman white swing bands—unlike their predecessors—no longer felt impelled to seek out and try to learn from the black jazz originators. For one thing, by the late thirties Oliver and his Lincoln Gardens had become a thing of the past, Fletcher Henderson no longer reigned at Roseland, and Harlem, past its heyday, no longer served as a strong magnet. For another, the black sounds had already become absorbed into white music, often modified as we have seen (if not watered down) and geared to the general public. Earlier, white New Orleanians like Paul Mares of the NORK and Nick LaRocca of the ODJB were quick to pay tribute to or (in LaRocca's case) deny the influence of the black sound they had adopted. But the white swing bands, at a generation remove, thought less and less in terms of African-American influences. In fact, the white swing musicians themselves were achieving such popularity and success that they themselves could now serve as role models—musicians such as Benny Goodman, Buddy Rich, Red Norvo, Bunny Berigan or Jack Teagarden.

(Actually the white exemplar had already materialized a decade earlier with Bix Beiderbecke. For Beiderbecke, although mesmerized by Armstrong's cornet playing, developed a style of his own. And while Armstrong had, undoubtedly, a more seminal influence on jazz, Bix himself had a very real impact on scores of musicians, both black and white, especially in terms of harmonic development, notably his use of the whole tone scale and his absorption, in his piano music especially, of the sounds of Ravel and Stravinsky.)

Interestingly, despite the progress of whites in the big band area, some musicians of both races were still surprised in the thirties to discover how far whites had come in a genre originally composed, performed and danced by blacks. In 1933, for example, Rex Stewart and his friends had heard about a jazzy white xylophonist/ vibraphonist named Red Norvo. Curious about the phenomenon, they wanted to check him out. Unfortunately, blacks weren't allowed into the clubs where Norvo played, and his records were distributed to white buyers exclusively. Finally, they managed to hear him in a New Jersey theater and couldn't believe their ears. "This cat had it!" they concluded, and henceforth always brought up Norvo's name "whenever somebody said ofays couldn't swing."[401] And in New York in the late 30s, Art Hodes was bowled over to discover that people actually came to listen to the band he was playing with—a *white* band—just as listeners used to flock to hear black musicians on Chicago's south side.[402] But by the end of the decade white musicians had come a long way and the white public had become far more knowledgeable than before in the realms of jazz and swing.

Graying of The Big Bands

The old stereotype of black-equals-hot-and-white-equals-sweet persisted as a widely held view well beyond the thirties. Yet, in reality—paralleling the trend seen in songwriters and vocalists—by the end of the decade and the approach of World War II, black and white swing bands resembled each other more and more and at times were racially indistinguishable. Charlie Barnet and Woody Herman were notable examples of white bands with a "black sound." Duke Ellington called Barnet's orchestra "the blackest white band of all."[403] And, addressing the old stereotype, Gunther

Schuller held that Woody Herman's band would have been more appreciated had he been black.[404]

Much of that apparent sameness in sound was due to the ubiquity of arrangers, mainly black arrangers, who wrote for both black and white bands. Fletcher Henderson's arranger, Don Redman, sold his services to Paul Whiteman and other leaders, black and white. In fact, Henderson and Whiteman would, at times, trade arrangements (although, poles apart. they still wound up with a dissimilar sound). Benny Goodman, besides hiring Henderson, bought orchestrations from Chick Webb's talented violinist, sax player and composer/arranger Edgar Sampson. Charlie Barnet bought scores from Benny Carter, Don Redman, Horace Henderson, Andy Gibson and Duke Ellington. The list goes on. On the other hand, some white arrangers sold scores to black bands, for example, Bill Challis and Will Hudson arranged for Fletcher Henderson, Russ Morgan for Louis Armstrong and Ken McComber for Charlie Johnson.

Hsio Wen Shih has noted the abundance of African-American arrangers working for black and white bands at the time, including the Hendersons, Edgar Sampson, Andy Gifford, Sy Oliver and Eddie Durham (who wrote for Glenn Miller and Artie Shaw among others), and he concludes:

> The increasing popularity of swing arrangements on the Henderson model led to a general similarity of style in all the big bands, Negro and white. Goodman, Shaw, the Dorseys, Barnet, Hines, Calloway, Teddy Hill, Webb were all approaching the same standards of proficiency . . . [405]

It should be noted that, while a good number of white bands had been absorbing and distilling the black sounds more and more proficiently, the black bands, while becoming smoother, and while including a repertoire of romantic numbers, were less apt to venture into the zone of saccharine music à la Guy Lombardo. True, Louis Armstrong favored some trite Tin Pan Alley tunes, and he was known to have expressed admiration for Lombardo, even slipping—or sinking—into the treacly Lombardo mode several times himself. But Armstrong, being Armstrong, could put a blessing on the most inane of numbers, and neither his ensembles nor the black bands considered here could ever wholly embrace the white society bands' brand of sweet music.

Thinking Small

White musicians who loved playing jazz felt necessarily hampered by the experience of performing in large dance bands. Before the swing era, the average white band, for commercial reasons, had held to a fairly pedestrian fare, leaving the serious jazz musician with a sense of frustration and unfulfillment. But even swing could not satisfy that musician's thirst for jazz, for, as we have seen, that music, with its written arrangements and structured approach, could only go so far toward an out-and-out jazz mode. Certainly, it afforded musicians only a minimum of opportunity for free play and improvisation. Consequently, from the early twenties through the thirties, white band players who wanted to indulge in the "real thing," the freer jazz most often associated with black musicians, usually did so in informal late night jam sessions, after an evening of performing a more standard fare.

They could also play a purer type of jazz in studios with small recording groups. Such recording engagements took place often on an *ad hoc* basis. In the twenties and thirties, for example, an Eddie Condon or a Red Nichols might gather together six or seven of the finest musicians available for this or that recording date, sometimes inventing a different jazz band name for each engagement.

Some white performers who recorded on a more or less free lance basis with small groups had been members of the early white Chicago Dixieland ensembles. For example, trombonist George Brunies of the NORK, tenor sax Bud Freeman, drummer Dave Tough, cornetist Jimmy McPartland, clarinetist/sax player Frank Teschemaker and banjo/guitarist Eddie Condon, had, all five, played in the Austin High School Gang. Frequently recording with them and others were notable sidemen such as clarinetists Mugsy Spanier, and Pee Wee Russell, trombonist Miff Mole, clarinetist/saxist Joe Marsala, trumpeters Wingy Manone and Max Kaminsky, drummer George Wettling and bass sax Adrien Rollini. Although a number of the players (Miff Mole, for example) have been accused of emphasizing technique at the expense of jazz feeling—a criticism often leveled at white players such as Jimmy Dorsey—recordings of these ensembles, clean, sharp and dexterous, have a verve and quality which continue to impress listeners today.

Small jazz recording ensembles seemed eminently suited to the late 1930s. For at that time a number of jazz aficionados, in rebellion against swing's big band brand of "diluted" jazz, strove to take jazz back to its roots, to preserve and promote it by presenting jazz ensembles in intimate Greenwich Village clubs and by recording small groups of jazz musicians.[406] Milt Gabler was one of the foremost figures in jazz recording of time, founding his Commodore Recording Company in 1938 for the preservation of the jazz he loved. Gabler frequently used the talents of the performers mentioned above but called as well on black stars such as Coleman Hawkins, Hot Lips Page and Billie Holliday for racially mixed recordings.

The mixing of the two races in small group recordings dated back to the earliest days of jazz recording, with Jelly Roll Morton—introduced to the studio as Cuban—collaborating with the NORK, and, even earlier, with Achille (Joseph) Baquet—passing as white—recording with Jimmy Durante's Original New Orleans Jazz Band in 1918. Although the average large black band had a relatively slim chance of getting good record engagements and air play, individual black performers of talent were often invited to record in small racially mixed groups. White musicians such as Eddie Condon and Joe Marsala were particularly active in organizing many such non-segregated recording ensembles.

As for the live interracial public performance, despite sporadic attempts in the thirties to make it happen, such a thing became truly possible only from the 1940s on. Before that, it occurred mainly on an informal, spontaneous basis. For instance, at the end of an evening, a Bix Beiderbecke might show up with his horn at Lincoln Gardens and be allowed, even invited, by Joe Oliver to join the band for a few choruses. Or, as Pops Foster told it, in Harlem, white Jack Purvis, a trumpeter and trombonist, stayed out in the sun for hours to look black enough for Louis Russell to let him sit in with his band.[407] But the customary venue for live interracial jazz playing was not the big band but the small group jam session. Here again, it was almost always a case of whites seeking to play with blacks, so such sessions usually took place on black territory.

The small interracial jazz ensemble became institutionalized in the latter part of the 1930s, after Benny Goodman started the practice of including the finest of African-American musicians in trios and quartets for performances before white audiences. Other bandleaders followed suit, creating their own "spin-offs" in which musicians of both races abandoned the customary swing arrangements for ensemble music with a greater focus on jazz.

Few, if any, people at the time realized that it was precisely, the small interracial jazz group rather than the big white band that would come to represent the future.

Evaluating the Big White Bands

For music lovers and commentators, the swing era, dominated by the large white ensembles, was either the greatest or rock bottom worst phase of jazz oriented popular music. As we shall see in a later chapter, the anti-swing band partisans were seemingly the most numerous—at least the most vocal. Critics such as Rudi Blesh, Peter Townsend, Al Rose and others lamented white swing's commerciality and found it sorely lacking when compared to black swing with its richer and more "authentic" brand of jazz.

In fact, generally speaking, when it came to comparing white band music against black, critics rarely put the latter on a par with the former. Albert McCarthy, who gave serious attention to white bands in *Big Band Jazz* and *The Dance Band Era,* wound up granting the whites faint praise in a kind of well-they-weren't-always-great-but-they-did-make-a-contribution stance. Gunther Schuller, in *The Swing Era,* entitled his section on white orchestras "The White Bands," whereas he called his section on black orchestras "The Great Black Bands." And other writers, wanting to give the white ensembles their due, have emphasized the fact that they had a different type of sound and given them credit less for the quality of their music than for bringing jazz "into the American mainstream."[408]

In evaluating the white swing bands, it is undeniable that although not many of them could match their black predecessors in richness, variety, depth and drive, the music of a Goodman, a Herman, a Dorsey or a Miller had a magic that completely captivated a generation of dancers and listeners in America and abroad. In the final analysis, the white bands played a vital role in the swing era, an era considered today as one of the highest points in the history of American popular music.

Notes

359 It has often been pointed out that downtown nightclub owners, unhappy with competition from the popular Harlem venues, made sure that reports of crimes in the area were perpetually featured in New York newspapers.

360 *Hot Man,* p. 48. Hodes attributes much of this enlightenment to new publications such as *Hot Discography, Jazzman* and *Jazz Information* and to the founding of small jazz recording companies like Blue Note, Commodore and Solo Art

361 *Swing Changes,* p. 84.

362 John Hammond, while flicking his car radio dial, happened across one of these "remotes" and chanced to discover his soon-to-be protégé, Count Basie.

363 According to Rex Stewart, Meyer Davis followed Jim Europe's Clef Club system and took over much of the society band business from the black bands. *Boy Meets Horn,* p. 90.

364 Trombonist Dicky Wells said, "I believe you can get too clean . . . everybody knows that the ofay's playing is clean . . ." *Night People,* p. 42.

365 *Early Jazz,* p. 70.

366 Vermazon, Bruce, in an internet article, "Al Hickman and his Orchestra," quotes a Hickman interview in the *San Francisco Examiner* of April 11, 1938, p. 6.

367 *Ibid.* Vermazon quotes *Examiner of October 30, 1920.*

368 *Kingdom of Swing,* p. 75.

369 *Jazz Masters of the Thirties,* p. 11.

370 Quoted in *Big Band Jazz,* p. 185.

371 See Chapter One of *Jazz Masters of the Thirties.*

372 Rex Stewart's phrase, *ibid,* p. 11.

373 Cited by Michael Brooks in documentation for CD, *Bix Beiderbecke, Singin'The Blues.*

374 *Op. cit,* p. 12.

[375] A number recorded by Goldkette's men but never issued.

[376] Such is the assessment of Loren Schoenberg in the documentation of the CD *Swingin' Uptown.*

[377] That is not the case, however, with Edgar Sampson's bluesy violin on Henderson's "House of David Blues." It adds rather than subtracts.

[378] One would think that Beiderbecke himself would have made jazz history once he recorded his own group. But unfortunately, the Bix Beiderbecke orchestra perpetuated the mainly sweet approach of Goldkette and Whiteman.

[379] Gunther Schuller held that Gifford borrowed heavily from black arranger, John Nesbitt, associated with McKinney's Cotton Pickers. See Chapter Fourteen, *infra*, concerning Richard Sudhalter's refutation.

[380] See, for example, Loren Schoenberg's squib on the Casa Loma orchestra in the documentation for CD *Anthology of Big Band Swing.*

[381] *Lost Chords,* p. 345.

[382] *The Big Band Era,* p. 61.

[383] *Pops,* p. 68.

[384] Dance, p. 55. According to Elmer Snowdon of the Ellington band, Henri Busse, Whiteman's main "spy," would sit in with Bubber Miley of the Ellington band, but Miley was too fast for him. Journalist Dave Peyton claimed that he saw Whiteman himself, in pursuit of musical information, offering Ellington's band $100 to play a certain number for him. See *The Duke Ellington Reader,* p. 26.

[385] P. 140.

[386] *Kingdom of Swing,* p. 60.

[387] See for example, his interview with Sudhalter in *Lost Chords.*

[388] Firestone, *Swing, Swing, Swing,* p. 85.

[389] *Ibid.,* p. 80.

[390] *Op. cit.,* p. 115.

[391] Cited in *Black Bottom,* p. 26.

[392] John McDonough in "Streamlining Jazz," *The Oxford Companion to Jazz,* p. 211.

[393] *Jazz in American Culture,* p. 69.

[395] *The Birth of Bebop,* p. 127. DeVeaux states earlier: ". . . With the Swing Era, the integration of dance music with other forms of mass-market entertainment was carried out on a scale and with a degree of technological sophistication never seen before. New

media . . . began to tie the vast American continent together into networks of production and dissemination controlled from New York and Los Angeles . . ." (p. 118).

396 Neil Leonard, *Jazz and the White Americans,* p. 103. This "standard product," a move away from black jazz with its polyphony and greater freedom, was pushed by moguls of the media. Leonard cites E.C. Mills, head of the Music Publishers' Protective Association and a director of ASCAP, who said "I think we should go back to the melody and let it serve instead of the noise . . ." (pp. 104-105).

397 As mentioned in the previous chapter, Lunceford had been paying his band next to nothing, whereas Dorsey could afford to make a lavish offer. Moreover, with Dorsey, Oliver would also have royalties, credit for his compositions and great artistic freedom. An offer he could not refuse.

398 P. 342.

399 *The Swing Era,* p. 686.

400 It is interesting that Gunther Schuller, a critic of great taste, does not discount Miller's music, as many jazz critics do. Although, in *The Swing Era,* he describes the Miller formula as "an attractive patina rather than the real thing . . . often connected to jazz by only the slimmest thread," he also finds it "often a music of considerable beauty" (p. 669). Further, he states ". . . it is hard to think of anyone with a sound quite so unique, quite so mesmerizing—and, more astonishingly, so resistant to becoming tedious."

401 *Jazz Masters of the 30s,* p. 76.

402 *Hot Man,* p. 45.

403 Cited in Shaw, *Black Popular Music,* p. 65. See also *The Duke Ellington Reader,* p. 254.

404 *The Swing Era,* p. 729.

405 See his chapter in Hentoff and McCarthy, *Jazz,* p. 186.

406 Critics have referred to such activities in the late thirties as part of a "Dixieland revival." But, as James Lincoln Collier has pointed out, many of these jazz musicians had had experience in swing bands and, consequently, provided a smoother and more polished sound than the Chicagoans of the early twenties (*The Making of Jazz,* p. 283).

407 *Pops Foster,* p. 140. Apparently, Purvis was successful.

408 See, for example the chapter entitled "The White Influx" in Collier's *The Making of Jazz.*

13

THE FALL OF SWING; THE RISE OF BOP

The Swing Era did not die dramatically—or even noticeably. As General Douglas MacArthur said of old soldiers, it simply "faded away." Rather than suddenly vanishing from the scene, swing held on as America's favorite music throughout World War II. A familiar and much loved commodity, it served as continuity and provided a morale booster for departed servicemen wherever they were stationed.

However, only a few years after swing had become a byword in American popular music, the big bands playing it had already begun to face serious problems. The number of band members had been steadily increasing, but economically, by the end of the thirties, big was no longer better. It became harder and harder, for example, to meet the payroll demands of large orchestras. Bands had to secure many bookings to meet costs, but new venues were not opening up for them. And booking agents discouraged competition from new bands starting up, in order not to eat into their profits.[409]

The outbreak of World War II took its toll in musical manpower. Bandleaders and performers were conscripted in the Armed Forces, forcing a number of orchestras to break up. And for those still in business, gas rationing and other wartime restrictions cut into their activities. Mobility on the road, whether by car, bus or railroad, posed problems for them; yet most of their profits had come from touring in various cities of the country. Further, the production of records was diminished by the Armed Forces' need for shellac. And worse was to come, namely, a thirty percent tax (later reduced to twenty percent) on nightclubs and cabarets where people danced to the sound of the bands. Not to mention a wartime midnight curfew one year later.

If all that were not enough, in the early forties major strikes drove wedges into the popular music business, adversely affecting the big swing bands. At the end of 1940, ASCAP (American Society of Composers, Authors and Publishers) demanded a yearly fee of up to nine million dollars for its music to be played on radio. Since that was double the sum previously paid to the Society, the radio administration would not agree to it. So, in early 1941, the radio networks banned music controlled by ASCAP from the air, and the ban lasted a full year, until both sides came to a compromise. Because the majority of the big band hits of the day constituted ASCAP material, bandleaders and performers could no longer play their theme songs and most popular numbers for radio listeners.

Some leaders, undaunted, found escape hatches. For instance, they began performing and recording swing arrangements of folk songs such as Stephen Foster's "Jeanie with the Light Brown Hair" and classics by Tchaikovsky or Debussy. In actuality, jazzing the classics had already been a trend in the thirties. But in 1941 the idea made practical sense, since bands were hurting for material, and folk and classic songs were in the public domain, well out of ASCAP's aegis.

Latin American music provided another outlet for big band creativity during the hiatus. As with folk and classic music, bands had already been swinging tunes from south of the border during the thirties, for Latin American songs and fashions had come very much in vogue in the era of Roosevelt's "Good Neighbor Policy." But around the time of the 1941 ban, such non-ASCAP material became a rich resource. Meanwhile, the radio networks had formed their own music publishing company, BMI (Broadcast Music Inc). And BMI happened to have in stock English language adaptations of Latin American numbers such as "Yours," "Green Eyes," "Perfidia" and "Amapola."[410] Like those songs, all recorded in 1941, other such imports temporarily bridged the gap for the repertory of big swing bands.

But shortly afterwards another calamity occurred: Between August, 1942, and September, 1943, the American Federation of Musicians imposed a recording ban while they launched a strike, demanding a fee for every record played on radio. That meant that during the strike period swing bands could not record at all. It was as if everything was conspiring to decimate the bands.

One important upshot of this latest disaster was that vocalists came to the fore. Although instrumentalists could not record during the ban, no ruling prevented singers from doing so. And so many did make records, backed up by vocal ensembles.

Actually, vocalists had already been gaining in importance on the big band scene. To remain commercially viable in the thirties, orchestras had to feature at least one attractive singer, often two, a female and a male—and, increasingly, the singers had been taking the spotlight. This trend seemed especially suited to the wartime mood. Separated lovers loved listening to nostalgic ballads, to singers reminiscing about times fondly shared together in the past. And now, with the AFM ban as a catalyst, vocalists such as Doris Day, Perry Como, Dinah Shore and Dick Haymes were ever more on the rise—at the eventual expense of the big bands, their leaders and instrumentalists.

Despite all such inroads on swing, it continued to survive, if not thrive, until the end of the war, fading out only in the late forties and fifties. Glenn Miller, for one, helped keep it alive by infusing the marching music of his Army Air Force band with lively swing sounds, in numbers such as "American Patrol" and "St. Louis Blues." (For some old-time partisans of Sousa's straightforward World War I march music, such innovations seemed as sacrilegious as jazzing "Ave Maria.") Like Miller's outfit, other swing bands provided music within the Armed Forces, while a number of civilian orchestras traveled to war zones to entertain the troupes under the auspices of the United Services Organization (USO). And in various Army, Marine and Air Corps bases in the States and abroad, GIs acting as disk jockeys spun the popular swing numbers and ballads on closed circuit radio stations for off-duty listening.[411] Playing that American-as-apple-pie music not only boosted morale but could even be considered a patriotic act. After all, Hitler had condemned swing as an arch-enemy of Nazism.

If the war helped prolong the life of swing, the patient's time would gradually run out, for several reasons, mainly financial ones. For example, in spite of a boom, fostered in large part by the manufacture of munitions and other war supplies, at the end of World War II, America was beset by a number of strikes and by inflation. The ever expanding swing bands, already scrounging to meet payroll and other demands, now suffered even more acutely. As David Stowe explains, promoters, in a bind, passed on expenses to customers by doubling the price of admission for dancing. It was a Catch-22, for as Stowe states,

> Consumers discouraged by high prices stayed home or went to movies; promoters went bankrupt paying high guarantees for what turned out to be sparse audiences; agencies found it more difficult to book bands at rates the musicians would accept . . . higher lodging and food costs prevented musicians from accepting lower salaries.[412]

Add to such problems the fact that newly introduced television was taking a greater and greater share of the big band audiences. Small wonder that by 1946 a dozen major swing band leaders, including Artie Shaw, Les Brown, Jack Teagarden, Benny Carter, Jimmie Lunceford and Benny Goodman himself, had dissolved their orchestras.

The black bands, were, of course, hit by the adverse developments in the music business. But since they had only rarely achieved the heights of fame and fortune attained by white bands, their comedown was less remarkable. In fact, as explained, during the post-1935 swing era they had been increasingly shut off from the commercial avenues open to whites. The most brilliant leaders among them, Duke Ellington and Count Basie, were able to make a go of it. Not merely because of strong promotion but because their talents transcended any one specific mode or mold such as standard swing. Indeed, they survived with their big bands until the end of their lives.[413] Lionel Hampton was another exception among black bandleaders. After achieving renown as a sideman with Benny Goodman, the vibraphonist formed his own band and continued leading well into the 1990s before his death in 2002. However, others less fortunate had to make do freelancing in occasional gigs or taking less glamorous jobs (leader Luis Russell, for example, became a chauffeur and shopkeeper after his career fell apart).[414]

But of course, whether in the black or white realm, swing's reign could not last indefinitely. In the early forties, folk and country music[415] and the great vogue of vocalists gave the once indomitable music strong competition. And like every musical fashion that preceded and followed it, swing had to change or give way to another one. So it went into a sort of eclipse, with leaders and sidemen increasingly regrouping into smaller, more economically viable units.

Swing's eclipse was only a partial one, however. Although another style, bop, would come into vogue, a number of musicians who adopted that style had been schooled in the big swing bands, for example, Dizzy Gillespie, Charlie Christian and Mary Lou Williams. Such musicians did not immediately abandon familiar swing techniques while experimenting with new ones. Moreover, much of swing's repertoire would resurface as "standards" adapted to the styles of later jazz musicians. And vintage swing era music survives today, not only on disk but with live swing bands echoing the old sounds or with "ghost bands" such as the Count Basie or Tommy Dorsey orchestras, which may boast one or two survivors from the original units. The old music continues and undoubtedly will continue to be played, for dancers, for nostalgic listening and, of course, for its particular charm and vitality.

Enter Bop

Not all jazz musicians and critics lamented the downfall of swing. In fact a number of them had been repelled by the blandness and commerciality of the post-Goodman bands and were more than ready to applaud the demise of such a sellout. But there was no general agreement about what should supersede the genre. For some, the solution was a return to the authenticity of traditional jazz. Thus the so-called Dixieland Revival of the forties, which did not offer an actual duplication of the New Orleans style but came close to it in its emphasis of ensemble styling by talented instrumentalists. Such a return to the sounds of old-time jazz was espoused by the likes of Milt Gabler and John Hammond and may be heard today in Gabler's excellent Commodore recordings. The Dixieland Revival also brought out of retirement some of the original contingent of New Orleans musicians, such as sixty-two year old Bunk Johnson, a contemporary of Buddy Bolden.[416]

Another avenue led not to the past but to the future. That avenue was bop, as it came to be called after the war (with the alternate labels "bebop". and "rebop"). Bop had been quietly developing during the war years. But wartime is no time for a change of president or musical style, and bop only became a public phenomenon years later, in the latter half of the 1940s. It was cultivated by musicians such as Charlie Parker, Dizzy Gillespie, Thelonius Monk, Charlie Christian, Bud Powell, Milt Hilton, Kenny Clarke and Max Roach.

Significantly, bop represented a racial turning of the tables. For while swing had been taken over and practically monopolized by whites, bop was not only created and developed by black musicians but remained fundamentally a black engineered product..

Bop musicians were already creating their sounds in the latter part of the 1930s, when white swing was still going strong, and in the early forties. They experimented in small groups, in after-hours jam sessions or in small Harlem clubs often located in basement rooms of subdivided Harlem tenements. One of the most famous and frequented of the clubs was Minton's Playhouse, a former hotel dining room, on West 118th Street. Talented black instrumentalists, venturing outside the mold of mainstream swing, would gather there and try out new musical ideas, each outdoing the other in inventing the unexpected. And in the process of creating and innovating, to a great extent they arrived at a sort of musical snobbery, an exclusiveness of the enlightened.

Until that time words like "snobbery" and "exclusiveness" would had seemed more appropriate to the white race. Certainly, almost any self-respecting white southern gentleman considered himself a good many levels higher than an African American, even at the time of the Second World War. As for "enlightened," given the relative lack of educational opportunities available to African Americans, the use of that word in connection with black musicians might seem surprising as well.

In the realm of popular music, however, those musicians, as we have seen, had already developed a type of swing that was deeper, richer and more sophisticated than the fare of most of the big white bands. That trend would intensify greatly with the advent of bop. And along with the marked complexity and sophistication of that new style of music came a heightened proprietary and elitist attitude on the part of bop musicians. Their stance appeared to be "This is our music, we invented it, we own it."

According to Dizzy Gillespie, it wasn't the music that led to the elitism of black musicians but the elitism which helped inspire the music. He explains:

> Some of us began to jam at Minton's in Harlem in the early 'forties. But there were always some cats showing up who couldn't blow at all but would take six or seven choruses to prove it. So on afternoons before a session, Thelonius Monk and I began to work out some complex variations on chords and the like, and we used them at night to scare away the no-talent guys. After a while we got more and more interested in what we were doing as music, and, as we began to explore more and more, our music evolved.[417]

Other contemporaries bear witness to Gillespie's and Monk's standoffish practice of discouraging outsiders with pre-rehearsed complexities. Some agreed that the *de facto* closed door policy did originate in order to keep inferior musicians away. Others maintained that bop became complex in order to exclude would be imitators or to ensure that outsiders didn't muscle in on the boppers' hard won jobs.[418] But there was undoubtedly another reason that lay behind the exclusiveness and esotericism of bop musicians. There was the matter of race.

It seems that for the very first time since black song and dance were discovered by white entrepreneurs and the white public—that is, the first time in a hundred years—African Americans were laying claim to their music. In the past, outside of a Joplin or a Handy, few of them had taken that music seriously. Even if they had, most black ragtime or jazz performers and composers understood that their only chance of monetary success in music lay in self-parody or imitations of white styles.

But the very whites who had adopted black music had now opened the way to black self-recognition. Following Benny Goodman's example, other white leaders had begun to desegregate their bands. And in the late thirties African-American musicians were achieving greater visibility, performing outside of Harlem, in downtown clubs. At that point, the white musical world was becoming aware of the talented black musical presence. And taking it seriously. That breaking down of barriers and that increasing awareness and esteem on the part of music loving whites must have sent a message to African-American performers—a self-confirming message. A further endorsement came from small recording companies of the early forties, forming on the heels of the Decca company's demise, for such companies were looking for new talent, and black artists helped to provide it.

Without hope, revolution is impossible. In the world of American popular music and in the field of jazz specifically, the strides of the late 1930s provided at least some rays of hope to the generation of blacks who would generate bop music. With a certain amount of optimism and self-awareness came the increasingly strong and articulated view that black music had repeatedly been taken away from blacks. And a determination not to let that happen again. So a sort of revolution occurred—not in militant demonstrations or racial protests of the 1970s variety, but in the minds and attitudes of African-American bop musicians.

Some of them maintained, at least among themselves, that they were creating a product that would finally be off limits to a white appropriation. As Billie Holliday put it, speaking of her experience with bop musicians,

> By the time the ofays got around to copping 'swing' a new style of music was already breaking out all over uptown. Ten years later that became the newest thing when the white boys downtown figured out how to cop it.[419]

In fact not many "white boys" could be said to have "copped" bop. But who could tell what would happen at that time? Mary Lou Williams related how, in the early forties, Thelonius Monk, believing that the blacks would never get credit for what they were doing, said, "We are going to create something that they can't steal, because they can't play it." So, according to Williams, Monk gathered together a group of instrumentalists who each contributed to extremely difficult arrangements. That may have discouraged outsiders, including ambitious white admirers, but, as Mary Lou Williams told it, the arrangements were so difficult that Monk's own band had trouble executing them![420])

This was not a case of inverse racism on the part of blacks, or what would later be termed "Crow Jim." The well-known bop musicians, on the whole, did not want to exclude whites from their music. On the contrary, the first bop band to play 52nd Street, Dizzy Gillespie's five-piece group at the Onyx Club, featured white pianist George Wallington. (Gillespie had previously included two white musicians in his small Philadelphia ensemble). Bop artists admired Woody Herman[421] and his bop styled group, Herman's Herd; they welcomed Benny Goodman's visits at Minton's, and at various times they played with pianist Lennie Tristano, tenor saxist Stan Getz, baritone saxist Gerry Mulligan, alto saxist Lee Konitz, trombonist Kai Winding and other white jazz artists on recordings and in live performances. Their caveats were not aimed at white musicians themselves but at the old and established practice of a commercial white takeover.

The Sounds of Bop

The schism between bop and its predecessor, swing, was not an absolute one. As with most fashions, there were links between the old and the new. Bop sounds had already been anticipated by swing musicians, developed by such predecessors as Coleman Hawkins and Lester Young.[422] Swing bandleaders like Earl Hines and Cab Calloway, although avowedly anti-bop, employed instrumentalists who introduced bop styling in their performances. Further, since most well-known bop musicians had experience playing in big swing bands, they naturally carried over techniques developed in swing. For example, the riffs that much of swing music had been built on would be featured in bop compositions.[423] Dizzy Gillespie, a creator, star performer and prime mover of bop music, never completely abandoned swing genres, playing an eclectic mix of styles throughout his career, including swing and Afro-Caribbean rhythms.

But such connections notwithstanding, in formulating their new sounds, the bop musicians left swing styling far behind them.[424] In fact, one of the clearest way to describe bop as a genre is to contrast it with swing.

To begin with, swing, as we have seen, had been tied very directly to the world of ballroom dancing. Bop, on the other hand, grew to maturity and developed its personality outside the confines of that world. Its instrumentalists, most of them unable or unwilling to make their living in big swing bands, no longer needed to concern themselves with accompanying and pleasing dancers.[425] Instead, theirs became a listening music, played in clubs and, more seriously, in concerts.

Without dancers, there was little need or care for the requisite of strict tempo: the steady 4/4 percussive bass beat that had been a *sine qua non* of jazz and dance bands at least since Bolden's time. Thus bop musicians were free to create far more irregular and complex rhythms than those heard in swing. In cases where a ground beat could be heard throughout a number, it was not swing's standard familiar, driving and danceable stress on the first and third beats, in the bass. Instead musicians commonly placed a bewildering emphasis on the second and fourth beats[426] with sounds like "be-*bop,* re-*bop.*" And they frequently used a steady succession of eighth notes, creating a highly undanceable beat. Further adding to the difficulties, instead of using the reliable bass drum for a simple and understandable tempo, percussionists such as drummers Kenny Clarke and Max Roach, tended to use the cymbals for the main beats and the bass drum more sparingly, for accents. In addition, they would intersperse throughout a piece a whole variety of ingenious rhythmic displacements.[427] All of these innovations presented obstacles to dancers. But what mattered for musicians, of course, were the breakthroughs in rhythm.

Rhythmic innovation had, of course, been an integral part of the African-American contribution to popular music. But now, with bop, harmonic changes came to the fore as well. From the start, new harmonic complexities accompanied the unusual rhythms—complexities very much at odds with swing, which aimed to please and be understood by its public. Most strikingly, bop musicians used unaccustomed chord combinations, creating a dissonance that conservative listeners considered jarring and bewildering. Bop musicians tended to favor the flatted fifth chord and introduced altered chords such as ninths or elevenths.

Such harmonies were not unknown to previous instrumentalists. Pianist Willie "the Lion" Smith, well acquainted with Debussy and Ravel, had already absorbed and made use of some of their innovative harmonic techniques. As he said, "[The bop musicians] talk about augmented chords, ninth chords, whole-tone progressions and all that. I've been using them for years but I didn't know what they were."[428] And Art Tatum, while not a bop musician, had developed, in addition to extremely complicated rhythms, very advanced harmonies. The bop musicians, however, made extensive use of such harmonies, seemingly pushing them to their outermost limits. To explain the phenomenon as simply as possible:

Swing harmony had, like previous harmony in popular music, most often built chords on a familiar sequence of alternate notes of the scale, for example, C-E-G, which spans five notes and is therefore called a "fifth." But bop musicians came up with a more interesting sound by lowering G, the top note of the chord, one half step, thus creating a "flatted fifth." They also made use of unaccustomed chords such as ninths and elevenths. For instance, to form a ninth, using that same C-E-G combination, they would introduce a D into the chord, thereby creating a dissonant sound. Musicians refer to such a chord as a "ninth," because D, the second note of the C scale, may be considered note number nine, since it also occurs right after the C that ends the eight notes of the scale. A third and last example of a chord creating a dissonance unfamiliar to previous jazz music is one that was taught to Dizzy Gillespie by Thelonious Monk. Commonly called a "minor seventh flat five," it consists of C, E-flat, G-flat and B-flat.

Such chords took in a greater range of notes than before, notes that would have been considered wrong and jarring in standard chords of swing music. And since bop instrumentalists based their improvisations on more and more complex and inclusive chords, they could now use almost any note in the scale. It was as if there were no more "wrong" notes. A masterful improviser like Charlie Parker managed to make it all work, but to the uninitiated or to those conditioned to swing music, such harmonic effects sounded highly abstruse and off-putting.

Creators of bop music were far more unpredictable in their inventions than swing arrangers. In fact, although bop musicians might pre-arrange and carefully rehearse their chordal progressions, they did not depend on the detailed professional charts essential to swing era music. On the contrary, most bop ensembles granted a much greater role to improvisation than the large swing bands could ever afford to do. Such improvisation was not always a case of musicians "making up" their parts with each and every performance. For, at times, as in the past, an instrumentalist and/or composer might work out individual variations that would be repeated in subsequent performances or recordings.[429] The emphasis, however, was now on free musical variations contributed by individual members.

The format generally adopted by bop musicians—a format that would characterize much of jazz to this day—reflected that free approach. It was certainly less strictly structured and codified than the format of swing. Customarily, the musicians would first launch into an introduction previously agreed on, an arranged section that might state or evoke the theme from a well-known number or from a new composition. They would follow that with improvisational solos by individual instrumentalists. Then finally, on cue, they would perform some pre-arranged ending. Such open-endedness would have been unthinkable in the context of the big swing bands. And even highly improvisational jazz heard in the twenties and thirties was generally more structured, arranged and cohesive than bop, its logic built on familiar chord structures and a steady beat.

In the realm of technique and performance, bop musicians liked to reach into higher registers than those previously used by the average swing instrumentalist. And since dancing was no longer an important factor in jazz composition or performance, they indulged in much faster tempos, introducing dizzying runs executed at breakneck speed. Bop provided ample opportunity for virtuoso playing, and its star players were, indeed, virtuosos.

These facts explain how and why the bop style started popular music on a far less accessible course than that of the swing bands and why, in the future, jazz would ultimately no longer qualify as "popular" music. But perhaps the most difficult, recondite aspect of bop for adherents of swing was its deconstruction not of rhythm, not of harmony but of melody. Because with the emphasis on improvisation and chord changes—a trend already anticipated in the work of black swing musicians,[430] the melody of a favorite song might start and finish a piece but only be alluded to, or neglected entirely, between the musical bookends. Small wonder that a number from Rodgers and Hart's Broadway show of 1939, *Let's Face It,* went: "I like to recognize the tune. I like to hear what the orchestra's playing. I keep saying 'Won't you play me a tune?'"[431]

In only a few years bop music had radically changed the course of jazz.

Bop and the Black Heritage

Paradoxically, the musicians who wanted to keep bop under black ownership took that music far afield of their own black tradition. For in doing away with standard danceable tempos and swing styling, in becoming more and more sophisticated and complex, they created music that veered away from the tempos of their African-American religious and cultural heritage. The lilting offbeat sounds of slave songs that had been perpetuated in ragtime and swing could not easily survive in the context of the new bop rhythms.

As for the blues, impressions and echoes of the twelve-bar genre did occur in bop. A musician such as Charlie Parker conveyed a recognizable and strong blues flavor in many of his pieces, and Dizzy Gillespie liked to include blues themes in his repertoire. Generally, however, the blues did not seem entirely at home in the new progressive music. Bop performers might use the twelve-bar pattern but impose their modern chord changes on it, dispelling much of the traditional blues feeling. According to Dizzy Gillespie, bop musicians shunned the blues as a part of their uncultured past. He stated: ". . . the bebop musicians didn't like to play the blues. They were ashamed."[432] If Gillespie's assessment was correct, the black heritage was, again, being cast aside by the new black artists.

LeRoi Jones disagreed with Gillespie. He saw, instead a strong relationship between bop and the blues, the two styles he personally favored and considered truly African-American. Bebop, he stated, "reestablished blues as the most important Afro-American form in Negro music by its astonishingly contemporary restatement of the basic blues impulse."[433] But, in fact, the basic blues impulse had well nigh disappeared in bop's new rhythmic and harmonic complexities.[434] For in the context of bop's modern progressions and improvisations, the blues lost their earthy drive, their message, their character and, except in rare cases (with Charlie Parker, for example), their very soul.

Taking bop even further away from the black tradition, in the place of black tradition, the bop musicians opted for patterns and techniques customarily associated with white European music, namely, classical music. For example, much of the harmonic complexity and dissonance of bop had been developed by classical composers such as Stravinsky, Bartók, Schönberg, Debussy and Shostakovich, composers much admired by Charlie Parker and other bop musicians.

In reality, few of the early practitioners and exponents of bop music were trained in classical music. Such training was generally not available to African Americans of the time, and a career in classical music would have been a most unlikely goal for them. But for decades a number of black jazz musicians, such as James P. Johnson, Fats Waller or Coleman Hawkins, had been drawn to classical genres, and some, like Scott Joplin or Duke Ellington, who wrote extended pieces outside the genre of ordinary dance music, attempted to bridge the gap between jazz and the classics. A number of whites in jazz, Bix Beiderbecke, for example, were drawn to that goal as well, but the black bop musicians were the first to infuse popular music systematically with classical elements.

Along with the classicizing of jazz music, the bop musicians created an atmosphere and a *modus operandi* to suit the seriousness of their style. Theirs was music to be listened to, if not reverently, at least as quietly as possible. The abstract, polysyllabic titles of some of their compositions, although self-mocking, may be seen as a sign of the new atmosphere and the new aspirations: Thelonius Monk's "Epistrophy," Charlie Parker's "Anthropology" or Benny Harris' "Ornithology."[435]

In classicizing jazz and elevating it to a "higher" level, bop musicians were not entirely successful in holding the attention of members of their own race. A good percentage of the New York black public that had flocked to the great battles of the bands and danced the night away to the music of Henderson, Basie or Webb, did buy bop records and listened to disk jockeys playing bop on radio. But African-American music lovers of the South and Southwest were generally not interested in the new music. For it could not excite them with the familiar beat of the foot-tapping swing or a good dose of the beloved blues. They—and in short order northern blacks as well—would turn instead to the more accessible rhythm-and-blues. As for the bop experimentalists, ironically, they wound up performing mainly for white audiences and white critics.

Early on, bop musicians, both black and white, were able to attract audiences with big bands, such as those of Woody Herman or Billy Eckstine. But if they wanted to keep dancers, they had to include, along with their bop numbers, sweet ballads or novelty songs with a standard dance beat. A progressive jazz artist like Dizzy Gillespie had to grapple occasionally with the problem of pleasing dancers while leading a bop oriented band in a ballroom venue. But such attempts were problematic. Gillespie and other bands playing the new music found a surer route to success—and were far more frequently heard—in recording, on stage and on concert tours in America and abroad. Europe, particularly, welcomed such bands—and individual bop artists—as celebrities, virtuosos and inventors of the latest American jazz style, to be listened to in concert.

All in all, despite the strong white connections and influences noted here, the bop style remained essentially an African-American genre, constantly developing within a black musical community. And in the last analysis, any fear of a white takeover proved unfounded. Although, as in the past, the agencies sponsoring bop music were controlled by whites, white performers, composers, bandleaders and entrepreneurs did not repeat history by swooping in on the new black sound, repackaging and marketing it. Perhaps because such a venture would have been unprofitable, lacking in mass appeal. Or, as Monk had predicted, a feat too difficult to execute. Or perhaps because the post-war American perspective on racial issues had had changed too much for such an attempt at expropriation. Or all of the above.

White musicians did participate in bop's reign. But more as admirers and emulators—or even colleagues—than as competitors or as a potential threat. After bop began to surface as the latest fashion in jazz, a number of white musicians eagerly adopted it. White bandleaders Charlie Barnet, Claude Thornhill and Woody Herman cultivated bop sounds. Individual white instrumentalists, such as Stan Getz, Gerry Mulligan, Gil Evans and Bill Evans played bop (but most notably later in the game, after bop's formative years). And as time went on, certain white musicians, a good percentage of them with classical training, would become known less as bop musicians than as practitioners of the later "cool" jazz.

But white usurpation of bop? It never became a reality.

Notes

409 See, for example, Scott DeVeaux's *The Birth of Bebop,* pp. 144-145. DeVeaux thought that such exclusivity on the part of bookers was probably responsible for Coleman Hawkins' failure at the time to succeed on the road as a newcomer in the big band business.

410 "Amapola" ranked as the most popular record of 1941. Like "Green Eyes" and "Yours," it was recorded by Bob Eberle and Helen O'Connell with Jimmy Dorsey's orchestra.

411 The War Department, through the Armed Forces Radio Services, issued, for military use only, ten- and twelve-inch records called "V-Discs," spinning at 78 rpm.

412 *Swing Changes,* pp. 192-193. Stowe gleaned this information from 1946 issues of *Down Beat.*

413 Ellington died in 1974, Basie in 1984. Ellington's band was taken over by his son Mercer. Basie, who had been forced to regroup with a smaller unit in 1950, resumed his big band performances in1952. Other top black bandleaders, such as Benny Carter, while no longer fronting big bands, maintained active careers in recording, live performances and on tours. Carter himself lectured at Princeton University, which awarded him an honorary doctorate in 1974, and he continued performing on sax until the late 80s.

414 Dizzy Gillespie noted that Dickie Wells, a trombonist with Fletcher Henderson, wound up as a bank guard (*To Be or Not to . . . Bop,* p. 66). Bandleader Teddy Hill, although minus a band, kept his musical connections as manager of Minton's Playhouse in the forties.

415 Genres adopted and promoted by BMI during the ASCAP ban.

416 Bunk's performances were controversial, extolled by some as the "real thing" and thought disappointing by others. According to

Frank Driggs and Harris Lewine, "Certain writers, record collectors, and budding jazz historians who hated swing and the new directions in which jazz seemed to be moving, had elevated . . . Bunk Johnson to a cult figure by the time he made his first records in 1942." *Black Beauty, White Heat,* p. 21.

417 *Hear Me Talkin' To Ya,* p 337.

418 *Ibid,* Chapter Nineteen, *passim.*

419 *Lady Sings The Blues,* p. 25.

420 *Hear Me Talkin,* p. 340.

421 Dizzy Gillespie's piece "Woody 'n You" was, indeed, a tribute to Woody Herman.

422 Art Tatum has often been cited as well as a predecessor of bop. This may be true only in the general sense that the prodigious Tatum had developed extremely complicated rhythms and advanced harmonies.

423 Leonard Feather found riffs "almost extinct" in bop versions of the blues (*Inside Jazz,* p. 52), but Parker, Gillespie and others made constant use of them in many of their compositions and improvisations. Take, for example, Parker's 1946 version of "Lady Be Good," Hawkins' and Monk's 1945 bop piece, "*Rifftide,*" or Gillespie's "Dizzy Atmosphere," to name just a few such numbers.

424 According to David Stowe (*Swing Changes,* pp. 204 *ff*), the continuities between swing and bop were more striking than the discontinuities. But Stowe is referring to bop mainly as a social, rather than musical, phenomenon.

425 Some bop musicians did attempt at some point to accommodate, rather than lose, their dancing clientele. Dizzy Gillespie did so when trying his hand at leading a big band. His "Stella By Starlight" (1956) is one example of a ballad played "straight" by his band, holding close to the melody and maintaining a steady dance beat throughout. But even outside the context of the big band ballroom scene, his is not always "pure" bop. For instance, his 1947 "Good Bait," recorded with a sextet, has one foot strongly entrenched in bop but is also redolent of swing.

426 A practice of drummer Art Blakey, on the hi-hat.

427 Because of his unaccustomed style of syncopated accentuation, Kenny Clarke was disparagingly dubbed "Klook-mop" by bandleader Teddy Hill.

428 *Music on My Mind.*

[429] But a brilliant instrumentalist/composer such as Charlie Parker could take the chances of an early Louis Armstrong and vary his improvisations from take to take.

[430] Coleman Hawkins' 1939 version of "Body And Soul" is a famous case in point, a *tour de force* even for present day listeners. Over a steady ground beat, Hawkins' saxophone initially states the musical theme, then weaves a steady string of improvisational patterns, a series of chromatic changes, throughout the piece. One by one, each pattern appears to meander "off course" momentarily but, with inescapable logic, comes to its inevitable resolution.

[431] Martin Williams' takes the title *Where's The Melody?* for a book on jazz. In his first chapter, similarly titled, he addresses the puzzlement of listeners exposed to bop and later jazz.

[432] *To Be or Not . . . To Bop,* p. 371.

[433] *Blues People,* p. 194.

[434] While LeRoi Jones does not explain in what way bop "reinstated" the blues, his description, in the same paragraph, of bop's treatment of the blues seems to point instead to the effect of drowning them in complexities: "In bop melodies there seemed to be an endless changing of direction, stops and starts, variations of impetus, a jaggedness that reached out of the rhythmic *bases* [his underlining] of the music. The boppers seemed to have a constant need for deliberate and agitated rhythmical contrast." (Ibid).

[435] Such titles may have had a tongue-in-cheek flavor, but subsequently, jazz pieces would often be given impressionistic, poetic or philosophical titles, a trend that has continued to the present day.

14

CRITICS AND CONTROVERSY

Over the years the subject of jazz has unleashed an avalanche of debates and disputes. At times the arguments have focused on the music *per se*, with critics debating what jazz is or what it should be. At others they have centered on the role of the races in jazz. But generally speaking, the two issues are not easily separated, and the racial question often comes into play when critics set about telling each other what is right or wrong about that all-important component of American popular music—jazz.

As for the music itself, there is one question that few, if any, can agree on: what qualifies as "true" or "real" jazz?

The Real Jazz

Invariably, each writer who attempts to explain or itemize the basic ingredients of jazz comes up with a different recipe. The most expert of experts propose definitions that are dizzyingly disparate. For some, any music worthy of the name "jazz" must depend first and foremost on improvisation. For others what counts is rhythm or drive. Jazz, according to Marshall Stearns, is "A semi-improvisational American music distinguished by an immediacy of communication, an expressiveness characteristic of . . . the human voice, and a complex, flowing rhythm."[436] On the other hand, Rudi Blesh opines that "Perhaps improvisation can be left out" but not the following three necessary components: 1) polyphonic variation (the interplay of tones or melodies), 2) polyrhythmic variation and 3) hot and vocal tone quality.[437] Further examples would show that the most qualified music historians offer definitions that may overlap but are never identical.

When it comes to questions such as, "Who plays authentic jazz? When and where could it be heard?" again answers will differ. The French critic Hughes Panassié had a fairly restrictive view, undoubtedly fostered by his friend, clarinetist Mezz Mezzrow. Panassié maintained in *The Real Jazz* (1942) that the "most genuine" jazz was played by the early New Orleans ensembles. He also praised those musicians who subsequently continued playing in the New Orleans tradition[438] and expressed admiration for black swing bands of the 1930s, such as Henderson's, Ellington's, Lunceford's, Basie's and Webb's.

A more stringent brand of purism may be found in *Shining Trumpets,* by Panassié's contemporary and well-known critic, Rudi Blesh. In his study Blesh maintained that the only truly authentic jazz was New Orleans jazz as heard and recorded before 1928.[439] He did not mean the "best jazz" but, as stated, the "only jazz." Like Panassié, he granted praise to certain ensembles playing New Orleans style music during the Dixieland Revival of the forties, but unlike the French writer, he essentially closed the door on any sounds that evolved after King Oliver in his glory days. In fact, according to Blesh, New York had "heard no real jazz apart from records since 1916."[440] In other words, genuine had to be synonymous with old.

Even Duke Ellington, in Blesh's view, never played jazz at all.[441] Instead, he was merely an "adroit technician" who made "effects for their own sake," someone who invented "seemingly complex arrangements" but whose "hodgepodge montages of sound effects" had "complexity without meaning."[442] Ellington's "Daybreak Express"—which Gunther Schuller saw as a "stunning lesson in the capacity of the jazz medium to equal or better anything that was being done in classical program music"[443]—was dismissed by Blesh as a "bit of theatrical 'corn."[444]

As for Louis Armstrong, none of his output after 1928 could satisfy the critic, mainly because the trumpeter had abandoned the New Orleans ensemble formula to execute his virtuoso solo improvisations. Not even Armstrong's brilliant "West End Blues" would do. For the piece did not conform exactly to the standard twelve-bar blues as sung by a classic icon such as Ma Rainey. The orchestration was deemed out of bounds, particularly Earl Hines' last solo, "built on harmonies that do not belong to the blues."[445]

Although other traditionalists, including those connected with the Dixieland revival, favored the old New Orleans ensemble style, not many went so far as Blesh in limiting the scope of what should or should not be included under the rubric of authentic jazz.

However, when it came to bop (or "bebop" as it was often called), a multitude of critics and musicians categorically turned their thumbs down. Sigmund Spaeth called it "a distortion of jazz." According to Tommy Dorsey, "Bebop has set music back twenty years." For the Moscow *Literary Gazette*, bop "bears the same relationship to music as tonsillitis."[446] Hughes Panassié stated that bop had nothing at all to do with jazz and offered quotes from various musicians who felt similarly. For example, trumpeter/arranger Buck Clayton, who said, "Be-bop is not, never was and never will be true jazz . . ." [447]

Now it seems that each new form of jazz evolving in history had been attacked by purists and traditionalists. Ragtime had its share of opponents ranging from newspaper and magazine writers to churchgoing homemakers (Eubie Blake's mother's "Take that ragtime out of my house!")[448] Later, New Orleans enthusiasts attacked big band swing. Then swing aficionados wanted to bury bebop. One would be hard put to say which new trend elicited the greatest opposition and anger.

Consider, for a moment, the polemics surrounding swing.

Like the future opponents of bop, a number of critics felt that swing—especially the post-Goodman brand of white swing—did not belong in the category of jazz at all. Al Rose, for instance, faulted swing for abandoning "the prime essentials of authentic jazz" by replacing pure ensemble work with "the solo concepts of what was called 'Chicago style.'"[449] A good number of books on jazz do not even discuss the white bands of the swing era, except possibly in relation to the black influence. For example, Floyd Levin's *Classic Jazz* includes no description of any of the contemporary white big bands. Joachim Berendt's *The Jazz Book* devotes a mere two paragraphs to one white leader, Goodman—and only in connection with Fletcher Henderson's arrangements.

Mark Gridley's *Jazz Styles* grants whole chapters to black bands but deals with white swing in three short paragraphs covering only Goodman, Tommy Dorsey and Artie Shaw. And Stanley Dance's *The World of Swing,* based on close to fifty interviews with black musicians, includes just one white leader, Benny Goodman.

As for Blesh, his view of swing, black or white, is decidedly, even angrily, negative. To quote the critic,

> Hot swing . . . has been simplified to a half-dozen screaming brass and bleating reed riffs. It is easy to prove that any swing is completely anti-jazz, completely anti-New Orleans, opposed to the real musical values which jazz represents . . . establishing no new art form, developing no older one, it is nihilistic, cynically destructive, reactionary.[450]

Beyond such esthetic, political and moral objections, Blesh has much of interest to say about the psychological effects of swing on its listeners:

> Hot swing, with its riffs, is a highly organized form of instrumental noise devoted to the superinducement of a wholly unnatural excitement . . . coming with the sounding of a handful of threadbare rhythmic tricks. The mass autohypnosis thereupon vents itself in anarchic, orgiastic, and dangerous excitement.[451]

Blesh, a highly knowledgeable jazz critic, offers concrete evidence to back up his stormy assessment. For example, he will compare a specific swing recording with a pre-1928 recording of the same number by a New Orleans band. His analyses are perspicacious, his conclusions highly subjective. To understand better where he is coming from, let us look at his comparison of King Oliver's "Dippermouth Blues" of 1923 and two recordings of the same piece (1925 and 1931) made by the swing band of Fletcher Henderson, who entitled both his versions "Sugar Foot Stomp."

Blesh justifiably calls Oliver's recording a great example of classic New Orleans [music]." Henderson's adaptations, on the other hand, receive poor grades from the critic. He finds the 1925 record a faulty imitation of New Orleans jazz. Its trio of clarinets emit a "sugary harmony, " and after Louis Armstrong's solo the music degenerates into "nauseatingly sweet portions interrupted by mechanized riffs." As for Henderson's 1931 version, it is too fast and represents merely the "swinging of a jazz classic."

Harsh words, indeed, for Blesh was not judging Henderson's work on its own merits but as compared against a fixed standard. He was right insofar as Henderson had not duplicated the New Orleans formula. But why on earth would he? Like Oliver in Chicago, Henderson in New York had updated his approach for a different audience and acquired an increasingly smooth and swinging style. Despite occasional sweet touches—which provide contrast to the general bounciness of the number—his 1931 "Sugarfoot Stomp" was an excellent piece of work.

More convincing is Blesh's comparison of Henderson's "The Chant," recorded in November, 1926, with Jelly Roll Morton's version of the number issued two months earlier. Since Blesh does not go into detail on the subject, let us explain that Morton's take is a beautiful example of tightly knit ensemble work. In the New Orleans tradition, soloists are granted breaks of only eight to sixteen measures (Henderson gives far more space to solo work). Yet when playing as a group, each instrument is clearly heard, limpidly weaving through the ensemble structure. Morton's piece is hot, lively and always interesting.

Henderson, on the other hand, drags the number for some reason, and it seems labored. But as someone said, "Shakespeare was not Shakespeare all the time," and, admittedly Henderson was not always at his best. To appreciate one of his finer pieces, we have only to listen to his "New King Porter Stomp" of 1932. At that later moment, although his arrangement and execution were now even farther away from the New Orleans style (granting long breaks to soloists, for example), his music had an irresistible drive and swing and was vibrant from start to finish.

But the point for so many proponents of "real jazz" appears to be that jazz was good in the good old days, the formula was right and the execution spontaneous. Whereas what came later—swing, with its sleek arrangements of Tin Pan Alley numbers, its vocals, its riffs, solo work, reed choruses and the rest, was "commercial" music—that is, inferior music geared to the lowest common denominator: a sellout.

Clearly, when critics praise the old-time jazz, they are not referring to the original music actually heard in New Orleans but to New Orleans jazz as recorded later, in the twenties, in Chicago, New York and elsewhere. For the jazz music that had been performed in New Orleans went unrecorded and was undoubtedly less polished than music subsequently played by New Orleanians in Chicago or New York. So, in fact, the jazz that these critics espoused was no longer the "real" thing; it had already changed and become smoother and more sophisticated. Still, some felt it was important to fix the music in time at that point and not let it evolve further. And especially to prevent it from becoming commercial.

In point of fact, jazz had always been commercial. Tin Pan Alley tunes, for instance, were no strangers to New Orleans of yore. For besides playing traditional blues like "Make Me a Pallet on the Floor" or stomp numbers like "Tiger Rag," early New Orleans musicians performed published favorites like "There'll be a Hot Time in the Old Town Tonight" or "Mr. Johnson Turn Me Loose." After Sophie Tucker came on tour there around 1911, Clarence Williams immediately regaled listeners with "Some of These Days" and "Alexander's Ragtime Band." And Williams later began to send away to New York for songs such as "Chinatown" and "That's A Plenty."[452] In Chicago, Joe Oliver often worked with stock arrangements of pop songs and cut off the titles, so onlookers wouldn't be able to identify the pieces.

Buddy Bolden and his contemporary New Orleaneans could certainly not be considered uncommercial. Hardly ivory tower artists, they vied with each other in attracting and pleasing the local dancers and regularly performed their favorite kinds of music. King Oliver and others would amuse audiences by introducing groans, wa-wa's and other sound effects made with cups or bathroom plungers. And some of the top black jazz artists of ensuing years were commercial in a variety of ways. Duke Ellington, for example, who knew the importance of pleasing his dancing public, and who let himself be touted by Irving Mills as "the greatest living master of jungle music."[453] And Louis

Armstrong who loved to mug for audiences and whose choice of songs often included banal Tin Pan Alley ballads and novelty numbers. Or Dizzy Gillespie who, despite the relatively esoteric, "serious" nature of bop music, could not resist dancing back and forth in front of a band and playing the clown. And more importantly, all the major jazz figures to the present time can be seen as commercial in that they had to deal with the realities of promoting and disseminating their music, whether through an agent/publicist or personally, in front of an audience.

But such evidence does not address the subject of commercialism in the music itself, as played after the glory days of King Oliver. As we have noted, Oliver's Chicago style had already become more commercial than it had been in New Orleans—smoother and more accessible to a relatively sophisticated northern, big city public. And had Oliver been able to stay in business as a bandleader,[454] he would undoubtedly have continued going in that direction. To compete with other bands, he would eventually have had to adopt innovations of Henderson and others and exchange his outmoded New Orleans sound for the black swing sounds of the late twenties and thirties.

That sort of evolution might have taken Oliver further in the direction of what people think of as commercialism. But it would have included him among the groundbreaking early black orchestras in New York and elsewhere, orchestras considered by most critics of today as examples of good American jazz. The word "commercial" could only be applied to them insofar as a number of them had eventually to sell out qualitatively in order to survive.

However, once the white big bands came to the fore from the mid-thirties on, jazz could certainly be accused of having become slicker and more commercial. Those bands, with their crowd-pleasing vocalists, their bandleader stars and their simplified, manicured arrangements, had turned jazz into a music for the masses and a product most profitable.

Was that a bad thing? Although much of white swing could, indeed, be thought of as a formulaic, even watered down jazz, at its best it had brilliance, vibrancy and drive while maintaining discipline and a high level of musicianship. It provided a perfect marriage of music and dance, it reached a multitude of listeners and it eventually opened the way to the recognition and appreciation of black jazz and black musicians.

The great seventeenth-comedy writer, Molière, said, "My greatest sin was in pleasing my public."[455] Perhaps that, too, was the greatest sin committed by swing.

As for the position that any real jazz must conform to a certain style or a particular point in time, let us leave the last word to that knowledgeable and most sensible critic, Gunther Schuller: "True jazz by its very nature cannot be held to a formula or be based on some stationary perfection. Indeed, the greatness of jazz lies in the fact that it never ceases to develop and change."[456]

A Music Most Black

Certain critics, both black and white, have maintained that since jazz was invented by African Americans, it should remain a black product, in black hands, and well outside the reach of would be white appropriators.

The first and most eloquent African-American critic to publish books in favor of black exclusivity was poet-essayist LeRoi Jones, who later took the name Amiri Baraka. In *Black Music*, recalling raids on African-American music by white minstrels and, later, by leaders like Whiteman and Goodman, he protested vigorously. He contended, for example that "the more intelligent the white, the more the realization he has to steal from niggers.[457] In opposing such perceived baseness, Jones painted whites in popular music not only as duplicitous and money grubbing but as nerdy and uncomprehending "freaks" who wrote stupid love songs although incapable of love.[458]

His resentment lead Jones to denigrate, or at least mistrust, moves that whites made in reaching out to black musicians. In *Blues People,* referring to Goodman's desegregation of his jazz ensembles, Jones wrote, "The spectacle of Benny Goodman hiring Teddy Wilson and later Lionel Hampton, Charlie Christian, and Cootie Williams into his outrageously popular bands and thereby making them 'big names' in the swing world seems to me . . . fantastically amusing."[459] Amusing because, as Jones notes, swing came from black jazz in the first place, but now it had "little to do with black America." And rather than applaud the reality that black musicians were being invited into the mainstream, Jones lamented that fact, for, as he said, more and more Negroes were becoming like whites.[460]

In another case, where a black musician received a high honor from the white establishment, Jones was upset, riled rather than proud. Thelonius Monk was to be the cover story of a *Time Magazine* issue. The magazine had to postpone the plan because, as Jones dryly put it "When President Kennedy was assassinated, another cover was substituted." He seemed surprised that the magazine actually came through and featured Monk the following year. But rather than applaud the choice, he asked why: "What, finally, does that mean?" Perhaps they were setting Monk up "for something bad to happen to his playing." A cover picture and article, he thought, might start the musician on a boring grind of playing himself out—but, finally, Jones doubted Monk would let that happen.[461]

It seems likely that Jones' problem with black musicians making it in a white world had to do not only with their loss of authentic blackness but, perhaps more importantly, with their loss of status as victims. For the victimization of blacks by whites is central to his thinking and feeling. And when black musicians enter the white establishment, in Jones' opinion, they not only lose their identity but they join the ranks of the enemy, that is, the victimizers. In the last analysis, an unspoken result of such crossing over by blacks is that there could eventually be no more victims and, therefore, no more cause for protest.

In a later book, *The Music; Reflections on Jazz and Blues,* Jones (who had changed his name to Amiri Baraka) and his wife, Amina Baraka, have cast the black/white opposition in a patently Marxist framework. Black musicians are now the "the people," in other words, the oppressed proletariat, and whites are bourgeois "corporate America." The quarrels between the two fall into the category of "class struggle." But change of name and Marxist vocabulary notwithstanding, Baraka's ideas remain exactly the same.

On the subject of music, some of Baraka's views on what type does or does not qualify as truly black may seem arbitrary. For example, although ragtime was invented by African Americans and was based on black rhythms, he faults the music for being un-Negro. Un-Negro because it has a formalized style and is European (meaning white) in nature. On the other hand, Baraka claims bop as a black genre because—in line with his militant perspective—he sees it as a music of protest. And further, according to Baraka, bop is black because it does not have European traits but, instead, is close to the blues and to African music. (Rather than digress here by disputing Baraka's ideas about bop and the blues and his denial of bop's European influence, I refer readers to the descriptions of bop in the preceding chapter. Let it be said, however, that Baraka's likening bop rhythms to African ones is not convincing, for unlike bop, African drumming, while complex, tends to maintain one specific rhythmic pattern over an extended period of time.)

Baraka is a knowledgeable critic with a most colorful style. He has thoroughly researched the subject of black music and he knows his jazz history. True, his outmoded Marxist pronouncements and rhetoric of the 1960s can be off-putting to twenty-first century readers. And since a good percentage of those readers could well be Caucasian, his anti-white pronouncements would doubtless induce only the most uninformed (or masochistic and guilt ridden) among them to swallow such statements whole. However, much of what he says is valid. And the man has obviously done his homework.

Frank Kofsky—although himself white—is a staunch believer in the white music establishment-as-oppressor theory. A Marxist like Baraka, Kofsky admires Baraka and shares many of his opinions. For example, in *Black Nationalism and the Revolution in Music*[462] and *Black Music, White Business,* he holds that jazz is not American music but strictly black music, that whites are exploiters and that black jazz is a renunciation of white western civilization. But he is more given than Baraka to *ad hominen* attacks on white music critics and jazz experts. According to Kofsky, Leonard Feather is a "misleader of the people,"[463] Dan Morgenstern of *Down Beat Magazine* writes "crap[464]" and Nat Hentoff, whose *Jazz Is* Kofsky happened to skim, as he tells it, dipping into a chapter here and there, offers only "pusillanimous" criticism.[465] In Kofsky's eyes, such critics and others are biased against blacks, and they don't address the issue of black nationalism.

In view of such attacks, it might seem odd that the two works of music criticism Kofsky finds worthwhile are André Hodeir's *Jazz: Its Evolution and Essence* and Gunther Schuller's *Early Jazz.* For neither of these works by white critics has anything to do with black nationalism, and neither author is more pro-black than Hentoff *et al.*

But other oddities are manifest in Kofsky's criticism. For example, he faults white entrepreneurs for holding to a "double standard" where African Americans are concerned. One might well imagine he is referring to inferior treatment of black musicians as opposed to white ones. But not at all. Rather than compare cases of specific blacks receiving worse treatment than their white counterparts, he offers instances of musicians in general—race unidentified—suffering at the hands of the establishment. In fact the one chapter devoted to describing a musician's plight focuses on a white musician, pianist/trombonist Mark Levine.[466]

The list of Kofsky's improbable assertions and contradictions is too long to be itemized here. To mention only a few: 1) Jazz is a minority taste in white America because it is Negro music.[467] (Actually, the public for jazz in America and Europe is mainly white.) 2) Recording companies subsidize classical music but not jazz because the latter is "nigger music."[468] (Here Kofsky does address the "double standard" principle, but his charge of prejudice is off the mark.) 3) Most white critics treating jazz are not musicologists.[469] (Nor is Kofsky.) 4) Black musicians have problems in nightclub work: low pay, people buying drinks during the music, no place to take a nap, etc.[470] (Had Kofsky interviewed white musicians, he would have heard exactly the same stories.) It goes without saying that when Kofsky speaks of bop, he includes only blacks among musicians worthy of note, without ever mentioning such as Lennie Tristano, Gerry Mulligan or other outstanding white instrumentalists.

Many other critics have equated jazz with the black race. Few, however, have gone to such extremes as Baraka and Kofsky in wishing to exclude white musicians entirely from the history and practice of jazz. Nevertheless, in the 1990s, African-American writers Albert Murray and Stanley Crouch have been faulted for taking such a stand. Their ideas, added to criticism such as the above, undoubtedly contributed to the publication of books and articles by end-of-the-century critics bent on "setting the record straight" and giving white musicians their due.

The White Side

James Lincoln Collier was one of the first critics to grant space in a book (*Jazz, the American Theme Song*) to addressing and countering the jazz-for-blacks-only argument. In opposing that position, he stresses white contributions throughout the history of jazz in America. His background information is useful and enlightening. Questions arise, however, when Collier develops the thesis that perhaps we cannot really attribute the invention of jazz to an African-American culture. Although he states, "Jazz was originally devised by blacks,"[471] he maintains that it did not spring from a black community or a common black experience, or "ethos." For in New Orleans, in addition to the freed blacks slaves, there were the very different Creoles of color, who also contributed so much to the music.[472]

That seems a bit of a stretch, since music historians fully understand that black jazz was not a pure and cohesive phenomenon. They are aware, for example, that the mélange of uptown and Creole musical talents of New Orleans must have contributed to the shaping of jazz. And although Collier's explanation of the Creole culture in that city is well worth reading, one wonders in what way it changes or dilutes the fact that jazz was essentially a black phenomenon.

In making a case for white musicians, Collier, like other critics, tends at times to overstate their importance. For example, he appears to give credence to white Nick LaRocca and his biographer Brunn who contend that LaRocca and other members of the ODJB invented jazz themselves. And he does not question LaRocca's and Papa Laine's improbable claims that they never listened to black jazz in New Orleans.[473]

Such a pro-white position on Collier's part, in 1993 is a far cry from his views in *The Making of Jazz,* published in 1978. That useful book is a straightforward history of jazz, beginning with the African roots and ending with John Coltrane, while considering important white musicians along the way. Interestingly, when it came to evaluating the white influence on jazz, he concluded:

"But undoubtedly the most important effect that the advent of whites had on jazz had nothing to do with the performance of the music at all. What the white players did was to bring jazz into the American mainstream . . ."[474]

So there was a great difference between a statement like that, one which would seem to downplay the role of white musicians, and the message of his later book, in which the white contribution to jazz is greatly magnified. At the risk of oversimplification, let us say that the difference, to a great extent, may be explained in two words: Wynton Marsalis. For in 1991 that talented and creative artist became director of the new program, Jazz at Lincoln Center, where his emphasis was on black musicians and black music. Although Collier does not mention Lincoln Center program or Marsalis,[475] his book was published in 1993, and he had to be aware of the program. (He would later become involved in debates about its apparent exclusion of whites.)

Unlike Collier, another critic, Gene Lees, has attacked Marsalis' approach openly in one of his books. In *Cats of Any Color* Lees counters Marsalis head on. He writes, for instance, that when Lincoln Center authorized the granting of commissions for the creation and performance of new jazz works, Marsalis awarded grants to himself and his friends. As for excluding white musicians from the program, Lees mentions that in a musical tribute to Monk, Marsalis substituted black musicians for the white ones who had actually performed with Monk, even though four whites who had played in Monk's final quartet were still living.

Lees attributes a good deal of such "reverse racism" to Stanley Crouch, whose policies and statements have shown an anti-white bias. He refers to the critic as "the *éminence grise*" in the career of Wynton Marsalis." Lees states that the relationship of Crouch and Marsalis is "the only known instance in jazz history, and perhaps all musical history, of a musician being controlled by a critic."[476]

Lees is clearly indignant on the subject of Marsalis and Crouch, and he counters their policies by emphasizing the contributions made by white musicians to jazz. But although his criticism is generally even-handed and realistic, it is difficult to agree with him when he, like Collier, uses as evidence the role of the Creoles in New Orleans jazz. Specifically, at one point he gives importance to white blood in Creole veins[477]—a reality that would seem to downplay the black origins of jazz. But as Lees himself would acknowledge, black jazz has always had an infusion of white blood and white culture. The fact remains that without blacks there is precious little chance that jazz could have happened.

It should be understood that neither Lees nor Collier nor most other prominent white critics targeting reverse racism in jazz were themselves racist. It is difficult to study the subject of jazz without opening one's mind and heart to the people who managed to develop a thing of beauty in the midst of so much darkness. As for Lees, his next book length publication after *Cats of Any Color* (which had been dedicated to Dizzy Gillespie) was a most empathetic study of four black jazz musicians.[478] It appears, however, that more than a few white critics of the day were, understandably, feeling the effects of acute *marsaliphobia.*

Such was undoubtedly true of another white jazz critic, Eric Nisenson. In *Blue, the Murder of Jazz,* he held that Albert Murray, Stanley Crouch and Wynton Marsalis (although all three of them opposed racism and black militancy), believed that only blacks could create and play jazz. In his book Nisensen set about refuting that viewpoint.

In point of fact Nisenson, like Lees and Collier, strongly admired black creativity and gave it its due in the book. What is more, he acknowledged jazz as a black genre and even recognized the superiority of black musicians in the music. "The deepest part of the jazz experience springs from the African-American experience,"[479] he wrote. And "There is no question that most of the greatest jazz musicians are black."[480]

However, there was Marsalis with his program, a program that appeared not only to close the door to whites but (and as Lees had pointed out as well) to seek only young, inexperienced musicians to boot. It was, Nisenson wrote, not a question of "trashing Marsalis;" since the trashing in his book was "at best only tangential."[481] Still, tangential or not, in his view the deed had to be done, for "There is no avoiding [Marsalis] if one wants to come to terms seriously with the current state of jazz."[482] In Nisenson's opinion, the current state of jazz—due to the museum like, restrictive approach of those on high-stifled all innovation and creativity and spelled "the murder of jazz."

Unlike Lees and Nisenson, writer Richard Sudhalter, whose *Lost Chords*[483] appeared in 1999, does not mention Marsalis or Crouch, by name in his book. Yet their emphasis on a black ownership of jazz undoubtedly contributed to his writing nearly 900 pages refuting such a stance. Only in his epilogue does he take direct aim at the Lincoln Center program. "Such cultural institutions as Lincoln Center in New York and the Smithsonian in Washington have created 'official' ensembles whose major purpose seems to be presentation of jazz as a kind of anthropological orthodoxy, existing in a cultural vacuum . . . [484]." As an antidote, Sudhalter demonstrates throughout his book ways in which a great number of white musicians have contributed to jazz since the time of the Original Dixieland Jazz Band.

Sudhalter's book is an important work of scholarship. Highly informed and well written, it contains a mine of useful information. And it does, as the title suggests, bring to light and emphasize the work of musicians who have not always had their due, specifically, white musicians. The problem with striving to set the record straight is running the risk of over- or understatement. And with Sudhalter as with Collier, the case for the white contribution to jazz is sometimes made at the expense of black creativity.

Throughout his study, Sudhalter grants credit and generous praise to black jazz artists. He could certainly not be accused of stinting in that respect. However, in aiming to place white musicians in the spotlight, he inevitably downplays African-American influences that helped to shape their music. For example, Paul Mares of the NORK, as we have seen,[485] testified to the fact that his group tried their best to imitate the black sound. His claim that they naturally did not succeed in capturing that sound may have been too self-effacing, for he and his band produced fine, swinging music worthy of their models. But Sudhalter passes off this case of whites eager to adopt black music by saying "Mares clearly admires Joe Oliver and wears his admiration proudly. Nothing remarkable here: it is what jazzmen have done throughout their music's history, taking inspiration from a favorite player in building a personal style."[486] Instead of seeing Oliver as the herald of an exciting, inspiring black sound, the critic cites him as simply a good musician to use as a model.

The same apparent minimizing of the black connection occurs in Sudhalter's coverage of Bud Freeman, Art Hodes and Eddie Condon. In their autobiographies all three emphasize the great effect the discovery of black music and black musicians had on their lives and careers.[487] But in treating the first two white instrumentalists Sudhalter mentions Oliver and other seminal black icons only casually—as names on a list of admired performers—and in Condon's case he makes no mention of the black influence. He may well have felt that that influence lay outside the sphere of his subject. Still, considering the strong emphasis the three men themselves placed on the role of black music in their professional development, one would have wished for at least a passing acknowledgement of it.

In an interview with Benny Goodman, printed in the book, Sudhalter asks the bandleader about such white musicians as saxists Adrian Rollini and Bud Freeman and arranger Eddie Sauter, musicians much admired by Sudhalter himself. Given that white music is the subject of the book, such questions were, of course, appropriate and natural. But it seems that the black component, so important in Goodman's career, was somehow closeted, and it was Benny himself who thought fit to speak not just of Beiderbecke, whom he admired, but of Johnny Dodds and Jimmy Noone, not just of Sauter (whom he passed off as "too fussy" an arranger) but of Fletcher Henderson and his role in Goodman's Palomar success.

Finally, in the process of setting the black-white record straight, Sudhalter is drawn into the who-got-there-first competition. For instance, he contests Gunther Schuller's belief that white arranger Gene Gifford had been inspired by the scores of John Nesbitt, an African American, and shows Gifford as the real creator. Both critics come up with persuasive evidence, but Sudhalter has the advantage of being the last one to rebut, so he automatically scores higher in the game. Sudhalter may be right in his assessment, but the subject is complex, and cross influences could well have been at play. As he himself put it, "No one worked in a vacuum."[488] Or as those in the know might have framed it more crudely, "Everybody was stealing from everybody."

In the final paragraphs of his book Sudhalter makes a strong statement designed to consign certain pro-black critics to a moral or intellectual purgatory. ". . . the 'blacks invented, whites appropriated' canon is based on either ignorance or a willful misreading of the historical record."

Of course few knowledgeable critics or musicians would accept the whole blacks-invented-whites-appropriated formula. Almost all have recognized that what the blacks created they did not accomplish in a vacuum. The French have an expression, "*Faire feu de tout bois*"—referring to someone's ability to make or achieve something with any material that happens to be at hand. Which is exactly what the black musicians did. Like the slaves who improvised their instruments using gourds, animal guts, bones, whatever; like the New Orleans musicians who could make a new kind of magic from a white quadrille or a military march; like jazz musicians of the thirties and forties building on sophisticated harmonies found in European music, they were able somehow to light a fire.

As for the whites appropriating black music—yes, indeed, they did. As we have seen amply, that happened a good number of times. And sometimes, as unjust as it must have felt, the appropriation wound up eventually for the benefit of the blacks.

But Sudhalter would probably not take issue with all that. What he is really objecting to are the extremists. And there we agree with him wholeheartedly.

Speaking From the Heart

Where race is concerned emotions can run high. As indicated here, critics and non-critics alike, considering black and white components of American jazz, have often stood in sharp disagreement. Of course different people, looking through the exact same lens, will come up with a different reading. Emotional astigmatism will, at times, fog or distort the picture.

When it comes to whites discussing black music and black musicians, rather than snobbery or animosity, we often encounter an empathy synonymous with love. Discovery of black music has brought a number of white fans into contact with African Americans and fostered strong feelings in them for the black race. Such was the case with John Hammond, and we have already seen how his love for jazz and the people engaged in it led to his activism in African-American causes. For admiration and affection often went hand in hand with the painful knowledge of what blacks had suffered at the hands of empowered whites. Said Bud Freeman,

> It was not just their music that moved me but the whole picture of an oppressed people who appeared to be much happier than whites who had everything. It was on the strength of this that I developed a love for them and their music and became a jazz musician.[489]

Other musicians testify to the link between love of black jazz and love for the black race. Art Hodes, speaking of his young co-musicians in Chicago, explained, "So it went, with most of us not only falling in love with the music but with the Race too."[490] For such as Hodes, to be accepted by black musicians, to be allowed into their circle, was an honor they wore like a badge. To quote Hodes again, "I came to be accepted by these people, as one of them, and believe me I never abused the privilege."[491]

Milton "Mezz" Mezzrow and Johnny Otis offer two extreme cases of white musicians who identified strongly with blacks. Indeed, each of these men felt he *was* black. Otis stated that he was "black environmentally, psychologically, culturally, emotionally and intellectually."[492] But it was possible for a white musician to go even further than that—if his name was Mezz Mezzrow. Mezzrow not only affected a Negro accent, tried to play blues in the black style, married a black woman (as had Otis), but when he went to prison for selling marijuana, he demanded to be put "with the colored group," insisting he was colored himself. His request satisfied, he was relieved to be away from the "grimy, grating" world of "ofays."[493]

Mezzrow's autobiography, *Really the Blues,* sheds light on much of this racial cross-dressing. A misfit and juvenile delinquent, while in reform school, he felt that the only people who seemed to care about him were the African-American inmates. He played jazz with them, they accepted him, and that same pattern was repeated in much of his adult life. To feel accepted by Negroes, to be one of the gang, possibly even complimented on his own (mediocre) playing—these were the honors he boasted of most proudly. As many have pointed out, much of his entrée into both black and white musical circles came from his ability to provide musicians with the highest quality marijuana available. Whatever the case, Mezzrow's identification with blacks was strong indeed.

Although few, if any, went so far as Mezzrow, other whites in music experienced a visceral, almost total, identification with black musicians and the black race. In *The Trouble With Cinderella,* Artie Shaw tells how he arrived in Harlem when he was jobless and hopeless and how he was "saved" by pianist Willie "the Lion" Smith. Smith, after some initial hesitation, allowed Shaw to play along with him and in so doing helped the clarinetist not only musically but morally and psychologically. Writing of his life during those months in Harlem, Shaw said,

> For the most part I was actually living the life of a Negro musician, adopting Negro values and attitudes, and accepting the Negro out-group point of view not only about music but life in general. In fact, on the few occasions when I was forced to realize I was a white man, I used to wish I could actually *be* a Negro.[494]

* * *

When it came to black musicians and their attitudes toward whites, quite naturally, close identification was not to be expected. Although there were, indeed, many cases of black musicians expressing admiration for individual white musicians or groups, fondness for the white race—a race that had oppressed blacks, marginalized them and competed with them while holding all the cards—would not have made sense.

African-American musicians must have resented the first white musicians who came into competition with them. But not until the late thirties and thereafter was such an attitude expressed openly. That is, not until white musicians began breaking down the barriers and inviting black into desegregated ensembles. Then, black musicians, understanding that whites could play jazz and that it was actually possible to work together, returned the favor. Whites were hired by Basie, Gillespie, Armstrong and others, and the pattern became the norm. It was then, however, that black musicians began to object with a sort of what's-going-on-here indignation. Then and later, black leaders hiring white musicians would hear "What is that white cat doing in the band? He can't play nothin'—he's white."[495]

Now, as we have seen, white bands, as a rule, have not usually had the swing of the black ones but, generally speaking, precision and technical expertise. However, individual white musicians could and did, indeed, swing—instrumentalists such as Jack Teagarden, Bunny Berigan, Mugsy Spanier, Pee Wee Russell or Red Norvo. According to a famous anecdote about Roy Eldridge, the trumpeter insisted that he could always tell the race of an unidentified performer simply by hearing him on disk. When put to the test by Leonard Feather, he scored quite low, as Lees put it, "well below the fifty percent he would have achieved by the law of averages."[496]

But for a good number of blacks in jazz, the white musician remained The Other, someone who did not belong on their turf. For a long time they gave him the label of "ofay," which, as noted above, some people have seen as an African word and others have interpreted as pig latin for "foe." Later, around the sixties, the tag was replaced by "whitey" (an epithet actually in use as far back as the early nineteenth century). With or without the labels, white musicians were often resented for being there, for taking a job that some worthy and needy black musician could have had. Many whites, feeling the hostility, simply packed up and quit.

In actuality, often the very blacks who protested against whites in jazz were eager to hire them. Gerard, Nisensen, Lees and others have pointed out that some of the most vociferous musicians on the subject of whites did just that. Art Blakey, often quoted as saying "The only way the Caucasian musician can swing is from a rope," used white sidemen in groups he organized. Archie Shepp, a militant anti-white, did exactly the same. As did Charlie Mingus, Ornette Coleman and Miles Davis, despite the many racial insults they delivered.

There was, clearly, an enormous ambivalence at work, and some blacks who took on white sidemen seemed caught in a dilemma and embarrassed about it. Ornette Coleman, for instance, felt he had to explain that he kept hiring white bassists because string instruments were more in the white than black musical tradition.[497] It seemed that nobody wanted to appear to have sold out and joined the enemy.

But at the same time, a good many black musicians continued to seek out the best in talent. And by the second half century, a large number of white musicians were, indeed, among the best.

At times interracial musical collaboration even promoted tolerance and understanding. Such was the case of Art Farmer (black flugelhorn player and trumpeter). At first Farmer could not understand Miles Davis' constant use of white musicians or Davis' stance that he didn't care of they were green blue or any other color so long as they played well. But later he said "the closer you get to the top, the more [racism] disappears."[498]

It was very often at the top of the musical ladder that black musicians have spoken of admiring and, at times, being influenced by white ones. Armstrong, Basie, Ellington, Sidney Bechet, Coleman Hawkins, Rex Stewart, Charlie Parker, Lester Young, Miles Davis—they are only a few of the greats who have paid tribute to white swing or jazz artists. Among the whites singled out: Bix Beiderbecke, Frankie Trumbauer, Jimmy and Tommy Dorsey, Benny Goodman, Woody Herman, Bud Freeman, Gil and Bill Evans.

Still, the cancer of racism can never be entirely expunged. Reverse racism undoubtedly contributed to attacks made on two of the greatest names in jazz: Louis Armstrong and Duke Ellington. During the fifties especially, Armstrong was harshly criticized by black critics. Musically, they objected to his fronting swing bands and playing the standard numbers of white Tin Pan Alley. From the racial standpoint, they criticized him for the Uncle Tom image projected by his mugging and eye rolling on stage. Blacks concerned with dignity thought that too evocative of the comic darky stereotype—an insult to the race. Politically, they complained he wasn't committed enough.

On the first count, it is true that Armstrong had an unfortunate liking for banal pop tunes. Still, although he came dangerously close the edge now and then—when he adopted the Lombardo style, for example—he had a way of turning Tin Pan Alley dross into pure gold. If people expected him to continue doing those brilliant trumpet improvisations of thirty years ago, they would, naturally, be disappointed. Armstrong had already done that, and besides, by that time his teeth ("my choppers") were in terrible shape. Much easier to deliver a pop vocal with style and gusto.

On the count of mugging, yes, Armstrong certainly did clown around when the chance presented itself. He was a born showman and entertainer, and once in front of an audience, he could not resist making people laugh and applaud. Early on, Dizzy Gillespie was one of those who viewed Armstrong as an Uncle Tom, as he put it, a "plantation image—handkerchief over his head, grinning in the face of white realism." But later, Gillespie realized he had misjudged him. "I began to recognize [my perceived image] as his absolute refusal to let anything, even anger about racism, steal the joy from his life and erase his fantastic smile."[499]

As for politics (and its supposed connection with music), Louis Armstrong was not involved in it. It is unlikely—in spite of an opinion commonly held—that his singing of "What Did I Do to Be So Black and Blue?" signified a strong protest against racism. The Razaf-Waller number, written under duress, as explained above, purposely sidestepped the issue of white prejudice.[500] And when Armstrong performed the number, he did not present it as a political statement. On the contrary, singing it before black soldiers during World War II, he diffused the serious implications of the song by ending it in a flourish of clowning that made his listeners break into laughter.

Open to the world, wanting to please, to be loved, Armstrong had no truck at all with racial militancy. He did not act according to some moral or political principle but according to common sense and feeling. In 1957, when he felt the injustice of Governor Faubus' refusal to desegregate the schools in Little Rock, Arkansas, he cancelled a State Department tour of Russia, saying in an interview that he did it because of the way the government was "treating my people in the South" and, further, that President Eisenhauer should go down to Little Rock and "take these colored children by the hand and lead them into the school."[501]

Even without such statements, made from the heart, the reality is that critics will come and go but Louis Armstrong remains.

When Duke Ellington, like Armstrong, was faulted for betraying his race, the criticism came not from an African American but from the well-known white activist, John Hammond. Among several negative articles he published about Ellington, an early one was entitled "The Tragedy of Duke Ellington,"[502] written upon hearing Ellington's first extended composition, "Reminiscing in Tempo." In his piece Hammond accused the bandleader of hiring "slick, un-negroid musicians" and of "aping Tin Pan Alley composers for commercial reasons." Ellington's music, according to Hammond, had become vapid and gutless. Why? Because the composer was uncommitted to racial activism, because he had "kept himself from any contact with the troubles of his people or mankind in general." It is as if Hammond—under the delusion that racial activism could foster music of quality—would have had Ellington go out into the political arena rather than take the few precious moments available to compose music.

Ellington, articulate but in possession of great dignity, was not about to strike back or lash out at Hammond, as Leonard Feather would do later in defending Ellington in 1943.[503] But in *Down Beat* of February, 1939, in an article on swing and its critics, he includes a paragraph on Hammond. In it he describes the man as a wealthy person involved in lost causes, one who identifies with minorities, and as a champion of the underdog "in the form of the Communist party." He ends the section with a certain *hauteur,* as though showing tolerance for a spoiled child: "Perhaps due to the 'fever of battle,' Hammond's judgment may have become slightly warped, and his enthusiasm and prejudices a little bit unwieldy to control."[504]

Here we have a case of a black musician neatly accusing a white critic of pro-black prejudice!

Whose Music Is It?

The racial issue has surfaced time and again in discussions and debates on jazz. Some have claimed the genre as an exclusively black product, taking it in the direction of a black monopoly. Others, protesting that stance and that outcome, have insisted on the biracial or increasingly multiracial nature of the music.

So whose music is it?

Duke Ellington, who always called what he composed and played "Negro folk music" or "the music of my race," had an answer to the question. In December, 1945, in an article published in *PM,* he stated,

> Twenty years ago when jazz was finding an audience, it may have had more of a Negro character. The Negro element is still important. But jazz has become a part of

> America. there are as many white musicians playing it as Negro . . . We are all working along more or less the same lines. We learn from each other. Jazz is American now. *American* is the big word.[505]

Ellington's jazz-as-Americana view would have been highly distasteful, unthinkable, to radical writers of the sixties and seventies. For it would have meant black musicians sharing honors with white ones, in other words undergoing a loss of black identity and integrity. However, at least a generation before that time, the situation in jazz had already changed too far in the direction of a biracial jazz for their point of view to be convincing or tenable.

Nevertheless, the issue of race in jazz—is it black, is it white, is it universal?—continues to occupy the minds of writers and critics in the twenty-first century. One example: In a three-day symposium entitled "Black, White and Beyond," published in *Jazz Times* in September, 2001, a panel consisting of Harry Edwards, Steve Coleman, Angela Davis, Nat Hentoff, Bruce Lundvall and Richard Sudhalter debated the continuing problem of race in jazz. All seemed to want to put the racial question behind them, with some asking why the subject of jazz always had to be reduced to black or white. Yet the question was clearly present, surfacing throughout the discussion and remaining, once again, unresolved.

It may always remain unresolved, for as long as *homo erectus* roams the planet people will continually view the Other as enemy or potential scapegoat. However, there have been precious moments when black and white jazz musicians have been able to create together, to delight in each other's sounds and through their musical collaboration come to understand one other as human beings. In view of that experience—an experience being repeated to this day—one might dare to hope. It is, perhaps, conceivable that at some future time the blatant inequities that continue to exist in marketing the music of the two races will have become a thing of the past. A time when white musicians in America will no longer view black attitudes as reverse racism. And when their black counterparts will understand that their music is far more than a private possession. Not a fiefdom but a contribution to all and a source of great pride.

Notes

436 *The Story of Jazz,* p. 282.

437 *Shining Trumpets,* p. 266.

438 Mezzrow's influence on Parnassié is evident from a reading of the clarinetist's *Really the Blues.* Mezzrow, for example, wanted musicians of his time to "stick with the original uncorrupted New Orleans style" (p. 141). His influence on Parnassié may also be seen in the area of racial polemics (discussed later in this chapter). For Panassié's 1942 book emphasized the black contribution to jazz in much the same way as did Mezzrow.

One result of the Panassié-Mezzrow connection: unlike other critics, Panassié granted a good amount of space and high praise to the clarinetist.

439 Especially jazz recorded between 1924 and 1928. See, particularly, pp. 253 and 261-262.

440 P. 338.

441 P. 281.

442 P. 280.

443 *The Swing Era,* p. 64.

444 *Op.cit.,* p. 281.

445 P. 286. On the subject of Armstrong's fronting big bands, Blesh, a leftist critic, deemed it nothing less than "counter-revolutionary (p. 259).

446 All quoted at the beginning of Feather's *Inside Jazz.*

447 *Op. cit,* pp. 74-75.

448 See Chapter Three, *supra.*

449 *I Remember Jazz,* p. 101.

450 *Shining Trumpets,* p. 290. He concludes on the following page ". . . swing is a form of rabble rousing that elicits . . . the same blind idolatry the demagogue or the dictator receives from the mob."

451 *Ibid,* p. 290. (With more time and less will power, it would be tempting to quote page after page.)

452 *Hear Me Talkin' To Ya,* pp. 29-33.

453 *The Cotton Club* (CD). See bibliography.

454 For one thing, he made the mistake of refusing a job at the new Cotton Club, deeming the pay too low.

455 *The Impromptu of Versailles,* a one-act play.

456 *The Swing Era,* p. 846.

[457] P. 206.

[458] *Ibid.*, pp. 205-207.

[459] P. 164.

[460] *Ibid.*, p. 165.

[461] The incident takes us beyond the time range covered by this book, for *Time* published Monk's picture and a cover story in February, 1964. But it is cited here as significant in the context of Jones' criticism, which appears on page 26 *ff* of his *Black Music.*

[462] At the time of writing this first book, in 1970, Kofsky was an assistant professor of History at Sacramento State College. From his preface it is clear he lacked the support of his colleagues and was unsure of his job there. He published both books with Pathfinder, a press specializing in Marxist and communist treatises.

[463] *Black Nationalism,* p. 82.

[464] *Ibid.*, p. 89.

[465] *Black Music, White Business,* pp. 18-20.

[466] *Ibid,* pp. 25 *ff*. The entire appendix of this book consists of copies of Levine's contracts and royalty payments.

[467] *Black Nationalism,* p. 185.

[468] *Ibid.*, p. 67.

[469] *Black Music, Black Business,* p. 99.

[470] *Black Nationalism,* p. 147-148.

[471] P. 218.

[472] *Ibid.*, pp. 189 *ff.*

[473] *Ibid.*, p. 200.

[474] *The Making of Jazz,* p. 139.

[475] He does criticize Crouch but only for an inadequate grasp of musicology and historiography (*Jazz, the American Theme Song* p. 257).

[476] *Cats of Any Color,* p. 228.

[477] *Ibid.*, pp. 178-179.

[478] *You Can't Steal a Gift*. New Haven, Yale Univ. Press, 2001.

[479] *Blue, the Murder of Jazz.*, p. 30.

[480] *Ibid.*, p. 31.

[481] *Ibid.*, p. 234.

[482] *Ibid.*, p. 13.

[483] The tome, weighing in at three pounds, is a rich, well documented source of information.

[484] P. 746.

485 See Chapter Ten, *supra.*

486 *Ibid.,* p. 33.

487 In *Crazeology,* Freeman tells how his group, the Austin High School Gang, heard Oliver after listening to the NORK. He said "We never went back to the New Orleans Rhythm Kings because when we heard the King Oliver band, we knew we were hearing the real thing for the first time" (p. 6). In *Hot Man,* Art Hodes explains that in starting out "The main thing I had to learn was the style, the idiom, which the blacks had and I didn't" (p. 16). And "Most of us Chicago lads learned from the great Negro players . . . They inspired us; we came, we listened, we learned" (p. 63). Eddie Condon, in *We Called it Music,* said "The white musicians who went to Lincoln Gardens, the Sunset Café, and the Nest, knew that however long they tried they would never more than imitate what they heard" (p. 162).

488 *Op. cit.,* p. 342.

489 *Crazeology,* p. 7.

490 *Hot Man,* p. 25.

491 *Ibid.,* p. 24.

492 Cited in Gerard, p. 108.

493 *Really the Blues,* p. 261 *ff.*

494 P. 228.

495 Cited in Lees in *Cats of Any Color* in connection with Oscar Peterson's hiring of white guitarist Herb Ellis (p. 188).

496 *Ibid.,* p. 209.

497 See Gerard, p. 28.

498 Cited in Lees, *Op. cit.,* p. 188.

499 *To Be or Not to . . . Bop,* pp. 395-396.

500 See Chapter Seven, *supra.*

501 Travis, Dempsey J., *Odyssey,* p. 116.

502 *Down Beat,* November, 1935, reprinted in *The Duke Ellington Reader,* pp. 118 *ff.*

503 See *The Duke Ellington Reader,* pp. 171-172, for debates on Ellington's work, originally printed in *Jazz* in spring of1943.

504 *Ibid.,* p. 137. Evidently, the allegation of a communist affiliation was common but groundless.

505 *The Duke Ellington Reader,* p. 254 (Ellington's emphasis).

15

THE DANCE CONNECTION

It is impossible to discuss American popular music apart from its ever-present partner, dance. Certainly, music and dance, universally allied from time immemorial, have been inextricably linked throughout the cultural history of America.

Moreover, like America's popular music, American dance has had a long history of black and white interrelationships. From the days of slavery on, black dance frequently appropriated elements of the white genre. And conversely, the early dances of white Americans—mainly imports from England, Ireland, Scotland and the continent—were eventually influenced by African-American styles. Like America's popular music, the dancing that tracked it every step of the way would demonstrate countless examples of racial crossovers and cross-fertilization in the course of the decades.

The most visible of such crossovers would be the adoption by white society of African-American styles of dance. That did not happen overnight. As with instrumental music and song, it would take some decades after Emancipation for the general white public to accept and begin performing indigenous black dances.

From Peasants to Princes: Upward Mobility of the Dance

The fact that black dance, like black music, would come eventually to have a strong impact on the white genre should not surprise us if we consider the origins of stylish European dances. It happened that nearly all, if not all, the dances performed by the nobility and upper classes of Europe, from the sixteenth well into the nineteenth century, were taken from lively backwoods peasant dances of various countries. Now American society had no noble class to boast of, and even its moneyed elite could not measure up to the enviable upper crust of England or France. It did, however, have a peasant class. Not the farmers, of course, for they were seen on a par with any other workers in democratic America. But the proletarian mass of slaves working the southern soil. People who, even when set free, still remained at the lowest level of society. So it is logical, if not inevitable, that innovations in dance, like innovations in music, should have emanated from inventions of African Americans.

In Europe, one could find numerous examples of the upward mobility of the dance, with the aristocracy and stylish bourgeoisie perpetually adopting dances of humble origins. The stately pavane of the sixteenth century, which came to the French court by way of Spain, was originally a popular dance of rural revelers. As its name indicates, it probably derived from *pavo,* the Latin word for peacock, and may well have been inspired by the strut of that animal. (The fact that the pavane and some other peasant-derived dances had parts where men and women kissed doubtless did not detract from their popularity.) Even the elegant minuet, danced at the French court from 1650 on to the music of Lully, came originally from a peasant dance of Poitou.

The dances imported and adopted by America in the eighteenth and nineteenth centuries, though originally rustic affairs, had been honed and polished in France by great dancing masters such as Beauchamp and Gardel, so that the members of the nobility and their bourgeois imitators could execute them with dignity and grace. Under the influence of ballet, the *contredanses* or country dances had been smoothed out. The quadrille and cotillion (the latter named for the peasant girl's petticoat or *cotte*) had lost their lively country jumping. Even the polka, that animated peasant dance from Czechoslovakia, had become tamed by the time it crossed over to America in the nineteenth century.

As for the waltz, that dance too had its rustic ancestry, likely deriving from Bavarian or Austrian peasantry or, as some have thought, from the reeling peasant *volta* introduced to French society in the sixteenth century. In any case, though graceful enough in its reformed and refined version, the dance scandalized many observers, with critics ranking it from "indecorous" to "obscene."[506] For the waltz abandoned the group formations of the quadrille and other square or circle dances and was executed by a man and woman in an actual embrace. Of course it was a chaste embrace, with the standard rule of several inches between partners. Moreover it was danced at a frenetic speed, one more conducive to perspiration than to titillation. Still, it made its way only very slowly to acceptance in nineteenth-century America.

Such dances, their humble origins long forgotten, became an intrinsic aspect of social life in American society North and South. For especially after the puritanical seventeenth century—a time when social dance enjoyed some popularity in the colonies but was generally frowned on—dancing became prominently featured in the social life of well-to-do white Americans. (George Washington himself granted it great importance.) So in the 1800s anyone who was anyone—or wanted to be—had to know quadrilles and cotillions and, later in the century, the lively mazurka, polka, schottische, galop—and even the controversial waltz.

In the South, many plantation owners gave periodic dances and attended them on other estates as well. Musical accompaniment cost little or nothing, because a plantation of any size would normally include competent slave musicians—sometimes hired out to friends and acquaintances as well. Guests might dance to the sound of a competent Negro fiddler or perhaps a slave trio, often including a banjo and a tambourine. A talented black set caller might shout out the moves in humorous homemade verses, while executing steps himself as he called them out.

Naturally, the slaves took it all in. They might have watched dances on the sidelines in the "big house" or observed them working as house servants, musicians or sight unseen. Or they could have been shown the figures by on-the-spot witnesses. Whichever the case, they appropriated the white dances that most appealed to them and, as we shall see, completely transformed them to their own style. So began one phase of the terpsichorean racial crossbreeding that would continue throughout the history of American popular dance.

Of course, at the same time slaves were observing the dancing of their white masters, the reverse held true as well. White plantation owners, their families and friends could not help be aware of the Negro dances. For those often took place right outside the slaves' huts on Saturday nights, on the Lord's Day—their one day off—on rare holidays and special occasions like corn shucking time or "crop-over" (harvesting) time. In some cases, slaves were known to dance even on week nights after hours of backbreaking labor, until the wee hours of the morning, when it was almost time to go back to laboring in the fields. (Such obvious joy in dancing has prompted many an apologist for slavery to insist that the slaves were "happy." Certainly, they did not dance out of happiness, but dancing allowed them, at least temporarily, to forget all misery.)

For white onlookers, the slave dances appeared strange, outlandish, amusing and often outrageous. Only the most adventurous nonconformists or the very young would be tempted to perform their steps as the slaves executed them. The lively black style did, undoubtedly, have some affect on white country dancing—a phenomenon that one critic has called "reverse acculturation."[507] And in the 1850s, some whites were observed finishing off an evening of country dancing with more unstructured Negro jigs.[508] However, the black dances remained—at least for a time—the property of the slaves. They might be copied informally for purposes of amusement or parodied on stage by black-faced minstrels but could not be literally transposed to the ballrooms of white society. A brief description of their dancing will demonstrate why this was so.

Slave Dancing and the African Tinge

The dances of the slaves recognizably retained features of African dancing. If the African heritage could not always be easily discerned in the songs of the slaves, it was highly visible in their religious and secular dances. For although singing in the slaves' native languages had been strongly discouraged on most plantations, their dancing was most commonly seen as a relatively harmless source of amusement and entertainment. So black dance lived on, along with its African styles of movement.

Two main types of black dance predominated: the slow and sinuous shuffle typical of the religious shout (described in Chapter One) and fast-stepping, jumping, whirling and kicking dances. These were not necessarily two separate genres, however, for very often dances would combine both styles.

Although the slaves performed a wide variety of dances, certain common traits may be culled from descriptions of witnesses during the eighteenth and nineteenth centuries. All of these commonalities hark back to features recurring in the various traditional dances of West and Central Africa. They are:

1. The contact of bare feet shuffling or stamping on packed earth or improvised board.
2. The upper torso leaning somewhat forward, often with convulsive shoulder movements.
3. Bent knees.[509] Body centered low, toward the ground.
4. Animal fluidity.[510] The entire body in play.
5. Sinuous body movement from the waist down. Pelvic rotation.
6. Obvious and aggressive sexuality.
7. Leg movement emanating from the hips.
8. Rapid jumping, stomping and kicking.
9. Improvisation.
10. Rhythm often progressing from slow to fast or frenetic.
11. Perfect timing of dancing to the rhythm of accompanying music or patting.
12. Challenge dances, e.g., males outdoing each other with speedy leg work and virtuoso moves.[511]

It should be clear from much of the above list that styles of slave dancing would remain outside the customary sphere of eighteenth- or nineteenth-century "polite society." Even without the sensuality of the black dances, the relaxed posture, looseness and wild abandon of the performers would have made them unacceptable for adoption in white salons. For most well bred whites were trained to dance in set, formal patterns, with an erect upper body frame, straight spines and legs, turned out toes and elegantly rounded arms. The slave's dancing, a far cry from such structured formality and dignity, appeared nothing less than grotesque to the average white viewer.

But the most foreign—and shocking—aspect of their dance was the frank sexuality of their movements. The notorious pelvic sways, especially shocking in females, had their precedent in African dancing, very likely in ancient fertility rites. And such sways seemed also a natural outcome of the way the slaves transported produce while walking. It is common knowledge that in North America, as in Africa, slave women often carried loads on their head. (Such a practice is still alive in peasant villages and mountain districts of Latin America, Asia and elsewhere.) That balancing of loads while walking would necessitate keeping the breast thrust forward and upper torso fairly immobile to prevent baskets or other articles from slipping or falling off the head. It would also mean keeping the lower body "grounded," encouraging a hugging-the-earth foot shuffle. And it would induce hip sway as one leg passed the other, as a way of keeping the walk horizontal and smooth rather than bumpy.

To the horror of many white onlookers, sensual hip sways could be seen even in the religious dances of the slaves. In the shout, for example, where they circled around, tapping sharply on a heel, then moving forward in a step or shuffle. A number of chroniclers have testified to the earthy and downright shocking hip and body movements of the participants.[512]

Such movements appeared positively lascivious when observed in a secular dance such as the highly popular *calenda* (or *calinda*). That dance, a Caribbean import, was performed in New Orleans' Congo Square and throughout many regions inhabited by the black slaves. It has been described variously, with details differing from area to area and from generation to generation. Often there is mention of women holding a handkerchief in one hand or clutching it by two corners while dancing.

The *calenda* appears to have been lively, with turns, pirouettes, shuffles and foot stamping. Sometimes it was seen executed in two lines, men facing women; at others it was described as performed in a circle, with a couple or couples dancing inside the ring. But in almost every case, despite an erect upper torso, the conduct of males and females toward one another, their striking thighs, even kissing during the dance, their twisting and writhing and, especially, the movement of the female pelvic region have either been characterized as indecent and lewd or said to defy description. Accounts of other Caribbean dances imported to the colonies, dances such as the *chica* or *bamboula*—which sometimes evoked the pursuit-and-evasion ritual of a cock-and-hen mating dance[513]—similarly make mention of sensual gestures and movements.

For most southern whites, however, even those of New Orleans, slave dancing meant not *calendas* or *bamboulas* but what they labelled "Negro jigs." That is, the fast stepping style, often called "buck" dancing or "breakdowns," of kicks, hops, stomps and whirls,[514] or, as Fanny Kemble saw them, "contortions, springs, flings, kicks and capers."[515] Some white observers of such dances might well have been reminded of Irish jigs. But such fast-paced stepping was so closely associated with the slaves that in the South the phrase "jig dance" stood for the lively Negro dancing. Similarly, the word "jig" was applied to various other types of black performance: "jig banjo," "jig tunes" and later "jig piano." And to the Negroes themselves.

Of all the slaves' lively recreational dances, one of the favorite, most widespread and enduring was the *juba,* whose name undoubtedly derived from the African *giouba,* originally a sacred dance. The dance was usually performed counterclockwise in a circle and, as with many other slave dances, often had a couple dancing inside the ring (sometimes one or two males). The dancers indulged in a good amount of twisting, turning, shuffling, hopping or kicking and capering. Critics and chroniclers have pointed to pre-Charleston moves in the juba, notably, the crossing and uncrossing of hands against knees that come together and spread apart with each beat.[516] The dance maintained a strong and steady rhythm, what with the metronomic foot stamping of dancers and the percussive beat provided by bystanders clapping hands, tapping feet and patting knees, thighs or chests ("patting juba").

One of the non-dancers would serve as "caller" shouting or singing out a sequence of steps for the dancers to perform. In fact, the lyrics of juba songs that have survived consist to a great extent of a list of specific moves for dancers to perform. For example,

> Juba jump and juba sing, Juba cut dat pigeon's wing
> Juba kick off Juba's shoe, Juba dance dat Jubal Jew.[517]

At the end of each verse the caller or those watching the dance would cry out "Juba!" Which was, apparently, a signal for the dancers to perform a specific step.

There are few concrete descriptions of most steps in Juba; for example "dat Jubal Jew" remains a mystery. However, the "pigeon wing," a step popular with slaves all over the South at the time, was probably a model for the "buck and wing" of minstrelsy, still performed in modern tap dancing. According to most accounts, in the "pigeon wing" a dancer, usually male, flapped or arched his arms like a bird's wing and hopped on one foot while circling the other one behind the calf of the hopping foot, in time to each hop. It has also been described as jumping up and kicking the legs together in mid-air.[518] Other steps mentioned in various versions of juba songs, are the "yaller dog," the "raise de latch" and its rhyming "long dog scratch," the last probably resembling a step called the "itch," in which dancers actually scratched themselves.

The juba songs, with their step-by-step instructions, like T. D. Rice's famous "Jim Crow" number, were early examples of here's-how-you-dance-it songs with in-built choreography. They would be followed by a whole string of such how-to numbers, popular well into twentieth century (*e.g.*, Ernest Hogan's "Pas Ma La" of 1895," "Ballin' the Jack" of 1913,[519] or, a white version, the "Varsity Drag"[520] from the 1927 show, *Good News).*[521]

A rare first-hand description by a white person of slaves dancing the juba may be found in James Hungerford's *The Old Plantation,* a fictionalized account of his stay at a plantation in southern Maryland in the summer of 1832. The dance, performed on the hard ground in front of a slave's hut, was directed by an eccentric house slave, Clotilda, who called out instructions to dancers "in a shrill, sing-song voice, keeping time to the measure . . . by beating her hands sometimes against her sides, and patting the ground with her feet."[522] The instructions had a satirical bent, in the African tradition. Clotilda made fun of the slaves in the group one by one, while instructing the dancers to imitate the butts of her satire. At one moment or other she had them copy the limping gait of one slave or the incessant tremors and shaking of another, while they moved about as directed. Their most difficult step was, apparently, the "juba reed," which must have been complex and acrobatic. Clotilda sang out:

> Try de Juber reed again;
> Try your bes' and try to win.
> Juber forrud, Juber back
> Juber dis way, Juber dat;
> Juber in, un Juber out;
> Juber, Juber, all ubbout.
> Juber![523]

But when they attempted the moves, all tripped and fell over each other in a burst of hilarity.

Among a host of other southern slave dances, animal dances, as in Africa, enjoyed great popularity. A prime example, the *buzzard's lope,* was usually danced in a circle, with participants singing, shuffling ahead and pecking, pretending to snatch the entrails and body parts of a dead cow—said "cow" being a slave lying in the middle of the rotating ring of dancers.[524] Although the buzzard's lope did not survive,[525] other animal dances or steps such as the *camel walk, snake hip* and *fish tail,* would continue in one form or another well into the twentieth century and find their way into white ballroom and stage dancing.

Buck Dancing, Master Juba and the Irish Question

The buck dancing of slaves was one of the most important sources of modern tap dancing. "Buck dancing," as noted, usually referred to the high-stepping fast "jig" dancing described in the above discussion of the juba. Since such dances were commonly executed by bare feet on packed earth, they might seem a far remove from the clickety-clack of today's tap. Yet many observers have testified to the rhythmic pounding sound of black feet on the white man's soil. And on occasion, a portable board, usually around six feet long, was used by (male) slaves for virtuoso dancing on the levee and in other areas as a platform, intensifying the sound level of their foot stomping and permitting a clearer articulation of their steps.[526]

The steps were not organized into set patterns but improvised, with step-hops and the whole store of traditional shuffles, struts, stomps, toe-and-heel taps, kicks, twists and grinds, plus any innovations or improvements that came to mind. Besides the "pigeon wing," described above, favorite moves included the "double shuffle" and the "eagle rock," the latter danced with arms outstretched like wings, head back and body swaying back and forth. Among innumerable other steps were the "weed corn," or "chuck corn," the undescribed "cut the buckle" and the "long J. Bow," executed by sliding one foot forward on the ground and tilting the toes upward to form a J. And the very same moves could be seen performed by blacks in almost any region of the country with a population of slaves or freedmen: in Philadelphia, New Jersey or in Albany, New York, where Joel Munsell observed slaves dancing "the double-shuffle-heel-and-toe-breakdown" at the Pinkster Festivals.[527]

Dance historians have theorized that black dancing before the Civil War combined with Irish jigs or step dances, and that this mélange eventually gave birth to modern tap dancing. It is a fact that as far back as the eighteenth century, Irish tinkers and other workers had settled in southern slave territories, notably the Carolinas. However, it is highly unlikely that plantation slaves would have had much contact with them or had been influenced by their dances at that time.[528] Instead, the slave dances clearly continued to follow the traditional African or Afro-Caribbean patterns described here. If black dance did, indeed, adopt features of the Irish jig, that would more likely have occurred up North around the 1840s, when waves of Irish immigrants entered the United States in the wake of Ireland's potato famine. Still, we find no concrete examples or reasonable proof in support of this presumed "Irishing" of black dance.

It is possible to point out similarities between Irish and African-American dances. But those similarities need not be attributed to an influence of one culture on another or to an early blending of cultures. Both styles of dancing traditionally involved fast and fancy footwork. Indeed, foot stomping and tapping were features not only of Irish or Negro dancing but of dancing all over the world. They could be found in the Spanish Flamenco *tapateo* of Moorish origin, in American Indian circle war dances, aboriginal Australian dancing and the English hornpipe and clog,[529] to offer just a few examples.

One might well be reminded of Carl Jung's theory of the "universal" or "collective unconscious" and his belief that similar forms of the psyche ("motifs" or "archetypes") were present everywhere, in the minds and mythologies of all civilizations. Such universal archetypes appear to have existed in art as well. Similar stylized depictions of animals have been found in the Paleolithic cave drawings of France and northern Spain, in Stone Age Bushmen drawings of South Africa, in fifth dynasty tombs of Ancient Egypt, and areas remote from trade and tourism. And in dance, with its universal themes (*e.g.*, religion, fertility, war), similar patterns of movement—primordial kinetic archetypes—have co-existed from earliest times, in many different cultures.

In America, eventually two such cultures, Irish and Negro, would meet on common ground. Their most noteworthy meeting place: New York City.

In the first quarter of the nineteenth century, New York had become the largest city in America, reaching up to 160,000, and by 1850 its population would number over a half million inhabitants. Technically, it belonged to a slaveholding state until 1827, although children of slaves were deemed legally free if born after July 4, 1799. By 1810, African Americans (including a minority of freedmen) made up over eight percent of New York City's population.[530] In the 1840s a good proportion of the growing black community could be found in lower Manhattan, where they would come in close contact with the Irish immigrants.

The Negro-Irish ethnological connection was perhaps nowhere more in evidence than in the notorious Five Points district, a high crime area situated in the vicinity of today's Chinatown. There

Irish and African Americans were nearly equal in number, often in racially mixed ménages with Negro males as heads of households. Narrow, filthy streets, tough inhabitants, saloons, dives, brothels and other assorted unredeeming features made of the place a sordid spot, one to avoid at all costs. Yet curiosity impelled some whites to venture there, specifically to see and later describe its dance halls and dancers.

It was in the Five Points region that the legendary William Henry Lane, or "Master Juba," lived and performed. A free Negro, born in Rhode Island, Lane, after winning a series of dance contests, triumphed as the undisputed "King of All Dancers."[531] He would often start his program by imitating the styles of various known dancers, then end the performance by "imitating myself." That is, he did what he alone could do and with greater panache than all the rest. Lane astounded onlookers with his amazing agility and sense of rhythm, with his grace, humor and versatility. On his visit to England (where he died in 1852 at the age of twenty-seven), his dancing inspired London critics to poetry.

Many chroniclers of black dance—perhaps the majority—believe that Lane, in close proximity with the Irish, naturally absorbed elements of Irish dancing and that it is with this great dancer that black and Irish elements formed a hybrid which was the ancestor of modern tap dancing. This widely held theory has yet to be proven by evidence contemporary with Lane. One might be well advised to study Charles Dickens' oft quoted description of his experience in a Five Points dance hall, where he witnessed a performance by an amazing black dancer.

In 1842, Dickens took what he called a "plunge into the Five Points," armed with two sturdy policemen. After venturing down "squalid streets" and past "leprous houses," the writer wound up at Almack's bar and dance house,[532] where a corpulent black fiddler provided the music. and an unnamed dancer held everyone in thrall. That dancer, by many accounts,[533] may well have been Master Juba himself. One might surmise as much from Dickens' description of the dancer's incredible technique.

> Single shuffle, double shuffle, cut and cross-cut; snapping his fingers, rolling his eyes, turning in his knees,

> presenting the backs of his legs in front, spinning about on his toes and heels like nothing but the man's fingers on the tambourine; dancing with two left legs, two right legs, two wooden legs, two wire legs, two spring legs—all sorts of legs and no legs—what is this to him?[534]

The shuffling in the above description, the finger snapping, eye rolling, knee angling and great elasticity clearly mark the performance (which Dickens called "a regular break-down"[535]) as a quintessential African-American product. What, then, if anything, had the dancer—Lane or a close second—absorbed from the Irish? Irish dancers were known for their speedy tapping—at times up to fifteen seconds per tap. But so were Negro dancers, who were often said to step faster than the eye could observe. And neither Lane nor other black dancers would have been prone to imitate the straight upper torso of Irish jigging, the hands firmly placed on hips,[536] leaving all dexterity to straight legs rather than moving from the hips down and giving the rest of the body free play as well.

It is quite possible that Lane incorporated a few moves from Irish jigs or reels. But there appears to be no shred of evidence of Irish techniques in all the existent descriptions of Lane's art. Rather, that art appears to have been a highly Negro phenomenon. To quote just two excerpts from other accounts of his dancing: "Such a combination of mobility of muscles, such flexibility of joints, such boundings, such slidings, such gyrations . . ." And "But the Nigger Dance is a reality . . . [Otherwise] how could Juba . . . tie his legs into such knots, and fling them about so recklessly . . . ?"[537]

Historians may have concluded that Irish and black dance began to blend with Lane because of the frequent use of the word "jig" in connection with his performances. But as we have seen, that word had been associated earlier with the dancing of the slaves and not conceived of as "Irish" but always "Negro jigs" executed in an African-inflected style.[538] Such was the style that characterized Lane's dancing.

Certainly, neither Lane nor other black dancers of his time would have had qualms about learning and borrowing their licks from others. However, in spite of the close commerce of the

Irish and African Americans in the Five Points area, there is little evidence that Lane or contemporary black dancers of the region adopted much of anything from the unsyncopated, albeit lively, Hibernian jigging. Let us note, too, that when Lane performed his popular imitations of other dancers, he was mimicking well known African-American dancers exclusively. One could point out that Lane's white rival, John Diamond, was born Irish and sometimes performed an Irish jig, "The Fireman's Hornpipe," in whiteface. But Diamond was generally billed as an "Ethiopian" minstrel whose business it was to execute traditional black dances. And in a judged competition with Master Juba, he would most surely have tried to match him in the traditional black style.

Although it is unlikely that a melding of Irish and black dance occurred with Master Juba, Negro dance would, eventually, demonstrate white (including Irish) influences. A notable example of such influence would be seen in the late days of minstrelsy, particularly in the realm of soft shoe dancing.

White Minstrelsy's Take On Black Dances

White minstrels in burnt cork sometimes introduced non-Negro dances into their shows, dances such as England's Lancashire Clog, for example. But early on, in the 1840s and 1850s, many of them made an attempt to reproduce southern black dances they had actually observed *in situ*. Thomas D. Rice had already set the example with his "Jim Crow" dance.[539] Later, in the 1850s, a white minstrel, Dave Reed, presented a dance he had learned from blacks on a Mississippi steamboat. It bore resemblances to the *buzzard's lope* and to traditional ring shouts.[540] The walkaround finales of minstrelsy were, similarly, staged representations of the Negro shouts, some of them even including. "patting Juba."[541]

By the time of early minstrelsy it had become customary to associate certain dances with specific states, and white minstrels were quick to exploit such names as the "Virginia Breakdown," the "Mississippi Breakdown," the "Louisiana toe-and-heel," the "Tennessee Double Shuffle," undoubtedly devising a mythical choreography for presentation to spectators who would, in any case, not know the difference between the real and the factitious.

If minstrels seeking authenticity had no first-hand knowledge of the South, they could, if they liked, witness the southern dances without traveling far afield. For New York City was minstrelsy's birthplace and its prime center of activity. And in New York's Catherine Market, not far from the wharves, slaves could be found dancing on holidays such as the Pinkster celebrations. There they would perform their jigs for money or for a dish of fried eels. No longer barefoot and pounding on warm southern soil, they competed with other slaves and free blacks, tapping out audible rhythms in hard soled shoes on their portable boards, or "shingles." (Although their steps and styling were traditionally black, some adopted the custom of English clog dancers who screwed pennies or pieces of metal to the heels of their boots for a higher decibel level.)

Still, the search for black authenticity was not a prime motive for most minstrels, who aimed simply to entertain and amuse with a bit of Negro exoticism. So like the songs of later minstrelsy, such as those of Stephen Foster or James Bland, the later dances did not have to imitate actual creations of the slaves. Instead, minstrels tended to make up their own, unsyncopated, dance numbers, including some kicks and shuffles, and give them colorful titles hinting at negritude, *e.g.:* "The Sugar Cane Reel," "The Congo Coconut Dance" or, even more improbably, "The Fling d'Ethiope."[542] A thick layer of black makeup did the rest.

After the Civil war, when the Negroes themselves began to form minstrel companies, they brought with them their own dances, performing them in their own manner. That was undoubtedly their greatest contribution to the minstrel stage. In songs, they could copy the ersatz darky numbers of white minstrels; in demeanor they could even parody themselves. But when it came to dance—their very bodies—they had to be themselves, and they excelled at it. So they appeared with their Negro jigs, their off-beat rhythms, their syncopated buck-and-wing, their time steps, their stop-time tapping, their precision lightening footwork and physical flexibility.

One of the most famous of black dances adopted by minstrelsy was the "Essence of Old Virginia." Although the dance would associated with the famous Negro minstrel, Billy Kersands, who performed it before Queen Victoria in the early 1900s, white minstrels had already discovered that "authentic . . . source material."[543] W. W. Newcomb was reputed to have originated the Virginia "essence" in the context of early white minstrelsy with a lively rendering of the dance's leaps, shuffles and glides. Dan Bryant is said to have perfected the dance in the 1850s but performing it slowly. The "essence" smoothed down over the decades. According to one of the clearest descriptions of the later style, made by composer Arthur Marshall, ". . . the performer moves forward without appearing to move his feet at all, by manipulating his toes and heels rapidly, so that his body is propelled without changing the position of his legs." Marshall also compared the dance to a person being towed around on ice skates.[544] Out of the "essence," the "waltz clog"[545] and similar styles of minstrelsy dancing developed the smooth soft shoe dancing.

This smoothing out of the Negro jigs and breakdown styles in white minstrelsy becomes obvious if one observes drawings of black-faced minstrel dancers depicted on covers of songbooks, sheet music or playbills throughout the years. In the early decades and at the height of minstrelsy, the dancers are invariably pictured with their knees pointed sharply outward in traditional black style, their arms outstretched or flying in the air, their bodies energetic. From the 1860s on, however, some are presented as poised, their postures far more restrained.[546]

It is not known to what extent Irish jigging or English clogging of the minstrel stage contributed to this evolution, but the white tendency to smooth and refine dancing did very likely play a part in it. For the original "buck" style of black dance had become far less unconstrained and improvisational. (This increased smoothness in late minstrelsy dancing may have been inevitable in any case, given the growing sophistication of American audiences.)

The epitome of the new smoothness in minstrelsy dance was, by many accounts, George Primrose (né Delaney) of Primrose and West Minstrels. A stylist rather than a technician,[547] he was known for his grace and elegance. His fluid technique influenced not only white dancers like Harland Dixon but black stars, such as Eddie Rector of the 1913 *Darktown Follies.* According to Marshall and Jean Stearns, his was "a style that transcended the stereotypes of the strutting or shuffling 'darky' and culminated in the suave 'class acts' of the 1930's and later."[548]

Tap dancing became known as such early in the twentieth century, in music halls, burlesque, vaudeville and musical comedy. It undoubtedly had gestated on the white and black minstrel stages as jigs smoothed out and soft shoe dancing became popular. Tap would not wind up as a white monopoly; black dancers remained brilliant exponents of the genre. However, due to discrimination, for decades African-American tap dancers would enjoy far less visibility on the stage than white ones.

By the time of vaudeville, black dancers had been learning from whites and whites from blacks. Although white dancers invented new moves to be emulated, both white and black tapping would continue to retain the store of traditional black moves mentioned above, such as the double shuffle, buck-and-wing or time step. And in the realm of tap—and dance in general—black dancers equaled or bested white ones in smoothness, style, agility, speed and precision. And class. The team of Rufus Greenlee and Thaddeus Drayton, for instance, the first blacks to perform in formal attire (including monocles) on Broadway, could scarcely be matched by dancers of either race in precision and elegance.

That black stage dancing was generally unbeatable is eminently clear from the numerous rave reviews of dancing in black shows of the 1910s and twenties, with their repeated comments concerning the superiority of black. show dancers over white ones. Tapdancers Alice Whitman ("Queen of Tap" in the early 1900s), Bill "Bojangles" Robinson, Eddie Rector and The Nicolas Brothers had their white higher-visibility rivals but were difficult, if not impossible, to match.

Only with Fred Astaire[549] in the 1930s would a white tap dancer reign supreme, when Astaire—phenomenally—combined soft shoe and tap with ballet, an aristocratic style of ballroom dancing and a worldly insouciance.

Nineteenth-Century Social Dancing: Some Crossovers

Until well after the Civil War, white social dancers held mainly to their quadrilles, their cotillions and their Scottish reels. As for the slaves, they adopted the most animated of the white dances, the Virginia reel, for example, but often executed them with wild abandon, introducing their own style of whirling, prancing, kicking—even "patting juba"—and generally showing off.

In time, the black liveliness influenced the square dances of the southern whites. While they would not indulge in capering, kicks and stomps, in country dances white participants did whirl partners around with a greater freedom than seen at formal city balls. Such relative informality may well have been induced by a fiddle playing slave caller regaling the company with tunes such as "The Hog-Eye Man" or "Old Zip Coon" (which would become known as "Turkey in the Straw") and shouting out comical instructions. James Hungerford, for example, noted the relatively relaxed and enjoyable atmosphere of a plantation country dance with an amusing slave caller, comparing the event favorably with the more staid dances of Baltimore.[550], [551]

Of course such freedom of dancing could only go so far in polite society, and the differences between a white reel and a black one remained visible. No matter how relaxed or informal, the former had to maintain its grace and dignity. The young white characters in *The Old Plantation* amused themselves watching the slaves dance. But when one young lady, unable to keep her feet still while listening to a slave fiddler play, attempted a black jig step herself, the author commented, ". . . she made even the jig graceful."[552]

Throughout the antebellum years and for decades afterwards these same distinctions between black and white dancing obtained. Perhaps the closest blending of the two was seen in the "Quadroon Balls" of New Orleans. At such events, female Creoles of color would attend dances to meet—and in some cases dally with—prospective white paramours. Technically, a young Creole woman (specifically, the daughter of a mulatto mother and white father) could only marry a Creole. Therefore, many a Creole girl was reared by her ambitious mother to become the mistress of a wealthy white man. Such a girl often had a genteel upbringing, a certain amount of education and—certainly when compared with darker-skinned counterparts—considerable refinement. So when she danced at the Quadroon Balls, she could perform all the fashionable white dances of the day. With great sensuality according to reports, but often more gracefully than the white women themselves.

This duplication of white dancing by a Creole caste did not survive after the Civil War, when Jim Crow legislation deemed all Creoles of color black and deprived them of their rights and privileges. Before that time authorities had held that one drop of white blood entitled a New Orleanian to the customary rights of the city's inhabitants. By the late nineteenth century, one drop of Negro blood made that person a Negro.

* * *

As the nineteenth century neared its last decade, the white dances were fast evolving. The old-fashioned quadrilles had become less popular, as had other square dances with callers and open sets of couples forming patterns. Schottisches, polkas and mazurkas, lively couples dances, were on their way out. Instead, dances with simpler walking and gliding steps became the fashion. Partners were now performing two-steps[553] to the strains of martial music in 2/4 time. In 1891, for example, Sousa's "Washington Post March" with its brisk walks and skips became a favorite in private parties and at fashionable balls. Waltzing was no longer a public scandal. Times were, indeed, changing.

Then, at the turn of the century, white America adopted its first black dance: the cakewalk. It did not become a social dance along with two-steps and waltzes but served mainly as an exhibition dance or in contest. It did, however, become a rage.

In the black context, the cakewalk had also served as a special occasion dance, used in contests. Often the slaves performed it walking along a chalk line with a tumbler of water balanced on the head. Whoever danced it best without spilling the water might win the cake (perhaps merely a modest corn cake), awarded by the plantation owners. The dance has been best remembered for its high prancing step with slave couples, dressed in finery, strutting along proudly, very likely in a parody of the elegant dancing of their white plantation owners.

The cakewalk was first introduced to New York in the all-black *Creole Show* of 1889 and quickly became a must in other black musicals, in minstrelsy and vaudeville. All manner of fancy steps were introduced, but the dance inevitably featured and ended with the old familiar prance or strut. The first official adoption of the dance by whites was either a cakewalk contest held in a New York ballroom in 1892, or, according to another theory, in 1897 at Madison Square Garden.[554] The rage had begun. Soon contest after contest took place along with the requisite award of a cake and. at times, far more lavish prizes.

If this unusual adoption of a black dance by white society was merely a fad, it was a significant one. Not only as a first but also because the cakewalk introduced the jaunty off-the-beat black rhythms that heralded ragtime and jazz.

The white dancing public would soon be stepping to those rhythms.

The 1910s: The Barbary Coast Dances

After the Civil War "jook or juke joints," dives where free blacks could gamble, dally and dance to their heart's content, flourished in the Tenderloin sections of towns North and South. At times in such establishments the clients danced the old white quadrilles—sprinkled with a good dose of black shuffling, stamping and "patting juba."[555] But very often they performed their versions of African-American dances such as the "black bottom," "twist," "funky butt," itch," "shimmy," "snake hips," "camel walk" or "slow drag." The last, sometimes danced by naked women in brothels,[556] would remain popular in black jukes, cabarets and dance halls well into the 1930s.[557] Couples often danced in a postage stamp space, simply grinding together to the languishing early morning strains of the blues.

Such dances—some of them merely steps or moves—having originated in the slaveholding South, survived all throughout the black diaspora, thriving especially in the large port cities. But it was San Francisco's "Barbary Coast" that would make several of them famous, thereby introducing black dance into the repertoire of the general white public.

Why San Francisco?

California itself had become a magnet since the Gold Rush of 1849. The flood of Americans immigrating to that state was further intensified by the creation in 1869 of the first trans-continental railway (later part of the Southern Pacific) and the Atchison, Topeka and Santa Fe in 1881. Although California was not a slave state, blacks in bondage had been brought there, many of them laying ties for the westward bound railroad lines. Then after the Civil War, a large number of freed blacks traveled or immigrated to the West,[558] some becoming gold miners, others merchants, cooks, cowboys or pony express drivers. And they carried their musical heritage with them.

Moreover, San Francisco, like New Orleans and Chicago, was a thriving port town, that is, a logical locus of a Tenderloin district with its black jazz and black dance. By the early 1860s, Old Sydney-Town already housed a goodly share of dives and dancehalls, and these increased in number over the years. At the turn of the century one could find numerous bars, jukes, opium dens and brothels—usually in cellars—near and along the docks.

This was the San Francisco's infamous "Barbary Coast," aptly named for the legendary North African region whose pirates captured and enslaved many a British subject throughout the seventeenth century. Although the San Francisco earthquake of 1906 took its toll on the area, popular Barbary Coast joints and dance halls were promptly rebuilt, and by 1910 around three hundred such places were doing business, clustered in the space of just a few blocks along Pacific Street. Among the most frequented of the dance halls were the Thalia, Spider Kelly's, the Hippodrome, the Midway and Purcell's So Different, with its Negro entertainers and strictly white clientele.

The early 1910s marked the beginning of America's great dance craze, and the Barbary Coast cabarets helped to spark the fad. For they became known as the scene of the lively black dances that would soon sweep the nation. A good number of these were animal dances, such as the "turkey trot," the "bunny hug" and the "grizzly bear." Of course most of them did not originate in the Barbary Coast, for the "turkey trot" and, as seen above, many other animal dances, had formerly been a specialty of the southern slaves.

The animal dances, performed to ragtime rhythms, captured the imagination of Americans and Europeans alike. In fact, people from all over the world came to San Francisco to see them. But the most sensational Barbary Coast dance, the "Texas Tommy," took its inspiration not from the animal kingdom but, quite possibly, from the whorehouse, since in that milieu, a "tommy" was a slang word for prostitute. The dance may well have emanated from Texas, but it was truly launched at the Barbary Coast's Purcell's—prime showcase for nearly all the new ragtime dances. Dancer Johnny Peters reportedly brought it there from the South, in 1911, but he undoubtedly re-created it, staging his own version of the number. Very similar to the popular "lindy" of the late 1920s, the acrobatic, syncopated "Tommy" hit viewers like a second earthquake. The great ballet star, Anna Pavlova—who had already fallen in love with the "turkey trot" of 1910—came to see it and gave breathtaking reports of it to newspaper reporters. Al Jolson made the trip as well and returned to Manhattan around 1911 with the "Texas Tommy's" interpreters, Johnny Peters and his partner, Mary Dewson. It was the first major introduction of an African-American Barbary Coast dance to the white public of New York City.

When Peters' partner became ill, he replaced her with dancer Ethel Williams. Dance teams had become popular at the time, and the couple were engaged to give demonstrations at the posh lobster palace and cabaret, Bustanoby's. There, in 1912, they presented new fashions in dance: the "maxixe," "tango," "one-step"[559] and, for their finale, the "Texas Tommy."

But such exhibitions reached only relatively few viewers. It took the New York stage to make the Barbary Coast dances known to a more general public. The "turkey trot" first appeared onstage in that city in 1910 in a show imported from San Francisco, *Over the River.* Then three years later it was performed by Irene and Vernon Castle in the musical, *The Sunshine Girl*. The *Ziegfeld Follies of 1911* featured the "grizzly bear" dance, and Peters and Williams introduced audiences to the "Texas Tommy" in the *Darktown Follies of 1913*. Ethel Waters performed the "shimmy" in her act around 1917, basing her performance on Spencer Williams song, the "Shim-Me Sha-Wabble;" a few years later white Gilda Gray brought the dance to larger audiences and greater fame in the *Ziegfeld Follies of 1922*.[560] The "Charleston" was presented in 1922 in *Liza*, the first black musical to play Broadway,[561] and in two numbers of the unsuccessful *How Come?* of 1923. But it truly became a hit that same year in a more popular black musical, *Runnin' Wild* (213 performances on Broadway). In that show, dancers garbed as redcap porters performed the dance to

James P. Johnson's immortal "Charleston." And as a final example, the "black bottom," first seen on a New York stage in 1924 in the play *Dinah,* became an international vogue upon its appearance in George White's *Scandals of 1926.*

It goes without saying that these dances, whether performed by black or white artists, did not duplicate the original, freewheeling and improvisational versions of slaves or free Negroes of the early nineteenth-century. For, as in the Barbary Coast cabarets and as in minstrelsy, the black dances were now arranged and presented as exhibition numbers for audience entertainment. A dance such as the Charleston, for example, had undoubtedly been originally inspired by a step seen in South Carolina and nearby areas of the South. It was perhaps a mere hop-kick with a number of improvised variations, performed to the familiar Charleston rhythm.[562] In the 1910s, Willie "the Lion" Smith saw "gullah" longshoremen from South Carolina and Georgia performing Charleston moves in the dives of Westside New York's "Jungle Alley."[563] But later, on the New York stage, those steps had obviously become adapted, modified, choreographed.

The complex choreographies of such dances could well have seemed daunting to inexperienced white viewers anxious to learn the new numbers. However, with the big dance mania sweeping America in the 1910s, a multitude of dance studios and schools sprang up, with teachers willing and able to simplify the dances, break them down and codify them into set patterns. The progenitor of Arthur Murray had arrived on the scene.

Whites Dancing Black

Before the 1910s, most social dancing of white society took place in private balls. Public dance halls were frowned on by middle class whites. Certainly a good percentage of such places were run as taxi dances, frequented by males who paid as little as a nickel per two-or three-minute dance with women of questionable respectability. Such places, some open to whites and others to blacks, flourished throughout America from the mid-nineteenth century to the Second World War. But even a more upscale sort of public dance hall would have been out of the question for the white middle class, since one simply did not rub elbows with "just anybody."

The situation changed radically in the first decade of the century, with the demise of Queen Victoria and Victorian strictures and attitudes. Modernity came to the fore with a search for new amusements, public venues in which to find them, and a greater freedom and daring in female behavior. Louis Erenberg, in his *Steppin' Out, New York Nightlife and the Transformation of American Culture, 1890-1930,* gives an excellent history of these changes, which clearly opened the way for the dance craze of the second decade and the adoption by whites of black dances. As the author explains, a new, exciting night life provided ample opportunity for modern amusement in the form of lobster palaces, cabarets, night clubs. By 1911 any hotel or restaurant of importance had added a dance floor for the pleasure of patrons and for demonstrations by professional exhibition dancers.

The huge popularity of dancing did not abate in the following years but, if anything, grew dramatically. To focus on only one year, 1923, and one publication, *Variety,* a headline of March 15 proclaimed "Huge Broadway Dance Hall," for the largest dance hall in the world (15,000 square feet) was soon opening at Broadway and 53rd Street.[564] A front page article of July 19 announced "'Dance lands' spring up all over town."[565] In fact, as the journal noted in yet one more front page article entitled "Dance Craze Sweeps On,"[566] legitimate theaters had become seriously concerned about their fate in the face of the snowballing popularity of dance halls and dancing.

The mania seemed unstoppable, although there were many who tried to stop it. For after the invasion of the Barbary Coast dances with their one-step prancing, their black ragtime inflexion and, especially, their close embrace, many observers saw the situation as out of hand. They raised their voices and pens in protest. Of course such protests were not a new development, since moralists had raised as great a storm anent the scandalous waltz, the mazurka and polka, despite the distance between partners and the frenetic speed of those old-time dances. The nineteenth-century church, for example, had warned Americans against "the abomination of permitting a man who was neither your [fiancé or serious suitor] nor your husband to encircle you with his arms and slightly press the contour of your waist."[567]

The dancing of white womanhood in the 1910s elicited a similar strong moral backlash. For one thing, the notorious *thés dansants* of the late afternoon drew many a married woman into the arms of some slick unattached male dubbed "dance gigolo," "lounge lizard" or "tango pirate." And elicited intense moral reactions. Erenberg, for instance, relates how a certain Eugenia Kelly, who frequented the cabarets night after night, was taken to court and legally made to repent and mend her ways. Erenberg concludes:

> Of all the cabaret's activities, the public character of dancing aroused the bitterest and most prolonged attacks. To reformers, the close physical contact . . . lifting of legs, the jerking of shoulders represented an unreserved demeanor on the part of youth and womanhood in general.[568]

The strident criticism of the intimate and suggestive dancing did not abate. In May of 1921 New York State enacted a law granting a state commissioner the right to censor dances. A New Mexico college newspaper of the same period published the opinion that "to jig and hop around like a chicken on a red-hot stove . . . shaking the body until it quivers like a disturbed glass of jello . . . would not be permitted in a semi-respectable road-house."[569] In 1922 the *Ladies Home Journal* issued this statement:

> Boy-and-girl couples leave the [dance] hall in a state of dangerous disturbance . . . the modern dance is producing little short of a holocaust. The statistics of illegitimacy in this country show a great increase in recent years.[570]

And in a vain attempt to stem the tide, a bill was introduced into the New York State Legislature to the effect that "Persons in dances shall at all times keep their bodies and faces free from each other."[571]

Of course, no one could turn the clock back. Young Americans continued to seek out the latest in black dances and attempt to perform each new step as it came in vogue. Protesters continued to protest, to no avail. But if nothing could be done to keep Americans away from such unrespectable dances, there was another solution at hand: the dances themselves could be made respectable.

Enter Irene and Vernon Castle. They were not truly innovators but stars. And through their teaching and, more importantly, through the example of their own elegance, dances of the black ghetto made their way—greatly modified—into the ballrooms of high society.

The Castles and the Whitening of Black Dance

News of the Barbary Coast dances reached the Castles in Paris in the early 1910s. Impoverished newlyweds, they were attempting to scrounge a living there as a dance team when they read an article about the new "grizzly bear" dance fad in America. After gleaning what little they could about the style of the dance, they introduced their concocted version of it to the French. Their interpretation of the "greezly" was a huge success and certainly helped launch their career.

Back in America, the Castles became nothing short of a sensation. Vernon's expertise and polish were finely matched by Irene's grace and beauty; her dancing was described by critic Gilbert Seldes as a "disembodied lightness."[572] The couple's talent, elegance and unquestionable sense of style—and their choice contacts within the finest of American society—made them idols of the nation and style setters.[573] They performed exhibitions, they danced in musical comedy, they taught, they set up a lavish institution, "Castle House," for lessons, demonstrations and dances. Where dance was concerned, their interpretation and precepts became close to gospel for anyone who was anyone. In fact, the Castles were, to a great degree, responsible for the shape and importance of ballroom dancing in America.

As for the Barbary Coast dances, although the Castles started out with the "grizzly bear" in Paris in 1911 and performed the "turkey trot" in *The Sunshine Girl* in 1913, by 1914 they had renounced such "primitive" styles. "Shuffles and twists and wriggles and jumps are no longer words to be used in connection with dancing," declared the Castles, and that included the "contorsions" of the "hideous" turkey trot and other such dances.[574] The rules of the Castles, offered as "suggestions for correct dancing," included these words,

> Remember you are at a social gathering, and not in a gymnasium. Drop the Turkey Trot, the Grizzly Bear, the Bunny Hug, etc. These dances are ugly, ungraceful, and out of fashion.[575]

According to these celebrated gurus of the dance, the goals would now be a flowing grace, beauty and dignity.

But if the Castles disdained the zoological fare of the Barbary Coast, they were not averse to the other dances inherited from the black tradition. Included in their repertoire were the Brazilian "maxixe," a mélange of an Afro-Lusitanian and European moves, and the Argentine tango, which had largely originated with black dancers of nineteenth-century Buenos Aires. Both dances, already smoothed out in South America, had become increasingly refined in Paris soon after 1900. The Castles would further tame the tango, cleansing it entirely of any hint of sexuality.

Others had already introduced such dances to the American public. Johnny Peters and Ethel Williams, newly arrived in New York from the Barbary Coast's Purcell's, had, in 1912, performed onstage precisely the dances the Castles would offer two years later: the maxixe, tango, one-step and waltz (although the Castles did not include Peters' and Williams' bouncy "Texas Tommy"). In fact, in an interview with Marshall Stearns, Ethel Williams said that Irene Castle had asked her for coaching in the steps.[576] And also, before the reign of the Castles, their arch-rivals, the team of Maurice Mouvet[577] and Florence Walton, had been presenting exhibitions of the tango and maxixe in restaurants, cabarets on the stages in New York and throughout America and Europe. Still, the Castles' talent and fame were such that their predecessors and their contributions have long been cast in the shadow.

The black elements in dancing did not evaporate entirely with the smoothing and refining of ballroom dance as exemplified by the Castles. Although the orchestra of James Reese Europe mainly provided a standard beat for their waltzes and other dances (the "Castle Walk," for example, has an even one-two, one-two rhythm), it did, at times, hint at a subdued ragtime. The one-step, a favorite of theirs, had been a customary feature of black ragtime dances.

Nonetheless, in the white milieus of the Castles' time, the African in African-American dance was fast fading. When the turkey trot appeared in *Over the River* in 1910, it was performed not to ragtime but to standard on-the-beat tempo of Irving Berlin's "Everybody's Doin' It." When white couples danced that or other Barbary Coast dances, they had to coordinate, to match steps, whereas in the black versions, each partner felt freer to do his or her own thing. For example, one of a pair—usually the male—might improvise fancy "shine" steps. Such was often the case in the "Texas Tommy," when the female was swung out of closed position and into a breakaway. The greater freedom and improvisation in black couples' dancing would continue to be seen throughout the twenties, thirties and forties.

For white males and females to execute the new dances "correctly," those who could afford it might choose from a wide range of available teachers. Many of them flocked to the dance academy of African-American dance expert Billy Pearce, the "Dancing Master of Broadway," who, besides teaching Harlem blacks tap and the current dances, attracted the patronage of such as Ramón Navarro, Ed Wynn, Louise Brooks, Anita Loos, Libby Holman, Lily Damita and other celebrities of the day.[578].But numerous other teachers, most of them white, opened studios as well. For as Irene Castle put it, "With the great boom in ballroom dancing, everybody rushed to hang out a shingle and proclaim themselves dancing teachers."[579]

A major problem was that one teacher might devise one way of dancing the maxixe, the "Tommy" or the tango and another's version could be quite different. So logically, associations were formed to standardize steps and codify rules and regulations. The American Society of Professors of Dancing became active around 1914. In Britain, a more proactive and influential association, the Imperial Society of Teachers of Dancing, founded in 1892, created its mission statement in 1904. It is interesting to note the extent to which that statement anticipated the work of Irene and Vernon Castle. The stated goal: "The elevation and advancement of the art of dancing and the preservation of its ancient prestige and dignity."[580] Quite naturally, such societies did not concern themselves with earthy fads like the Barbary Coast animal numbers but mainly with smooth, "refined" dances that would endure in the ballroom dancing repertoire of the future.

So important were the ideals of elevation and dignity in dance that when the Imperial Society of Teachers of Dancing took on the sensual Argentine tango they cleansed and reformed it by creating the purified "international tango." That is, something resembling a gracefully turning one-step, with a bit of Latin zip only by way of occasional head jerks. Done today in long feathery gowns, it looks quite beautiful, but one might well conclude that the Imperial Society had taken the tang out of the tango.[581]

White Ballroom Dancing in the Big Band Era

Not all white dancers could afford the luxury of dance lessons. In fact the majority simply picked up the skill from family, friends or by observing and learning as they went along. But whether tutored or not, they danced the same dances. Their favorites: the foxtrot of 1914 and the imperishable waltz, dances which would remain staples of social dancing throughout the big band era of the 1920s and 1930s. The foxtrot and waltz were performed by dancers of both races but associated primarily with the white ballroom clientele. For African-Americans were less known for their smooth or staid ballroom dancing than for their unusual inventions in lively black jazz dance.

Despite its animal name, the foxtrot, danced in *andante* 4/4 tempo, may well have been a white invention. Its origins, however, remain problematical. According to one version, Vernon Castle so liked James Reese Europe's slow playing of Handy's "Memphis Blues," that Europe suggested the Castles invent a dance to go with that tempo, and so the foxtrot was born.[582] Noble Sissle, however, stated that Vernon Castle first saw the dance performed "in an exclusive colored club[583] and then adapted it. But most dance historians have pointed to white entertainer Harry Fox as the actual originator of the dance. Fox is known to have performed a trotting step on stage in New York in 1914, and that, evidently, became known as Fox's Trot, or the "foxtrot."

Certainly, the foxtrot of the dance hall differed greatly from Fox's original stage performance. A teacher/choreographer Oscar Duryea claimed to have smoothed Fox's trot (likened to "a nervewracking movement")[584] into a smooth glide. Charles Coll maintained that when first danced by couples it amounted to "one continuous romp from beginning to end," but that Philadelphia dance teachers deserved credit for "taming reynard."[585] In 1914, the year of the foxtrot's birth, the fledgling American Society of Professors of Dancing made it its business to standardize the steps of the dance.

Whatever the actual origin and early look of the foxtrot, its slow-quick-quick pattern, codified by the powers that were, endured throughout the ballroom dance era as a favorite form of white social dancing. Faster versions of the dance became popular by the early twenties, the "Peabody" in America and the "quickstep" in England, but by and large the standard foxtrot and waltz remained the perennial staples of the white ballroom dancers. They were the main dances done to the music of white units such as the Casa Loma Orchestra, Art Hickman, Lester Lanin and Paul Whiteman. Or to Fletcher Henderson's band at Roseland, where the black band played to white dancers exclusively. And the foxtrot and waltz would remain mainstays well after the introduction of black jazz dances of the twenties and latin dances of the thirties, forties and fifties.

Black Dancing in the Big Band Era

Unlike white ballroom dancing of the twenties and thirties, black social dancing did not usually conform to set patterns. It is true that in some venues, such as the Renaissance Ballroom in Harlem, black dancers of the thirties wanted standard waltzes and smooth Whiteman style music for their social affairs.[586] However, in small clubs and cabarets of Harlem or in crowded Chicago dance halls, most patrons would not be executing codified steps or figures from Arthur Murray's how-to diagrams. They simply danced. Often, in such places, they might be seen shuffling their feet in one chosen spot or doing a form of slow drag known as the "bump and mess-around."

But the black inventiveness still continued to spawn its sprightly innovations. Throughout the twenties and thirties especially, scores of new steps and dances were created and introduced to a public now eager to adopt the latest in African-American dance fads. A prime breeding ground and showcase for such fads: Harlem's famous Savoy Ballroom. Constructed and opened in

1925, occupying a whole block on Lenox Avenue between 140th and 141st Streets, with a capacity for 3,500 to 4,000 dancers, the ballroom was Harlem's most dazzling dance venue. The following description by Barry Singer bears this out.

> . . . a truly sumptuous, legitimate dance palace on a monumental scale, from the dazzling, capacious lobby dominated by a towering cut-glass chandelier and marble staircase to the hall itself . . . appointed in orange and blue, heavily carpeted, laced with tables and settees, a soda fountain, and a 250-by-50-foot, sleekly varnished wood dance floor, laid out before two bandstands and a 'disappearing' stage . . . a gift to black Harlem, savored by black Harlemites from the Savoy's first moments for the simple reason that *anyone* could dance there.[587]

One of the most remarkable features of the Savoy related not to its décor but to the fact that anyone could, indeed, dance there. For the Savoy admitted white couples who danced in the same space as blacks, not in a roped-off area as in other dance halls with both races in attendance. One even saw interracial partnering in the memorable Harlem ballroom.

It was at the Savoy that African-American dancers produced what would become undoubtedly America's most famous national dance: the "lindy." (or, as it also came to be known, "jitterbugging" or "jive"). Although dancers referred to it as a "hop" early on, it acquired the name the "lindy hop" in 1927 after Charles Lindbergh's famous transatlantic solo flight that year.[588] The dance was similar to the "Texas Tommy" and incorporated traditional black breakdown moves but performed in a somewhat smoother, more horizontal style. It generally had a count of eight,[589] the basic closed position step alternating with flinging the female partner out into breakaways. During such breakaways highly acrobatic feats were executed by the dancers; for example, the female partner being hoisted between the man's legs, up over his back and down to face him. Some believe that the "lindy" became increasingly acrobatic to impress white onlookers and possibly discourage them from imitation.

The dance called lindy flourished throughout the thirties, accompanied by vogues such as the "Big Apple," a circle dance, late in the decade. As the lindy evolved it absorbed a whole assortment of new moves, some of them first seen on the stage of the Cotton Club. "Truckin'"—a 1933 foot shuffle accompanied by the right index finger waving in the air—enjoyed great popularity, as well as the 1936 "Suzy-Q"—a shuffle on both feet, toeing left and right, similar to a Charleston step—and the 1937 "pecking," a pigeon-like neck bobbing from the traditional black stock of animal moves.[590] At one point the dance even incorporated the old "itch," popular at the turn of the century.

Harlem's lindy was adopted by white teenagers during the thirties. Nothing less than a sensation, it featured in dance marathons, exhibitions and soon—to the dismay of an older generation—made its way into the most dignified of white ballrooms. Rather belatedly, in 1942, the Society of Teachers of Dancing, unable to ignore the controversial "jitterbugging" any longer, adopted it into their syllabus as "Jive." If they could not make it go away they could at least try to tame it on the dance floor.

* * *

In discussing black and white relationships in music, the subject of dance has recurred as an important leit-motif throughout this book. For popular music and popular dance have long functioned as two sides of the same coin. So it should not surprise us that when the glory days of big band music faded into the sunset, the social ballroom dance so intimately tied to that music would fade as well.

The following may help clarify the reasons for the eclipse of ballroom dance in America during the second half of the twentieth century.

Destiny of the Dance

People have long debated whether, historically and pre-historically, 1) dance preceded music or 2) music came before dance. Some have thought the first theory correct, holding that from earliest times human beings danced and that musicians were inspired by their dancing. For clearly, great composers like Bach, Beethoven, Mozart and many others found inspiration in dancing and repeatedly built their compositions on dance themes.

However, if we consider the example of African-American music and dance, we find that the reverse is true, that dance continually followed the patterns of music.

In the traditional African context, music—specifically percussive music—came first taking precedence over the dance. For the drums contained the important rhythms that summoned the African gods, and dance, like song, had to adapt to those pre-established rhythms. Then, during slavery in America, in the absence of drums or other instruments, patting had usually set the tempo for dances. And as we have seen, the singer of the juba songs called out the cues to dancers who went through their paces as pre-arranged and directed by the singer. Later, the rhythms of popular ragtime music demanded a new style of dancing, and so the one-step and various Barbary Coast dances were invented to match the music.

Then in the twenties and thirties, big band swing music demanded still another kind of dancing. It is significant that the Savoy Ballroom served as a prime locus for the gestation of swing dances such as the lindy hop and its variations. For from the ballroom's inception, big bands such as the Fletcher Henderson Orchestra had been playing there, and their swing music inspired a new, swinging type of dance. Stearns and Stearns have pointed to 1932 as a notable year in the effect of Savoy big band music on dancers, for that was the year Bennie Moten's Kansas City band came there with trumpeter "Hot Lips" Page and tenor saxist Ben Webster. As the authors describe it, "Moten's band generated a more flowing, lifting momentum. The effect on the dancers was to increase the energy and speed of execution, a necessary preliminary for the acrobatics to come."[591] And, certainly, the irresistible rhythm and drive of the Chick Webb Orchestra, the Savoy's resident band for much of the thirties, had a great effect on the style of the "lindy hoppers." Lastly, when big band swing, both black and white, smoothed out over the years, swing dance had to smooth out as well.

In other words, each new invention or style in American popular dance found its inspiration in the music being played and shaped itself accordingly.

However, at the end of the 1930s, when a mostly white swing began to give way to black bop, ballroom dancing as it had been known reached an impasse. Factors other than bop music have been held responsible for its eventual doom. For example, the economic problems forcing the big dance bands out of business (see Chapter Eight) or, later, the nightly attraction of television. But in fact, despite statements by bop musicians like Gillespie that bop music could be danced to, it was not truly danceable. Dance had been following music all along, and now there was no music to follow. The famous black and white big bands of the twenties and thirties had been dance bands, and the pieces they played were composed and arranged with dancers in mind.[592] The bond between dancers and musicians had been strong and continuous. Always in communication with each other, orchestras and dancers forged, as Rex Stewart put it, "an unbreakable chain of reflected creativity."[593] That unbreakable chain, however, had broken.

For dancers to dance, a new kind of music was necessary. Rock and Roll eventually supplied it with its driving, understandable beat. But couples could, only with difficulty, attempt to dance together smoothly to it and execute a variety of steps in sync. For rock and roll had pared music down to a near primitive simplicity. Its rhythm was neither rich nor varied but most often reduced to a one-dimensional and continuous repetitiveness. Its melodies were similarly reduced, restricted to a smaller gamut, closer to the range of the blues. In other words, rock and roll had taken popular music outside the realm of the more sophisticated ballroom and swing dance styles and reafricanized it. Dancers had little choice but to accompany it back to Africa.

So would begin several decades of dancers (of both races), usually in pairs but dancing apart, standing in one spot, each doing his or her or own thing. The vogue would get under way in 1960 with Chubby Checker's introduction of the song, "The Twist," when immediately people of all ages, dancing apart, started rotating their hips as though propelling imaginary hula hoops. But outside of the "hustle" of the seventies, done to disco music, attempts to introduce other dances or steps were short lived. Generally, for quick-tempo rock and roll the general style of dance became simple gyrations with occasional unstructured foot patting or shuffling. For slow numbers the solution was—and still is—a glomming onto one's partner in a cleaned-up version of the slow drag. Since the old three-minute limit on dances no longer applies, with the wrong partner or a bum leg any dance could feel like a marathon.

As an alternative, these days some have opted to specialize in specific dances, such as Argentine Tango, Country and Western, Zydeco and East- or West-Coast Swing. Or to go with traditional ballroom dancing. Witness the ballroom dance revival of the present time. Much admired and regularly featured on television, ballroom dances are now executed by committed enthusiasts (often engaged couples learning waltzes or foxtrots for their wedding receptions—or seniors who never stopped dancing them). Their music of choice is most often the best fit: songs of the big band era. A mainly white phenomenon at this writing, the future of ballroom dancing is anybody's guess.

If there is a more modern and creative route for American dancers, it will most probably be inspired by the example of some new, contagious style of music. In the past, African Americans have mined their rich heritage to produce innovations in American popular music and dance. Once again, it may take some sort of cross-fertilization (racial or perhaps international) in music to produce a truly new and exciting form of American popular dance.

Notes

[506] From the sixteenth century on, various ancestors of the waltz were continually condemned for immorality throughout Europe. See Reeser, *The History of the Waltz.*

[507] Sanjek, Vol. I, p. 409.

[508] Knowles, p. 12.

[509] An old Congo proverb contained this advice: "Dance with bended knee, lest you be taken for a corpse." Cited in Knowles, p. 23.

[510] Robert Farris Thompson writes, "To say that a person dances as if he or she had no bones is one of the highest compliments a Liberian Dan, Nigerian Tiv, or Zairois Yanzi can bestow." *African Art in Motion*, p. 9.

[511] These characteristics have been drawn from observation of traditional dances in videos such as *Africa; JVC/Smithsonian Folkways Video Anthology* and works such as Stearns' and Stearns' justifiably celebrated *Jazz Dance*, Emery's comprehensive *Black Dance From 1619 to Today*, Thompson's *African Art in Motion* and other studies and chronicles included in the Bibliography.

512 See, for example, Emery, pp. 120 *ff.*

513 Moreau de St. Méry, writing the end of the eighteenth century, described the Caribbean *chica* as a struggle in which all the ruses of love are put into play: fear, hope, disdain, tenderness, caprice, pleasure, refusal, delirium, flight, inebriation, fainting away [*anéantissement*]." *De la Danse,* p. 44.

514 Such dances—jigs, fandangos and breakdowns—were also performed in Congo Square in the early 1900s.

515 *Journal of a Residence on a Georgia Plantation.*, p. 131.

516 More specifically, in the Charleston, when the knees come together the hands are crossed (right hand on left knee and vice versa). Then, with knees wide apart on the next half beat, the hands uncross and pat the extended knees. At the same time, the feet swivel back and forth, toeing inward when knees come together and outward when they spread apart.

517 Recalled by W.C. Handy in his *Blues: an Anthology,* cited by Emery, p. 97.

518 See Nathan, *Dan Emmett and The Rise of Early Negro Minstrelsy*, p. 85.

519 "First you put your two knees close up tight,
You swing 'em to the left and you swing 'em to the right.
Step around the floor kinda nice and light,
And you twist around, twist around with all your might.
Spread your lovin' arms way out in space,
And you do the eagle rock with such style and grace.
You put your left foot out and then you bring it back.
That's what I call Ballin' the Jack."

520 "Here is the drag, see how it goes:
Down on the heels, up on the toes,
That's the way you do the Varsity Drag . . ."

521 Although the slaves' juba is a likely ancestor of such songs, one may also be reminded of children's ring dances ("You put your little foot in, you take your little foot out). Or of Humperdinck's *Hansel and Gretel* with its ditty,
"Hansel come and dance with me. Both my hands I offer thee
Right foot first, left foot then, round about and back again."

522 Hungerford, p. 196.

523 *Ibid.,* p. 198. Such lively dances could be seen up North as well, where slaves and free blacks, especially during holidays, tried to outdo each other, often on improvised boards, in places such as New

York City's Catherine Market or the center of Albany (at Pinkster Festival time). At times New Jersey slaves could be found competing with Long Island ones or with free blacks, for a cash prize. See, for example, Malone, p. 48

As for the juba song, Rudi Blesh theorized that it had an off-the-beat syncopation, and, accordingly, he had a friend create a syncopated annotation which Blesh included in an appendix of *Shining Trumpets.* Such a "jazzy" version might appear improbable, for wherever verses to the juba are found, they have the same "sing-song" trochaic meter as the ones quoted here. And examples given of Juba tunes in Nathan's *Dan Emmett* (p. 446) are all unsyncopated. However, it is quite possible that the patting and dancing helped to create irregular syncopation and that the style of singing itself transformed the even meter. For an off-the-beat version of the Juba dance, see the video *Dancing; New Worlds, New Forms.*

524 In a version of the dance performed by a black family for Lydia Parrish, one person patted, another one danced in a circle around a third who lay prone, as the dead cow, while a fourth called out the cues. See Parrish, p. 111.

525 "Pecking," however, as an imitation of the pigeon's head and neck movement, became popular with lindy hoppers in the late 1930s.

526 Such devices were used by freed blacks of all regions and were observed as late as the 1940s by travellers to the South, who were greeted at train stops by the sight of young blacks dancing for money on portable planks of tin (for lighter carrying and an enhanced sound).

527 Vol. II, p. 56.

528 According to Jerry Ames, the influence of white dancing on blacks can be traced back to the boats transporting slaves to America, where the white crewmen "did their native step dances for the benefit of their first black audiences" (*The Book of Tap,* p. 31). Ames also theorized that in the early 1800s, Irish dancers from the North "paid frequent visits to the southern estates" (*Ibid.,* p. 33.) This author, however, has not found evidence in support of either of those statements.

529 Athough Dutch, English and German clog dancing probably did combine with African dance in the country dancing of the Appalachian region.

530 W.T. Lhamon, Jr.'s *Raising Cain* (pp. 16-17) offers more data on black and white demographics in New York based on Shane White's *Somewhat More Independent: the End of Slavery in New York City, 1770-1810*. Athens, Univ. of Georgia Press, 1991. See also pp. 2-3 of Stuart Blumin's introduction to Foster's *New York by Gaslight*.

531 Having won several challenge matches against Master John Diamond, an expert white dancer of the time. Three judges (or more) were usually involved in such contests: one for time, one for style and one for execution. The last often sat underneath the stage, the better to judge the beat of the steps.

532 In 1850, an American, George Foster, following the examples of Dickens in England and Eugène Sue in France, exploited the vogue of exposing the seamy side of big cities. He, too, described a dance hall in Five Points, one owned by a Pete Williams. Although Dickens named Almack as the dance hall he visited, Pete William's house was familiarly called "Dickens' Place," since the author also went there on his 1842 visit to that district.

533 Hannah Winter, for example (in a chapter of *Chronicles of the American Dance*, p. 50), cites a squib of May 8, 1848, in the *London Illustrated News* concerning Dickens' experience of Lane's dancing.

534 *American Notes*, pp. 88-90.

535 *Ibid.*

536 Only later, in the twentieth century, did Irish dance masters insist on arms rigidly down at the sides.

537 Both quotations from Winter, p. 50.

538 Emery, noting the case of a Negro minstrel who called himself a jig dancer but auditioned by patting Juba, concluded: "Perhaps the dances called Jigs were in reality the Juba dance." P. 194. As explained earlier in this chapter, "jig" was, indeed, the name given by whites to lively slave dancing.

Hans Nathan, citing a pamphlet "based on the authority of the well-known minstrel Charles White," wrote: "Jig Dancing . . . had its origin among the slaves of the southern plantations . . . It was original with them and has been copied by those who in the early days of minstrelsy made that a feature of their business . . ." P. 70, *op. cit.* And an Englishman, Andrew Burnaby, referred to the southern "jigg" as "a practice originally borrowed, I am informed, from the Negroes" (quoted in Knowles, p. 12). Dana Epstein (*Sinful Tunes*, p. 122), wrote à propos of slave jigs, "Not one contemporary witness has associated the Negro jig with jigs known in the British Isles, although they used the same word for both, leading to unfortunate ambiguity."

[539] Discussed in Chapter Two.

[540] The dance is described in *Dan Emmett*, pp. 75-76.

[541] See Toll, 44-47 for the use of authentic black material in dances of early white minstrelsy.

[542] See Emery, p. 194

[543] Winter, p. 55.

[544] Quoted in the Marshall and Jean Stearns' *Jazz Dance*, p. 50.

[545] A 3/4 time step that would be perfected by Bill "Bojangles" Robinson.

[546] See illustrations in Nathan, pp. 74-80.

[547] As described in an interview with dancer Harland Dixon in *ibid.,* p. 52.

[548] *Ibid.,* p. 127.

[549] Who lost to "Bojangles" Robinson in a 1929 buck-and-wing contest.

[550] *Op. cit,* pp. 135-136.

[551] The mixture of black and white country dances was much more pronounced in the Appalachian Mountain region, where African dances blended with English, Irish and Dutch or German styles.

[552] *Ibid.,* p. 199.

[553] A two-step is usually based on the *chassées* used in box steps. For example, one might step left on the left foot, slide the right foot next to it—changing the weight to the right foot—and take another left step. That is: left-together-left, to the tempo quick-quick-slow.

[554] See Stearns and Stearns, p. 122.

[555] *Ibid.,* p. 23. According to the Stearns' sources, Negro versions of the quadrille continued from the Civil War to early twentieth century, with 4/4 time replacing the original 6/8 tempo.

[556] As in New Orleans of 1869, according to Al Rose (*Storyville,* p. 9).

[557] One can, for example, see film footage of Bessie Smith dancing it in the thirties in the video *Cotton Club.*

[558] Through the years the African-American population of California expanded exponentially. Between 1900 and 1920 it increased from 11,045 to 38,763, according to a census report cited in Stoddard, p. 155.

[559] The maxixe is a graceful Brazilian dance with flowing arm movements. The tango is well known. The one-step is simply one step to a beat, as though marching: left, right, left, right.

[560] Mae West performed a sizzling shimmy in 1928 in the musical *Summertime.*

561 After seeing *Liza,* Heywood Broun stated that all the other dancers he had ever seen "did nothing but minuets." Stearns and Stearns, p. 143.

562 See James P. Johnson's description of the dance, cited in Singer, p. 113.

563 P. 83.

564 Vol. 70, No. 4, p. 7.

565 Vol. 71, No. 9.

566 Vol. 69, No. 7. In No. 9 of that volume, *Variety* announced that the *Chicago Journal* had added a column on (ballroom) dance in January of that year.

567 Sanjek, Vol. II, p. 95.

568 P. 81.

569 *Chronicle of the Twentieth Century*, p.

570 Quoted in Charters and Kunstadt, p. 124.

571 *Variety*. January 19, 1923, Vol. 69, No. 9, p. 3.

572 *Castles in the Air*, p. 87.

573 Irene, particularly. When she cut her long hair in 1914, hordes of women followed suit. When people flocked to their performances, she suspected it was often because women wanted to see what she was wearing in order to copy her new fashions.

574 *Modern Dancing*, pp. 39 and 170.

575 *Ibid.*, p. 177.

576 Stearn and Stearns, p. 128.

577 Mouvet discovered the tango in Paris at the age of fourteen (1902) when he was in Europe with his family. He helped popularize it in the States in the early 1910s and was especially known for his apache routines. It is commonly thought that Mouvet created the American tango as it is taught today. Mouvet and Walton were married in 1911, the same year their rivals, the Castles, took their vows.

578 Cuney-Hare, pp. 136-137.

579 *Castles in the Air*, p. 87.

580 Imperial Society of Teachers of Dancing mission statement may be found on www.istd.org.

581 Eventually, the I.S.T.D. incorporated African-American dances into its program. For example, it adopted and codified steps and a syllabus for Harlem's "lindy" (naming it "jive") and for sensual Afro-Caribbean dances of the late 1930s, the1940s and 1950s, e.g., the rumba, samba and cha-cha. All these, including jive, are now grouped by the I.S.T.D. as "latin," a separate category from waltz, foxtrot and tango which are labelled "smooth."

582 See Stearns and Stearns, p. 98.

583 According to Charles Coll in 1919, in *Dancing Made Easy*, p. 46.

584 So described in a 1914 article in the British *Dancing Times*, quoted in Stephenson and Iaccarino, p. 35.

585 *Op. cit.,* pp. 46-47.

586 See DeVeaux, p 51.

587 *Black and Blue*, p. 157.

588 According to many reports, "Shorty" George Snowdon, an outstanding black dancer of the time, came up with the name when asked what the dance was called. Snowden was also the inventor of the "Shorty George," a step used in the "lindy" breakaway.

589 Standardized over the years and now known as "swing," the basic eight-step pattern begins with two quick triplets, the man dancing a left-right-left to the left side, then a right-left-right to the other side. This is followed by steps seven and eight: a back-and forward step or "back break" consisting of left foot back and right forward. The "lindy" is usually distinguished from "swing" in its elimination of the second triplet. That is, it is a left-right-left triplet, then a back break. Lindy moves are often incorporated in swing dances.

590 In "pecking," a dancer, keeping the head level, moves it forward and back like a pigeon. Also in the realm of animal moves, a charming strut familiarly dubbed the "chicken walk" is featured in swing and jive performances to this day.

591 *Op. cit.*, p. 325.

592 Erenberg wrote, "It is no accident that from [World War I] on, Tin Pan Alley decreed that a successful song had to be danceable." P. 153.

593 *Boy Meets Horn*, p. 138.

16

CONCLUSIONS

SYMBIOSIS

Like the interlacings of a tenacious vine on a sturdy trellis, the black and white musics evolved both singly and together. Examining their interconnections in these chapters, we have discovered leitmotifs, patterns repeated again and again from the time of slavery through minstrelsy, ragtime, swing and bop. We have discussed recurrent themes, such as the imitation and adoption of the music of one race by the other and the constant "boomerang" effect of black and white musics. And we have noted commonly recurring modes of behavior in personal dealings between blacks and whites throughout the years, in areas such as show business, recording, songwriting, big band music and dance.

Still, despite the familiar motifs and themes and despite our sense of *déja vu,* black and white interrelationships in popular music have been too complex, too variable—that is, too human—to be categorized easily. The concept of *symbiosis,* used throughout this text and in the title of its conclusions, cannot completely explain or sum up the intricate interweavings of black and white musicians and their music. To a great extent, however, that concept can help to put those interweavings into perspective.

In symbiosis (from the Greek "living together") members of two different species connect or combine for a specific purpose or purposes. Biologists point to three main types of such linking: "parasitism" (A takes something from B to the detriment of B); "commensalism" (A takes something from B without affecting B at all); "mutualism" (A and B take from each other to their mutual benefit).

Concerning the realm of popular music, one might be tempted to see the role of American whites as parasitical, given their repeated appropriation—or expropriation—of black music. Yet, as foregoing chapters have demonstrated, the connection between African Americans and whites in music, although never a truly equal partnership, has worked to a great extent to the benefit of both races. In the final analysis, "mutualism" is the more applicable term.

The natural world provides thousands of examples of mutualism in symbiosis. To cite just two: The Egyptian plover hops into the open mouth of a crocodile, and even if the crocodile is hungry, the bird remains unscathed. The explanation is two-fold: 1). The plover removes harmful parasites from the crocodile. 2). In exchange for the beneficial cleansing, the plover is entitled to a meal of the parasites. And consider the case of the clown fish and the sea anemone. The colorful little clown fish, vulnerable to predators because of its bright hue and poor swimming skills, sends signals to a dangerous sea anemone. The giant anemone allows the clown fish—at times several of the species—to make a home within its deadly tentacles—and does nothing to harm it. The trade-off? The clown fish brings food to the sea anemone; the anemone shelters the clown fish from outside predators. Even without viewing the crocodile and anemone as Mafiosi protectors à la Al Capone, such lessons in basic science can well apply to the subject at hand.

Let us first look at the situation from the perspective of whites. From early on, even in the context of southern slavery, many whites saw black music as a commodity. The musical talent of the slaves could be of practical value to a plantation owner. For, as we have seen, talented slave musicians not only furnished accompaniment at no cost for dances in the "big house," they could also be hired out as callers, singers, dancers and players to others. In such cases, a slave might receive some little recompense, but his or her master could well turn a profit on the deal. (One can almost hear the gritting of a master's teeth when, in trying to retrieve a runaway slave, he describes the person as a fine musician, adding that the escapee took his fiddle with him.)

Then once discovered by entertainers and entrepreneurs of the North, the black music became highly marketable. From minstrelsy through vaudeville and musical comedy, from ragtime through swing, in Tin Pan Alley and the recording industry, in song and in dance, whites imitated, adopted and promoted the black style, adapting it to white audiences and, once more, turning a profit.

What counted primarily in the white appropriation of black music was its *difference.* It injected a new voice, a new rhythm and a new life into white sphere, and, eventually, into its music and dance. It caught on with the public because it was infectious. It was praised by those in the know because it was good. And because it was good it would greatly affect the course of white popular music.

The key factor for white entrepreneurs, however, was not so much its quality as its marketability. And that attitude explains much of the white side of the black and white symbiotic equation.

As for the black musicians, from the time of slavery, they too took what they wanted, or needed, from the music of the Other. Bereft of their African heritage, they used the white hymns as fodder and an existent scaffolding on which to build their songs. Once liberated, in order to succeed and survive, they adopted white formulas such as the minstrel show and the coon song, along with the darky stereotypes of those genres, and later, the Tin Pan Alley ballad, white innovations in big band orchestration and the smoothing of jazz and dance styles.

But especially, what black musicians needed and accepted from whites was protection, marketing and promotion. To survive, black minstrels and show people usually had to have recourse to white producers and managers, especially when it came to touring in the danger laden South. To become marketable, gifted ragtime artists who played strictly by ear depended on white musicians to notate their music and amend it for publication. To make a showing, black entertainers, recording artists or bandleaders needed white agents for recording dates, stage and night club appearances or tours and, generally, to facilitate, sponsor, produce, publicize and promote their work.

Symbiotic mutualism in nature does not always amount to an equal contribution by both parties in the "partnership." One of the species may, at times, take aggressive action against the other. In the context of black and white relationships in music, the main feature is not aggression (on that score, white entrepreneurs have mistreated whites just as blacks have harmed their own race) but, rather, an imbalance. For, as we have seen, the whites have traditionally held the highest cards and the greatest power in the field. Still, even given that imbalance, the concept of mutualism is still operative, since it has clearly been a case of need and opportunism on both sides and of meshing functions which have ultimately generated benefits for both black and white.

* * *

One reality has especially informed the chapters of this book and has been present or implicit on almost every page. That is, the reality of the black contribution. Discussions of interconnections, interweavings and cross-fertilization of black and white music—and the foregoing analogy of mutualism—might appear on the surface to equate the two musics or put them in the same package. However, the black inventions can only be seen as unusual. In America, the popular and classical musics of a traditionally white public, although often outstanding and of the highest quality, have generally traveled the European route rather than producing earth-shaking indigenous innovations. The different and vital qualities of black music energized the music of America, helping it—indeed, causing it—to become a national and international phenomenon.

The Chinese philosopher Lao Tzu wrote[595]:

"Thirty spokes meet at a hollowed-out hub;
  the wheel won't work without its hole.
A vessel is molded from solid clay;
  its inner emptiness makes it useful,
To make a room, you have to cut doors and windows;
  without openings, a place isn't livable.

To make use of what is here,
    you must make use of what is not."

There can be no doubt that the Africans transplanted to America had to make use of what was not. Deprived of their freedom, their language, their past, their very identities, and offered little or nothing to fill the emptiness, they created a music out of the dearth. Using anything at hand—a calabash, the guts of an animal, a Baptist hymn—they improvised spirituals of anguish and hope. Freed, yet discriminated against and disenfranchised, they carried with them the soul-stirring sounds of their blues and the ingrained rhythms that would evolve into ragtime and jazz.

The white involvement played a large role in the shape and fate of the black musical creativity. But without the black heritage and black inventiveness, American popular music would, of course, be bereft of its most original and outstanding component, jazz.[596]

Notes

[595] In his *Tao Te Ching*.

[596] Ken Burns has called it "the only art form created by America." Commencement address, Boston College, May, 2009.

Selected Bibliography

Abbott, Lynn and Oldaeus, Per. "'For Ofays Only': An Annotated Calendar of Midnight Frolics at the Lyric Theater," *The Jazz Archivist.* Tulane Univ., Hogan Jazz Archive. Vol. XVII (2003)

The African American Theater Directory. Peterson, Bernard L., Jr., ed. Westport, Ct., Greenwood Press, 1997

The African Diaspora; a Musical Perspective. Monson, Ingrid, ed. N.Y., Garland Publishing, 2000

Albertson, Chris. *Bessie.* N.Y., Stein and Day, 1972

Allen, Frederick L. *Only Yesterday; An Informal History of the Twenties.* N.Y., Harper and Row, 1964

American Ballads and Folk Songs. Lomax, John A. and Alan, eds. N.Y., Macmillan, 1934

American Hymns Old and New. Christ-Janer, Albert; Hughes, Charles W.; Smith, eds. Carleton Sprague, eds. N.H., Columbia Univ. Press, 1980

American Popular Music. Rubin, Rachel, and Melnick, Jeffrey, eds., Amherst, Univ. of Massachusetts Press, 2001

Ames, Jerry and Siegelman, Jim. *The Book of Tap.* N.Y., David McKay, 1977

Armstrong, Louis. *Satchmo: My Life in New Orleans.* N.Y. Da Capo Press, 1986

Aspects of the History of Irish Dancing. Cullinane, Dr. John, ed. Cork City, Ireland, Litho Press, 1987

Badger, Reid. *A Life in Ragtime; A Biography of James Reese Europe.* N.Y., Oxford Univ. Press, 1995

Bagneris, Vernel, and Touchet, Leo. *Rejoice When You Die: The New Orleans Jazz Funerals.* Baton Rouge, Louisiana State Univ. Press, 1998

Ballanta, Nicholas George Julius (Taylor). *St. Helena Island Sprituals.* N.Y., Schirmer, 1925

Baraka, Amiri (LeRoi Jones) and Baraka, Amina. *The Music; Reflections on Jazz and Blues.* N.Y., William Morrow, 1987

Barker, Danny. *Buddy Bolden and the Last Days of Storyville.* Shipton, Alyn, ed., Cassell, London and N.Y., 1998

______________ *A Life in Jazz.* London, Macmillan, 1986

Barlow, William, and Finley, Cheryl. *From Swing to Soul; An Illustrated History of African American Popular Music From 1930 to 1960.* Washington, D.C., Elliott and Clark, 1994

Batterberry, Michael and Ariane. *Fashion; the Mirror of History.* N.Y., Greenwich House, 1982.

Batterson, Jack A. *Blind Boone; Missouri's Ragtime Pioneer.* Columbia, Missouri, Missouri Univ. Press, 1998

Bean, Annemarie, Hatch, James B., McNamara, Brooks, eds. *Inside the Minstrel Mask; Readings in Nineteenth-Century Blackface Minstrelsy.* Wesleyan, Wesleyan Univ. Press, 1996

Bechet, Sidney. *Treat it Gentle.* N.Y., Da Capo Press, 1978

Bell, Malcolm, Jr. *Major Butler's Legacy; Five Generations of a Slaveholding Family.* Athens, Ga, Univ. of Georgia Press, 1987

Bergreen, Laurence. *As Thousands Cheer: The Life of Irving Berlin.* N.Y., Viking, 1990

______________ *Louis Armstrong; An Extravagant Life.* N.Y., Broadway Books, 1997

Berendt, Joachim. *The Jazz Book; from New Orleans to Rock and Free Jazz.* N.Y. Lawrence Hill, 1975

Berlin, Edward A., "Cole and Johnson Brothers' *Evolution of Ragtime.*" *Current Musicology.* 1983, Issue 36, p. 21ff

______________ *Ragtime; A Musical and Cultural History.* Berkeley, Univ. Of Calif. Press, 1980

Berlin, Ira. *Generations of Captivity; A History of African-American Slaves.* Cambridge, MA, Belknap Press of Harvard Univ. Press, 2003

______________ *Many Thousands Gone; The First Two Centuries of Slavery in North America.* Cambridge, MA, Belknap Press of Harvard Univ. Press, 1998

Berry, Faith. *Before and Beyond Harlem; Langston Hughes, a Biography.* New York, Citadel Press, 1992

Bindas, Kenneth J. *Swing, That Modern Sound.* Jackson, MI, University Press of Mississippi, 2001

Blesh, Rudi, and Janis, Harriet. *They All Played Ragtime; the True Story of an American Music.* N.Y., Knopf, 1950

______________ *Shining Trumpets; A History of Jazz.* N.Y., Knopf, 1953

______________ *The Blues Line.* Compiled by Eric Sackheim. N. Y., Grossman Publishers, 1969

Boardman, Gerald. *American Musical Theatre.* N.Y., Oxford Univ. Press, 1978

Bremer, Frederika. *Homes of the New World; Impressions of America.* N.Y., Harper and Brothers, 1853

Broughton, Viv. *Black Gospel; an Illustrated History of the Gospel Sound.* Poole, Dorset, Blandford Press, 1985

Bowdich, T. Edward. *Mission From Cape Coast Castle to Ashantee, With a Statistical Account of that Kingdom, and Geographical Notices of Other Parts of the Interior of Africa.* London, J. Murray, 1819

Brunn, H. O. *The Story of the Original Dixieland Jazz Band.* Baton Rouge, Louisiana State Univ. Press, 1960

Buerkle, Jack V., and Barker, Danny. *Bourbon Street Black.* N.Y., Oxford Univ. Press, 1973

Burns, Ken, Commencement address at Boston College, May, 2009.

Cable, George W. "The Dance in Congo Square." *Century Magazine.* Feb., 1886, vol. xxxi, No. 4, p. 52 *ff*

Calhoun Plantation Songs. Hollowell, Emily, ed., Boston, C.W. Thompson, 1907

Calloway, Cab, and Rollins, Bryant. *Of Minnie The Moocher and Me.* N.Y. Thos. Crowell, 1976

Carey, James T., "Changing Courtship Patterns in the Popular Song," *American Journal of Sociology.* Vol. 74, May, 1970 (songs of the 50s and 60s)

Castle, Irene, with Duncan, Bob and Wanda. *Castles in the Air.* N.Y., Doubleday, 1958

Castle, Mr. and Mrs. Vernon. *Modern Dancing.* N.Y., Harper, 1914

Chafe, William H. *The American Woman.* N.Y., Oxford Univ. Press, 1972

Charters, Ann. *Nobody: The Story of Bert Williams.* N.Y., Macmillan, 1970

Charters, Samuel B., and Leonard Kunstadt. *Jazz, A History of the New York Scene.* Garden City, N.Y., Doubleday, 1962

Chase, Gilbert. *America's Music: From the Pilgrims to the Present.* Urbana and Chicago, Univ. of Illinois Press, 1987

Chicago Defender Newspaper. (Founded 1909) Issues from 1917-1930

Chronicle of the Twentieth Century, Daniel, Clifton, ed. Mt. Kisco, N.Y., Chronicle Publications, 1987

Chronicles of the American Dance: From the Shakers to Martha Graham. Magriel, ed. Paul. N.Y., Holt, 1948

Ciment, James. *Atlas of African-American History.* N.Y., Media Projects, 2001

Clarke, Donald. *The Rise and Fall of Popular Music.* N.Y., St. Martin's Press, 1995

Cobb, Buell E., Jr. *The Sacred Harp: A Tradition and Its Music.* Athens, Univ. of Georgia Press, 1978

Cockrell, Dale. *Demons of Disorder; Early Blackface Minstrels and Their World.* Cambridge, Cambridge Univ. Press, 1997

Cohn, Lawrence. *Nothing But the Blues.* N.Y., Abbeville Press, 1993

Coll, Charles, and Rosière, Gabrielle. *Dancing Made Easy.* N.Y., Clode, 1922

Collins, David R. *Bix Beiderbecke; Jazz Age Genius.* Greensboro, N.C., Morgan Reynolds, 1998

Collier, James Lincoln. *Benny Goodman and The Swing Era.* N.Y., Oxford Univ. Press, 1989

______________ *Jazz; The American Theme Song.* N.Y., Oxford Univ. Press, 1993

______________ *Louis Armstrong; An American Genius.* N.Y., Oxford Univ. Press, 1993

______________ *The Making of Jazz; a Comprehensive History.* N.Y., Delta Books, 1978

Condon, Eddie. *We Called It Music.* N.Y., Henry Holt, 1947

Cone, James H. *The Spirituals and the Blues.* N.Y., Seabury Press, 1972

Conway, Cecilia. *African Banjo Echoes in Appalachia.* Knoxville, Univ. of Tennessee Press, 1995

Cook, Bruce E. *Listen to the Blues.* N.Y., Scribner's, 1973

Courlander, Harold. *Negro Folk Music U.S.A.* N.Y., Columbia Univ. Press, 1963

Cowley, John. *Carnival, Canboulay and Calypso; Traditions in the Making.* Cambridge, Cambridge University Press, 1996

Crouch, Stanley. *Notes of a Hanging Judge; Essays and Reviews, 1979-1989.* N.Y., Oxford Univ. Press, 1990

Crumpacker, Bunny and Chick. *Jazz Legends.* Layton, Utah, Gibbs Smith Pub., 1995

Cuney-Hare, Maud. *Negro Musicians and Their Music.* N.Y., Da Capo Press, 1974

Curtis-Berlin, Natalie. *Negro Folk Songs.* Hampton Series. N.Y., Schirmer, 1918

Daly, John J. *A Song in His Heart* [biography of James Bland]. Philadelphia, John C. Winston, 1951

Dance, Stanley. *The World of Swing.* N.Y., Scribner's, 1974
Davis, Angela. *Blues Legacies and Black Feminism.* N.Y., Random House, 1998
Davis, Francis. *The History of the Blues.* N.Y., Hyperion, 1995
DeLong, Thomas A., *Pops: Paul Whiteman, King of Jazz.* Piscataway, N.J., New Century Publishers, 1983
DeVeaux, Scott. *The Birth of Bebop.* Berkeley, Univ. of California Press, 1997
Dickens, Charles. *American Notes; a Journey.* N.Y., Fromm International, 1985 (published in 1842)
Dictionary of the Black Theatre. Woll, Allen, ed. Westport, Ct., Greenwood Press, 1983
Dixon, Robert, M.W., and Godrich, John. *Recording the Blues.* N.Y. Stein and Day, 1970
Douglass, Frederick. *Narrative of the Life of Frederick Douglass, an American Slave.* N.Y., Signet, 1968
The Duke Ellington Reader. Mark Tucker, ed. N.Y., Oxford Univ. Press, 1993
Ellington, Duke. *Music is My Mistress.* Garden City, N.Y., Doubleday, 1973
Ellison, Ralph. *Shadow and Act.* N.Y., Random House, 1953.
Emery, Lynne Fauley. *Black Dance From 1619 to Today.* Princeton, N.J., Dance Horizons, 1988
Epstein, Dena J. *Sinful Tunes and Spirituals; Black Folk Music to the Civil War.* Urbana, Ill., Univ. of Illinois Press, 1977
Erenberg, Lewis A. *Steppin' Out; New York Nightlife 1890-1930.* Chicago, Univ. of Chicago Press, 1981
_______________ *Swingin' the Dream; Big Band Jazz and the Rebirth of American Culture.* Chicago, Univ. of Chicago Press, 1998
Ewen, David. *The Life and Death of Tin Pan Alley.* N.Y., Funk and Wagnall, 1964
_______________ *Panorama of American Popular Music.* Englewood, N.J. Prentice-Hall, 1959
Farnsworth Marjorie, *The Ziegfeld Follies.* N.Y., Putnum, 1956.
Feather, Leonard and Gitler, Ira. *The Biographical Encyclopedia of Jazz.* N.Y., Oxford Univ. Press, 1999
_______________ *Inside Jazz* (originally titled *Inside Bebop*). N.Y., Da Capo Paperback, 1949

Firestone, Ross. *Swing, Swing, Swing: the Life of Benny Goodman.* N.Y., Dutton, 1992

Fisher, Miles M. *Negro Slave Songs in the United States.* Ithaca, N.Y., Cornell, 1953

Fletcher, Tom. *100 Years of the Negro in Show Business.* N.Y., Da Capo Press, 1984

Floyd, Samuel A., Jr. *The Power of Black Music.* N.Y., Oxford Univ. Press, 1995

Foreman, Ronald Clifford, Jr., *Jazz and Race Records, 1920-30: Their Origins and Their Significance for the Record Industry and Society.* Ph.D. Thesis, Urbana, Ill., Univ. of Illinois, 1968.

Forte, Allen. *The American Popular Ballad of the Golden Era, 1924-1950.* Princeton, N.J., Princeton Univ. Press, 1995

Foster, George G. *New York by Gas-Light and Other Urban Sketches.* Berkeley, Univ. of California Press, 1990

Foster, Pops, *Pops Foster, The Autobiography of a New Orleans Jazzman,* as told to Tom Stoddard. Berkeley, Univ. of California Press, 1971

Fox, Ted. *Showtime at the Apollo.* N.Y., Holt, Rinehart and Winston, 1983

Freedland, Michael. *Irving Berlin.* N.Y., Stein and Day, 1974

Freeman, Bud. *Crazeology; The Autobiography of a Chicago Jazzman,* as told to Robert Wolf. Urbana and Chicago, Univ. of Illinois Press, 1989

Garden, Allen D. *The Missouri Harmony.* Lincoln, Nebraska. Univ. of Nebraska Press, 1994

Gelat, Roland. *The Fabulous Phonograph, 1877-1977.* N.Y., Macmillan, 1977

Gerard, Charley. *Jazz in Black and White: Race, Culture and Identity in the Jazz Community.* Westport, Conn., Praeger, 1998

Giddins, Gary. *Visions of Jazz; The First Century.* N.Y., Oxford Univ. Press, 1998

Gillespie, Dizzy, with Fraser, Al. *To Be Or Not to . . . Bop.* N.Y., Doubleday, 1979

Gridley, Mark C. *Jazz Styles; History and Analysis.* Englewood Cliffs, N.J., Prentice Hall, 1988

Gitler, Ira. *Jazz Masters of the Forties.* N.Y., Da Capo Press, 1983

______________ *Swing to Bop,* N.Y., Oxford University Press, 1985

Goldberg, Isaac. *Tin Pan Alley.* N.Y., John Day, 1930

Goodman, Benny, and Kolodin, Irving. *The Kindom of Swing.* N.Y., Frederic Ungar, 1961

Green, Harvey. *The Uncertainty of Everyday Life (1915-45).* N.Y., HarperCollins, 1992

Green, Stanley. *Broadway Musicals.* N.Y., Hal Leonard, 1990

Gridley, Mark C. *Jazz Styles.* Englewood Cliffs, N.J., Prentice-Hall, 1988

Hadlock, Richard. *Jazz Masters of the Twenties.* N.Y., Macmillan, 1956

Hajdu, David. *Lush Life; a Biography of Billy Strayhorn.* N.Y., Farrar Straus Giroux, 1996

Hammond, John. *John Hammond on Record.* N.Y., Summit Books, 1977

Hamon, W.T., Jr. *Raising Cain; Blackface Performance From Jim Crow to Hip Hop.* Cambridge, MA, Harvard Univ. Press, 1998

Handy, W.C. "The Heart of the Blues." *The Etude.* March, 1940, Vol. lviii, No. 3, pp. 152 *ff*

_______________ *A Treasury of the Blues.* N.Y. Charles Boni, 1949

Harrison, Daphne D. *Black Pearls; Blues Queens of the 1920s.* New Brunswick, N.J., Rutgers Univ. Press, 1988

Haskins, James. *Black Music in America; a History Through its People.* N.Y., Thomas Y. Crowell, 1987

Hasse, John Edward. *Ragtime; its History, Composers, and Music.* New York, Schirmer, 1985

Haverly, Jack. *Haverley's Negro Minstrels Burnt Cork Specialties.* Chicago, Frederick J. Drake, 1903

Hearn, Lafcadio. *An American Miscellany.* Vol. I. New York, Dodd, Mead and Co., 1924

_______________ *Creole Sketches.* Cambridge, MA, The Riverside Press, 1924

Hentoff, Nat. *The Jazz Life.* N.Y., Dial Press, 1961

Hennessey, Thomas J. *From Jazz to Swing; African-American Jazz Musicians and Their Music, 1890-1935.* Detroit, Wayne State Univ. Press, 1994

Herskovitz, Melville. *The Myth of the Negro Past.* N.Y., Harper, 1941

Heyward, Dubose. "Porgy and Bess; Return on Wings of Song." *Stage Magazine.* October, 1937, pp. 25 *ff*

Hill, Errol C. and Hatch, James V. *A History of African American Theatre.* Cambridge, Eng., Cambridge Univ. Press, 2003

Hodeir, André. *Jazz; Its Evolution and Essence.* N.Y., Grove, 1956

Hodes, Art, and Hansen, Chadwick. *Hot Man; The Life of Art Hodes.* Urbana and Chicago, Univ. of Chicago Press, 1992

Hogsbawm, Eric. *The Jazz Scene.* N.Y., Pantheon, 1993

Holloway, Joseph E., and Vass, Winifred K. *The African Heritage of American English.* Bloomington, Indiana Univ. Press, 1993

Hooley's Opera House Songster; American Ballads and Songs. N.Y., Dick and Fitzgerald, (n.d.; Civil War era minstrel songs)

Hughes, Langston. *The Big Sea.* New York, Hill and Wang, 1940

Hungerford, James. *The Old Plantation.* New York, Harper, 1859

Hugill, Stan. *Shanties from the Seven Seas.* London, Routledge and Kegan Paul, 1961

Hyland, Wm. G. *The Song is Ended.* N.Y., Oxford, 1995 [World War II era]

______________ *In Their Own Words: A History of the American Negro, 1619-1865.* Milton Meltzer, ed., N.Y., Thomas Y Crowell Co., 1964

Jablonski, Edward. *Gershwin.* N.Y., Doubleday, 1987

Jasen, David A., and Jones, Gene. *Black Bottom Stomp; Eight Masters of Ragtime and Early Jazz.* N.Y., Routledge, 2002

______________ *Spreadin' Rhythm Around; Black Popular Songwriters, 1880-1930.* N.Y., Schirmer Books, 1998

______________ *That American Rag; the Story of Ragtime from Coast to Coast.* N.Y., Schirmer Books, 2000

Jasen, David A, and Tichenor, Trebor Jay. *Rags and Ragtime.* N.Y., Seabury Press, 1978

Jazz; The First Century. Hasse, John Edward, ed. N.Y., William Morrow, 2000

The Jazz Makers. Shapiro, Nat, and Hentoff, Nat, eds., N.Y., Rinehart, 1957 *Jazz Times Magazine.* Sept. 2001

Johnson Guion Griffis. *Ante-Bellum North Carolina.* Chapel Hill, Univ. of North Carolina Press, 1937

Johnson, Guy B. *Folk Culture on Saint Helena Island, South Carolina.* Hatboro, Penn., Folklore Associates, 1968

Johnson, James Weldon. The Autobiography of an Ex-Colored Man. N.Y., Penguin Books, 1990

______________ *Black Manhattan.* N.Y., Knopf, 1930

Jones, Jacqueline. *Labor of Love, Labor of Sorrow: Black Women, Work and the Family from Slavery to the Present.* N.Y., Basic Books, 1985

Jones, LeRoi. *Black Music.* Westport, Conn., Greenwood Press, 1980

_______________ *Blues People.* N.Y., Morrow Quill, 1963

Jordan, Winthrop D., *White Over Black: American Attitudes Toward the Negro, 1550-1812.* Chapel Hill, Univ. of North Carolina Press, 1968

Jubilee Songs: As Sung by The Jubilee Singers of Fisk University. Compiled by Seward, Theodore F., and White, George L. N.Y., Biglow and Main, 1872

Kaminsky, Max. *My Life in Jazz.* London, Deutsch, 1964

Keepnews, Orrin, and Grauer, Bill, Jr. *A Pictorial History of Jazz.* N.Y., Crown, 1966

Kemble, Frances Anne (Fanny). *Fanny Kemble's Journals.* Clinton, Catherine, ed.. Cambridge MA, Harvard Univ. Press, 2000

_______________ *Fanny Kemble; the American Journals.* Mavor, Elizabeth, ed. London, Weidenfeld and Nicolson, 1990

_______________ *Journal of a Residence on a Georgian Plantation in 1838-1839.* N.Y., Knopf, 1961

King, Johnny. *An Insider's Guide to Understanding and Listening to Jazz.* N.Y., Walker and Co., 1997

Kings of Jazz. Stanley Green, ed. South Brunswick and N.Y., A.S. Barnes, 1978

Kirk, Andy. *Twenty Years on Wheels.* As told to Amy Lee. Ann Arbor, Univ. of Michigan Press, 1992

Kmen, Henry A. *Music in New Orleans; the Formative Years, 1791-1841.* Baton Rouge, Louisiana State Univ. Press, 1966

Knowles, Mark. *Tap Roots: the Early History of Tap Dancing.* Jefferson, N.C., McFarland, 2002

Kofsky, Frank. *Black Music, White Business.* N.Y., Pathfinder, 1998

_______________ *Black Nationalism and the Revolution in Music.* N.Y., Pathfinder, 1970

Krasner, David. *Resistance, Parody, and Double Consciousness in African American Theatre, 1895-1910.* N.Y., St. Martin's Press, 1997

Krehbiel, Henry Edward. *Afro-American Folksongs; A Study in Racial and National Music.* Portland Me, Longwood Press, 1976. Reprint of 1914 Schirmer edition

Kubic, Gerhard. *Africa and the Blues.* Jackson, Miss., Univ. Press of Mississippi, 1999

Lanier, Sidney. *Florida, its Scenery, Climate, and History.* Philadelphia, Lippincott, 1875

______________ *The Science of English Verse.* N.Y. Scribners, 1894. Folcraft Library Editions, 1978

Latrobe, Benjamin Hanry. *Journals, 1799-1820, From Philadelphia to New Orleans.* Vol. III. New Haven, Yale Univ. Press, 1980

Laurie, Joseph, *Vaudeville; From the Honky-Tonk to the Palace.* N.Y., Holt, 1953

Lees, Gene. *Cats of Any Color; Jazz, Black and White.* N.Y., Oxford Univ. Press, 1994

______________ *Singers and the Song II.* N.Y., Oxford Univ. Press, 1998

______________ *You Can't Steal a Gift.* New Haven, Yale Univ. Press, 2001

Leonard, Neil. *Jazz and the White Americans.* Univ. of Chicago Press, Chicago, 1970

Levin, Floyd. *Classic Jazz.* Berkeley, Univ. of Califormia Press, 2002

Levine, Lawrence W. *Black Culture and Black Consciousness; Afro-American Folk Thought From Slavery to Freedom.* N.Y. Oxford Univ. Press, 1977

Lewis, David Levering. *When Harlem Was in Vogue.* N.Y., Penguin, 1997

Lhamon, W.T., Jr. *Raising Cain; Blackface Performance from Jim Crow to Hip Hop.* Cambridge, Ma., Harvard Univ. Press, c1998

Lomax, Alan. *Mister Jelly Roll.* N.Y., Duell, Sloan and Pearce, 1950

Lomax, John and Alan. *The Folk Songs of North America.* N.Y., Doubleday, 1960

______________ *American Ballads and Folk Songs.* N.Y., Macmillan, 1934

______________ *Negro Folk Songs as Sung by Lead Belly.* N.Y., Macmillan, 1936

Lovell, John, Jr. *Black Song: the Forge and the Flame.* N.Y., Macmillan, 1972

MacAdams, Lewis. *Birth of the Cool: Beat, Bebop, and the American Avant-Garde.* N.Y., The Free Press, 2001

McCarthy, Albert. *Big Band Jazz.* N.Y., Berkley Publishing Co., 1977

______________ *The Dance Band Era (1910-1950).* N.Y. Chilton Book Co., 1971

McDonagh, Don. *Dance Fever.* N.Y., Random House, 1979

Mailer, Norman. "The White Negro" in *Advertisements for Myself.* N.Y., Putnam, 1959

Malone, Jacqui. *Steppin' On the Blues.* Urbana, Univ. of Illinois Press, 1996

Marks, Edward B. *They All Sang.* N.Y., Viking Press, 1934

Marquis, Donald M. *In Search of Buddy Bolden.* Baton Rouge, Louisiana State Univ. Press, 1978

Melnick, Jeffrey. *A Right to Sing the Blues; African Americans, Jews and American Popular Song.* Cambridge, Harvard Univ. Press, 1999

Merod, Jim, "Singing in the Shower: Ralph Ellison and the Blues." La Folia.com online musical review, April, 2001

Mezzrow, Milton "Mezz," and Wolfe, Bernard. *Really the Blues.* N.Y., Random House, 1946

Minstrel Songs With Guitar Accompaniment. Boston, Oliver Ditson Co., n.d.

More Than Dancing; Essays on Afro-American Music and Musicians. Irene V. Jackson, ed., Center for Ethnic Music, Howard University. Westport, CT, Greenwood Press, 1985

Moreau de St. Méry. *De la Danse.* Parme, Rodini, 1801

________________ *Description topographique, physique, civile, politique et historique de la partie française de l'isle Saint-Domingue.* Paris, Société de l'histoire des colonies françaises, 3 vols., 1958

Morgan, Thomas L., and Barlow, William. *Cakewalks to Concert Halls; an Illustrated History of African American Popular Music From 1895 to 1930.* Washington, Elliott and Clark, 1992

Munsell, Joel. *Collections on the History of Albany From its Discovery to the Present Time,* Vol. II. Albany, N.Y., J. Munsell, 1867

Nathan, Hans. *Dan Emmett and the Rise of Early Negro Minstrelsy.* Norman, Oklahoma, Univ. of Oklahoma Press, 1977

New Grove Dictionary of Jazz. 2 Vols. Kernfeld, Barry D., ed. N.Y., Macmillan, 2000

The Night People; The Jazz Life of Dicky Wells, as told to Stanley Dance. Washington, D.C., Smithsonian, 1991

Nicholson, Stuart. *Ella Fitzgerald.* N.Y., Da Capo Press, 1995

Nisenson, Eric. *Blue, The Murder of Jazz.* N.Y., St. Martin's Press, 1997

Oakley, Giles. *The Devil's Music; A History of the Blues.* N.Y., Da Capo Press, 1997

Odum, Howard W., and Johnson, Guy B. *The Negro and His Songs.* Westport, Conn., Negro Universities Press, 1925

Oliver, Paul. *Blues Fell This Morning: the Meaning of the Blues.* N.Y. Horizon Press, 1960

________________ *Savannah Syncopators; African Retentions in the Blues.* N.Y., Stein and Day, 1970

_______________ *The Story of the Blues.* Philadelphia, Chilton Book Co., 1969
Olmstead, Frederick Law. *The Cotton Kingdom.* N.Y., Knopf, 1962
Ostransky, *Jazz City, The Impact of Our Cities on the Development of Jazz.* Prentice Hall, Englewood Cliffs, 1978
Oxford Companion to Jazz. Bill Kirschner, ed. N.Y., Oxford Univ. Press, 2000
Panassié, Hughes. *The Real Jazz.* N.Y., A. S. Barnes, 1942
Papachristou, Judith, and Wald, Carol. *Myth America; Picturing Women l865-1945.* N.Y., Pantheon Books, 1975
Park, Mungo. *Travels in the Interior Districts of Africa.* London, W. Bulmer, 1799
Parrish, Lydia. *Slave Songs of the Georgia Sea Islands.* Hatboro, PA, Folklore Associates, 1942
Paskman, Dailey. *Gentlemen Be Seated! A Parade of the American Minstrels.* N.Y., Clarkson N. Potter, 1976
Pasternak, Judith M. *Dixieland; the Birth of Jazz.* Life, Times and Music Series. N.Y., Friedman/Fairfax, 1995
Peretti, Burton W. *The Creation of Jazz; Music, Race, and Culture in Urban America.* Urbana, Univ. of Illinois Press, 1992
Piersen, William D. *From Africa to America; African American History From the Colonial Era to the Early Republic, 1526-1790.* N.Y., Twayne, 1996
Plante, Ellen M. *Women at Home in Victorian America.* N.Y., Facts on File, 1997
Popular Music; An Annotated Index of American Popular Songs. Vols. I-VIII. [from 1900] Shapiro, Nat.; Stratyner, Barbara C., Pollack, Bruce, eds. Detroit, Gale Research and N.Y., Adrian Press, 1964-1988
Ragtime; Its History, Composers, and Music. Hasse, John E., ed. N.Y., Schirmer Books, 1985
Reading Jazz: A Gathering of Autobiography, Reportage, and Criticism From 1919 to Now. Robert Gottlieb, ed. N.Y., Pantheon Books, 1996
Reeser, Dr. Eduard *The History of the Waltz.* Stockholm, Continental Book Company, ca. 1936
Riis, Thomas L. *Just Before Jazz; Black Musical Theater in New York, 1890-1915.* Washington, Smithsonian Institution Press, 1989
_______________ *More Than Just Minstrel Shows: the Rise of Black Musical Theatre at the Turn of the Century.* I.S.A.M. Monographs,

No. 33. Brooklyn College Institute for Studies in American Music, 1992

Roach, Hildred. *Black American Music: Past and Present.* Boston, Crescendo, 1976

Roberts, John Storm. *Black Music of Two Worlds.* N.Y., Praeger, 1972

______________ *The Latin Tinge; The Impact of Latin American Music on the United States.* N.Y., Oxford Univ. Press, 1999

Rogers, Agnes. *Women are Here to Stay; The Durable Sex in its Infinite Variety Through Half a Century of American Life.* N.Y., Harper and Bros., 1949

Rose, Al. *Eubie Blake.* N.Y., Schirmer Books, 1979

______________ *I Remember Jazz.* Baton Rouge, Louisiana State Univ. Press, 1986

______________ *Storyville New Orleans.* Birmingham, Alabama, Univ. of Alabama Press, 1974

Rose, Al, and Souchon, Edmond. *New Orleans Jazz; a Family Album.* Baton, Rouge, Louisiana State Univ. Press, 1967

Rosenberg, Rosalind. *Beyond Separate Spheres; Intellectual Roots of Modern Feminism.*New Haven, Yale Univ. Press, 1982

Rothman, Sheila M. *Woman's Proper Place; A History of Changing Ideals and Practices, 1870 to the Present.* N.Y., Basic Books, 1978

Rourke, Constance. *American Humor.* N.Y., Doubleday, 1931

Rublowsky, John. *Black Music in America.* N.Y., Basic Books, 1971

Russell, Tony. *Blacks, Whites and Blues.* London, November Books, 1970

Rust, Brian. *Jazz Records 1897-1942.* 3 vol. New Rochelle, N.Y., Arlington House, c1978

The Sacred Harp. Sacred Harp Publishing Co., Cullman, Alabama, 1991

Sampson, Henry T. *Blacks in Blackface.* Metuchen, N.J., Scarecrow Press, 1980

______________ *The Ghost Walks: A Chronological History of Blacks in Show Business,* 1865-1910. Metuchen, N.J., Scarecrow Press, 1988

Sanjek, Russell. *American Popular Music and its Business; the First Four Hundred Years.* Vols. I-III. N.Y., Oxford Univ. Press, 1988

Sanjek, Russell and David. *American Popular Music Business in the 20th Century.* (Abridgement of Vol. III, previous entry.) N.Y., Oxford Univ. Press, 1991

Scarborough, Dorothy. *On the Trail of Negro Folk-Songs.* Cambridge, MA, Harvard Univ. Press, 1925

Schafer, William J. and Riedel, Johannes. *The Art of Ragtime; Form and Meaning of an Original Black American Art.* Baton Rouge, Louisiana State Univ. Press, 1973

Schneider, Dorothy, and Schneider, Carl J. *Slavery in America From Colonial Times to the Civil War.* N.Y., Facts on File, 2000

Schuller, Gunther. *Early Jazz; Its Roots and Musical Development.* N.Y., Oxford Univ. Press, 1968

______________ *The Swing Era.* N.Y., Oxford Univ. Press, 1989

Shack, William A. *Harlem in Montmartre.* Berkeley, Univ. of California Press, 2001

Shapiro, Nat, and Hentoff, Nat., eds. *Hear Me Talkin' to Ya; The Story of Jazz as Told by the Men Who Made It.* N.Y., Dover, 1955

Shaw, Arnold. *Black Popular Music in America.* N.Y., Schirmer Books, 1986

______________ *Let's Dance.* Bill Willard, ed. N.Y., Oxford Univ. Press, 1998

Shaw, Artie. *The Trouble With Cinderella.* N.Y., Da Capo, 1979

Shipton, Alyn. *Groovin' High; The Life of Dizzy Gillespie.* N.Y., Oxford Univ. Press, 1999

______________ *A New History of Jazz.* London and N.Y., Continuum, 2001

Simon, George T. *The Big Bands.* N.Y., Schirmer Books, 1981

______________ *Glenn Miller and His Orchestra.* N.Y., Da Capo, 1974

Simpson, Anne Kay. *Follow Me; The Life and Music of R. Nathaniel Dett.* Metuchen, N.J., Scarecrow Press, 1993

Silverman, Jerry. *Good Times, Hard Times and Ragtimes.* Pacific, Mo., Mel Bay, 1992

Singer, Barry. *Black and Blue: The Life and Lyrics of Andy Razaf.* N.Y., Schirmer, 1992.

Slave Songs of the United States; the Classic 1867 Anthology. Allen, W. F., Ware, C. P., Garrison, L. M., eds. N.Y., Dover, 1995

Smallwood, Arwin D., with Elliot, Jeffrey M. *The Atlas of African-American History and Politics from the Slave Trade to Modern Times.* N.Y., McGraw-Hill, 1998

Smith, Willie the Lion with Hoefer. George. *Music on My Mind.* Garden City, N.Y., Doubleday, 1964

Southern, Eileen. *The Music of Black Americans: A History.* New York, W.W. Norton, 1971

_______________ "An Origin of Negro Song," *The Theater of Black Americans: a Collection of Critical Essays.* 2 Vols. Hill, Errol, ed. Englewood Cliffs, N.J., Prentice Hall, 1980

_______________ *Readings in Black Popular Music,* N.Y., W.W. Norton, 1983

Squire, Russel N. *Church Music; Musical and Hymnological Developments in Western Christianity.* St. Louis, Bethany Press, 1962

Stampp, Kenneth M. *That Peculiar Institution; Slavery in the Ante-Bellum South.* N.Y., Knopf, 1967

Starr, S. Frederick. *Bamboula! The Life and Times of Louis Moreau Gottschalk.* N.Y., Oxford Univ. Press, 1995

Stearns, Marshall W. N.Y. *The Story of Jazz.* N.Y., Oxford Univ. Press, 1958

Stearns, Marshall and Jean.. N.Y. *Jazz Dance; the Story of American Vernacular Dance.* N.Y., Macmillan, 1968

Stein, Charles W. *American Vaudeville As Seen by its Contemporaries.* N.Y., Knopf, 1984

Stewart, Rex. *Boy Meets Horn,* Claire P. Gordon, ed. Ann Arbor. Univ. of Michigan Press, 1991

_______________ *Jazz Masters of the 30s.* N.Y., Macmillan, 1972

Stoddard, Tom. *Jazz on the Barbary Coast.* Berkeley, Calif., Heyday Books, 1998

Stowe, David W. *Swing Changes.* Cambridge, MA, Harvard Univ. Press, 1994

Sudhalter, Richard M. *Lost Chords: White Musicians and Their Contribution to Jazz; 1915-1945.* N.Y., Oxford Univ. Press, 1999

_______________ *Stardust Melody; The Life and Music of Hoagy Carmichael.* N.Y., Oxford Univ. Press, 2001

Sudhalter, Richard M., and Evans, Philip R., with Dean-Myatt, William. *Bix, Man and Legend.* New Rochelle, Arlington House, 1974

Tango, the Dance, the Song, the Story. Collier, Simon, advisory editor. London, Thames and Hudson, 1995

The Theater of Black Americans, Vol. I. Hill, ed. Errol. Englewood Cliffs, N.Y., Prentice-Hall, 1980

Thompson, Robert Farris, *"An Aesthetic of the Cool: West African Dance," African Forum.* Vol. II, No. 2 Fall, 1966

_______________ *African Art in Motion.* Berkeley, Univ. of Calif. Press, 1974

______________ *Tango: the Art History of Love.* N.Y., Random House, 2005

Thornton, John. *Africa and Africans in the Making of the Atlantic World, 1400-1800.* Cambridge, Eng., Cambridge Univ. Press, 1997

Thorpe, Edward. *Black Dance.* Woodstock, N.Y., Overlook Press, 1989

Tirro, Frank. *Jazz; A History.* N.Y., W.W. Norton, 1977

Toll, Robert C. *Blacking Up; The Minstrel Show in 19th-Century America.* N.Y., Oxford Univ. Press, 1974

Townsend, Peter. *Jazz in American Culture.* Jackson, MI, Univ. Press of Mississippi, 2000

Travis, Dempsey J. *The Louis Armstrong Odyssey; From Jane Alley to America's Jazz Ambassador.* N.Y., Urban Research Press, 2000

Tracy, Stephen C. *Langston Hughes and the Blues.* Urbana, University of Illinois Press, 2001

Tucker, Sophie. *Some of these Days.* Garden City, N.Y., Doubleday Doran, 1945

Turner, Lorenzo Dow. *Africanisms in the Gullah Dialect.* N.Y., Arno Press and the New York Times, 1969

Turner, Frederick. *Remembering Song.* N.Y., Viking, 1982

Ulanov, Barry. *A History of Jazz in America.* N.Y., Viking press, 1957

Van de Leur, Walter. *Something to Live For; the Music of Billy Strayhorn.* N.Y., Oxford Univ. Press, 2002

Variety Magazine. Dec. 6, 1905, Issue No. 1, and *passim* to 1950.

Ward, Andrew. *Dark Midnight When I Rise; The Story of the Jubilee Singers.* N.Y., Farrar, Straus and Giroux, 2000

Ward, Geoffrey C., and Burns, Ken. *Jazz; A History of America's Music.* N.Y., Knopf, 2000

Waldo, Terri. *This is Ragtime.* N.Y., Hawthorn Books, 1976

Walton, Ortiz. *Music: Black, White and Blue.* N.Y., William Morrow, 1972

Waterman, Richard A. "African Influence on the Music of the Americas," *Proceedings and Selected Papers of the XXIX Congress of the Americanists.* Pp. 207-217. N.Y., Cooper Square Publishers, 1952

______________ "'Hot' Rhythm in Negro Music," *Journal of the American Musicological Society.* Vol. I, No. 1. Spring, 1948, pp. 24-37

Wells, Dicky. *Night People* (As told to Stanley Dance). Boston, Crescendo Publishing, 1971

Wilder, Alex. *American Popular Song: the Great Innovators, 1900-1950.* N.Y., Oxford, Univ. Press, 1972

Williams, Iain Cameron. *Underneath a Harlem Moon: the Harlem to Paris Years of Adelaide Hall.* London, Continuum, 2002

Williams, Martin. *Jazz Masters of New Orleans.* N.Y., Macmillan, 1967

Witmark, Isidore, and Goldberg, Isaac. *From Ragtime to Swingtime; the Story of the House of Witmark.* N.Y., Lee Furman, 1939

Work, John W. *American Negro Songs and Sprituals.* N.Y., Crown Publishers, 1940

Wyman, Bill, with Havers, Richard. *Bill Wyman's Blues Odyssey.* N.Y., DK Publishing, 2001

Zeidman, Irving. *The American Burlesque Show.* N.Y., Hawthorn Books, 1967

Ziegfeld, Richard and Paulette. *The Ziegfeld Touch.* N.Y. Harry Abrams, 1993

Zinnser, William. *Easy to Remember; The Great American Songwriters and Their Songs.* Jaffrey, N.H., David R. Godine, 2000

DISCOGRAPHY

Anthology of Big Band Swing (1930-1955) (CDs). N.Y., GRD-2-629. MCA Records, 1993

Anthology of Sissle and Blake's "Shuffle Along" (LP). NW 260. New World Records, 1976

At the Jazz Band Ball: Bix Beiderbecke (1924-1930) (CD). AJA 5080. England, Living Era, 1991

Art Tatum; Classic Early Solos (CD). GRD-607. Decca Jazz. N.Y., MCA, 1991

Authentic New Orleans Jazz Funeral (CD). MG 1012. New Orleans, La., Mardi Gras Records, 1991

The Bebop Era (CD). CK 40972. N.Y., CBS Columbia. 1987

The Ben Pollack Orchestras (1928-1938) (CD). Jazz Archives 161. Czechoslovakia and Sussex, England Flyright Records, EPM 2000

Benny Goodman Live at Carnegie Hall (Cds). GK40244-40246 N.Y., Columbia, 1986, from recordings of January 16, 1938

Bessie Smith and Louis Armstrong Together (CD). CECD 013. London, TKO Magnum Music, 1996

Best of the Big Bands: The Dorsey Brothers (CD). CK 48908 DIDP 077410. N.Y., Sony, 1992

Best of Big Bands: Glen Gray (CD). CK 45345. DIDP 072204. N.Y., CBS Records, 1990

The Best of Jelly Roll Morton (1926-1939) (CD). 158012. Jazz Archives 16. EPM, Paris, 1993

Bill Wyman's Blues Odyssey (CDs). DOCD-32-20-2. England, Document Records, Ltd., 2001

Bix Beiderbecke: Singin' The Blues (Cds). CK 45450 DIDP 072207. N.Y., CBS Records, 1990

Chick Webb, Ella Swings the Band (LP). MCA 1327. Jazz Heritage Series Vol. 28. N.Y., MCA Records, 1980.

Chick Webb and His Orchestra (1929-1934) (CD). France, Classics Records, 1992

Chick Webb, Stomping at the Savoy (1934-1939) (CD). 159722. Jazz Archives #161. France, 2000

The Chronological Benny Goodman and His Orchestra (1934-1940) (Cds). Stemra Classics 744-1098. France, Classics Records, 1994-1999

Clarence Williams (CD). 836 829-2. Jazz Classics. Australian Broadcasting Corp., 1989

Collector's History of Classic Jazz (LPs). N.Y., Murray Hill Records

The Colored Sacred Harp; Winegrass Sacred Harp Singers (CD). 80433-2 DICX 018902.

N.Y., New World Records. Recorded Anthology of American Music, 1993

The Commodore Story (Cds). CMD 20400. N.Y., GRP Records, 1997

The Cotton Club. (CD). AJA 5031 R. London, Academy Sound and Vision, 1984

The Definitive Duke Ellington (CD). CK 61444 DIDP 101776. Ken Burns Jazz Series. N.Y., Sony, 2000

Dixieland (CD). UAE 30632 MCPS. Holland, TKO Records, 1996

Dixieland; The Birth of Jazz (CD). A26417. Life, Times and Music Series. N.Y., Sony Music, 1995

Dizzy's Diamonds; Best of the Verve Years (Cds) 314 517 2852-287 2. N.Y. Jazz Series. Polygram Records, 1992

Early Jazz (1917-1923) (CDs). FA 181. France, Frémeaux, 2000

The Early Minstrel Show (CD). 80338-2 DIDX034774. N.Y., New World Records, 1985, 1998

The Eighty-Six Years of Eubie Blake (LP). C25847. N.Y., Columbia Records, 1969

Ella Fitzgerald (CD). 314 549 087-2. Ken Burns Jazz. Universal City, CA, Verve, 2000

Ella Fitzgerald; Priceless Jazz (CD). GRD 9870. N.Y., GRP Records, 1997

Encyclopedia of Jazz on Records (LPs). DL 8398. N.Y., Decca, 1957

Expression; John Coltrane (CD). GRD-131. N.Y., MCA, 1993

Fingerbreaker: Classics of Ragtime and Early Jazz Piano (CD). 289 460 499-2. London, Decca, 1999

The Fletcher Henderson Story; A Study in Frustration. Thesaurus of Classic Jazz (Cds). C3K 57596 CK 57597-9 DIDP 081409-11. N.Y., Sony Music Entertainment, 1994

Georgia Sea Island Songs for Everyday Living, Vols I-XIII (CDs). Rounder 1701-1713. Cambridge, MA, Rounder Records, 1998

The History of Jazz; the Be-Bop Revolution (CD). PLAT CD 715. Enfield, England, Prism Leisure, 2001

I'll Dance Till the Sun Breaks Through; Ragtime, Cakewalks and Stomps from 1898 to 1903 (CD). N.Y., Musical Heritage Society, 1999

The Indispensable Bix Beiderbecke (1924-1930) (CDs). Jazz Tribune. RCA 66540-2 B. France, BMG, 1992

An Introduction to Art Tatum; His Best Recordings (1933-44) (CD). DK 003. France, Best of Jazz; The Swing Era 4022, 1995

King Oliver and His Dixie Syncopators (1926-1928) (LP). BL 58020. Brunswick Collectors' Series. N.Y., Brunswick Radio Corp., 1950

King Oliver's Jazz Band (1923-1926) (CD). Classics 639. DK003. France, Classics Records, 1992

King Oliver/Luis Russell; The Alternative Takes in Chronological Order (1923-1930) (CD). RP2022. Vienna, Neatwork, 2000

James P. Johnson, Harlem Stride Piano (1921-1929) (CD). 158953. France, Jazz Archives, 1997

Jammin' For The Jackpot; Big Bands and Territory Bands of the 30s (LP). NW 217. N.Y., New World Records, 1977

Jazz Piano (CD). DIDP 071804. Smithsonian. N.Y., CBS Records, 1989

Jazz Legends (Cds). Mastertone 0705. N.Y., BMG Music, 1998

Jelly Roll Morton: Great Original Performances (CD). BBC CD 604. Australian Broadcasting Corp., 1985; BBC Enterprises, 1986

Jelly Roll Morton: Kansas City Stomp. (CDs). Library of Congress Recordings Vols. I-III. Recorded by

Alan Lomax. Rounder CD 1091. Cambridge, Ma, 1993

Jelly Roll Morton: Last Sessions (CD). CMD-403. N.Y., Commodore Recordings, 1997

Jelly Roll Morton: The Pearls (CD). 6588-2-RB. N.Y., BMG Music, 1988

Jim Europe's 369th U.S. Infantry "Hell Fighters" Band (CD from 1919 recordings). MA 7020. Memphis, Memphis Archives, 1996

Ladies Sing the Blues (1923-1939) (CD). AJA 5092. London, Living Era, 1992

Louis Armstrong; The Hot Fives and Hot Sevens (Cds). CK44253-44422 DIDP 07111-071373. N.Y., CBS Records, 1989

Louis Armstrong On The Road (CD). 15 798. Los Angeles, Delta Music Inc., 1992

Louis Armstrong, Satchmo's Classics (CD). PML 1002. Germany, Planet Media, 2000

Louis Prima (CD). CDP 7 94072 2. Hollywood, CA, Capitol Records, 1991

Making Choices: Evolutions in Jazz (1920 to 1960} (CD). No catalog number. N.Y., Museum of Modern Art, 2000

Music from the New York Stage, 1890-1920 (Cds, Vols. II-IV). CD 9053-9061. E. Sussex, England, 1993

The Music Goes Round and Round, The Golden Years of Tin Pan Alley (1930-1939) LP). BF 75090.

Westinghouse Broadcasting. N.Y., New World Records, 1970

Negro Blues and Hollers (CD). Library of Congress Archive of Folk Culture. Recorded by Alan Lomax,

John W. Work and Lewis Jones in 1941-42. Rounder 1501. Cambridge, MA, Rounder Records, 1997

Negro Folk Music of Alabama (LPs). FE 4417 and 4418. N.Y., Folkways, 1960

Negro Work Songs and Calls (CD). Library of Congress Archive of Folk Culture. Rounder 1517. Cambridge, MA, Rounder Records, 1999

New Orleans Rhythm Kings (and Jelly Roll Morton) (CD). MCD 47020-2 DIDX 01242. Berkeley, CA, Milestone Records, Fantasy, Inc., 1992

Old Curiosity Shop; a Treasury of Immortal Performances (LP). LCT 1112. RCA Victor, n.d.

Pyramid: The Modern Jazz Quartet (CD). 1325-2. N.Y. Atlantic Recording, 1960

RCA Victor Jazz; The First Half Century (CDs). 07863 66085-2 to 666089-2. N.Y., BMG Music, 1992

The Roaring Twenties (CDs). Intersound 1401-1404. Roswell, Ga., 1998

Roots of the Blues, Southern Folk Heritage Series. Recorded in the field and edited by Alan Lomax (CD). DIDX 010765. From New World Records 80252-2, 1977

Rough Guide to Classic Jazz (CD). RGNET 1012. London, World Music, 1997

Songs We Taught Your Mother (CD). BV 1052. Alberta Hunter, Lucille Hegamin and Victoria Spivey. Berkeley, Calif., Prestige Bluesville Records, 1992

Soultrane John Coltrane (CD). PRCD-7142-2 Berkeley, CA, Fantasy, 1999

Steppin' On the Gas; Rags to Jazz (1913-1927) (LP). NW 269. N.Y., New World Records, 1977

Steppin' Out; Mackie Burnette With Panorama (steel drums ensemble) (CD). No catalog number. Cambridge, Ma, Brarnak Studios, 1999

Sweet and Low Blues, Big Bands and Territory Bands of the 20s (LP). NW 256. N.Y., New World Records, 1977

Swingin' Uptown; The Big Band (1923-1952) (CDs). 07863 66746-2. N.Y., RCA Victor, 1998

This Is Society Dance Music, Lester Lanin and His Orchestra (CD). 473656 2 BIEM/SDRM. N.Y., Sony, 1993

Tribal, Folk and Café Music of West Africa (LPs). Recorded and edited by Arthur S, Alberts. Documentation text by Melville J. Herskovits, Richard A. Waterman, Duncan Emrich and Marshall W. Stearns. No catalog number. N.Y., Field Recordings, limited edition, 1950

The Ultimate Charlie Parker (CD). ULT 40412. Holland, Ultimate Music Collection, 2000

West Africa Drum, Chant and Instrumental Music (CD). 79709-2. From 1976 recording. N.Y., Nonesuch Records, 2002

The World of Swing (CD). CK66080 DIDP 101266. N.Y., Sony, 2000

The Yoruba/Dahomean Collection (CD). RCD 10405. Smithsonian Endangered Music Project. London, Rykodisc, 1998 (project of Melville Herskovits)

FILMS AND VIDEOCASSETTES

Africa; JVC/Smithsonian Folkways Video Anthology of Music and Dance of Africa. Vols. I-III. Victor Company of Japan, Ltd., 1996

The African American Cinema, Vol. II. (Footage of Sissle and Blake). Library of Congress Video Collection, c. 1995

African Drumming by Babaunde Olatunji. Brattleboro, Vt., Interworld Music Associates, 1993

At the Jazz Band Ball. Newton, N.J., Yahoo, n.d.

Benny Carter, Symphony in Riffs. N.Y., Rhapsody Films, 1989

Cavalcade of Old Time Dances. Jim and Betty Montgomery. Jim Forest Videos

The Cotton Club. Evanston, Ill., Altschul Group Corp. 1982

Dancing: New Worlds, New Forms, Program V and *Dancing in One World,* Program VIII., Public Media Home Vision Series, (WNET and BBC-TV)

The Devil's Music; 1920s Jazz. PBS Video, 2000

Irene and Vernon Castle: Footage of dancing. New York Museum of Modern Art, N.Y.

Jazz, a Film by Ken Burns. Four episodes: "Gumbo," "The Gift," "Our Language," "The True Welcome." Burbank, CA, Warner Home Video, 2000 1979)

The Lullaby of Harlem. Hollywood, CA, Passport International Productions, 1998

Riverdance. Culver City, Calif., Tyrone Productions, 1997.

Roots of Rhythm: A Worldwide Celebration of Latin Music, from Africa to the Caribbean and America. Narrated by Harry Belafonte. 3 vols. N.Y., New Video Group, 1997

Swing. Denmark, Storyville Records, 1993

That's Dancing! Culver City, CA, MGM/UA Entertainment, 1985

Uncle Tom's Cabin, or, Slavery Days. Thomas A. Edison, 1903, and *Uncle Tom's Cabin,* a Minot Film Release, 1914. Both on one Matinee Classics cassette. 198?

Vaudeville. An American Masters Production. WGBH, Boston, Oct., 1999

MUSICAL SCORES

Cook, Will Marion and Dunbar, Paul Louis, *In Dahomey, a Negro Musical Comedy*. London, Keith, Prowse, 1903

Europe, James Reese. *Castle House Rag* and *Castle Walk*. Arranged by Gunther Schuller. Newton, MA, Margun Music, 1984

Gottschalk, L.M. *Collected Works for Piano*. N.Y., G. Schirmer, 1995

Jones, Sidney, and Rubens, Paul A. *The Girl from Utah*. (vocal score) London, Chappell, 1913

Ragtime Jubilee; 42 Piano Gems, 1911-21. Ed. By Jasen, David A. Mineola, N.Y., Dover Publications, 1997

Index